AF722817

Bill,

Thank you for visiting #SMB. I hope you find this interesting + helpful.

Best wishes
Dave Johnson
November 26, 2012

Medical Licensing and Discipline in America

Medical Licensing and Discipline in America

A History of the Federation of State Medical Boards

David A. Johnson and
Humayun J. Chaudhry

Lexington Books
Lanham • Boulder • New York • Toronto • Plymouth, UK

Copublished with the Federation of State Medical Boards

Published by Lexington Books
A wholly owned subsidiary of The Rowman & Littlefield Publishing Group, Inc.
4501 Forbes Boulevard, Suite 200, Lanham, Maryland 20706
www.rowman.com

10 Thornbury Road, Plymouth PL6 7PP, United Kingdom

Copublished with the Federation of State Medical Boards

British Cataloging in Publication Information Available

Library of Congress Cataloging-in-Publication Data

Johnson, David A., 1959–
Medical licensing and discipline in America : a history of the Federation of State Medical Boards / David A. Johnson and Humayun J. Chaudhry.
p. ; cm.
Includes bibliographical references and index.
ISBN 978-0-7391-7438-8 (cloth : alk. paper)—ISBN 978-0-7391-7439-5 (pbk. : alk. paper)—ISBN 978-0-7391-7440-1 (electronic) 1. Medicine—Practice—Standards—United States. 2. Medicine—Practice—Standards—United States—History. 3. Medical policy—United States. I. Chaudhry, Humayun J. II. Federation of State Medical Boards of the United States. III. Title.
[DNLM: 1. Federation of State Medical Boards of the United States. 2. Licensure, Medical—history—United States. 3. Clinical Competence—standards—United States. 4. Government Regulation—history—United States. 5. History, 20th Century—United States. 6. History, 21st Century—United States. 7. Malpractice—history—United States. W 40 AA1]
R728.J645 2012
610.71—dc23 2012020227

∞™ The paper used in this publication meets the minimum requirements of American National Standard for Information Sciences—Permanence of Paper for Printed Library Materials, ANSI/NISO Z39.48-1992.

Printed in the United States of America

Contents

Acknowledgments

Telling the story of an organization whose history spans a century requires time, patience, and the assistance of many friends and colleagues. We have been particularly fortunate in this regard and have benefited from the support of many individuals. Our gratitude and appreciation go out to several people in particular and we would be remiss if we failed to acknowledge their contributions.

Betty Burnett, Ph.D, assisted with research and background materials for chapters 6 and 7. In addition, she provided wise counsel and suggestions at the beginning of this book project based upon her experience authoring a history of the National Board of Osteopathic Medical Examiners. Several of our Federation colleagues deserve special recognition. Federation Librarian Linda Jordan, M.L.S., proved invaluable in tracking down and obtaining source materials—both those obtained with relative ease and some well off the beaten trail. Frances Cain, the Federation's director for assessment services, contributed generously with her keen editorial eye and insightful comments in reviewing all early draft chapters for this book. Our colleague Aaron Young, Ph.D., Federation senior director for research and analytics, offered cogent suggestions and guidance on the presentation of statistical data throughout the text. Conversations with Federation colleagues Kelly Alfred, M.S.; Martha Bucholz; Kevin Caldwell; Drew Carlson; Bradley Dunn; David Hooper; Randy McCullough; Tim Miller, J.D.; Michelle Turner, M.Ed.; and Lisa Robin, M.L.A., added immeasurably to the authors' understanding of specific Federation initiatives and activities taking place in recent years as well as those occurring several decades ago.

Many others outside the walls of the Federation's offices graciously provided time to review portions of this manuscript. We are deeply appreciative for the insights and helpful advice they provided and which strengthened the text immeasurably. The authors would like to thank the following individuals for their assistance: John Bulger, D.O.; Janet Carson, J.D.; Gerard Dillon, Ph.D.; Norman Gevitz, Ph.D.; Kenneth Ludmerer, M.D.; Donald Melnick, M.D.; John Prescott, M.D.; Thomas Ryan, J.D.; Barbara Schneidman, M.D.; Stephen Seeling, J.D.; and James Thompson, M.D.

This book has benefited greatly from these individuals and the others whose contributions (both great and small) have strengthened this story of the Federation and the evolution of America's state-based system for medical licensure and discipline. The success of this book is attributable in part to our friends and colleagues. Their observations and feedback have helped us to avoid the inevitable missteps in any book project. Naturally, any deficiencies, errors or omissions are the sole responsibility of the authors.

The authors would like to offer a special note of thanks to the members of the Federation's Centennial Advisory Panel who strongly encouraged us to pursue this project as part of the organization's overall plans for its centennial. We salute Doris Brooker, M.D.; Robin Hunter Buskey, M.P.A.S.; Gary Clark; Cissy Dillon; Larry Dixon; Eugene Oliveri, D.O.; and Dinesh Patel, M.D., and Cheryl Vaught, J.D. for their contributions. Their encouragement, as well as the support of the Federation's board of directors—especially Chair Lance Talmage, M.D., Immediate Past Chair Janelle Rhyne, M.D., and Past Chair Freda Bush, M.D., who reviewed later drafts of the manuscript and offered helpful comments—are deeply appreciated. We would also like to thank our Federation colleagues on the executive management team—Michael Dugan, M.B.A., Todd Phillips, M.B.A., Lisa Robin, M.L.A. and Sandra Waters, M.E.M.—for their graciousness and understanding of the time commitment represented by this book.

We would also like to credit the many organizations and entities that have kindly granted permission to reprint photographic or tabular material. The authors would like to recognize the Federation of State Medical Boards; the National Board of Medical Examiners; the State Archives of Florida; Special and Digital Collections, Tampa Library, University of South Florida; the U.S. National Library of Medicine; the Shelby White and Leon Levy Archives Center, Institute for Advanced Study, Princeton, New Jersey; Johns Hopkins University Press; the Ohio State Medical Association; the Association of American Medical Colleges; the U.S. Library of Congress; the Congress Hotel, Chicago, Illinois; the Kansas State Historical Society; the Yale University Harvey Cushing/John Hay Whitney

Medical Library; the North Carolina Medical Board; Orange County (New York) Medical Society; and the Colorado Medical Board.

We are indebted to our families—Lydia, Katherine and Zachary Johnson; Nazli, Shaun and Haris Chaudhry—for their continuous support of our labors on this project, especially when multiple tasks sacrificed our time with them. Writing is an art and knowledge is a gift freely shared among friends and colleagues, teachers and mentors. We are grateful to those who have encouraged and inspired us—Carol Clothier, Clayton Eichelberger, Uzi Parnes, Harris M. Sarney, Katherine Hill and Elizabeth Kramer.

Finally, in telling this story we are reminded of the words written by the renowned British historian George M. Trevelyan:

> The poetry of history lies in the quasi-miraculous fact that once, on this earth, on this familiar spot of ground, walked other men and women, as actual as we are today, thinking their own thoughts, swayed by their own passions, but now all gone, one generation vanishing into another, gone as utterly as we ourselves shall shortly be gone, like ghosts at cockcrow.

We have been inspired by the rich history of the Federation, its state medical and osteopathic board members and those "ghosts" who preceded us. We dedicate this book to them and all those who will follow in our collective footsteps.

Authors' Notes on the Text

This narrative represents our attempt to not only tell the history of the Federation of State Medical Boards, but to do so within the broader context of the evolution of medical regulation within the United States. The story we tell weaves one organization's history over the past century into the larger fabric of the development of medical regulation from its colonial antecedents to the birth of the modern medical licensing system in the late nineteenth century and into the present day. We have crafted our narrative in such a way that the reader encounters a story that shifts focus periodically between micro- and macro-level history in detailing events and developments in the growth of medical regulation. We believe this blending of Federation-specific and state-level detail with national forces and trends creates a complementary narrative framework enabling the reader to more fully comprehend the context within which our state-based system for medical regulation developed.

Any extended written work presents its own unique stylistic issues requiring an authorial decision. We would like to point out several of these and how we have attempted to resolve them. One stylistic issue concerned how we would refer to the various state boards/agencies empowered to license and discipline physicians and the often unique and unwieldy titles associated with each. Here we took guidance from Shakespeare, who famously asked 'What's in a name?' and then answered his question by stressing the importance of essence rather than title. We concur with the Bard and have adopted his approach by using the phrase "state medical board" (or a close variance such as "state board" or "medical board") throughout the text as the standard verbiage for the legally constituted state agency assigned the task of overseeing physician regulation. This generalized terminology has been used for all medical licensing bodies within the United States and its territories, particularly in the earlier portions of the narrative. Unless otherwise indicated, this naming has been used regardless of whether that board licenses allopathic (M.D.) or osteopathic (D.O.) physicians or both.

The achievements of the Federation over the last century have stemmed largely from the contributions of many people—some serving as staff at this organization and others as a part of the Federation's governance. Many, however, served on their respective state medical board and we felt it important to recognize this connection. The reader will notice that many names in this text are followed by a parenthetical listing of a state. Where appropriate, we have added this parenthetical identifier listing the state medical board upon which the individual served, for example, Walter Bierring (Iowa). As state medical boards were composed solely of physician members until the 1960s, we have foregone use of the title "Dr." or insertion of the medical degree after the individual board members' names.

Titles commonly associated with various positions on state medical boards have changed over the past one hundred years. In the nineteenth century, the senior executive staff member guiding a state medical board was often titled "secretary," with the board headed by its "President." Today, the senior staff member is more often designated "Executive Director," with the board led by a "chair" or "president." To avoid confusion we have opted to standardize these position titles by giving the modern usage unless the context of the passage seemed to warrant utilizing the older titles. A similar evolution occurred with Federation titles. Since 2004 the senior Federation staff member has been titled president, with leader of the board of directors titled chair. Previously, these positions were titled secretary-treasurer or secretary (1912–1993) and executive vice president (1994–2003) for the senior staff member and president for the elective position (1912–2003). We have generally utilized the title appropriate for that time period in most references throughout the text.

Any written history of the Federation and the medical regulatory field runs inevitably into a bewildering array of names for organizations, agencies and licensing examinations whose full titles would be wearisome to repeat in full with each appearance in the text. Thus, we have provided the commonly used acronyms for such entities after the first use of the full name, for example, National Board of Medical Examiners (NBME). Thereafter, these commonly cited entities are typically identified by their acronym or a shortened version of the name. To assist the reader, we have included a complete list of all acronyms used in this text as a part of the book's end materials.

Finally, we would offer a few words about references and citations. Source citations have been provided as notes to each chapter of the text.

The first citation for each source appears in full; subsequent citations to the same source appear in shortened format with author name, the work cited and page number. If there has been no intervening source after the first citation, then *Ibid.* has been utilized. Rather than the standard bibliography, we have opted to provide a bibliographical essay guiding the reader to critical source materials rather than a redundant listing of all the sources. All citations have been drafted in compliance with the *Chicago Manual of Style,* 16th edition.

Foreword

In the opening passages of *Medical Licensing and Discipline in America: A History of the Federation of State Medical Boards*, the authors astutely point out that the story of medical regulation is also a story of our nation. They deftly weave into this fascinating narrative, on the occasion of the centennial founding of the Federation of State Medical Boards, engaging anecdotes about health care in the colonies and in Europe, and the positive impact on health care and medical regulation of such visionary and pragmatic leaders of the Federation as Walter Bierring, David Strickler, Herbert Platter, Harold Rypins, Robert Derbyshire, Ray Casterline, and Frederick Merchant.

This book reviews the gradual transformation of state medical licensure and discipline laws over time, in a nation that was driven from its inception to excellence "in order to form a more perfect Union"—from the American Revolution through the Civil War. Ultimately, ever greater concern for the public in the latter half of the 1800s led to the modern-day establishment of state medical and osteopathic boards committed to protecting the public and promoting quality health care.

A story such as this is also a history of public health and medicine and I am pleased that highlighted throughout the book are some of the many advances that have occurred in public health, particularly in the last century, and in clinical and scientific medicine. The authors' retelling of the inability of physicians in 1799 to save the life of George Washington, who appeared to be suffering from an upper respiratory infection, using the remedies that were then available, is a particular reminder of how far we have come in our understanding of disease pathophysiology, diagnosis and treatment. Better disease control ultimately resulted from improvements in sanitation and hygiene, the discovery of antibiotics, and the implementation of universal childhood vaccination programs. Such scientific and technologic advances remain the bedrock for today's disease surveillance and control systems.

When the Federation was founded in 1912, through a merger of the National Confederation of State Medical Examining and Licensing Boards (itself founded in 1890) and the American Confederation of Reciprocal Examining and Licensing Boards, the top three causes of death in the United States were pneumonia (much of it due to influenza, then considered a bacterium), tuberculosis and diarrhea. Public health action to control infectious diseases in the twentieth century was effective primarily because of the late-nineteenth-century discovery of microorganisms as the cause of many serious diseases such as cholera and tuberculosis.

In 2009, the most recent year for which we have data from the Centers for Disease Control and Prevention, the three leading causes of death in the United States were heart disease, cancer and chronic lower respiratory diseases. The estimated age-adjusted death rate, which accounts for changes in the age distribution of the population, decreased to 714.0 per 100,000 persons that year. Life expectancy at birth for the total population in 2009 was 78.2 years (75.7 for males, 80.6 for females). Although the drop in the age-adjusted death rate in 2009 is a record low and life expectancy for all ethnic and racial groups has generally increased over time, these trends belie a need on the part of all of us to become a more healthy and fit nation. Although America provides some of the world's best health care and spent over $2.5 trillion for health in 2009, the United States still ranks below many countries in life expectancy, infant mortality and many other indicators of healthy life.

In June 2011, I had the honor of presenting the nation's first ever National Prevention and Health Promotion Strategy, a critical component of the Patient Protection and Affordable Care Act (upheld by the U.S. Supreme Court in June 2012), which was developed by a National Prevention, Health Promotion and Public Health Council that I chaired. The Council comprised seventeen heads of departments, agencies and offices across the Federal government who are committed to promoting disease prevention and wellness. Poor diet, physical inactivity, tobacco use and alcohol misuse are just some of the challenges we face as a nation. We also know that many of the strongest predictors of health and well-being fall outside of the health care setting, which is why housing, transportation, education, workplaces and the environment are major elements that are included in the strategy. Our goal is to increase the number of Americans who are healthy at every stage of life.

The year before being nominated by President Obama to become the eighteenth U.S. surgeon general, I served as chair of the Federation of

State Medical Boards. I was honored to have been given such an important responsibility and look back with very fond memories on our efforts on behalf of the state boards to ensure that the processes by which physicians and physician assistants are licensed in the United States and its territories are robust, that state board actions against disciplined physicians and physician assistants are shared among the state boards and accessible to the public, and that medical licensure portability through such means as the Uniform Application for Physician Licensing (UA) and expedited telemedicine licenses, to name just two examples, ultimately facilitate the nation's efforts to improve the health and quality of life for individuals, families and communities.

I am pleased to see that as the Federation enters its second century of operations it remains focused on excellence and quality in all of its activities, as state boards consider implementing a program for Maintenance of Licensure (MOL), as the United States Medical Licensing Examination (USMLE) undergoes a comprehensive update (in partnership with the National Board of Medical Examiners), and as the Federation Credentials Verification Service (FCVS) completes its modernization.

I would like to offer my sincerest congratulations to the Federation of State Medical Boards on the occasion of its one-hundredth birthday. I would also like to recognize the many men and women who tirelessly serve our nation through their dedicated work on state and territorial medical and osteopathic boards. It is to all of them that this book is ultimately dedicated.

Regina M. Benjamin, M.D., M.B.A.
U.S. Surgeon General
January 20, 2012

Message from the FSMB Chairman

It is a great honor to introduce this special publication by Mr. Johnson and Dr. Chaudhry celebrating a century of achievement by the state medical and osteopathic boards of America. The fact that the Federation of State Medical Boards is celebrating such a remarkable milestone says volumes about the importance of medical regulation in America. The practice of medical regulation dates back almost as far as the practice of medicine itself in our country.

Medical regulators have always played a crucial role in our health care system. Protecting the public is a role that is often unnoticed, unfortunately. But the diligence and dedication of our member boards to public protection has had a tremendously positive impact on public health for more than a century.

Medical Licensing and Discipline in America: A History of the Federation of State Medical Boards is the story of a profession responding to the high call and privilege of self-regulation. As a largely self-regulating profession, physicians have had society's permission to set and maintain standards for entering the profession, for working in the profession, and the right to set rules for when and how members may be removed from the profession. As society has evolved and grown more diverse, state boards have responded by enlarging their tent to include new voices in the story of medical regulation: public members and representatives from other health care professions. The FSMB and its member boards have been at the center of this story as it has unfolded over the last century.

On this historic occasion, the FSMB salutes the many devoted men and women of our medical regulatory community who have diligently worked to protect the citizens of this great country. As the ninety-first elected leader or chair of our organization, I am deeply aware of the long chain of fine leaders who have preceded me—on whose shoulders I now stand. Now it is our hour, the time to forge the first link in the second century of the stirring story of medical regulation.

Much work has been accomplished during the last one hundred years. Much work remains to be done. We are in a time of great transition in our public health care system, and together we stand united as we enter a new era of medical regulation. Congratulations to you for all you have achieved!

Lance Talmage, M.D., Medical Board of Ohio
Chair, FSMB Board of Directors

Chapter 1

The Birth of Medical Regulation in America

Energy and persistence conquer all things.

—Benjamin Franklin (1706–1790)

On a breezy, sunlit day in Chicago in the spring of 1908, four years before the first meeting of the Federation of State Medical Boards, a young man by the name of John Brinkley arrived in town to become a doctor. Chicago was home to not only the nation's largest physician organization, the American Medical Association (AMA), but also to several medical schools reflecting a variety of philosophic approaches to the practice of medicine—allopathic, osteopathic, homeopathic and eclectic. Having spent a year in Tennessee apprenticed to a trickster who dispensed miracle tonics for impotence, Brinkley considered his options carefully as he became enamored with the "new aristocracy" making its home in the castles and fortresses along the waters of Lake Michigan. Avarice, impatience, and a tendency to imbibe alcohol to excess would fatefully lead him off the beaten path.

Brinkley shopped around at first, writes Pope Brock in the bestseller *Charlatan*, and soon settled on Bennett Eclectic Medical College, a less competitive alternative school of medicine that focused its teachings on herbal remedies. Borrowing $25 for the school's entry fee from a loan shark, Brinkley studied for a time but never completed its curriculum. In 1915, he instead "bought" a medical diploma, enabling him to become licensed over time in eight states. Over the next several years—from Greenville, South Carolina to Judsonia, Arkansas, to Milford, Kansas—Brinkley methodically and fantastically plied his ill-begotten trade. Like other quacks, according to Brock, men like Brinkley "struck in one town, vanished to the next, and taught their tricks to others." Over time, Brinkley amassed a fortune by claiming to cure impotence by transplanting live goat testicles into humans before he was finally stripped of his licenses and died nearly penniless after a large number of malpractice and wrongful death suits.[1]

A man of Brinkley's sheer ambition and chutzpah, one might surmise, would not get very far in today's world. Eclectic schools of medicine no longer exist, for one thing, and one can't simply purchase a medical degree, at least not legally. Admission into an accredited U.S. medical school (allopathic or osteopathic) requires successful performance on a standardized admissions test and completion of prerequisite courses of study in a bona fide educational program leading to a baccalaureate degree. Obtaining a state medical license requires graduation from medical school, a year or more of supervised training in an accredited graduate medical education (GME) training program and successful performance on a multistep standardized medical licensure examination, not to mention a criminal background check (required by a majority of state boards) and cross-matching against national databases listing malpractice and disciplinary actions from all state and territorial licensing jurisdictions in the United States. The system, in short, provides significantly more checks and balances to safe medical practice than it did a century ago. But the system is not foolproof, judging by the caseloads of today's state medical board investigators and the more than 6,000 substantive disciplinary actions (everything from a temporary licensure suspension to permanent revocation for such activities as inappropriate prescribing of opioids, falsification of training credentials or several other categories of unprofessional conduct) taken annually against physicians who are legitimately licensed (or, less commonly, unlicensed) and reported to the Federation of State Medical Boards.

So how did the medical regulatory system (the term used here to describe the oversight of medical licensure and discipline) of a hundred years ago enable a man like Brinkley to discreetly buy a medical degree and obtain the right to practice medicine? What mind-set prompted patients to eschew traditional forms of medicine in favor of unproven cures or procedures? What kinds of criteria, other than the ability to pay tuition, were required to enroll in medical school in the first place? More fundamentally, what role have state boards played since—individually and collectively, under the aegis of the Federation—to promote higher standards for medical school admission, undergraduate and graduate medical education, medical licensure and examination, medical discipline, and the continuing professional development of physicians to protect the public from charlatans like Brinkley?

This introductory chapter addresses the first three of these questions, focusing on the evolution of medical practice, education and regulation in North America—particularly the English influence upon what would emerge as a decidedly American style of medicine—from the 1600s through the late 1800s. The chapters that follow address the remaining question and focus on the formation, evolution and growth of the Federation and its continuing role on behalf of the nation's seventy state and territorial medical boards.

The history of medical licensure and discipline in the United States, to be sure, is also a story of the nation and its laws. These statutes evolved in fits and starts—including a remarkable refresh following a thirty-year period in the early 1800s when nearly all regulatory laws for all professions were abolished—to govern the medical regulation of literally hundreds of thousands of physicians and, later, physician assistants. It is a story of advancements in our understanding of medical science, including public sanitation and germ theory, and of the establishment of full-bodied centers of learning and research for undergraduate and graduate medical education.

While this book is not by any means intended to be a history of medicine or medical science, nor of medical education, any treatise about medical regulation during the past century must include references to some of the contemporaneous advances that were occurring in these areas and, where appropriate, these have been mentioned. Finally, this is also a story of the countless men and women—doctors, lawyers, investigators and members of the public—who serve on state and territorial boards of medicine and on the staff, committees, working groups and governance of the Federation, to better protect the public by permitting only the learned and skilled to practice medicine.

OLD WORLD AND COLONIAL ANTECEDENTS

While a handful of physicians accompanied Columbus on his maiden voyage to the New World and municipal tribunals of physician examiners (also known as protomedicato) had attempted to regulate physicians in Mexico and Peru during the 1500s, the earliest attempt to regulate the practice of medicine in the English colonies took the form of legislation enacted in 1639 in Virginia. After colonists complained about excessive costs for the health care they increasingly needed, leaders in Virginia sought a means to control the fees charged by physicians and other health practitioners. Enforcement of such statutes appears to have been haphazard, however, and more likely nonexistent, as Virginians a century later would again find themselves proposing similar legislation. With the colonial population growing and the credentials of self-professed healers uncertain except by reputation, authorities increasingly felt compelled to act.[2]

A 1649 regulation passed by the Massachusetts Bay Colony, and mirrored by New York in 1665, was as elaborate as the ordinance passed by Virginia and among the first to acknowledge the danger to its citizens of unscrupulous and/or unqualified health practitioners. The law sought to regulate physicians, surgeons, midwives or others who were working "at any time about the bodye [*sic*] of men, women or children, for preservation of life, or health . . . without the advice and consent of such as are skillful in the same Art."[3] The city of New Amsterdam (later New York) even passed a law in 1657 employing doctors in the detection of crime: "To all Chirurgeons . . . when they are called to dress a wound they shall ask the patient who wounded him and that information thereof be given to the Schout" (i.e., sheriff).[4]

Lacking medical schools and any secure way of validating the credentials of those who claimed to be physicians, colonial Americans struggled with how they should identify and recognize such individuals, often acquiescing to a physician's reputation in the community. One of the first known efforts by a colonial legislature to formally issue an honorary "license" for the practice of medicine dates to 1652, when the Connecticut General Assembly granted a license and annual retainer to Thomas Lord "for setting of bones and otherwise, as at all times, occasions and necessities may require."[5] Rhode Island bestowed the title of "Doctor of physsicke and chirrurgery" in 1654 to Captain John Cranston, though it is unclear what actual training or expertise he possessed. Similarly, Jonas Wood was recognized with a license to practice medicine by an act of the New York legislature in 1677. Because the goal of such legislative action was primarily to recognize exemplary physicians for commendation and to encourage their work, these early colonial licenses were largely honorifics intended for those who possessed skills in the healing arts and not designed to penalize unlicensed practitioners. Lacking a hospital within its precincts, New York City's government even paid some physicians, at a rate of £5 a year in 1687, for treating the poor. Records from this time also show a request by a physician, addressed to the Proprietors and Freeholders of Hempstead, Long Island, for eighteen to twenty acres of land in return for settling among the community, tilling the land and practicing his art.[6]

Most of the medical licenses granted by the colonies before independence from Great Britain were salutatory rather than salutary and simply attested to the fitness and experience of an eminent practitioner. In 1760, however, the Colonial Assembly of New York expressed great alarm about the abuses being committed by "many ignorant and unskilful [*sic*] persons in physic and surgery." The assembly soon passed legislation that forbade any person to practice medicine or surgery in New York City unless first *examined* by a committee of colonial officials, a group that included the Mayor and the King's Counsellor. Such a move was the first of its kind for a city in British America and an important milestone in the history of medical regulation in the United States. New Jersey became the first of the original colonies to have such an examination requirement (1772) and New York extended the New York City regulation to the entire state in 1797.[7]

In 1781, the value of an examination of a physician's knowledge and skills was embraced beyond a state's legislature for the first time when the new Massachusetts Medical Society—which would go on to publish the *Boston Medical and Surgical Journal* (later the *New England Journal of Medicine*) in 1812—enacted a comparable requirement for membership. This was important for two reasons. First, medical societies of practicing physicians were attempting to exert some measure of professional control through motives that combined pecuniary self-interest and the best interests of the public. Second, the efforts of these societies to raise professional standards complemented a legislative trend that saw many states looking to these bodies as adjunct partners in medical regulation. New York, South Carolina, Maryland, New Jersey, and Connecticut soon required that a medical license could only be obtained by membership in a medical society comprised of physician peers or by passing an examination administered by such a society. In some of the more sparsely populated regions, individual physicians were designated to serve as examiners when numbers were insufficient for a medical society or an official licensing authority.[8]

This evolving regulatory model predicated upon localized control by nongovernmental bodies that were comprised of a physician's peers made sense. The questionable diagnostic and therapeutic value of much of the practice of medicine in the colonies at this time also meant the profession was truly more of an art than a science. As such, direct experiences with, and supervision by, physician peers represented a reasonable attempt to ensure a modicum of professional expertise; and in the overwhelmingly rural America of that time, it represented the only practical model.

The practice of medicine remained a universally empirical and experiential art for much of the Enlightenment in the colonies, often passed on through apprenticeship. A young man would spend four to seven years with a doctor's household (sometimes in indenture), keep casebooks, and learn the art of medicine from close observation for a typical fee of about $100. Much of the actual practices of physicians in early America were, in fact, no different from the practices of physicians elsewhere in Europe and quite similar to the practices of medicine worldwide. They lacked knowledge of basic concepts such as bacteria, infection, and contagion and diagnosed disease based upon observed symptoms (e.g., fever), a practice which understandably led to incorrect categorization and treatment of different diseases. This proved doubly problematic as the incorrect diagnoses made it difficult, if not impossible, to test the efficacy of any treatment.[9] As knowledge of the sciences gradually advanced, and physicians began to prosper as members of a learned profession, the depth and breadth of medical practice that physicians should engage in became a topic of great interest.

EUROPEAN VERSUS AMERICAN MODEL OF MEDICAL PRACTICE

In the years leading up to the American Revolution, and for many years thereafter, Americans' scorn of hierarchy and aristocracy was so strong and pervasive that it eventually led to the grounding in the United States of a particularly egalitarian brand of medicine. This "general undifferentiated medical practice" model would ultimately become the normative model in much of the Occidental world. The differences between the American and European approaches to medical practice at this time were striking and are worth reviewing because they explain, in part, how the American model prevailed.

In England, the medical profession clearly reflected a hierarchical structure. Physicians were recognized as members of a learned profession, part of a cultural elite that was distinct from the "lower orders of surgeons" said to simply practice a craft, or the apothecaries who compounded medicines and were felt to merely follow a trade. Each of the three groups had their own guild organizations that dated to the sixteenth century and had defined boundaries and privileges. Physicians were recognized as gentlemen who typically declined to work with their hands, focusing instead on the more lofty and cerebral activities of "observation, speculation and prescription." The typical English physician, writes historian Daniel Boorstin, looked every bit the part of the gentleman with "powdered wig, a coat of red satin or brocade . . . and a gold-headed cane."[10]

By contrast, surgeons in England were not allowed to call themselves doctors and engaged primarily in manual tasks such as amputations, excisions of boils and cancers, and setting bone fractures, though they were permitted to prescribe medicine. In medieval Europe, many years earlier, barbers had conducted surgical procedures because the physicians of the day were priests forbidden by their Christian faith to shed blood. Surgeons who were employed specifically for amputations and wound excisions of soldiers on the battlefield became distinct from barbers only over time, though many served as "barber-surgeons," ostensibly practicing both crafts. From 1540 to 1745, surgeons and barbers belonged to the same guild in England, with surgeons agreeing not to shave their patients and barbers agreeing not to shed blood. Surgery as a separate specialty within the practice of medicine in the United States, in fact, would remain uncommon until the late 1800s because the earliest anesthetics were not well understood and postoperative infections remained a persistent and daunting problem for which there were no easy solutions.[11]

The apothecaries who carried out a physician's orders and stocked medicines to be mixed in their shops were the most numerous of the three practitioners of the healing arts in England. They also had the right to attend to patients and prescribe but could only charge for the medications they prepared, not for their advice. Even lower on the totem pole were the so-called wise women, ministers, farriers (blacksmiths for equine hoof care), and others who claimed to possess some specific skill or ability to heal or provide care.[12]

Because European physicians had no real incentives to migrate across the Atlantic, the earliest "doctor" in the English colonies in the Americas therefore tended to be the surgeon-apothecary, the midwife and the apothecary, each of whom would sometimes be known as a physician.[13] The boundaries of profession and trade blurred in America, however, as European class distinctions were already anathema to the colonists. The earliest doctors in the colonies, therefore, did it all: diagnose disease, perform surgeries, deliver babies, and sell drugs. The modern vestige of this notion can still be found in many countries and in states like New York, where qualified physicians—whether they ultimately practice in a specialty of medicine or surgery—still receive a license to practice "Medicine and Surgery."

With medicine primarily an art, one might question the need among the colonists at this time for formal medical education and training beyond apprenticeship. It was the prestige and perceived knowledge base underpinning a formal medical degree that prompted many an enterprising and ambitious individual to seek just such an opportunity overseas, a practice that began in the late seventeenth century. Not surprisingly, many did not return after completing their training as financial prospects for new physicians were much more appealing in Europe than at home. No medical schools existed in America until 1765, so colonists like William Bull, of South Carolina, traveled abroad in 1734 to receive a medical degree.[14] By the time of the Revolutionary War, it was estimated that there were 3,500 individuals in the thirteen colonies who called themselves physicians, no more than 350 of whom were said to be graduates of European medical schools. In 1790, the year of the first census conducted by the United States government, the general population was estimated at 3,929,214, suggesting a workforce of 89 physicians per 100,000 persons.[15]

As colonial physicians became better established and more affluent at home many more sought formal medical education in Europe. Cities such as Paris, Leyden, Vienna, Parma, Padua, London, Dublin, and Edinburgh (where more than one hundred Americans received medical degrees before 1800) offered American physicians and others interested in medical careers an unrivaled opportunity to improve their abilities and skills. Noticing the great wealth and opulence of European physicians while abroad, American physicians like John Moultrie, Isaac Cathrall, Thomas Cadwalader, Thomas Bond, Benjamin Rush, William Shippen Jr., John Morgan, and Abraham Chovet returned with considerable energy and ambition to create their own medical societies and medical schools, hoping to perhaps achieve the "prestige, standards and dignity" for their growing profession that physicians seemed to enjoy overseas. Though the Massachusetts General Court issued a call for the formal study of "physicke and chirurgery" and the teaching of human dissection as early as 1647, it would take more than a century before the first medical school was established.[16] The story of John Morgan and the response to his bold ambitions for medical education in the colonies upon his return from abroad in 1763 illustrates how a distinctly American form of medicine was destined to dominate in this country.

THE FIRST MEDICAL SCHOOL IN THE UNITED STATES

The first son of an immigrant from Wales, John Morgan trained in the colonies as an apothecary and then as an apprentice to a practicing physician before going abroad for three years of medical study in Edinburgh, where he received his medical degree, and then on to London, Paris, Parma and Padua, where he reportedly met Giovanni Morgagni, the great Italian anatomist. Excited by his experiences, Morgan returned to Philadelphia and announced his determination to engage in medicine "without turning apothecary or practising surgery." Though he pleaded in vain for his colleagues to adopt the European style of a "separate and regular practice of physic" (that is, apart from surgery and apothecary), he was chastised for not appreciating the essentially democratic nature of the colonists and their antipathy toward class distinctions, even in medicine. This was hardly surprising given that colonists had already rejected, on similar grounds, British customs and practices such as primogeniture and a nationalized church. A second reason, at least as important, arose from concern about disrupting the economic status quo. Formally splitting fees with surgeons and apothecaries was inappropriate, prominent contemporary physicians argued, because Philadelphians were said to be accustomed to paying a single comprehensive fee for medical services; besides, it was stated, a proper physician was identified as much by his high calling fee as by his dress and education.[17]

Morgan reluctantly demurred and issued his famous apology, delivered at the public commencement of the College of Philadelphia in 1765, for "attempting to introduce the regular mode of practicing physician." While he did not succeed in getting his original model adopted by his colleagues, he did manage to persuade the trustees of the college to establish what would become America's first medical school (later the University of Pennsylvania School of Medicine), where he served as its first Professor of the Theory and Practice of Medicine. Two years later, a second medical school was organized in New York as King's College (now Columbia University College of Physicians and Surgeons). King's College holds the distinction of being the first medical school in the colonies to formally offer the M.D. (doctor of medicine) degree, beginning in 1767.[18]

What Morgan did not realize was that in the English provinces outside of London, and even in Edinburgh, the tides were beginning to turn in favor of a general practice model of medicine that was seen to be more efficient and comprehensive, combining all three branches (medicine, surgery and apothecary). Morgan's accompanying discourse on the value of a formal medical education nonetheless served as an important template for the founding of many other medical schools in the United States, including Harvard Medical School, established in 1782. Morgan went on to serve from 1775 to 1777 as the colonists' second "chief physician and director general," an early name for the U.S. surgeon general, of the Continental Army.[19]

THE RIGHT TO PRACTICE MEDICINE: STATE MEDICAL SOCIETIES VERSUS MEDICAL SCHOOLS

With the establishment of the first medical school (Pennsylvania) and the first use of a medical society by a colonial government to examine those seeking to practice medicine (Massachusetts), medical regulation in the United States seemed poised to advance quickly. Instead, the seeds of a major conflict were sprouting that would need to be resolved before regulation could advance. If the governmental regulation of medicine by the states was going to be effective, it could occur in conjunction with medical societies or with medical schools, but perhaps not both. The sociologist

William Rothstein saw this as an emerging question after the nation's independence: Who should take the lead as individual states considered the prospect of regulating or licensing physicians—the medical societies or medical schools?[20] The medical societies had already received the power to license physicians from many of the colonies prior to independence and most colonies exempted medical school graduates from licensing. Medical societies were beginning to assert that they should require all physicians, even those trained at the nation's newest medical schools, to obtain licenses. The medical schools, in turn, felt their diplomas should be adequate for the lifelong practice of medicine. After all, they argued, in England the medical degrees of Oxford and Cambridge were recognized as a credential sufficient to authorize their holders to practice medicine.

The conflict reached a turning point in Massachusetts in 1788 when Harvard's medical school sent its first and only two students to be examined by the board of censors (examiners) of the Massachusetts Medical Society. Though aware of the school's reluctance to present its students for examination because of a nagging belief by the school that additional examination was unnecessary, the society committed a tactical error. Fearing that the licensing of medical students would "encourage the school's proponents to expand its curriculum and grant degrees" without limit, the medical society promptly rejected the graduates, despite their having performed well. In response, a Harvard faculty member defiantly instituted a formal course of lectures with the intention of awarding a medical degree at commencement later that year. The medical society's members tried in vain to urge Harvard's president, Joseph Willard, and the school's Board of Overseers to halt the courses. By the end of the year, an examination was held by the school and the two students again performed well. Realizing that they would be confronted with a fait accompli, the society decided to hold a reexamination of the two men in the week before the students' commencement. The men passed and at graduation received the degree of Doctor in Physic, formally enabling Harvard's first medical graduates to practice medicine.[21]

Going forward, the Harvard medical degree would suffice for the lawful practice of medicine in Massachusetts without further examination or endorsement by the state's medical society.[22] This Boston contretemps presaged a struggle that would unfold more fully in the nineteenth century when medical schools proliferated and the medical profession splintered along philosophical lines unimaginable in the eighteenth century.

THE NEW NATION IN THE EARLY 1800s

The first decade of our nation's history has been described as the most crucial in American history because it set precedents and "established in palpable fact what the Constitution had only outlined in purposely ambiguous theory." For the future of medical regulation in these now United States, the Tenth Amendment to the Constitution became the underpinning for the entire system. Following several years of discussion and debate, the states' ratification of this amendment as part of the Bill of Rights concluded on December 15, 1791. It explicitly avowed that powers not granted to the federal government, nor prohibited to the states by the Constitution, would be reserved to the states or to the people, a notion that would be recognized as both a truism and a tautology. Half a century later, Alexis de Tocqueville would remark on the advantages he saw while touring the new nation of having both government centralization (for "the relations of the people with foreigners") and administrative decentralization (for "the undertakings of the township").[23] While the interstate commerce clause of the Constitution has been used in more modern times to legitimize increased federal authority, particularly in areas outside of health care, the Tenth Amendment remains a living codification of states' rights and is routinely cited by state medical boards today to justify the authority delegated to them by their state legislatures.

Medical society membership continued to offer a convenient mechanism for medical regulation in the earliest years of the new republic. In 1799, the *Raleigh Register* suggested in an editorial that it would be "extremely useful" if the newly chartered medical society of North Carolina, which was planning to formally organize later that year, could enable "the community to distinguish the true Physician from the ignorant pretender; and . . . suppress the fatal and criminal practices of Quacks." A report of the society's meeting from 1800, presided over by Richard Fenner, an army surgeon who served during the Revolution, records that licensure candidate Charles Smith passed the society's examinations for admission into the organization and for licentiate status. Though the society's members were said to be "able and progressive physicians," the organization survived only five years, for reasons that are unclear.[24]

In 1806, New York's state legislature enacted what some have characterized as "the most elaborate medical law" for its time in the United States. It called upon medical practitioners in every county in the state to form societies and then to elect censors to examine prospective candidates for admission to the society. Medical students would be examined only after they successfully completed three years of medical study. The Medical Society of the State of New York (MSSNY), established on April 4 of the same year, convened delegates representing all of the state's county societies and was authorized by the state legislature to serve as an appellate court for unsuccessful candidates rejected by the county society for licensure. Despite such an elaborate law, between 1806 and 1827 the only penalty for the unlicensed practice of medicine in New York was a prohibition on suing in the state's courts to collect outstanding fees.[25]

New York's experience, while perhaps not wholly satisfactory in the eyes of the public or that state's physicians, was typical of the direction of most licensing laws in the first decades of the 1800s. In most instances, state legislatures looked to work in concert with medical societies as the best mechanism for regulating the practice of medicine within their state. Often it was state legislation that established a state's medical society—years before the AMA and the American Osteopathic Association became umbrella organizations for the societies—and empowered the society's members to control membership criteria as the sole pathway to a license to practice medicine. Perhaps not surprisingly, this approach sometimes faltered in larger states where the population (including that of physicians) was widely dispersed and where primitive frontier conditions prevailed. The experiences of North Carolina, Ohio, Pennsylvania and Virginia fall into this category. Ohio, in particular, witnessed a bewildering series of laws, none of which took root, such that a "disgusted" legislature repealed all licensing laws from the books in 1833.[26]

In Texas, the newly formed Republic established a Board of Medical Censors on December 14, 1837, for the purpose of granting licenses to practice medicine and surgery. Signed into law by Sam Houston, the Republic's legendary first president, it required the board to consist of one physician, a graduate of medicine and surgery from an authorized college or university, from each state senatorial district. A twenty-dollar fee for licensure was collected from those who passed an examination, without which physicians could not collect unpaid fees from patients in court. The board was scheduled to meet annually but transportation over long distances and unstable frontier conditions frequently prevented annual meetings, and the board was eventually discontinued by a state legislative act in 1848.[27]

Medical schools—which should have been a growing source of supply for physician candidates appearing for membership in the medical societies—were experiencing problems of their own. Prior to 1810, approximately ten medical schools operated in the United States. Situated primarily along the East Coast, the schools produced reasonably well-educated individuals with knowledge of the natural sciences, mathematics, foreign languages (almost exclusively Latin), materia medica (pharmacology) and service spent in a medical apprenticeship. Attempts to emulate European counterparts did not always work. Those medical schools in America that offered both a bachelor's degree and a medical degree, as European medical schools did and many still do, soon discovered that students receiving their bachelor's degree after a year of study rarely came back to study for their medical degree. The medical school at the College of Philadelphia bowed to this reality when, in 1789, it eliminated the bachelor's degree from its curriculum, instead requiring one course in natural and experimental philosophy (or its equivalent) as a prerequisite for its medical degree. Elsewhere in the United States, medical schools were seeking and often receiving statutory accommodations with medical societies. In Connecticut, for example, the state legislature in 1810 created an examining board that consisted of an equal number of faculty and nonfaculty members of the Connecticut Medical Society, making sure that graduates of the new Medical Institution of Yale College had an equal opportunity to qualify for medical licenses. Others such as the Berkshire Medical Institution in Massachusetts gained the same privileges for its graduates to practice medicine as those enjoyed by Harvard through recourse to the state legislature.[28]

After the War of 1812, medical schools began to proliferate in the United States, particularly west of the Appalachians, as the nation's seemingly inexorable westward expansion accelerated and its rural population grew. By 1840, there were thirty-three schools of varying size and quality; by 1875, the number approached eighty. Despite the notable exception of Elizabeth Blackwell, who graduated from the Geneva Medical School in New York in 1859, most medical schools remained overwhelmingly male bastions of learning well into the mid-1900s. Most of the nation's medical schools in these early 1800s were also commercial, proprietary endeavors lacking state support, a reality that continued throughout the nineteenth century. Invariably these institutions were of poor quality and noticeably lacking in resources. Most of the revenue supporting these schools stemmed from the physician faculty, who charged fees and distributed tickets for attendance at their lectures.[29]

Alarmed by an increase in the number of medical schools and their class sizes, New York's medical society proposed in 1826 that either the mode of compensation of faculty members at medical schools be changed in that state to reduce the economic incentive toward larger enrollment, or that the license be separated entirely from the degree, with the latter simply becoming "a professional distinction" without practice privileges. In part, the president of MSSNY was responding to a clear trend in which the number of licenses issued by medical societies was steadily being eclipsed by the number of students receiving medical degrees. With lax enforcement of licensing laws and obstacles in place at medical societies as the guardians of the licensure pathway, it appears that fewer individuals bothered to pursue a license at all. Figures derived from the medical societies in New York, Connecticut, New Jersey and Maryland for the second quarter of the nineteenth century all reflect a similar trend.[30] This lack of interest in medical regulation, on the part of both physicians and the public, stemmed in part from the limitations of traditional medicine in being able to consistently and assuredly alleviate the effects of disease and suffering.

THE RISE OF ALTERNATIVE MEDICAL PHILOSOPHIES IN THE 1800s

Descriptions of the conditions in the 1800s in the cities and towns of the United States, particularly those deep in the American interior, revealed the harsh realities and medical challenges of an agrarian lifestyle as well as the conditions facing individuals in more densely populated locations such as New Orleans, St. Louis, Philadelphia, New York and Baltimore. Humans and their animals lived in dangerously close proximity. Waste from both, along with household garbage and animal carcasses, was disposed of haphazardly. Crude cesspits passed for sanitation.[31]

Perhaps not surprisingly, a series of devastating epidemics of yellow fever, malaria and cholera swept portions of the United States in the first decades of the 1800s. Though the causes of these outbreaks and their treatments were poorly understood, cities such as New Orleans, New York, Boston and Washington, D.C., established temporary health boards to combat such diseases with seasonal street cleaning, the only measure that seemed to curb morbidity and mortality. What these epidemics also laid bare were the clear limitations of medical science at this time. The 1832 cholera epidemic is perhaps most instructive in this regard. Physicians of the day, as in epidemics centuries earlier around the world, remained divided over the causes of disease and illness. In the case of cholera, physicians attributed its origin to factors ranging from atmospheric conditions and unclean living conditions to moral failings on the part of the afflicted. Lacking an understanding of contagion theory and unaware of the existence of bacteria, physicians prescribed treatments for cholera that reflected the harsh remedies of the so-called "heroic" age of medicine, such as bloodletting and liberal doses of calomel, a mercury compound.[32]

The methods employed by physicians for attacking and treating epidemic diseases, as well as for more routine health matters, underscored the profession's long-standing limitations in the therapeutic realm. The frequent failures of *traditional* medicine soon opened the door to alternative treatment philosophies and methodologies, such as Thomsonian medicine, homeopathy, eclectic medicine and, much later, osteopathic medicine (described in chapter 3). In some cases, these alternative schools of medicine attracted so many adherents and such broad public support that schools devoted to these medical philosophies contributed significantly to the proliferation of a wide variety of medical schools in the 1800s.

Individual physicians and reformers became drawn to various movements and theories as part of their faith or because the medical therapeutics of the day were often as lethal as the diseases they purported to cure. For example, Benjamin Rush, the noted physician and signatory to the Declaration of Independence, sought, like many of his peers, a universal theory to explain illness and disease to help rid the practice of medicine of its complexities and mysteries. Rush soon came to equate the European taxonomy of hundreds of diseases as reflective of aristocracy and monarchy. He sought to create instead an enlightened practice of medicine that even ordinary people in the new nation could understand and comprehend. Rush reduced all diseases to fever, which he claimed was caused by tension in the blood vessels. Thus, Rush's recommended treatment for all diseases, from consumption (tuberculosis) to cancer, involved reducing vascular tension through purging and bloodletting. Acknowledged as the most well-known physician in America at the time of his death in 1813, Rush is also known to have caused the deaths of many of his patients through bloodletting—an outcome attributable in large part to his overestimation of the amount of blood in the human body.[33]

In this regard and despite his zeal, Rush fell squarely in line with the harsh treatments that were offered in this heroic age of medicine. Patient treatments that involved scarification and cupping, blistering, bloodletting, induced vomiting via tartar emetic, intestinal purging through calomel, or profuse sweating with diaphoretics remained the bane of suffering patients well into the 1800s. Bloodletting, in particular, continued to be utilized for specific illnesses for decades, and as late as 1912 was recommended for the treatment of pneumonia by Sir William Osler, widely recognized as the father of modern medicine, though the blood loss he called for was relatively minimal.[34]

A firsthand account by three prominent physicians—James Craik, Elisha Cullen Dick and Gustavus Richard Brown—of the illness and death in 1799 of their most prominent patient, George Washington, illustrates both the inadequacy of medical care at the time and the helplessness of physicians to offer more to the nation's great hero, founding father and first president.

> Some time in the night of Friday . . . having been exposed to rain on the preceding day, General Washington was attacked with an inflammatory affection of the upper part of the windpipe. . . . The necessity of bloodletting suggesting itself to the General, he procured a bleeder in the neighborhood, who took from the arm in the night, twelve or fourteen ounces of blood. . . . Upon the arrival of the first of the consulting physicians, it was agreed, as there were yet no signs of accumulation in the bronchial vessels of the lungs, to try the result of another bleeding, when about thirty-two ounces were drawn, without the smallest apparent alleviation of the disease. Vapours of vinegar and water were frequently inhaled, ten grains of calomel (mercury) were given, succeeded by repeated doses of emetic tartar, amounting in all to five or six grains, with no other effect than a copious discharge from the bowels. The powers of life seemed now manifestly yielding to the force of the disorder. Speaking, which was painful from the beginning, now became

> almost impracticable, respiration grew more and more contracted and imperfect, till half after eleven o'clock on Saturday night, when, retaining the full possession of his intellect, he expired without a struggle.[35]

Years later, Brown wrote Craik defensively about that fateful night: "You must remember he (i.e., Dick) was averse to bleeding the General, and I have often thought that if we had acted according to his suggestion when he said, 'he needs all his strength—bleeding will diminish it,' and taken no more blood from him, our good friend might have been alive now. But we were governed by the best light we had; we thought we were right, and so we are justified."[36]

Brown and Craik, like the majority of educated physicians throughout the world, adhered to Galen's humoral theory of medicine, itself based on Aristotelian doctrine, that the body was composed of four cardinal elements (water, fire, air and earth) comprising four principal humors (phlegm, blood, bile and black bile). Galen's theories had been taught for centuries throughout Europe and Asia and were contained in Avicenna's celebrated *Canon of Medicine,* which remained the premier medical textbook in the world for six centuries following its publication in 1012. According to the theory, excessive quantities or improper temperature of these humors resulted in disease. Dietary measures, herbal remedies and phlebotomy, therefore, were routinely employed to secure a proper humoral balance in case of disease.[37] As the medical historian Paul Strathern adeptly notes about the persistence of this point of view, "The Roman Empire would fall . . . the Middle Ages would pass, the Renaissance would come and go, before humanity conceived of better explanations." Still, some American physician leaders did appreciate the opportunities and challenges before them. David Arnell, secretary of New York's Orange County Medical Society, described well the difficulties of reconciling the value of clinical experimentation with limitations in medical knowledge. In an 1807 address, Arnell cited the deadening effect of "absurd systems of ancient physicians" and the equally "preposterous" theories of some of his contemporaries who minimized the need for "experimentation . . . to precede conjecture." Arnell questioned blind adherence to any overarching philosophy of medicine when "our knowledge of Nature is too limited and our collection of materials too scanty to enable even the most diligent and ingenious to form a correct theory."[38]

Samuel Thomson of New Hampshire emerged as one of the first of the challengers to the status quo in medicine. Deeply suspicious of "orthodox" physicians and their harsh mineral-based treatments (e.g., mercury, arsenic), Thomson developed a botanical-based theory of medicine predicated upon the idea that the source of all disease stemmed from cold, with heat as the key therapeutic treatment, such as steam baths and "hot" botanicals such as cayenne pepper. Thomson's popular 1822 work, *New Guide to Health; or Botanic Family Physician,* not only sold well, it created a mass

Table 1.1. Bacteriological Origin of Select Diseases

Disease	*Microorganism*	*Year Relationship Established*
Anthrax	*Bacillus anthracis*	1876
Malaria	*Plasmodium malariae*	1880
Diphtheria	*Bacillus diphtheria*	1884
Pneumonia	*Diplococcus pneumonia*	1884
Typhoid fever	*Bacillus typhosus*	1884
Dysentery	*Bacillus dysenteriae*	1898

Source: Adapted from Nathan Colwell, "Medical Education, 1915" in U.S. Dept. of the Interior, Bureau of Education, *Report of the Commissioner of Education* (Washington, DC: Government Printing Office, 1915), 191.

following of Thomsonians in rural America who embraced the notion of reclaiming medicine from the hands of the privileged and placing it in the hands of the people. Thomson's intellectual "descendants" later established thirteen "physio-medical" schools committed to botanical medicine and foreswearing mineral-based drugs. Meanwhile, Samuel Hahnemann, a well-educated German physician, established the principles of homeopathic medicine that reached the United States in the 1820s. Hahnemann's homeopathic philosophy was built upon two concepts: the notion that "like cures like" and a so-called law of infinitesimals. The resulting drug therapies stemming from these principles involved administering drugs in such small doses as to have minimal effect; in effect, leaving nature to do the work of healing. The eclectic branch of medicine of the type pursued by John Brinkley in 1908 comprised the other major alternative group of medical practitioners that originated prior to the Civil War. Like the Thomsonians, the eclectics relied heavily upon botanical or herbal remedies; unlike them, however, they advocated medical treatments guided by physicians, rather than placed in the hands of the layman.[39]

The significance of these medical philosophies and their adherents, often characterized by orthodox physicians as "irregular" practitioners in the 1800s, was their success in establishing strong, viable challenges to traditional medicine beginning in the 1830s. Alternative practitioners and their philosophies continued to gain traction because an understanding of the germ theory of disease, and the definitive identification of the specific pathogens responsible for several major diseases, was still decades away (see table 1.1). Thomsonian, homeopathic and other alternative philosophies of medicine proffered an apparently coherent vision of medicine that was generally understandable to the public. Additionally, the lack of constraints around the establishment of medical schools allowed practitioners of such philosophies to set up numerous homeopathic and eclectic schools. Consequently, when licensing laws reemerged in the 1870s, after their collapse in the Jacksonian Era, state legislation often gave a statutory imprimatur to these philosophies by establishing separate boards for the licensing of these practitioners or ensuring their representation on state medical boards.

THE JACKSONIAN ERA AND THE FOUNDING OF THE AMERICAN MEDICAL ASSOCIATION

As evidenced by the circumstances surrounding President Washington's death, the absence of consistently dependable treatments for disease in the United States in the early 1800s helped promote a notion that popular knowledge was perhaps as accurate as the knowledge of experts. Such a radical proposal found a receptive social climate during America's Jacksonian Era (1828–1840) when the long political shadow of the political giant and hero of the Battle of New Orleans, President Andrew Jackson, inculcated a reverence for the wisdom of the common man. The era coincided with the acceleration of the nation's Second Great Awakening, when religious revivals energized existing churches (particularly Baptist and Methodist but also Presbyterian) and generated new ones, including the Seventh-day Adventists, Christian Scientists, Jehovah's Witnesses, and Mormons. Looking back, one might also argue that the inadequate scientific underpinnings for medicine in those days meant that a physician's education or training simply did not matter to most patients and was largely irrelevant to treatment outcomes. It seems likely that at some level this was understood intuitively by much of America's citizenry. Thus, the rationale for legally limiting the practice of medicine struck many Americans as questionable at best.

The rugged individualism and anti-regulatory climate of the first half of the nineteenth century, combined with the democratization of medicine as espoused by Thomsonians and others, led directly to what modern observers might find shocking: the wholesale collapse of medical regulation in the United States. Nearly every state repealed its penalties for the unlicensed practice of medicine, with Illinois leading the way in 1826, followed over the next quarter century or so by Alabama, Ohio, Mississippi, Georgia, Massachusetts, Maine, South Carolina, the District of Columbia, Maryland, Vermont, Connecticut, New York, Texas, Michigan, and, in 1852, Louisiana. Only New Jersey appears to have managed to avoid repealing its medical licensing laws throughout much of this period. Caught in a democratic upheaval just fifty years after the nation's founding, America's physicians and their loose patchwork of county and state medical societies felt publicly and effectively humiliated by the revocation of their profession's licensing authority. Attempts later in the century to reestablish a regulatory system would prove quite challenging, though gradual progress would be made beginning around the time of the Civil War. Even so, as late as 1894 the impact of the Jacksonian Era could be detected, when physicians were being registered by the Oklahoma Territorial Board of Health on what was essentially an honor system: the board registered anyone presenting what appeared to be a diploma from a medical school or an affidavit stating that the medical diploma had been lost.[40]

As the governmental basis for medical regulation largely disappeared in the 1830s and 1840s, most practicing physicians simply pursued their vocation as best they could under the new circumstances. Others, however, felt a need to speak up and sought to mobilize their colleagues to action in areas where they believed progress could be made. In 1844, the same year that New York repealed its medical licensure laws, MSSNY explored the possibility of raising the standards in the state for medical education. The motives behind this initiative were a mixture of altruism (improving the quality of physicians treating the public) and self-interest (slowing the wide number and variety of physicians entering practice by means of raising educational standards). The state's medical schools presented a significant challenge to this practical proposal, however, with their understandable concern that if other states did not similarly pursue increased standards, students would abandon the New York schools and simply transfer their tuition and fees to other states. Recognizing a need for national action on the matter, MSSNY's leaders issued a call for a national convention of all of the country's state medical societies and medical schools to be held in New York in 1846. Only eleven medical schools sent representatives, fewer than hoped, ostensibly because of concern that they might be called upon to unilaterally raise admission and graduation standards. One significant historic action did emerge from the gathering, however—the decision to establish a permanent national medical society, an action which formally came to fruition the following year when the group convened in Philadelphia.[41]

Several hundred delegates representing forty state medical societies and twenty-eight medical schools from across the United States gathered in the "City of Brotherly Love" in 1847. The new organization, it was agreed, would be called the American Medical Association (AMA) and its founding president would be thirty-year-old Nathan Smith Davis—the same New York physician who led that state's medical society in its reform efforts a year earlier. Davis would later serve as the first editor of the *Journal of the American Medical Association (JAMA).*

Despite national calls for reform of curricula and admission requirements at the nation's medical schools, the AMA was no more successful than MSSNY had been in New York because neither organization had the legal right to impose penalties on substandard medical schools. In part, this may have stemmed from inherent tensions within the physician community in attempting to address the quality of America's medical schools, which remained largely commercial, proprietary endeavors of individual or groups of physicians. While most physicians may have viewed progress on this front as essential to improving the profession's status, others vigorously opposed such efforts as an assault on their financial interests in these schools. Additionally, relations between state medical societies and the medical schools, as they had been in the early years of the new nation, remained strained. The medical societies thus faced an existential problem: if they insisted on higher standards for admission into their society, membership would decrease and they would struggle to survive; if they admitted large numbers of physicians without regard to high standards they would be unable to insist on higher standards later and their membership could fracture.[42]

One approach the AMA did consider and could act upon without dissent, and which was likely to garner support from both traditional medical schools and practitioners of traditional or "regular" medicine, was to confront practitioners of alternative medical philosophies. The AMA Code of Ethics, adopted in 1847, squarely confronted the homeopathic challenge first. Homeopathy had grown sufficiently by then to have organized its own national organization in 1844, the American Institute of Homeopathy. The subsequent perceived success of homeopathic physicians in treating cholera patients in the late 1840s, as measured against the more aggressive treatments of orthodox practitioners, won additional converts to the homeopathic system. The Code's consultative clause explicitly prohibited AMA members from case consultation with sectarian practitioners.[43] The growing lines of division separating regular from so-called irregular practitioners spawned a vigorous counterattack from adherents of alternative philosophies who later waged successful state legislative battles that established separate licensing boards for homeopathic, eclectic, and, later, osteopathic physicians.

CIVIL WAR AND THE RETURN OF MEDICAL LICENSING LAWS

By the mid-1800s, the proliferation of all varieties of medical schools with few requirements for admission contributed to an increasing number of physicians of many stripes ostensibly possessing medical degrees. Superimposed upon the general collapse of the legislative structures that had supported medical regulation at the start of the Jacksonian Era, the physician holding a medical license in the 1800s in the United States possessed a credential of limited utility. Where an earlier generation of the profession had rightly viewed the medical degree leading to a license as a path to socioeconomic prestige and financial advantage, this was no longer the case. As for the public, they seemed uninterested in the sectarian debates among physicians. As one historian describes it, the public "remained indifferent to progress in pathology, new germ theories of disease, or . . . primitive ideas that ascribed ills to the influence of the stars, provided they were relieved of their pain and freed from the bonds of sickness."[44]

The public increasingly viewed the credentials of a physician (whether by medical degree or license) as irrelevant. These notions would continue unabated as long as the diagnostics and therapeutics of the practice of medicine remained poorly understood and as long as the value of appropriately trained and licensed physicians remained elusive.

By the time the Civil War began, the medical licensing system in the country was virtually destroyed or abandoned in nearly all of the states. Historians have found little to say in defense of American medical practices, regulation or education at this time. Typically, the period has been characterized as a "dark ages" for the profession in the United States, when medical schools of all types were often "incredibly bad" and practitioners of varying philosophies and training were generally ineffective in the face of disease.[45]

Against this indolent backdrop occurred one of the central traumatic events in America's collective memory that was also an important milestone, as it were, for the practice of medicine and surgery, the advancement of public health, and the belated recognition of a need for robust, state-based medical licensure and discipline. The 1861 onset of the Civil War represented a watershed moment in the practice of medicine, leading eventually to both a greater scrutiny of those who called themselves physicians and a higher regard for the enforcement of proper sanitation and public hygiene. From the time that hostilities commenced at Fort Sumter on April 12, 1861, to the final surrender at Appomattox Court House on April 9, 1865, more than 620,000 soldiers and countless numbers of civilians died in the conflict. Though the Civil War remains America's deadliest war, two-thirds of the deaths were said to be the result of medical illnesses such as typhoid and dysentery in grossly unsanitary encampments rather than at the end of a bayonet or a bullet.

One of the first challenges facing the North and the South during the conflict was identifying a qualified cadre of physicians prepared to treat sick and wounded soldiers. Prewar statistics offer some insight into the scope of the problem. From 1841 to 1849, only 55 out of 170 candidates for Army surgeon (the term then used to describe all military physicians) managed to pass the Army Medical Board examinations, while 77 of 175 passed the Navy Medical Board examination. Obtaining what the military deemed acceptably qualified physicians proved challenging. At the start of the Civil War, there were only 64 commissioned medical officers in the United States Army. Expanding the pool of military physicians also proved difficult as the Army's written examinations demonstrated very clearly the ill-training, inadequate knowledge and near illiteracy of many prospective medical officers. The average military physician candidate, it was said, conveyed a "vague and confused" understanding of medicine in "barbarous" English with the result that nearly three-quarters failed the examination. Once inducted into the Union army, the uneven quality of the candidates further manifested itself in a court-martial/dismissal rate estimated by one historian as 5 percent—nearly twice the rate for the Union army as a whole.[46] It quickly became apparent that physician and governmental efforts to preserve the health and well-being of soldiers were wholly inadequate to the medical challenges posed by the war.

Physicians and civilians tried to collaborate on major voluntary initiatives on behalf of the war effort. In 1861, a New York physician named Elisha Harris established a voluntary organization called the Women's Central Relief Fund and pressured the Union's secretary of war, Simon Cameron, to accept the voluntary services of a first-ever sanitation commission. Despite initial reservations about the utility of such a group, federal authorities acquiesced to the recommendation and in 1861 President Abraham Lincoln signed legislation creating the United States Sanitary Commission. The Commission's investigation found that there was a lack of fresh food and medicines for soldiers, poor levels of medical care for the sick and wounded and scant hospital facilities. In addition to distributing fresh fruits and vegetables to all the regiments and ensuring a regular supply of medicines, the Commission pressured the Army Medical Corps, which was initially hostile to outside efforts, to adopt new policies to prevent typhoid and prevent the spread of disease through isolation. These sanitary reforms in the military would later have a direct and positive impact on the civilian population when Union troops began to impose, as they did in New Orleans, new sanitary programs upon local health authorities. They also acquainted some cities and regions with the efficacy of governmental action in the public health arena. In addition, the practical experiences gained in the field by physicians in the Civil War led to a better understanding of anesthetics and surgical care. By the time of the Battle of Antietam in 1862, which saw upward of 23,000 casualties in a single day, army surgeons had developed and implemented procedures and processes for the Union Army that would lay the foundations for the development after the war of both a civilian ambulance corps and emergency room triage in cities across the reunited United States.[47]

With the Civil War becoming such a dominant presence in all aspects of the American experience between 1861 and 1865, it is not surprising that issues left simmering or pushed aside at the start of the war reemerged with even greater force in the aftermath of war and Reconstruction. The reinstitution of a medical regulatory system in America can be traced to many factors, though perhaps the greatest of these was a general reassessment of what government regulation in the guise of licensing represented. Where once the licensing of physicians had been equated with "power and privilege," the concept now became more closely linked to a genuine effort at protecting the general public as well as the interests of independent educated professionals, both of which now seemed vulnerable in the emerging age of industrial titans like Rockefeller, Carnegie and Vanderbilt. The Reconstruction era witnessed the birth of large corporations that seemed to threaten the idealized American vision of a nation driven by the economic engines of the yeoman farmer, artisan and small businessman. Recognizing the value of qualified physicians to help promote the public's health, not to mention the value of qualified engineers and architects, occupational licensing developed anew, starting in the 1870s. The basic idea, of course, was not entirely new since the colonies had licensed auctioneers and peddlers. The type of licensure familiar to us today for doctors, nurses, pharmacists and lawyers soon blossomed in the late nineteenth century. While the justification was the same for almost all of the occupations, ostensibly to protect the public, this was considered the most obvious and persuasive argument in the case of doctors.[48]

North Carolina was one of the first states to emerge out of the professional and regulatory dark ages, even before the Civil War had commenced. The state's medical society, first established in 1799 and long dormant, was reconstituted in 1849. The state's first medical practice act became effective with the creation of the North Carolina Medical Board on April 15, 1859, following what has been described as a "spirited debate." Graduation from medical school was not a requirement for medical licensure but the applicant, who paid a one-time license fee of $10, needed to be at least twenty-one years of age, of good moral character and able to pass the board's examination. The names of the licensees were to be published in two newspapers within thirty days of medical licensure. The legislation also contained a "grandfather" clause exempting those who were already actively practicing medicine from the board's examination requirement. Texas adopted its medical licensing authority and created county boards of medical examiners in 1873 (its state board of examiners, replacing its county system of regulation, was created in 1907), Nevada in 1875 (its board of medical examiners was created in 1899), Alabama and California in 1876, Illinois in 1877, Minnesota in 1883, Colorado and Washington in 1881, New Mexico in 1882, Virginia in 1884 and Oklahoma in 1890.[49] It is important to note that as licensing laws began to reappear throughout the United States, and in the absence of a national body among regulators to promote sharing of ideas or reach consensus on common standards, there was predictable and considerable variation among adopted state legislation. As will be discussed more fully in later chapters, the impact of poorly written or inadequate legislation would prove challenging for state boards for years to come. Additionally, the variance in standards embedded in the legislation provided fertile ground for questionable practitioners seeking the lowest common denominator in state qualifications for licensure who were anxious to remain one step ahead of authorities by crossing state lines.

Nearly all of the states had licensing boards and independent examinations of their own in place by 1910. And once states began insisting upon an examination as a prerequisite for medical licensure, proprietary schools (some of which were little more than diploma mills) could no longer blatantly exploit state law with abandon.[50] With greater emphasis on the quality of examinations administered to physicians to qualify for state licensure, test security now became an important concern. The minutes from a 1911 meeting of the North Carolina Medical Board record one of the very earliest reports of cheating on a medical licensing examination when a security breach resulted in a physician candidate obtaining an advance copy from an elevator attendant at the hotel where the test was being administered.[51]

On the western coast of the United States, states like California recognized the value and need for medical regulation for their own reasons. The territory saw its first population boom in and around San Francisco because of the 1850 gold rush. Later, the southern part of the state became the focal point for questions about the quality of medical practitioners. Because of its "healthy climate," thousands of invalids—and a large number of physicians to take care of them—had migrated to the southwest portions of the state. One doctor remarked in 1875, "We in Los Angeles have a larger percentage of doctors in relation to the population than in any other city I know." That number was estimated to be 165 doctors for a city of 70,000 inhabitants. Because of large numbers of what it saw as "quack doctors and quack remedies," the California legislature passed its first Medical Practice Act in 1876.[52]

The new law provided for the state's medical society to appoint a Board of Examiners consisting of seven members. The new board required all physicians in the state holding medical degrees or licenses to exhibit them, along with an affidavit of their authenticity, to any state board member upon request. Those physicians who had never graduated from a medical school nor had a medical license to practice from another jurisdiction were required to present their names to the board as candidates for examination. Soon thereafter, two additional boards (Eclectic; Homeopathic) were created in 1878 that, like the Medical Board of Examiners, had their membership chosen by their respective medical societies. Between 1875 and 1901 these three boards issued 8,535 certificates to practice medicine at $5 each, netting an income in excess of $42,000—enough to sustain the regulatory bodies, with surplus funds reverting to the state. Soon after 1900, when there were well over one hundred allopathic, homeopathic and eclectic medical schools and a dozen osteopathic medical colleges, every state required an examination of its own to obtain a license to practice medicine, though the scope of the exams would vary from among oral, written and practical exams, often supplemented with an interview.[53]

The pattern seen in North Carolina and California of having the medical society play an active role in medical licensure was typical of laws in the late 1800s. The medical society served either as a recommending body for appointments to the state medical board (or the source for board members) or it provided some degree of oversight by virtue of its role in examining prospective candidates. Eventually, the fledgling state medical boards challenged state medical society oversight and influence with growing assertions of state governmental authority and independence. In California, that challenge came in 1903 when the dean of the California College of Physicians and Surgeons initiated legal proceedings in the state's Supreme Court to have the members of the state's Board of Examiners ousted because the medical society appointing the board was a private corporation and had no right to appoint public officials. Other states around the country took this cue to change their practice—sometimes reactively and sometimes in anticipation of a challenge. The overlapping but not wholly complementary interests of state medical societies and state licensing boards sometimes led to tense discussions. One physician member of Oklahoma's Greer County Medical Society recalled an extraordinarily intense meeting in 1905. While the exact subject of the dispute was not recorded, the minutes noted an exchange of "hot words" made all the more tense by attendees intermittently resting a hand on holstered revolvers.[54] Today, state medical societies have a limited role, if any, in the makeup of state boards, whose voting members are usually appointed by a governor and include physicians, lawyers and members of the public.

A narrative explaining the rebirth of medical licensing laws in the mid- to late 1800s in America might reasonably draw upon multiple additional factors: professional aspirations for greater prestige; competing schools of medicine striving for recognition; a burgeoning number of medical schools; advances in medical science; and growing public awareness of, and perhaps impatience with, the ramifications of a laissez-faire economic system upon individual consumers. According to legal scholar Lawrence Friedman, the tremendous volume of laws passed in the areas of public health and sanitation between 1850 and 1900 can be characterized as a failure of pure free-enterprise theory. Quality goods should, in theory, ultimately drive out bad ones in the market, according to Friedman, or force lower prices.[55] But many people, including the producers of quality goods and the providers of health care services (i.e., physicians), were not willing to wait for the hidden hand of the marketplace. The discovery, validation and better understanding of germ theory between 1857 and

1890, and the dangers of bad food and bad water (which could now be sterilized and processed to avoid contaminants), provided almost a moral impetus for enactment and/or refinement of laws designed to protect the public. Likewise, it may be argued, scientific and medical advancements meant that the public and legislators could no longer afford to wait for good doctors to drive out bad doctors in the competitive marketplace.

Most of the health laws during this period were in the form of criminal statutes targeting the unlicensed practitioner. This was an understandable approach but not the only option. The courts, Friedman argues, might have strengthened the law of warranty but intentionally chose a different direction. After all, anyone could use the civil courts to sue a seller whose goods or services were shoddy or caused harm. But realistically, the average citizen had neither the time nor desire to pursue litigation over a single faulty product or service—or in this case, the outcome of a physician-patient interaction. Under criminal law, by contrast, the state assumed the cost and burden of enforcement. Thus, the establishment of licensing laws that placed enforcement under criminal statutes represented the commitment of a governmentally based regulatory system to intercede on behalf of the public.

By the twentieth century, as opposed to the nineteenth century, it made a substantive difference to a patient in the United States where and how his physician was educated and trained. What would now be needed for the medical regulatory system to work were effective laws in every state and quality medical schools everywhere, to prevent a medical student at a deficient school from obtaining a license in a different state where the law was lax or nonexistent. As state licensing boards began to understand the importance of their role better, and as concerns about the rigors of an undergraduate medical education increased, the seeds were now planted for the establishment of national bodies devoted to both these areas.

PROMOTING QUALITY MEDICAL EDUCATION

Major developments in medical education were occurring simultaneous with the advent of the licensing laws of the late 1800s. The U.S. Census Report of 1870 listed 110 schools teaching medicine in the United States, 77 of which could be classified as orthodox, with 62,383 persons claiming medicine as their profession. Historian Kenneth Ludmerer notes that medical schools of all philosophies and backgrounds at this time were remarkably deficient in the delivery of their curricula. Course work was accelerated and highly "superficial" with the second of two sixteen-week terms essentially repeating its content. Laboratory work was minimal as few schools possessed true laboratories. The physical facilities were usually small, often sharing space with another business. The entire faculty might consist of a handful of instructors who, not coincidentally, were often the owners of the school. Rare was the school that possessed any legitimate relationship or affiliation with a university or hospital, as evidenced by responses to medical schools on questionnaires circulated in 1849 and 1873.[56]

Despite this discouraging state of affairs, steps toward genuine progress and standardization in medical education lay ahead. In retrospect, one sees a two-prong offensive that would soon be under way in medical education reform. The late nineteenth century witnessed the rise of academic medicine as evidenced by the structural model established at Johns Hopkins, Harvard and elsewhere. Much of this initiative was internally driven by medical schools committed to educational reform and supported by the push for increased standards by state medical boards and, later, the Association of American Medical Colleges, the national umbrella organization for traditional medical schools. The second prong in the reform movement unfolded later in the second and third decades of the twentieth century when state medical boards proved quite effective and instrumental in dismantling the remaining inferior, mostly proprietary, medical schools unwilling (or unable) to meet the statutorily mandated minimum standards.[57] This demarcation was hardly precise though as one of the most comprehensive efforts to curb blatant excesses in medical education occurred in Illinois years earlier. That state's 1877 legislation had created a Board of Health, under the leadership of John Rauch, marking the start of a vigorous attempt to verify credentials, assess qualifications, identify bogus medical diplomas and eliminate fraudulent practitioners. The Illinois board also introduced a classification system for medical schools that predated later national efforts. This soon became a de facto "authoritative" listing of schools for all medical licensing boards. Additional help to standardize the quality of medical education occurred almost simultaneously with the creation in 1876 of the AAMC and its efforts to improve medical education. Though the group's aspirations proved untenable early on—the organization disappeared from 1882 to 1890 when its members fell out over a proposal concerning the duration of a medical education curriculum—the momentum toward meaningful medical education was clearly building.[58]

Two U.S. Supreme Court decisions during this time period upheld the states' rights to regulate medicine under the Tenth Amendment. In the 1889 case, *Dent v. State of West Virginia*, the court upheld the right of the West Virginia Board of Health in its refusal to grant a medical license to a graduate of the American Medical Eclectic College of Cincinnati. Justice Stephen Field delivered the court's unanimous opinion, stating that certain circumstances might prompt states to exclude people without licenses from practicing medicine and that in medicine, because of the careful nature of its training, the large knowledge of the human body required of doctors, and the nature of life-and-death circumstances with which doctors dealt, reliance needed to be placed on the assurance of a license. Nearly a decade later in 1898, the Supreme Court went further in *Hawker v. New York* by upholding a state law preventing convicted felons from practicing medicine, even when the felony conviction occurred before the law was enacted, thereby ruling that character can also serve as an important qualification for doctors wishing to obtain a medical license.[59]

Representatives of sixty-six M.D.-granting colleges of medicine attended a reorganization meeting of the AAMC in 1890 and in the following year the AAMC agreed, in conjunction with the newly established National Confederation of State Medical Examining and Licensing Boards (one of two predecessor organizations of the FSMB that are discussed in greater detail in the next chapter), to recommend a three-year medical course of instruction; by 1894 the AAMC had raised its recommendation to four years of medical instruction. By 1896 the National Confederation was also recommending high school graduation as a minimum requirement for premedical education and this was made AAMC policy in 1900. Though the state medical examining boards set up before 1900 had widely differing standards and procedures, through the National Confederation they began to singularly and collectively force commercial medical colleges out of existence, more than a decade before Abraham Flexner issued his scathing indictment of proprietary medical schools.[60]

Alarmed at dwindling medical incomes and the continued proliferation of diploma mills—despite the nascent and welcome efforts of such entities as the state medical boards, the National Confederation and the AAMC—a reorganized and strengthened AMA in 1902 established a committee to take up with the U.S. Congress a proposal for a national medical licensing board that would be appointed by the president of the United States to promote "sufficiently high" standards; the idea was quickly dropped, however, as constitutionally challenging. The right to license physicians was vested in the states, and the states were unlikely to press for the constitutional amendment necessary to set up such a central or national agency. The National Confederation's member boards formally voted down the idea but after it merged with the American Confederation of Reciprocal Examining and Licensing Boards to become the Federation of State Medical Boards in 1912, it did express support for a national medical examining board. This idea was supported by the AMA, subsidized by the Carnegie Foundation for the Advancement of Teaching and resulted in the formation of the National Board of Medical Examiners in 1915. In its strong defense of the proposal, the Federation's leadership provided continuous assurances to its state medical boards that the new National

Board was intended only as a qualifying body, that it would never have licensing powers and would not reduce the state boards' revenue.[61]

Almost simultaneous with these initiatives, innovations in medical knowledge spurred significant changes and educational reforms at health care institutions, starting on the East Coast. The opening of a hospital (1889) and a medical school (1893) at Maryland's Johns Hopkins University were the first steps in what would widely be recognized as the finest hospital and medical school in America. Founded and built upon a German model of medical education, the medical school would be among the first to insist on strict entrance criteria, including the requirement of an undergraduate college degree and successful passage of a medical school entrance examination. The school emphasized scientific method in its curriculum, provided four years of study in the basic and clinical sciences, offered hands-on training for students with patients cared for at the bedside, promoted laboratory research and developed innovative postgraduate internships, residencies and fellowships for additional advanced study in medicine and surgery.[62]

Johns Hopkins was hardly alone in its progressive approach to education, it should be said. Northwestern University had instituted a three-year curriculum for its medical school in 1859; in 1871, Harvard University's president insisted that its medical school have both a three-year curriculum and the requirement of an academic degree for admission. In 1877, the University of Pennsylvania adopted a graded sequential curriculum with clinical courses following scientific courses and abandoned faculty-collected fees in favor of a tuition model. The University of Michigan incorporated similar procedures in 1877 in addition to a rapid expansion in the use of laboratory instruction. One by one in the 1890s, however, medical schools visited the Baltimore campus and began establishing full-time clinical professorships in the manner Johns Hopkins had, though the costs for such reforms were prohibitive for many schools. The typical proprietary school could ill afford to lengthen its curriculum, establish laboratories for research or pay its professors competitive salaries. A clear separation in the quality of medical education was under way. The "have-nots" of medical education were witnessing a new era in which financial pressures for such schools to close, merge or seek university affiliation would steadily increase, quite apart from increasingly effective outside pressures for reform. Moreover, this wave of educational reform—largely internally driven by progressive schools— reflected the commitment to a model of academic medicine consistent with the higher standards sought by state medical boards and consistent with the aspirations of most within the profession.[63]

For state medical boards, the educational curriculum and training introduced by Johns Hopkins and other preeminent schools in the late 1800s created a standard for excellence that would ultimately become the basis for formal evaluation and recognition of all medical schools within their jurisdictions. The curricular model of teaching basic sciences, followed by clinical sciences, and then providing direct patient interaction in a hospital setting would ultimately inform state medical boards' concept of what constitutes a minimally acceptable education and training experience for all physicians. The legal status and authority of state medical boards would serve as a complementary statutory lever driving improvements in medical education and training. Working in concert with voluntary organizations such as the AMA and the AAMC, the state board community supported improvements that within the first several decades of the twentieth century led to the advent of a truly modern medical education.

Nearly three centuries of slowly evolving medical regulation placed the nation, in 1900, on the cusp of what would be termed the "health century," enabling life expectancy to soar, infant mortality to decline, better control of infectious and nutritious diseases, as well as advance our understanding and management of deadly diseases such as cancer, heart disease and stroke.[64] America's medical regulatory community reemerged in the latter half of the 1800s, ready for broader and deeper improvements in the next century as undergraduate, graduate and continuing medical education reforms took shape; as undergraduate, licensing and graduate examinations and assessments became more standardized, computerized and validated; and as medical licensure and discipline by state boards of medicine itself became more rigorous and collaborative. A number of voluntary, nonprofit national organizations devoted to supporting each of these areas arose to nurture and facilitate major transformations in health care and public protection. The Federation of State Medical Boards would be among them.

NOTES

1. Pope Brock, *Charlatan: America's Most Dangerous Huckster, the Man Who Pursued Him and the Age of Flimflam* (New York: Broadway Books, 2009), 10–11.

2. John Tate Lanning, *The Royal Protomedicato: The Regulation of the Medical Profession in the Spanish Empire*, ed. John Jay Tepaske (Durham: Duke University Press, 1985), 20, 24–30; Robert Derbyshire, *Medical Licensure and Discipline in the United States* (Baltimore: Johns Hopkins University Press, 1969), 2; John Duffy, *From Humors to Medical Science: A History of American Medicine* (Urbana: University of Illinois Press, 1991), 39.

3. Felix Swope, Juanita Mayo, et al., *The Virginia Board of Medicine: 1884 to 2000 and Beyond* (Richmond: Virginia Board of Medicine, 2000), 1; Joseph F. Kett, *The Formation of the American Medical Profession: The Role of Institutions, 1780–1860* (New Haven: Yale University Press, 1968), 7–8.

4. Maurice Bear Gordon, *Aesculapius Comes to the Colonies: The Story of the Early Days of Medicine in the Thirteen Colonies* (Ventnor, New Jersey: Ventnor Publishers, 1949), 152.

5. Richard Harrison Shryock, *Medical Licensing in America, 1650–1965* (Baltimore: Johns Hopkins University Press, 1967), vii; George O. Sumner, "Early Physicians in Connecticut," *Connecticut State Medical Journal* 6 (1942): 459.

6. Kett, *Formation of Medical Profession*, 7; Gordon, *Aesculapius*, 154.

7. Robert R. Hannon, "Medical Licensure in New York State," *Federation Bulletin* 30 (July 1943): 194, 197; Shryock, *Medical Licensing*, 17.

8. Kett, *Formation of Medical Profession*, 12–13.

9. John S. Haller Jr., *American Medicine in Transition, 1840–1910* (Urbana: University of Illinois Press, 1981), 193; William G. Rothstein, *American Physicians in the 19th Century: From Sects to Science* (Baltimore: Johns Hopkins University Press, 1985), 27.

10. Paul Starr, *The Social Transformation of American Medicine* (New York: Basic Books, 1982), 37–38; Daniel J. Boorstin, *The Americans: The Colonial Experience* (New York: Random House, 1958), 234.

11. Rothstein, *American Physicians*, 252–53.

12. Duffy, *Humors to Medical Science*, 7–8.

13. Kett, *Formation of Medical Profession*, 5.

14. Arthur M. Schlesinger Jr., *The Almanac of American History* (New York: Barnes and Noble Books, 2004), 84.

15. Haller, *American Medicine in Transition*, 194; "Pop Culture: 1790," U.S. Census Bureau, accessed January 13, 2012, www.census.gov/history/www/through_the_decades/fast_facts/1790_fast_facts.html.

16. Haller, *American Medicine in Transition*, 195; Gordon, *Aesculapius*, 11.

17. Kett, *Formation of Medical Profession*, 11.

18. Haller, *American Medicine in Transition*, 195–96; Starr, *Social Transformation*, 43; "A Brief History of Columbia," Columbia University, accessed January 7, 2012, http://www.columbia.edu/content/history.html.

19. Boorstin, *The Americans*, 235; Kett, *Formation of Medical Profession*, 5, Duffy, *From Humors to Science*, 55.

20. Rothstein, *American Physicians*, 104–5.

21. Ibid.; Duffy, *Humors to Science*, 139–40.

22. Rothstein, *American Physicians*, 104–5; Shryock, *Medical Licensing*, 25.

23. Joseph J. Ellis, *Founding Brothers: The Revolutionary Generation* (New York: Alfred A. Knopf, 2001), 11–12; Alexis de Tocqueville, *Democracy in America*, ed. Harvey C. Mansfield and Delba Winthrop (Chicago: University of Chicago Press, 2000), 82.

24. Ivan M. Proctor and Dorothy Long, *One Hundred Year History of the North Carolina State Board of Medical Examiners, 1859–1959* (Raleigh: Edwards & Broughton, 1959), 1; Christina Apperson, *Protecting the Public, Strengthening the Profession: A One Hundred Fifty Year History of the North Carolina Medical Board, 1859–2009* (North Manchester, Indiana: HF Group, 2009), 1–2.

25. Kett, *Formation of Medical Profession*, 16–17.

26. Rothstein, *American Physicians*, 74–75.

27. "Board of Medical Censors," Texas State Historical Association, accessed October 9, 2011, www.tshaonline.org/handbook/online/articles/mdb07.

28. Rothstein, *American Physicians*, 105.

29. Haller, *American Medicine in Transition*, 199; Paul Strathern, *Medicine from Hippocrates to Gene Therapy* (New York: Carroll and Graf 2005), 268; Duffy, *Humors to Medical Science*, 133.

30. Rothstein, *American Physicians*, 106.

31. "Population of the 33 Urban Places: 1800," U.S. Bureau of the Census, accessed January 13, 2012, http://www.census.gov/population/www/documentation/twps0027/tab03.txt; Mary Beth Norton, David Katzman, et al., *A People and a Nation: A History of the United States to 1877* (Boston: Houghton Mifflin, 1982), 229, 233; Dorothy Porter, *Health, Civilization*

and the State: A History of Public Health from Ancient to Modern Times (New York: Routledge, 1999), 147.

32. Charles Rosenberg, *The Cholera Years: The United States in 1832, 1848 and 1866* (Chicago: University of Chicago Press, 1962), 42, 66, 72, 75.

33. Gordon S. Wood, *Empire of Liberty: A History of the Early Republic, 1789–1815* (New York: Oxford University Press, 2009), 725–26.

34. Rothstein, *American Physicians*, 182.

35. Gordon, *Aesculapius*, 43.

36. Ibid., 43–44.

37. Mona Nasser, Aida Tibi, and Emilie Savage-Smith, "Ibn Sina's Canon of Medicine: 11th Century Rules for Assessing the Effects of Drugs," *Journal of the Royal Society of Medicine* 102 (2009): 78–80.

38. Strathern, *Hippocrates to Gene Therapy*, 34; David Arnell, *Secretary's Reports, 1806–1857, Volume 1* (New York: Orange County Medical Society), 18–19.

39. John S. Haller Jr., *Kindly Medicine: Physio-Medicalism in America, 1836–1911* (Kent, Ohio: Kent State University Press, 1997), xiii; Duffy, *Humors to Medical Science*, 81–84.

40. Kett, *Formation of Medical Profession*, 13, 30–31; Richard Green, "Oklahoma Medical Board History: Part I," *Journal of the Oklahoma State Medical Association* 96 (November 2003): 531.

41. Rothstein, *American Physicians*, 114–15; Kett, *Formation of Medical Profession*, 170.

42. Kenneth M. Ludmerer, *Learning to Heal: The Development of American Medical Education* (1985; repr., Baltimore: Johns Hopkins, 1996), 27; Starr, *Social Transformation*, 45–46.

43. Duffy, *Humors to Medical Science*, 85; Haller, *American Medicine in Transition*, 237.

44. Haller, *American Medicine in Transition*, 192.

45. Kett, *Formation of Medical Profession*, vii.

46. Anton Sohn, "19th Century Academic Examinations for Physicians in the United States Army Medical Department," *Western Journal of Medicine* 160 (May 1994): 172; Haller, *American Medicine in Transition*, 213; Ludmerer, *Learning to Heal*, 11, 15; Thomas P. Lowry and Terry Reimer, *Bad Doctors: Military Justice Proceedings against 622 Civil War Surgeons* (Frederick, Maryland: National Museum of Civil War Medicine, 2010), 105–6.

47. Porter, *Health, Civilization and the State*, 149–50; Chuck Gordon, "Antietam: Forging the Modern Military Medicine System," accessed January 13, 2012, www.army.mil/-news/2009/07/24/24859–antietam-forging-the-modern-military-medicine-system/

48. Starr, *Social Transformation*, 103; Lawrence Meir Friedman, *A History of American Law* (New York: Touchstone, 2005), 340.

49. Ronald Hamowy, "The Early Development of Medical Licensing Laws in the United States, 1875–1900," *Journal of Libertarian Studies* 3 (1979): 113–14; Apperson, *Protecting the Public, Strengthening the Profession*, 4–5.

50. Apperson, *Protecting the Public, Strengthening the Profession*, 4; Hamowy, "Early Development of Medical Licensing Laws in the United States," 113–14; Haller, *American Medicine in Transition*, 224.

51. Ledger 1, Meeting Minutes for June 14, 1911, Archives of the North Carolina Medical Board, Raleigh, North Carolina.

52. Linda McCready and Billie Harris, *From Quackery to Quality Assurance: The First Twelve Decades of the Medical Board of California* (Sacramento: State of California, 1995), 2–3.

53. Donald Melnick, Gerard Dillon, and David Swanson, "Medical Licensing Examinations in the United States," *Journal of Dental Education* (May 2002): 595–99.

54. Green, "Oklahoma Medical Board: Part I," 531–32.

55. Friedman, *History of American Law*, 342–43.

56. Haller, *American Medicine in Transition*, 201; Kenneth M. Ludmerer, *Time to Heal: American Medical Education from the Turn of the Century to the Era of Managed Care* (Oxford:

Oxford University Press, 1999), 4; William Norwood, "Critical Incidents in the Shaping of Medical Education in the US," *JAMA* 194 (November 15, 1965): 717.

57. See chapters 6 and 13 of Kenneth Ludmerer's *Learning to Heal: The Development of American Medical Education* for an assessment of state medical boards' role in what originated as an internally driven reform movement by progressive medical schools.

58. Clinton Sandvick, "Enforcing Medical Licensing in Illinois: 1877–1890," *Yale Journal of Biology and Medicine* 82 (June 209): 68–72; Kenneth Schnepp, "Medical Licensure in Illinois: An Historical Review," *Federation Bulletin* 64 (March 1977): 72–73, 82; Haller, *American Medicine in Transition*, 222.

59. "129 US 114 Dent v. West Virginia," Open Jurist, accessed January 13, 2012, http://openjurist.org/129/US/114.

60. Rosemary Stevens, *American Medicine and the Public Interest* (Berkeley: University of California Press, 1998), 59–60.

61. Ibid., 61–63.

62. Haller, *American Medicine in Transition*, 222; Rothstein, *American Physicians*, 4–5.

63. Haller, *American Medicine in Transition*, 218; Stevens, *American Medicine and the Public Interest*, 58; Ludmerer, *Learning to Heal*, 53–56.

64. Ludmerer, *Time to Heal*, xix.

Chapter 2

The Roots of the Federation of State Medical Boards

Mighty things from small beginnings grow.

—John Dryden, *Annus Mirabilis*, 1667

The roots of the Federation of State Medical Boards stretch more than twenty years prior to its formal establishment in 1912. They extend into the last decades of the nineteenth century when America's medical regulatory system grew into the broad framework characterizing it to this day. In reconstructing a state-based system for medical regulation after its previous demise during the pre–Civil War era, state legislators and physicians were responding to both public pressure and professional interests. Admittedly, these were relatively unequal forces at work. Despite the boisterous laissez-faire milieu of late-nineteenth-century America, public sentiment coalesced slowly around the need for modest measures of governmental protection against unqualified practitioners. Even stronger, however, was the desire of a hopeful medical profession striving for greater autonomy and prestige—a desire that manifested itself directly in support of the creation of medical licensing boards. As this chapter will show, professional interests and public sentiment cultivated the landscape of medical regulation and brought forth two major organizations committed to serving the medical licensing community.

When addressing the Federation's origins, published histories of medical licensure and regulation in the United States have typically alluded to the merger of two predecessor organizations as the genesis of the Federation: the National Confederation of State Medical Examining and Licensing Boards and the American Confederation of Reciprocating Examining and Licensing Boards.[1] These published histories have not, generally speaking, gone beyond referencing the merger to look more closely into the history of these predecessor organizations and the larger issues they confronted which prompted not only their creation, but that of the Federation itself. The history of these organizations, particularly the key issues spurring their genesis (principally medical education and license reciprocity), reflected the multiple priorities and tensions at work within the medical profession and the emerging licensing community at the close of the nineteenth century.

THE NATIONAL CONFEDERATION OF STATE MEDICAL EXAMINING AND LICENSING BOARDS

The National Confederation of State Medical Examining and Licensing Boards (hereafter cited as the National Confederation) represented the elder of the two predecessor organizations. The National Confederation was established in 1890 with its first annual conference held the following year in conjunction with the annual meeting of the AMA. John Rauch, a physician and longtime head of the Illinois State Board of Health, provided the initial impetus for the National Confederation and served as its president until his death in 1894.[2] The involvement and selection of Rauch does not surprise given the stated emphasis of the organization "to establish a uniform standard of requirements" for both medical schools and the state medical licensing boards which would subsequently be evaluating the schools' graduates. Previously, Rauch had served as a catalyst in the early efforts of state medical boards to raise the educational standards of medical schools, starting with Illinois's 1878 legislation restricting the issuance of a medical license to graduates of approved schools with clear standards for premedical and medical education.[3] Throughout its twenty-two-year history, the National Confederation devoted considerable attention and resources to issues related to medical education and the minimum standards that should be required for medical licensure. This emphasis—specifically the insistence upon raising educational standards as the best long-term means for achieving uniformity in standards for licensure—ultimately created a fundamental disagreement within the licensing community among those pressing for more immediate progress on practical issues such as medical license reciprocity, that is, the prerogative of one state board to recognize and authorize for its jurisdiction the licensure decisions made by another state.

Upon Rauch's death, leadership of the organization passed to William Warren Potter, a Buffalo, New York, physician who served as editor of *American Medical Quarterly*. Potter served the organization in multiple capacities over the next decade. Under his tenure the National Confederation drafted and presented to its members a constitution and bylaws. This represented an important formalizing development in medical regulation given that nearly three-quarters of all state boards were represented by the time of the organization's 1895 annual meeting.[4] The National Confederation's stated objectives were threefold: (1) Providing a mechanism for "mutual aid and counsel" in the discussion of methodologies used by medical boards; (2) acting as a clearinghouse for the "collection, compilation and dissemination" of information on medical licensure; and (3) issuing "advisory" rulings reflecting the consensus of medical boards collectively. Papers formally presented at the organization's 1896 meeting underscored not only the informational nature of these gatherings but also the medical profession's concern for two of the most pressing issues of the day: medical educational requirements set by state medical boards and interstate recognition of state licenses.[5] On the former subject, Potter's keynote address to the National Confederation's membership on the relations of state medical boards to the medical schools garnered considerable attention in the medical journals of the day.

Potter set forth three particular reforms in 1896 that, in his opinion, enjoyed consensus support within the licensing and medical professional community: higher matriculation standards for medical education; a longer, more robust medical education curriculum; and "separate examination by a state board of examiners" with said exam open only to candidates holding a degree from a "legally registered school." He additionally called for an "entrance examination" into medical school for those not presenting a high school diploma and spoke against the concept of a "National Examining Board" which had gained adherents recently.[6]

Potter's speech mirrored the early focus of the National Confederation on matters of medical education relative to licensure. As early as 1891, the organization's member boards had passed a resolution calling for a minimum of three years of medical training prior to the issuance of a medical license. In 1897, the organization reviewed an early draft report by its Committee on Minimum Standards for Admission to Medical College that laid out suggested matriculation requirements to be enforced by any medical college in good standing. However, in discussing the report some argued that medical schools should utilize solely an examination rather than rely upon acceptance of a high school certificate or diploma. Citing his experience on the Tennessee board, one attendee said, "The average certificate from the average high school is not worth much more than the average diploma of the average medical college ten years ago." The National Confederation's final report, adopted by its member boards in 1899, followed three years of diligent discussions and research on premedical education standards required by individual states as well as the standards set forth by groups such as the Association of American

Medical Colleges, the Southern Medical College Association, the National Confederation of Eclectic Medical Colleges and the Inter-Collegiate Committee of the American Institute of Homeopathy. The report called for a minimum matriculation standard of a 4-year course of study in high school or the passing of an examination in specified subjects (e.g., Latin, English Grammar and Composition, Arithmetic, Algebra, Geometry, Physics, Botany and Zoology) conducted by the respective state licensing board. The National Confederation's report acknowledged that not all states met the minimum standard but called for raising the requirements in those states not meeting the minimum. The report further cited the good work of groups such as the AAMC to "elevate" medical education but stressed that only the state licensing boards possessed the legal authority to set or enforce these standards to the benefit of the public and the medical profession.[7]

That the early leaders of state-based medical licensure placed so much emphasis upon common standards for medical education is not surprising. It seems hardly coincidental that the National Confederation arose in the same year (1890) as the reorganized AAMC. After an initial push for higher standards in medical education, the AAMC essentially disappeared between 1883–1889 when its earliest members withdrew their membership in protest over the "too rapid" application of higher standards for medical entrance requirements and curricula. Gaining support for higher standards proved just as challenging later on as evidenced by the fact that by 1910 only one-third of the nation's medical schools were AAMC members.[8] The problems inherent to the largely unregulated practice of medicine in the latter half of the nineteenth century provided a natural intersection of interests between state medical boards and medical educators on the issue of educational standards.

Even when the National Confederation provided assistance in its functions as an informational clearinghouse, the focus invariably returned to medical education. Attendees of the organization's 1895 meeting crafted a document summarizing practice requirements for the various states and territories. Despite antiquated verbiage and imprecise classifications, the document reveals much about the state of medicine and medical regulation prior to the turn of the century (table 2.1). At one end of the regulatory spectrum, twenty-three states or territories required an examination before a medical examining board prior to issuance of a medical license. At the opposite end, the laws in eleven states or territories were deemed to be either so loose or nonexistent that essentially anyone could practice medicine within those jurisdictions. The sectarian splits plaguing medicine in the mid- to late-nineteenth century are also evident in the seven states that had multiple licensing boards within them. The presence of these multiple licensing boards provides perhaps the best indicator of ho-

Table 2.1. Survey on Medical Regulation in U.S. States and Territories, 1895

Medical Law Permits Practically Anyone to Open an Office to Practice Medicine	Alaska, Arizona, District of Columbia, Idaho, Kansas, Michigan, Nevada, New Hampshire, Texas, Wisconsin, Wyoming
Medical Law Supervises Issuance of Diploma	California, Kentucky, Missouri, Nebraska
Medical Law Requires Licensing Exam but Accepts Diploma of Certain Colleges in Lieu of Examination	Arkansas, Colorado, Connecticut, Illinois, Indian Territory, Choctaw Nation, Iowa, Massachusetts, New Mexico, Oklahoma, Rhode Island, South Dakota, Tennessee, Vermont
Medical Law Requires Passing Examination before Board of Examiners prior to Issuance of License	*Before Single Examining Board* Alabama, Oklahoma Territory, Cherokee Nation, Maine, Minnesota, Mississippi, Montana, New Jersey, North Carolina, North Dakota, Oregon, South Carolina, Utah, Virginia, Washington, West Virginia *...Two Examining Boards*[a] Delaware, Florida, Louisiana, Maryland *...Three Examining Boards*[b] Georgia, New York, Pennsylvania

Note: Survey conducted by the National Confederation of State Medical Examining and Licensing Boards
[a] Regular and Homeopathic
[b] Regular, Homeopathic, and Eclectic

Source: "Medical Legislation in the United States—Work of the National Conference of State Medical Examining and Licensing Boards—The Stringent New York Laws," *Indiana Medical Journal* 15 (April 1897): 424–425.

meopathic and eclectic physicians' success in garnering both public and political support for their respective schools of medicine.[9]

The National Confederation also looked at the "standard of qualifications" being utilized by the various medical boards. Three areas were reviewed: premedical education; medical education; and knowledge assessment by the state examining board. In terms of premedical education, most boards simply deferred to the assessments being done by individual medical schools. However, New York and Illinois were specifically cited as positive examples where state law supported the purview of the state medical board to establish minimum requirements in this area. Additionally, the National Confederation determined that the emerging standard for medical education among the states and territories was a diploma reflecting three years of medical instruction with "parts of these 3 years . . . *spent in a medical school*" (italics added). While this was still well-removed from the four-year curriculum that the AAMC would be espousing a decade later in 1905, this standard apparently reflected a late-nineteenth-century reality confronting state medical boards—older physicians presenting themselves for licensure reflected multiple paths to becoming a physician beyond the vehicle of a degree-granting medical school, such as apprenticeship, serving as a "house pupil" in a hospital setting, study in Europe, etc.[10]

The National Confederation also looked at the state licensing examinations that were then being offered to qualify for medical licensure. They determined that as many as thirty-five state jurisdictions were examining the licensure candidate's knowledge of medicine. However, in twelve of these jurisdictions an examination was only utilized when the candidate did not possess a diploma from a medical school recognized by the licensing board. For the remaining boards, an examination was required in all instances. The National Confederation specifically cited the New York State Medical Examining Board as a salutary example of the protection such legislation afforded both the public and the profession. The New York board's examination in seven branches of medicine not only spanned three and a half days, it was apparently a rigorous standard that many found challenging. The National Confederation noted with some pride that during the period 1893–1897, 29 percent of the 2,832 candidates presenting themselves to the New York board for examination were "found deficient."[11]

Later on, the dialogue among National Confederation members shifted toward the specifics of licensing examination content and test administration. Consensus slowly emerged supporting "mixed" examinations for licensure, that is, combinations of written, oral and practical components within a single examination administration. Increasingly as the first decade of the twentieth century drew on, the published summaries of the National Confederation meetings included detailed discussion and sharing of data showing applicants' performance on a given state board's examination. These were often presented showing pass rates for applicants from specific medical schools. The AMA expanded upon this practice by collecting examination data from all state boards and publishing detailed performance results broken down by individual medical schools beginning in 1905.[12] In a consensus action by its member boards in 1909, the National Confederation adopted a resolution recommending that state medical boards take appropriate measures to gain the statutory flexibility to incorporate a practical component to their examinations. By 1908, according to the Ohio medical board secretary, George H. Matson, nine states had adopted a practical component to their medical qualifying examinations. Concerns remained, however, about the feasibility of adopting this type of assessment. Skeptics pointed to the political nature of state medical board appointments as a factor not always conducive to selecting those with sufficient experience and aptitude for developing examinations. This point carried some weight at the time as most of the physicians serving on state boards had themselves likely never taken a licensing examination. Others rightly pointed out the logistical challenges for states with larger licensee populations that would have to establish working relationships with medical schools and hospitals in order to implement practical examinations.[13]

While the focus on uniform standards for medical education continued to dominate much of the National Confederation's earliest discussions, more pragmatic issues also received periodic attention. For example, at the group's 1897 annual meeting, discussions turned to the flight of physicians from one jurisdiction to another after being found deficient by a state medical board. Attendees passed a resolution calling for notification of sister boards in other states when one jurisdiction revoked or suspended a physician's license. However, it seems telling that neither the resolution calling for such action nor the meeting summary spoke to the necessary administrative mechanics behind such a notification system. The concept of a "national registration bureau" arose naturally, meanwhile, from discussions by state boards concerning physician and interstate mobility. The idea involved establishing the nineteenth-century equivalent of an information clearinghouse containing the names of "legally qualified and reputable physicians" to facilitate their movement from one state to another without losing the "privileges . . . [for] the practice of medicine."[14]

The National Confederation's predominant focus over the next decade continued to be medical education. A Committee on Uniform Curriculum for Medical Colleges was established in 1902 with annual reports issued between 1903 and 1905. The Committee's 1904 report represented an exhaustive work based upon survey results from 124 medical colleges. Committee Chair George Webster, the AMA's librarian since 1892 and a physician member of the Illinois board, characterized the results as indicative of a "woeful lack of uniformity" in curricula with even the best schools varying widely relative to enforced entrance requirements. The adopted report called for a standard curriculum for the M.D. degree to include course work in four terms spanning four calendar years; each term consisting of thirty weeks; the entire course consisting of 3,600 hours over four years; elective work offered *in addition* to the minimum standard; and clinical work that comprised 25 percent of the 3,600 required hours.[15] The curriculum standards adopted by the National Confederation mirrored those set by the AAMC. Symposia on clinical instruction for medical students took place in 1909 and 1910 with the National Confederation as a contributor. At its 1911 annual meeting, the National Confederation took up the question of state control of medical colleges—prompted, undoubtedly, by Abraham Flexner's influential 1910 report, "Medical Education in the United States and Canada."[16] (See chapter 3.)

In retrospect, the efforts of the National Confederation to facilitate "uniform standards" in the requirements set forth by both state medical boards and medical schools appear to reflect a strategic approach to resolving a seemingly intractable issue. The period of the mid- to late nineteenth century witnessed a proliferation of medical schools with many dedicated to specific philosophies of medicine. Because medicine was only just acquiring valid scientific underpinnings for its study and practice, the field was rife with practitioners—"sectarians" according to the more cynical critics—with minimal or no qualifications for practice and a dubious knowledge base. Lacking a legitimate therapeutic basis for its work, the medical profession struggled to acquire the gravitas necessary to set even minimum standards without accusations of "protectionism"—an updated version of the Jacksonian Era anti-privilege accusations that destroyed earlier legislative attempts at medical regulation.[17] Voluntary associations such as the AMA or the AAMC, while potentially influential, lacked the authority to drive needed change. The only recourse was legislative. As the duly constituted legal authority regulating the practice of medicine within each state or territory, the state medical boards were poised to accomplish what others could not: establish or strengthen standards that protected the public from incompetent and unsafe practitioners. By the mid-1890s, twenty-seven states had established (or re-established) state oversight of the practice of medicine through the creation of a medical licensing and examining board. According to one source, in sixteen of these twenty-seven states the requirement for a diploma from a "recognized medical college" was mandated for the issuance of a license.[18] The National Confederation's twin priorities of uniform standards for both medical education and licensure reflected not merely the vision of its early leaders but the reality of state medical boards actively weighing in on the educational standards of the day.

The National Confederation and its president, William Warren Potter, a former Civil War–era surgeon, were applying a long-term strategy to achieve higher uniform licensure standards by raising medical education standards nationally, a laudable commitment serving the best interests of the public and patient care.[19] But in playing such a long endgame dependent upon statutory changes among the various states, the organization risked sacrificing short-term victories that might address the more immediate concerns of all licensees. The key issue for many was license reciprocity. From his editor's desk at the *Buffalo Medical Journal* and within the pages of the *American Medical Quarterly*, Potter downplayed the viability of reciprocity without first establishing uniform standards. "It is . . . out of place to expect that . . . reciprocity can be established . . . while the methods of education are so different." For Potter, reciprocity represented the "final stage of the great reform" and a "finishing stroke" that could not be "seriously considered until all the conditions precedent thereto are fulfilled." Later, sensing perhaps the need for quicker movement toward reciprocity and the inherent legislative obstacles to implementing a single uniform standard for admission to medical practice, Potter threw his support behind a proposal calling for the identification and adoption of several tiered standards. These would be sufficiently inclusive to cover virtually all state medical boards and allow for rapid endorsement of credentials, if not outright reciprocity, between states or territories falling under the same standard. The National Confederation's appointment of a Committee on Reciprocity in 1900, however, came too late to forestall those looking for more rapid progress from devising methodologies of their own.[20]

THE AMERICAN CONFEDERATION OF RECIPROCATING EXAMINING AND LICENSING BOARDS

The genesis of the Federation's other predecessor organization—the American Confederation of Reciprocating Examining and Licensing Boards (cited hereafter as American Confederation)—can be found in countless stories like that of Edwin Klebs. This well-known German physician had achieved a considerable measure of professional success by isolating and linking the diphtheria bacillus to the disease. In 1895, Klebs relocated to North Carolina where he intended to practice at an Asheville sanatorium and continue his research into tuberculosis. Until 1907, however, North Carolina state law required every physician entering the state to sit for its medical board's examination. Indeed, the board enjoyed no discretion in exceptions to the examination mandate. Similarly, no allowances were provided to the board for establishing reciprocal relations with other states that might have precluded the need for an examination. This minor contretemps involving a prominent physician exposed the North Carolina board to criticism and embarrassment despite Klebs's willingness, and subsequent success, in passing the board's examination. Licensed physicians less sanguine than Klebs often balked at mandated examinations and pressed state medical boards and legislatures for license reciprocity.[21]

The immediate impetus for the American Confederation, however, can be traced to an 1899 meeting of the Wayne County (Michigan) Medical Society. The society's president, R. H. Bonner, established a committee charged with assessing what might be done to assist Michigan physicians by facilitating greater uniformity in licensing laws. The activities and discussions that followed would place the society center stage in the emerging national discussions of medical license reciprocity. Their conversations led directly to efforts by the state medical boards in Michigan, Wisconsin, Illinois, and Indiana to address license reciprocity on a regional basis for their respective boards.[22]

Representatives from these states moved quickly to place this topic at the forefront of the June 1900 meeting of the National Confederation. At that meeting, two physicians, Emil Amberg of Michigan and William Spurgeon of Indiana, made a forceful push on the issue of license reciprocity, arguing that such an initiative could move forward in parallel with the organization's ongoing efforts to support higher standards in medical education. Amberg urged a tactical approach that would mobilize the profession and draw in the "lay press" as an ally in the "improvement of medical laws." Amberg also cited Michigan's positive experience with the lay press in the legislative battle that established a medical regulatory system for that state. Spurgeon then introduced a resolution before the member boards of the National Confederation calling for the creation of a Committee on Interstate License Reciprocity.[23]

If published reports are reflective of the meeting's discussions, many National Confederation leaders were less than enthusiastic about entering this territory. Former President Potter, President J. N. McCormack and Vice President James Egan echoed doubts about the prospects for successfully addressing the issue of reciprocity. Potter warned against "hasty action" and raised his familiar refrain about addressing reciprocity only after medical education standards had been more fully addressed; Egan deemed it "useless" to hope for uniformity coming from legislative bodies. McCormack openly questioned the motives of some states by claiming that reciprocity for some represented little more than an attempt to jettison "surplus medical men." Indeed, McCormack struck a protectionist tone and pointedly identified several states whose failure to establish sufficient standards undercut any serious advances in reciprocity. Despite this vocal opposition, the delegates voted in the end to support formation of a reciprocity committee.[24]

The committee reported back one year later, at the June 1901 meeting. The published transactions of the organization for that year appeared in the *Bulletin of the American Academy of Medicine*, the National Confederation's official publication. The proceedings offer a seemingly terse treatment of license reciprocity as an issue for consideration by the organization's membership. The report was "received and filed" and the committee thanked for its work; then they were formally "discharged." While the transactions did not convey any of the prior year's contentious tone, the treatment of the committee and its report clearly rankled. It was no coincidence that representatives from the Illinois, Wisconsin, Indiana and Michigan boards gathered less than six months later in a meeting that culminated in the formation of the American Confederation. Looking back at this development, the National Confederation's secretary, A. Walter Suiter, admitted the causal chain of events leading to the American Confederation's genesis. He acknowledged that the National Confederation "summarily disposed" of the reciprocity topic in a manner leading directly to the formation of the American Confederation. Suiter further regretted the creation of yet another "association" drawn from the state medical board community; and particularly one whose name was sure to create confusion as it mirrored the elder organization so closely. Still, his assessment that the issue of license reciprocity had received more "attention . . . than its importance really deserves" and that interstate legislation was premature reflected a fundamental disagreement over the utility of a national organization attempting to resolve an issue arising from state-specific circumstances.[25]

The American Confederation was established in January 1902 through a meeting of representatives from the Illinois, Indiana, Michigan and Wisconsin state medical boards. The representatives present at the meeting passed a resolution organizing themselves as the American Confederation of Reciprocating State Medical Examining and Licensing Boards, elected officers—J. R. Currens, Beverly Drake Harrison and James M. Dinnen—established their own committee on reciprocity and passed a resolution calling for medical license reciprocity along two lines of qualification:

> Qualification 1: Possession (for at least one year) of a medical license presented by virtue of a "satisfactory" medical diploma and an examination by a state medical board; or
>
> Qualification 2: Possession (for at least one year) of a medical license presented by virtue of a "satisfactory" medical diploma and upon the "recommendation" of that state medical board in lieu of an examination.[26]

Subsequent meetings of the American Confederation's membership refined these qualification standards for reciprocity over the next several years. By 1904, Qualification 1 was revised to specify a minimum score (75 on a scale of 100) on the examination and a possible "supplemental examination" for subjects not covered under the original examination. Qualification 2 was further refined to clarify that the medical school issuing the diploma had to be in "good standing" at the time of its issuance and that the diploma must date to a time period before an examination requirement had been enacted in the issuing state.[27]

The American Confederation's executive board secretary, Beverly Drake Harrison, soon drafted an open letter to state medical licensing boards across the country, alerting them to the fledgling organization and its adopted policy on reciprocity while leaving the individual states to address qualifications relative to premedical and medical education. Citing the efficacy and power of even a relatively small number of boards acting in concert, Harrison presented an argument for the power of cooperating state medical boards to facilitate physician mobility while simultaneously strengthening educational standards in the process. A fundamental premise of the organization held that reciprocity "should only be made upon equal terms" with no state forced or intended to accept a lesser standard presented by prospective licensees from other states. Harrison and the American Confederation leadership understood that reciprocity necessitated interaction with state legislatures, bodies almost certain to prove challenging. He specifically acknowledged the mistrust felt by many legislators—especially from rural districts—who viewed any regulation of medicine as "class legislation" and a protection of the "Doctors' Trust." Finally, Harrison could not resist chiding the National Confederation, stating the group might have achieved more if not for the presence of so many members "indifferent" to the cause of reciprocity.[28]

It bears noting that the impetus for the American Confederation perhaps received a boost from an earlier abortive initiative to establish a national examining board. An 1896 editorial from the *Public Health Journal,* reprinted in the *International Journal of Surgery,* called for a "National Examining Board" broadly empowered to "examine physicians and grant certificates to practice . . . [and] endorse the certificates of State boards." Proponents of such a body argued that this represented the best means for resolving the difficult practical issues stemming from the varying standards for licensure among the states and territories. They chafed at the "inelastic" nature of the U.S. Constitution, which they said seemed more reflective of eighteenth century sociopolitical values and mores that feared placing trust in the people, as opposed to the progressive American spirit at the dawn of the twentieth century. Inevitably, opponents of such a national licensing board forestalled these proposals by playing their Constitutional trump card, the Tenth Amendment reserving rights not otherwise elucidated to the individual states. Even calls for a *voluntary* national licensing board, such as those championed by the AMA's William Rodman and discussed in the previous chapter, proved premature. With a national solution to challenges arising from license reciprocity seemingly off the table, those pressing for progress on this issue turned naturally to organizations like the American Confederation. Not surprisingly, neither the American Confederation nor the National Confederation strongly supported Rodman's later call for a voluntary national licensing board.[29]

The constitution adopted by the American Confederation clearly set forth the goal of the organization: "to establish reciprocal relations between the medical examining and licensing boards" such that "well-qualified physicians . . . legally authorized to practice" in one state might do so in another "without a repetition of the tests of qualification." A review of this constitution reveals the strong regional orientation of the organization at the time of its inception as all the signatories were from the Midwest. That a similar regional approach evolved separately in New England testifies to the perceived value of this geographically focused approach that many championed as the most effective means for addressing license reciprocity. Certainly, there was strong desire in many quarters to make progress on this front as evidenced by the seventeen boards that joined the American Confederation by 1904.[30]

Late in 1902, the American Confederation's Beverly Harrison pointed proudly to the progress being made in eighteen states and territories toward fostering contiguous-state and regional models of partial or full reciprocity. This successful start offered a striking rebuttal to the criticism conveyed in an AMA report chiding state medical boards for failing to work actively within and amongst themselves, as well as with legislators, to enact meaningful change. Despite such optimism, significant challenges remained. Among the greatest of these was the continued perception within the medical profession that the American Confederation's Qualification 2, as a basis for reciprocity, entailed lowering the legislative bar with a resultant "unrestricted migration" of incompetent and questionable practitioners from one state to another. Though Harrison and other leaders of the American Confederation argued that only "graduates of reputable colleges" were included in the language of Qualification 2, this charge became a frequent refrain requiring a repeated response.[31]

The concern that this allegation could gain further traction and damage the organization's efforts led the American Confederation to ultimately adopt a Qualification 3, requiring "moral and professional character." This called for candidates under reciprocal licensure to provide "evidence" of having been a member in good standing for at least one year in "county, state and national medical organizations of the school or system of [his] practice" and to present a "recommendation issued . . . by vote" from the society in which his membership originated. While certainly not a panacea, it appeared to represent a good faith attempt at addressing the "charlatans" and ethically questionable practitioners who might be "able to pass an examination . . . [and] systematically secure license in every state . . . possible" as a means for rapid relocation after being "exposed or convicted in one place." To help combat such a scenario, the American Confederation also adopted a measure calling for state medical boards to secure an "affidavit" from the reciprocal licensure candidate that provided a "good faith" intention to abandon practice in the prior state and become a permanent resident of the new one.[32]

That many state medical boards were successfully utilizing reciprocity in at least some form is clear from statistics reported by the American Confederation within several years of its founding. Between 1905 and 1908, more than 2,500 "reciprocal registrations" were issued by twenty-one reporting state boards. The detailed statistics for 1905–1906 reveal that the vast majority of physicians (938 out of 1,187) were issued reciprocal licenses under Qualification 1.[33] This seems particularly telling as it would seem to indicate that boards were working effectively with candidates presenting themselves based upon their license having been obtained through examination in another state. As the ubiquity of medical licensing examinations was relatively recent, it appears that younger physicians were finding fewer barriers than their older colleagues who, because they were less likely to have taken a licensing examination, had to pursue a reciprocal license under Qualification 2. That category, predicated upon a diploma from a medical school in good standing and a license issued prior to the requirement for an examination in the issuing state, saw the reciprocating board often issuing a license to older practitioners. This decision may have felt like one made in good faith based upon several assumptions. For example, the reciprocating board presumed the original licensing board had verified the candidate's bona fides; and that the board's attestation of the candidate's good standing represented an informed appraisal of the physician. Matters might be even more complicated if the candidate were an "irregular" practitioner, terminology often assigned to homeopathic and eclectic physicians. Thus, it is not surprising that far fewer reciprocal licenses were being issued under this qualification.

The introduction by New Jersey's delegation of a series of resolutions before the member boards in support of medical license reciprocity at the 1904 meeting of the National Confederation, and the subsequent unsuccessful outcome of these resolutions, underscored the persistence of this issue and the apparent inability of the American and National Confederations to find common ground. The New Jersey resolutions detailed a reciprocity model predicated largely upon individuals who obtained their license through presentation of a medical diploma *and* successful completion of a licensing examination. The detailed response of the American Confederation's Harrison was published in a series of objections to the proposed model in the pages of *JAMA*. These focused primarily upon the constitutionality of a model facilitating license portability for only that small percentage of licensees who obtained their medical license based upon an examination by the state medical board (estimated at 10 percent) while remaining silent about the vast majority, primarily older physicians, not covered by the proposal. Specifically, Harrison criticized the proposal for its failure to address reciprocity for those physicians who had obtained their license by virtue of the medical diploma presented to the medical board as well as those physicians who presented an examination successfully passed before a medical faculty recognized by the state medical board. That the National Confederation tabled the New Jersey resolutions, and that the American

Confederation apparently had no interest in deviating from the Qualifications model set forth in its constitution, spoke volumes about the state of affairs between the two organizations.[34]

Less clear was the extent to which the existence of two apparently competing organizations created mutually exclusive camps within the medical licensing community or the impact of the American Confederation on the membership roster of the National Confederation. Membership in the National Confederation was open to all medical licensing boards and each of their actively serving board members. Unfortunately, existing records fail to indicate which boards belonged to the National Confederation and the meeting summaries reported in journals of the day refer almost exclusively to the *individuals* in attendance, though news items in 1910–1911 mention the Oregon, Louisiana, Utah and Arkansas (Medical and Eclectic) boards as new members.[35]

This contrasts markedly with the reported proceedings of the American Confederation, which consistently listed and promoted the number of state medical boards in their active membership. Though it retained its strong regional flavor, by 1911 there were fourteen member boards in the American Confederation: Georgia, Indiana, Iowa, Kansas, Maryland, Michigan, Nebraska, Nevada, North Dakota, Ohio, Oklahoma, Utah, West Virginia, and Wisconsin. While this doubled the original seven signatory boards to the American Confederation in 1903, it hardly represented a massive shift in state board allegiance. It also seems telling that the National Confederation's officers and executive board during much of this period drew heavily from the membership of state boards unaffiliated with the American Confederation, such as New York, Pennsylvania, Connecticut, and Tennessee.[36]

While there is evidence for some degree of exclusivity between the two organizations, fluidity and overlap were inevitable simply by virtue of the National Confederation's membership categories which allowed for individual members. For example, Illinois and Ohio board members such as George Webster and Augustus Ravogli assumed leadership positions within the National Confederation despite their state boards' commitment to the American Confederation.[37] Thus, membership appears not to have represented a zero-sum game for either organization. One likely outcome of this reality was that neither organization perceived membership as an issue requiring them to bridge their differences; nor did it appear to threaten derailing pursuit of their respective agendas.

As the end of the first decade of the twentieth century approached, the prospects for common ground, much less a union, between the National and American Confederations seemed mixed at best. In March 1910, however, the chairman of the AAMC's Committee on State Medical Boards struck a hopeful note. Reflecting on his committee's interactions with the two organizations, he deemed a union of the two as "extremely probable." Only a few months later, however, published reports in the *St. Louis Post-Dispatch* commented at length on failed merger talks between the two organizations.[38] Such mixed signals are indicative of the research challenge, a century later, in seeking to untangle the actions and motivations of the parties involved. As best the extant sources can tell us, this is what we know.

The primary work and respective focus of both organizations continued unabated throughout the first decade of the 1900s. The National Confederation continued its focus on strengthening medical education standards and resisting efforts that would require licensed physicians to reexamine before a state medical board as part of any licensure endorsement model. Likewise, the American Confederation maintained its efforts on behalf of license reciprocity while also moving to address medical education reform as evidenced by its creation of committees on preliminary medical education and college inspection.

As the work of the American and National Confederations unfolded, certain perceptions of both organizations—not always positive—developed, many of which found their way into the contemporary press and medical journals. Whether accurate or not, increasingly a perception took hold of a pro-AMA bias on the part of the National Confederation. In part this perception arose from the fact that several prominent leaders at the National Confederation (J. N. McCormack; George Webster; T. J. Happel; Augustus Ravogli) also had deep ties to the AMA. More important, the perception deepened after 1904 when the AMA established its formidable Council on Medical Education, which moved quickly to adopt minimum standards for medical education (i.e., four years of high school; four years of medical school) consistent with those advocated by the National Confederation and the AAMC. At the same time, the Council began a series of surveys and assessments of U.S. medical schools that culminated in their invitation to the Carnegie Foundation for the Advancement of Teaching to lead the effort that produced Abraham Flexner's influential report of 1910. The National Confederation supported these reform initiatives but in doing so inherited the opponents and critics of the AMA. Accordingly, the harshest criticism of the National Confederation arose within the medical profession along sectarian lines. *Medical Century*, the national journal of homeopathic medicine, characterized the National Confederation as "part and parcel" of the AMA. This growing suspicion stemmed from concerns that the National Confederation was doing the work (either intentionally or by default) of the AAMC and AMA Council on Medical Education to significantly reduce the number of medical school graduates in the United States at the expense of so-called "irregular" practitioners, such as eclectics, homeopaths, and so on. Thus, in some quarters, the perception grew that the National Confederation was so firmly entrenched within the medical establishment as to no longer be a viable change agent for reform efforts.[39]

On the other hand, it is quite telling that some of the strongest support for the American Confederation arose from the ranks of the irregular practitioners within the medical community. The homeopathic physicians, in particular, lauded the American Confederation for its effectiveness and impartiality, describing it as "the one body that has ever been fair to all schools of medicine." This support is not surprising given the "Qualification" model set forth by the American Confederation as the basis for reciprocal licensing. In essence, the examination and recommendation components removed all issues of the relative merits of a given school of medicine from the equation. Practitioners educated in homeopathic or eclectic medical schools had already seen considerable success legislatively in either gaining representation on state medical boards or having a separate board constituted for their practitioners.[40] Consequently, they looked favorably upon the American Confederation's efforts at reciprocal licensing agreements among state boards as this would only serve to further legitimize these practitioners and offer additional practice opportunities. In addition, the American Confederation's vigorous program for having state licensing boards inspect the medical schools within their state seemed less threatening than a process under the control of the AAMC and the AMA Council on Medical Education.[41]

MERGER CREATING THE FEDERATION OF STATE MEDICAL BOARDS

From 1910 to 1912, the American and National Confederations engaged in a series of meetings that culminated in the 1912 merger of the two organizations. With the benefit of hindsight, these maneuvers seem less a courtship dance than a cross between an arranged marriage and a shotgun wedding. Some of the motives for a merger of the two organizations are clear. First, neither organization appeared to possess significant financial resources or the infrastructure for a truly sustainable national organization. The home office of each organization appears to have resided with whichever physician held the office of president or executive secretary. It is no coincidence that both organizations met annually in connection with the annual meeting of the American Medical Association. By far the largest gathering of physicians in the United States, the AMA's annual meeting represented an opportunity for multiple groups to hold ancillary meetings of their own organizations that otherwise would not have convened, or if they did convene, with a greatly reduced membership. A second motive arose from the understanding, both within and outside the medical licensing community, that the interests of the public and medical regulation were not well served by two national organizations operating within this realm and sometimes directly at cross purposes. Even the founders of the American Confederation publicly acknowledged the missed opportunity represented when the license reciprocity movement foundered within the National Confederation, thus spawning their organization. Virtually all parties recognized the efficacy of one organization rather than two as the national voice of the licensing community. Third, by 1911, half of the National Confederation's officers and executive committee were drawn from the Arkansas, Illinois and Ohio boards—all of which were members of the American Confederation. It seems reasonable to speculate that these individuals' exposure to the American Confederation through their respective boards' participation created a familiarity that may have transcended philosophical differences between the two organizations. Finally, there seems to have been a clear push from the AAMC and AMA Council on Medical Education acting as mediators to bring about a union of the American and National Confederations. Indeed, as early as 1908 one hears a gentle but direct chiding of both organizations from speakers at the AMA Council on Medical Education. "You gentlemen . . . ought to organize a body that will bring together all states."[42]

As mentioned before, the year 1910 witnessed mixed messages concerning the likelihood of a union between the two organizations. The AAMC representative to both organizations saw a probable union in the future of the two organizations. Yet one major newspaper reported failed talks between the two organizations. Perhaps the most telling comment, however, came from the American Confederation's president, who stated that the "primary purpose" behind that organization's founding had been "to a large degree fulfilled." Whether so intended or not, this seemed a clear signal of receptiveness to further merger discussions. At their March 1910 meeting, the American Confederation's member boards authorized their president, William A. Spurgeon, to solicit exploratory talks for "amalgamation" of the two organizations. Interested parties moved quickly to facilitate merger talks.[43]

According to the American Confederation's Harrison, exploratory discussions between the two organizations took place starting in June 1910 though no formal actions resulted from these talks. Failure to generate any definite plans from this meeting may have stemmed from the fact that these discussions appear to have involved solely parties from the two organizations, with no outside participants present to play a mediating role. A broader conference took place on February 25, 1911, at the Congress Hotel in Chicago. Representatives from the American Confederation

(William Spurgeon, Beverly Drake Harrison), the National Confederation (Charles Tuttle, George Matson); the AAMC (William Harlow, Fred Zapffe); the AMA Council on Medical Education (Nathan P. Colwell, Arthur Bevan); and the Carnegie Foundation for the Advancement of Teaching (Abraham Flexner) met and concluded that a merger of the two organizations was "desirable" and in the best interests of the nation's state medical boards. Another meeting was called for March 2, with both state board confederations asked to designate negotiating teams. The progress of the talks and prospects for merger appeared positive. A proposed name for the new organization was put forth by George Matson of the Ohio medical board—the National Federation of State Medical Boards. Consensus also emerged as to membership in the fledgling organization (restricted to state medical boards only) while roles were defined for former members of state boards (who would be known as Fellows) and for those interested physicians not affiliated with state medical boards (who would be known as Associates). The following day the American Confederation met for apparently the last time, receiving a positive report from their Committee on Amalgamation with the National Confederation. Anticipating success based upon the consensus from preliminary talks, the draft program for the National Confederation's February 1912 meeting included topics appropriate for the proposed merged organization, such as "What can a National Federation of State Boards do? and "What should be the requirements for membership in a National Federation of State Boards?"[44]

With an agreement in principle for union, the two parties set about arranging to establish a constitution and bylaws for the new organization, agreeing that it should be called the Federation of State Medical Boards (FSMB). Tuttle, Matson, Harlow, Colwell and Albert Brown represented the National Confederation's negotiating committee for the new organization's constitution and bylaws. In the absence of the other members of his negotiating team, Beverly Drake Harrison acted on behalf of the American Confederation.[45] On February 28, 1912, the two committees agreed upon the general framework for a constitution and bylaws for the Federation. Election of officers took place the next day with the following results: President Arthur Brown (Louisiana), Vice Presidents Charles Cook (Massachusetts) and Pearl H. Tatman (Arkansas) and Secretary-Treasurer George Matson (Ohio). The Federation's first executive committee included James Duncan (Ohio), Charles Tuttle (Connecticut), W. Scott Nay (Vermont), Lee H. Smith (New York) and Fred Murphy (Arkansas).[46]

With the first annual meeting of the Federation not slated until 1913, there remained considerable interim work to be done and this proved highly contentious. The greatest source of contention was a proposed addition to the new organization's constitution by the American Confederation delegation. The American Confederation proposed that the Federation establish a Standing Committee on Medical College Inspections and Ratings, with seven members "representing the five schools of practice" that then existed on state medical boards. Three were to be drawn from the "regular" (allopathic) medical schools plus one each from the homeopathic, eclectic, physio-medical and osteopathic medical schools. The National Confederation delegates initially agreed but later declared this proposal unacceptable. The American Confederation delegates subsequently proposed a compromise that would remove physio-medical and osteopathic representation from the standing committee. After consultation with the AMA Council on Medical Education by the National Confederation delegates, this proposal, too, was rejected. Ultimately, the original constitution and bylaws of the Federation did not list any standing committees. However, as will be seen, the American Confederation's delegates were more successful in getting desired language around the issue of license reciprocity.[47]

Looking back, it appears that the National Confederation held considerable sway in the nascent Federation. None of the significant players from the American Confederation's governance (Harrison, Spurgeon, etc.) held an officer position within the newly established Federation, in either 1912 or 1913, though Harrison became deeply involved in the new organization. For example, he chaired several committees looking at the classification of medical schools. Similarly, the National Confederation's opposition to a Standing Committee on Medical College Inspections and Ratings appeared to signal an accommodation made with the AMA Council on Medical Education and the AAMC in which leadership in the arena of medical education reform would reside with these organizations rather than the medical licensing community. This seems somewhat surprising given the National Confederation's historic interest and activity in efforts to raise medical education standards but perhaps represented an acknowledgment of the limited resources the Federation had at its disposal, compared to the AMA, to lead such an undertaking as inspecting the nation's medical schools. Yet with the notable presence of representatives from the AMA Council on Medical Education and AAMC in establishing the Federation, and the sudden absence of medical education issues on the program of the first Federation annual meeting in 1913, it is not hard to see why there were some individuals unsure of just what the future might hold for this new body representing the medical licensing community.[48]

NOTES

1. Derbyshire, *Medical Licensure and Discipline,* 49–50; Shryock, *Medical Licensing in America,* 55, 58–59.

2. Joseph C. Guernsey, "Medical Examining Boards and Medical Legislation," *Journal of the American Institute of Homeopathy* 4 (1911): 570; "National Confederation of State Examining Boards," *Transactions of the Medical Society of State of New York* (Albany: Medical Society of New York, 1897), 19.

3. *18th Annual Report of the State Board of Health of the State of Illinois* (Springfield: E. F. Hartman Printer, 1896), xli; "John Henry Rauch," *Dictionary of American Biography* (New York: Charles Scribner's Sons, 1935), 390; "Medical Education in Illinois," *Medical Record* (June 15, 1878): 480.

4. "William Warren Potter," *Who's Who in New York City and State* (New York: L. R. Hamersly, 1904), 470; *18th Report of Illinois Board of Health*, xlii.

5. *Transactions of the Medical Society of New York*, 19; "Physicians in Congress," *New York Times*, May 5, 1896.

6. "Relations of Medical Examining Boards to the State, to the Schools and to Each Other," *Medical and Surgical Reporter* 74 (May 9, 1896): 600; "A National Examining Board," *International Journal of Surgery* 9 (July 1896): 199.

7. Dean F. Smiley, "History of the Association of American Medical Colleges, 1876–1956," *Journal of Medical Education* 32 (July 1957): 515–16; "Report of the Delegate to the National Confederation of State Examining and Licensing Boards," *Twentieth Annual Report of the State Board of Health of the State of Connecticut, 1897* (New Haven: Tuttle, Morehouse & Taylor, 1898), 235–36; "National Confederation of State Medical Examining and Licensing Boards: Report of the Committee on Minimum Standards for Admission to Medical Colleges," *Cincinnati Lancet-Clinic* (August 5, 1899): 136–44.

8. Ludmerer, *Learning to Heal*, 89.

9. "Medical Legislation in the United States—Work of the National Conference of State Medical Examining and Licensing Boards—The Stringent New York Laws," *Indiana Medical Journal* 15 (April 1897): 424–25.

10. Ibid., 425; Ludmerer, *Learning to Heal*, 16–18, 88.

11. "Medical Legislation . . . National Conference," 424–25.

12. "State Board Examination Results During 1904," *Journal of the American Medical Association* 44 (May 6, 1905): 1454–82.

13. "National Confederation of State Medical Examining and Licensing Boards," *JAMA* 53 (July 10, 1909): 134; "National Confederation of State Boards," *JAMA* 58 (February 10, 1912): 432–33; "National Confederation of State Medical Examining and Licensing Boards," *JAMA* 58 (April 13, 1912): 1143–44.

14. "National Confederation of State Medical Examining and Licensing Boards," *Bulletin of the American Academy of Medicine* 3 (1899): 58; "Reciprocity in Medical Licensing," *New York Medical Journal* (June 5, 1897): 771.

15. George M. Webster, "Report on the Curricula of American Medical Colleges," *Quarterly Bulletin of the Northwestern University Medical School* 6 (June 1904): 356–57, 360, 364; Morris Fishbein, *A History of the American Medical Association 1847 to 1947* (Philadelphia: W. B. Saunders, 1947), 1075–76.

16. Smiley, "History of AAMC," 518; Guernsey, "Medical Examining Boards and Medical Legislation," 571–72.

17. B. M. Griffith, "Report of the National Confederation of State Medical Examining and Licensing Boards," *18th Annual Report of the State Board of Health of the State of Illinois* (Springfield: F. Hartman State Printer, 1896), xli; Starr, *Social Transformation*, 54–59.

18. Eugene Porter, ed., *North American Journal of Homeopathy*, Third Series 12 (1897): 75.

19. Potter's reminiscences of his Civil War service have been reprinted as *One Surgeon's Private War: Doctor William W. Potter of the 57th New York Consult* (John Michael Priest, Editor). He published a shorter reminiscence which appeared as "Three Years with the Army of the Potomac—A Personal Military History," *Buffalo Medical Journal* 67 (July 1912): 678–83.

20. William Warren Potter, "Interstate License Reciprocity," *American Medical Quarterly* 1 (April 1900): 371; William Warren Potter, "How Shall Reciprocity in Licensure Be Established?" *Buffalo Medical Journal* 56 (September 1900): 123–25.

21. Proctor and Long, *North Carolina Board of Medical Examiners,* 9–10.

22. Emil Amberg, "Cooperation of the Medical Profession of the United States with the National Confederation of State Medical Examining and Licensing Boards in Establishing Interstate Reciprocity for the License to Practice Medicine," *Medical Record* 58 (July 7, 1900): 493.

23. Ibid., 495–96; "National Confederation of State Medical Examining and Licensing Boards," *Medical News: A Weekly Journal of Medical Science* (June 9, 1900): 926.

24. Amberg, "The Cooperation of the Medical Profession . . . ," 493–96; "National Confederation," *Medical News,* 917; "National Confederation of State Medical Examining and Licensing Boards," *JAMA* (June 23, 1900): 1625.

25. "Transactions of the National Confederation of State Medical Examining and Licensing Boards," *Bulletin of the American Academy of Medicine* 5 (June 1902): 861–62, 866, 872.

26. Ibid., 866–67.

27. B. D. Harrison, "Unconstitutionality of Indorsement," *JAMA* 43 (August 13, 1904): 481.

28. "Transactions of the National Confederation," 870–71.

29. "A National Examining Board," *International Journal of Surgery* 9 (July 1896): 199; C. F. Taylor, "National Medical Legislation," *Medical World* 20 (May 1902): 180–81; Beverly Drake Harrison, "Medical Reciprocity or Interstate Exchange of Licensure," *Medical Record* 62 (October, 4, 1902): 523–24; "National Examining Board," *International Journal of Surgery,* 199.

30. "Constitution of the American Confederation of Reciprocating and Examining and Licensing Medical Boards," *Wisconsin Medical Journal* 2 (October 1903): 344; "Progress in the Movement for Reciprocity in Licensure," *JAMA* (November 5, 1904): 407.

31. Harrison, "Medical Reciprocity," 522, 525.

32. "Progress in the Movement for Reciprocity in Licensure," *JAMA* 48 (November 5, 1904): 1407; "The American Confederation of Reciprocating Examining and Licensing Boards," *JAMA* 49 (May 13, 1905): 1558.

33. "American Confederation of Reciprocating Examining and Licensing Boards," *JAMA* 46 (May 5, 1906): 1394; "Council on Medical Education of the American Medical Association Secretary's Report," *JAMA* 48 (May 18, 1907): 1707; William Rodman, "Report of the Committee on Reciprocity, AMA Council on Medical Education" *JAMA* 46 (June 16, 1906): 1869; "American Confederation of Reciprocating Examining and Licensing Boards," *JAMA* 52 (June 5, 1909): 1862.

34. E. L. B. Godfrey, "Indorsement in Lieu of Reciprocity Between State Licensing Boards," *JAMA* 43 (August 13, 1904): 480–81; Harrison, "Unconstitutionality of Indorsement," 481–82.

35. Guernsey, "Medical Examining Boards and Medical Legislation," 571; "From the Field," *Bulletin of the American Academy of Medicine* 11 (August 1910): 433; "National Confederation of State Medical Examining and Licensing Boards," *California State Journal of Medicine* 9 (May 1911): 218.

36. "American Confederation of Reciprocating Examining and Licensing Boards," *JAMA* 56 (March 25, 1911): 919; "National Confederation of State Medical Examining and Licensing Boards," *Bulletin of the American Academy of Medicine* 9 (August 1908): 254.

37. "Annual Session of the National Confederation of State Medical Examining and Licensing Boards," *Texas Medical News* 16 (July 1907): 468.

38. Fred C. Zapffe, "Report of Committee on State Medical Boards," *Bulletin of the American Academy of Medicine* 11 (December 1910): 757; "Recent Admissions of the Trust Doctors as to Their Real Purpose in Seeking National Legislation," *Twentieth Century Magazine* 2 (August 1910): 464.

39. Susan Skochelak, "A Century of Progress in Medical Education: What About the Next 10 Years?" *Academic Medicine* 85 (February 2010): 197; "A Medical Comedy," *Medical Century* 48 (April 1911): 120–21.

40. In 1912, eclectic medical boards operated in Arkansas, Connecticut, District of Columbia, Florida, Georgia and New Hampshire. Those same states, along with Delaware, Louisiana and Maryland, also had homeopathic medical boards in operation. See Ronald Hamowy, "Early Development of Medical Licensing Laws in the United States, 1875–1900," *Journal of Libertarian Studies* 3 (1979): 119.

41. "A Medical Comedy," 122; "American Confederation of Reciprocating Examining and Licensing Medical Boards," *Bulletin of the American Academy of Medicine* 11 (December 1910): 755–57; Starr, *Social Transformation*, 106–7.

42. James A. Duncan to Charles H. Cook, June 3, 1911. Federation of State Medical Boards Archives, Euless, Texas; "Council on Medical Education of the American Medical Association," *JAMA* 50 (June 20, 1908): 2097.

43. J. N. Baker, "The Federation: Its Origin, History and Obligations," *Federation Bulletin* 23 (March 1937): 76; "American Confederation of Reciprocating Medical Examining and Licensing Boards," *JAMA* 54 (March 19, 1910): 994.

44. Baker, "The Federation: Its Origin," 76–77; Walter L. Bierring, "The First Decade of Federation Activities," *Federation Bulletin* 9 (March 1923): 58–59; "Report of Committee on Amalgamation with the National Confederation," *JAMA* 56 (March 25, 1911): 919; "National Confederation of State Board," *JAMA* 53 (February 10, 1912): 432.

45. The other members of the American Confederation's delegation unable to attend were A. W. Alvord (Michigan), E. A. Carr (Nebraska), H. H. Baxter (Ohio), and William A. Spurgeon (Indiana).

46. Bierring, "First Decade," 59; Baker, "The Federation: Its Origin," 77.

47. E. Arthur Carr, "A Matter of Historical Record," *Journal of the American Institute of Homeopathy* 6 (March 1914): 833; "Constitution and By-Laws of the Federation of State Medical Boards of the United States," *Quarterly of the Federation of State Medical Boards* 1 (October 1913): 90–93.

48. "Executive Session of the Federation," *Federation Bulletin* 3 (April 1917): 14; "A Constructive Program for the Federation," *Federation Bulletin* 7 (March 1921): 59; Carr, "Matter of Historical Record," 834; "Medical Comedy," *Medical Century*, 121–22.

Chapter 3

Beginnings, Growth, and Challenges, 1912–1929

> Perhaps the entire country may some day be covered by a national organization engaged in protecting the public health against . . . ignorance, incompetency, commercialism and disease.
>
> —Abraham Flexner, 1911

While much of the country followed the unfolding political drama of the 1912 U.S. presidential campaign and the tightly contested race among New Jersey Governor Woodrow Wilson, incumbent President William Howard Taft and former President Theodore Roosevelt, representatives from the American and National Confederations labored quietly to put the finishing touches on an acceptable constitution and bylaws for the proposed Federation of State Medical Boards. Their efforts proved successful, though it seems clear that accommodations and compromises were made on both sides. A close reading of the Federation's original constitution and bylaws provides some telling insights into what transpired in these negotiations and the regulatory environment within which the organization came into being.

The Federation's constitution identified its primary mission as facilitating "high and uniform standards" for medical licensure. To achieve that end, the Federation cited three objectives it would endeavor to pursue. The first dealt with educational standards (both preliminary and medical) as adopted by state medical boards. This objective was consistent with the National Confederation's historical focus on raising educational standards and the more recent interest sparked by the Carnegie Foundation's issuance of Abraham Flexner's influential report on medical education in the United States and Canada. What is telling, however, is that the stated objective was "to obtain accurate knowledge" of these educational standards rather than to engage state medical boards directly in the inspection, review and classification of these schools.[1] This activist role had been pursued by the American Confederation previously through special committees on premedical education and medical college inspection; meanwhile, the National Confederation had been moving away from this role. During the negotiations on merger and later in drafting a constitution, representatives of the American Confederation had pushed unsuccessfully for a standing committee of the Federation on medical college inspection. As the Flexner Report and the ongoing work of the AMA Council on Medical Education and the AAMC addressed educational standards in a manner consistent with the position of the National Confederation, it was deemed unnecessary to carve out this function as a stated objective in the new Federation's constitution.

A second stated objective of the Federation called for "further[ing] interstate endorsement of licensure." This was the raison d'être for the American Confederation and here they gained everything that Harrison and his colleagues had hoped for in the Federation's founding documents. The bylaws contained a section on "minimum standards" that Federation member boards were required to uphold. The subsequent description of "qualifications for indorsement of state licenses" drew almost verbatim from the qualifications criteria set forth previously by the American Confederation. Specifically, this included licensure by endorsement based upon a medical diploma from a recognized medical school and either passage of a licensing examination or a license in good standing held in a prior state. This appears to have been the single major concession to the American Confederation and its stated priorities in drafting the Federation's constitution and bylaws.[2]

The third objective called for publishing a "Bulletin by which . . . information may be disseminated among the members." That the Federation's constitution would expressly mandate a written communication vehicle may strike a twenty-first-century audience as an unusually specific operational matter to have included. But in 1912, though the telephone was available in large cities, efficient communication among and between state medical boards represented a significant barrier to achieving the greater uniformity in standards that all parties recognized as beneficial. Correspondence among National Confederation members predating the negotiations over the Federation's constitution spoke of the potential value of such a bulletin and the plentiful source material available through the state medical boards. They envisioned a bulletin reporting on a wide range of subjects such as physician impostors and changes in medical legislation. But more important, they saw the bulletin as a tool "in the campaign for higher and better standards of medical licensure" and a tool for unifying boards.[3]

Two other aspects of the original constitution and bylaws warrant mention. In addition to defining its core membership (state medical boards), the constitution also identified individuals who would henceforth be eligible for membership in the Federation, that is, fellows and honorary fellows. The latter category comprised former members of state medical boards, the former represented current members of state medical boards. A category for Associate Members consisted of individuals who were not gubernatorial appointments to state medical boards but "interested in medical education and state licensure."[4] That the Federation carved out a specific nonvoting membership designation for individuals not serving on state medical boards is not surprising when one recalls that the Federation, and prior to that, the National and American Confederations, held its annual sessions in conjunction with the meetings of the AMA Council on Medical Education and the AAMC. Leaders from both of these organizations helped broker the merger of the two confederations. Undoubtedly, issues of common interest to both groups—medical education; licensure examinations and, later, hospital internship—offered natural touch points where the expertise of each organization benefited the other.

A potentially more significant section of the Federation's bylaws dealt with the eligibility criteria for state medical boards seeking membership in the new organization. Article I of the Federation's bylaws spoke of "uphold[ing] the minimum standards of the Federation" and then set forth standards for preliminary and medical education, the licensing examination and criteria for licensure by endorsement. Specifically, the educational standards meant that Federation member boards required graduation from high school and a four-year medical school, while the examination standard demanded a test of sufficient length and subject matter coverage to "thoroughly test the candidates' fitness to practice medicine." What is striking is that membership in the Federation was predicated not simply upon the presence of such standards in state statutes or regulations but on actual *enforcement* of these standards. The bylaws explicitly tied a state medical board's membership to satisfactorily demonstrating to the Federation's executive committee that the applying board "is actually enforcing the minimum requirements of the Federation." Thus, under its original constitution and bylaws the Federation was more akin to a voluntary association than a membership organization in the truest sense. As an association of like-minded member boards with similar goals and standards, membership was not an automatic function derived from a state board's sui generis status under their medical practice act. Instead, membership derived from the enforcement of common standards which served to differentiate the more progressive boards from those not yet willing or able to meet such standards.[5]

In the view of at least some of the Federation's founding fathers, this was a critical distinction. What these founders sought was an organization comprised of "progressive boards" who might act as a de facto "national force" influencing other states to seek the same "degree of excellence."[6] By linking membership directly to maintaining minimum standards for licensure, the Federation signaled its willingness to start small, with a cadre of progressive, forward-thinking medical boards, and then expand over time as more boards raised their standards sufficiently to meet the Federation's eligibility criteria for membership. Like a rising tide lifting all boats, the Federation and its twenty-two charter member boards committed themselves to what they believed were inexorable and compelling forces leading toward heightened standards in medical regulation nationwide. (See appendix for a list of original charter member boards.)

Meanwhile, news of the Federation's establishment, as well as its founding documents, circulated widely and found a receptive audience in the mainstream press. It is striking to hear the early aspirations for the Federation from observers and commentators at the time of its founding. Their sentiments reflected the hopefulness of many Progressive Era activists who placed great faith in the salutary effects of concerted governmental action on behalf of its citizenry; and sometimes little faith in the collective judgment of that same citizenry. A 1913 article in *Harper's Weekly*, the politically influential periodical, offered a "hearty welcome" to the Federation as a vehicle for fostering greater uniformity of standards for physicians while simultaneously raising those same standards. The commentator noted the challenge awaiting the Federation in "educating public opinion" against the medical "quacks" and "incompetent practitioners" sure to oppose heightened standards. Reflecting upon the patent-medicine industry's opposition to the 1906 Pure Food and Drug Act and the coalition of forces that opposed the concept of a "National Health Department," *Harper's* envisioned the Federation—through its collective membership—serving as a "natural . . . agency of reform" on a national scale.[7] A *New York Times* editorial several days later evinced this same call to arms on a national level. The *Times* editor called for the Federation to "campaign" for the creation of a federal department of health. Their rationale was simple and echoed a refrain not uncommon in that day. According to the *Times*, "the treatment of disease is a public, rather than a private, concern."[8]

This call to action mirrored the already considerable faith of many Progressive Era politicians and reformers as well as much of the American middle class that an appropriate role existed for the federal government in the realm of public health and safety. Precedents already in place included the 1902 Biologics Control Act and the Pure Food and Drugs Act only a few years later. The former gave authority for federal regulation of biological products (e.g., diphtheria vaccine) by establishing hygienic standards for laboratory production of such materials. The latter piece of legislation stemmed from the demands of the public, journalists and social crusaders against unsanitary conditions in food processing and persistent concerns about false or deceptive advertising of patent medicines.[9] That the *Harper's* and *Times* writers both alluded to the potential role for, or the impact of, the Federation hints at an early perception that this new organization, through its collective membership, might be able to provide a national voice in addressing problems viewed previously as local or regional issues.

Looking back, these aspirations for a broadly influential Federation, while flattering and well intentioned, expected perhaps too much from the fledgling organization. In some ways and at a fundamental level, writers such as those from *Harper's* and the *Times* misunderstood the true nature and authority of the Federation. They seemed to conflate an annual gathering of representatives from individual state agencies with a truly national body akin to a federal agency—or at least one possessing the voice, if not the power and authority, of a national body. This was not the case with the Federation at the time because the obstacles to fulfilling such a role were significant. At a very tangible level, the early Federation lacked sufficient resources to play the role that some envisioned for it. The organization had no permanent office or headquarters. The work of the organization took place in the private homes and business offices of its officers. It initially possessed neither permanent paid staff nor monetary resources. Indeed, the first financial statement for the organization in 1913 showed a balance of $250. Even several years later, in 1916, the Federation coffers showed receipts and disbursements leaving a mere $400 net balance. The single largest budget item for the Federation in its early years involved the printing costs for the organization's monthly publication, the *Federation Bulletin*. Yet, even this important vehicle for the Federation proved difficult to sustain at times. Twice in the late 1920s the Federation sought and obtained financial relief from the AMA for printing costs associated with the *Bulletin*.[10]

Despite these challenges the prospects for the Federation were bright. In part, this stemmed from the organization's clear understanding of the major impediments and challenges facing state medical boards in the United States at that time. Based upon the Federation's constitution and bylaws alone, two of the obvious challenges facing the state medical boards pertained to educational standards for medical licensure and licensure by endorsement. By 1917, the Federation's newly elected president, David Strickler, could confidently list several other issues as those deemed most in need of attention by medical boards: greater uniformity in states' medical practice acts; the content of licensing examinations; classification systems for medical schools; and the requirement of a hospital internship year as a requirement for medical licensure. A survey of state medical boards commissioned by Strickler in that same year identified a number of other issues that were increasingly demanding the attention of state boards: New York cited the activities of drugless practitioners and/or "cults;" New Jersey urged annual registration of licensees; Utah advocated for clear minimum standards before states chartered educational institutions; California lamented the lack of a central bureau to track disciplined physicians as well as the need for greater uniformity in administrative records; and Vermont lamented public opinion that was too often averse to, or disinterested in, the role of state medical boards.[11] If the minutes of the Federation's annual meetings and the pages of the *Federation Bulletin* are indicative of the organization's priorities and focus during its first two decades, these issues consumed not only the energy of the FSMB but those of the country's state medical boards as well.

EXAMINATIONS FOR MEDICAL LICENSURE

If today the American public generally associates the phrase "medical examiner" with forensics, no such connotation existed in the popular imagination a century ago. It was not by happenstance that both of the Federation's predecessor organizations integrated the phrase "Examining and Licensing Boards" into their full names. One need only note the ubiquitous presence of the term "examiner" in the name of the vast majority of early-twentieth-century state medical boards—a holdover term still used among some modern-day state medical boards—to recognize that one of their primary functions involved personally examining the fitness to practice of their licensure candidates. In this particular area, state medical boards throughout the United States experienced considerable success in their public protection role, even before the Federation's founding in 1912.

Almost from the beginning of the second wave of medical licensing laws enacted across the United States starting in the 1870s, provision was made for an examination of physicians by duly constituted examining boards. Early on, however, the examination component was usually not a requirement but one of several alternatives for being licensed in a given state. For example, an examination might be required if a physician could not present a medical school diploma, a certification from a state or country medical society or proof that he or she had been in practice a prescribed number of years in that state. One researcher's review of state statutes covering the period from 1867 to 1895 concluded that twenty-three states either required an examination or offered one as a mechanism for obtaining a medical license. In most instances, the examinations were written in longhand by candidates. However, an oral examination before the board seems also to have been likely since various state statutes often spoke in terms of the board's authority to "examine" a candidate without reference to the format of the examination. The rigor behind such an examination varied greatly between a pro forma exercise and an in-depth assessment stretching over several days.[12]

As one might anticipate, content for these examinations varied markedly between states. However, some areas appear to have been commonly covered by most states. The Texas medical board's licensing examination may serve to illustrate the development of these exams both from the perspective of what they covered and, even more tellingly, what they omitted. The 1873 Texas Act to Regulate the Practice of Medicine is generally credited as one of the earliest, if not the first, modern Medical Practice Act (MPA) in the United States. The legislation created a "board of medical examiners" charged with undertaking a "thorough examination" of prospective candidates for licensure. Whether for reasons of political expediency or simply because the legislature was satisfied to leave content decisions to the board, there was no attempt to delineate what a thorough examination might constitute. Content does not appear to have been explicitly identified until 1885 when a Texas legislative bill required an examination covering anatomy, physiology, pathology, chemistry, surgery and obstetrics. Less than a decade later, in 1894, additional legislation left the required content coverage intact but clarified that the state had no intent to test physicians within their specific "school of medicine."[13] The purpose behind this language is clear. Up to that time, Texas opted not to examine physicians in either therapeutics or *materia medica* as these two branches led inexorably into philosophical differences among physicians along specific approaches to the treatment of illness and disease. With "regular" physicians, homeopaths and eclectics equally represented on the Texas board, the clear accommodation was to assess licensure candidates in the calmer waters of the commonly agreed main branches of medicine while avoiding the shoals of branches such as therapeutics. In this way, the Texas board avoided sectarian pitfalls in the contested waters surrounding the *practice* of medicine.

However, not all medical boards were reluctant to assess in contested areas such as therapeutics and *materia medica*. Naturally, in states such as Florida and Arkansas where separate homeopathic and eclectic boards had been established, examinations could assess areas such as these without touching off contentious arguments with physician colleagues representing other schools of medicine. On occasion, even those states with a single examining board, such as Missouri, addressed these areas directly, despite the inherent potential for conflict. The Missouri State Board of Health's 1906 examination tested candidates in the commonly accepted fundamental branches as well as therapeutics and medical "practice." Missouri may have been atypical in this regard. The Texas approach—omitting contentious fields from the explicitly identified content of the medical licensing exam—more closely reflected the norm in those states where a single board had been established.[14] (See the appendix for sample questions from Missouri's 1906 licensing examination.)

By 1907, a year after Frederick Hopkins suggested that a lack of vitamins caused scurvy and just four years after Willem Einthoven developed electrocardiography, a deepening understanding of the science underpinning medicine led Texas to expand the content coverage of its medical licensing examination. Bacteriology and histology were added to the required content. Public health initiatives had developed sufficiently, and with significant success, to warrant adding hygiene and medical jurisprudence, as well. Additionally, physical diagnosis and gynecology were now included in the examination.[15]

While states were expanding the depth and breadth of coverage of their medical licensing exams, a simultaneous move to make them mandatory rather than an alternative to obtaining a license was also under way. In 1915, the Federation's secretary-treasurer, Walter Bierring, as chairman of a Federation Special Committee on Medical Licensure, proudly claimed that all states utilized some form of medical licensing exam.[16] Progress in reaching this point had not come easily, however. Indeed, it appears that by 1907—and perhaps even earlier—all forty-six states, the New Mexico and Arizona territories, and the District of Columbia were administering some form of written examination for medical licensure as evidenced by the annual state board issue of *JAMA*. What is less obvious are the requirements surrounding these examinations—specifically, whether they were mandated for all licensure applicants. Here the record is less clear, though available evidence would seem to indicate that by the time of Bierring's statement only New Mexico did not mandate an examination as part of its medical licensure requirements.[17]

With virtually every state medical board administering a licensing examination, the question arises, "How significant a challenge did these exams present for physicians?" In attempting to answer this question, the annual state board issue of *JAMA* was reviewed for multiple years covering the first three decades of the twentieth century. From a national perspective, one overall trend for medical licensing examinations was a steady but pronounced increase in the pass rate. Aggregate data combining the results from all states' examinations showed a pass rate between 78 and 81 percent during the period 1904–1914. The pass rate improved to 84–88 percent over the next ten years and then from 1925 to 1932 increased further to 90–94 percent (table 3.1). One explanation for this improvement on state medical board licensing examinations stems from the post-Flexnerian landscape of medical education. The decade prior to Flexner's 1910 report witnessed an ebb and flow in undergraduate medical education facilities with 50 new schools of various types appearing on the scene and school closings and consolidations impacting 70 more. Even more significant was the post–Flexner report contraction from 133 medical schools in 1910 to 65 approved medical schools in 1932 and the rapidly shrinking ranks of commercial, proprietary schools. One might reasonably conclude that this resulted in fewer marginally or inadequately

Table 3.1. Registration of Physician Licensure Candidates by State Boards[a], 1904–1932

Year	*# Examined*	*# Passed*	*% Failed*
1904	7,039	5,676	19.4
1905	7,179	5,688	20.8
1906	8,035	6,368	20.7
1907	7,274	5,726	21.3
1908	7,773	6,087	21.7
1909	7,290	5,860	19.6
1910	7,005	5,713	18.4
1911	6,963	5,581	19.8
1912	6,880	5,467	20.5
1913	6,447	5,248	18.6
1914	5,573	4,373	21.5
1915	5,318	4,491	15.6
1916	4,854	4,127	15.0
1917	4,741	4,072	14.1
1918	3,643	3,160	13.3
1919	4,749	4,073	14.2
1920	4,793	4,059	15.3
1921	4,814	4,218	12.4
1922	4,012	3,520	12.3
1923	4,712	4,013	14.8
1924	5,374	4,738	11.8
1925	5,990	5,438	9.2
1926	5,819	5,353	8.0
1927	5,467	5,080	7.1
1928	5,547	5,170	6.6
1929	5,729	5,362	6.4
1930	5,525	5,208	5.7
1931	5,577	5,226	6.3
1932	5,624	5,191	7.7

[a]Includes Medical, Homeopathic and Eclectic Boards

Source: Adapted from "Medical Licensure Statistics for 1932," *Journal of the American Medical Association* 100 (1933): 1246.

trained physician candidates sitting for medical licensing examinations. In tracking state medical board statistics on the sources of their licensed physicians, graduates from approved medical schools constituted a steadily increasing percentage of all licensees—reaching nearly 94 percent in 1932.[18] With this growing cohort of presumably better-trained physicians, improved performance on licensing examinations represents an outcome that one might reasonably have expected.

Another factor apparently at work was the typical practice in some states of crediting extra points, or an additional percentage, to the examination results of established practitioners who were previously licensed in another state. Texas, Illinois, and Massachusetts utilized this practice. At one time, Illinois's medical practice act called for crediting the examinee with "5 per cent" toward the required 75 percent passing rate for every five years in active practice. Though it is unclear how many states were actually implementing such a practice, the lack of negative comments concerning this practice in the extant literature would seem to indicate this was neither uncommon nor unexpected. Indeed, it appears to represent a political compromise of sorts, designed to assuage the concerns of both "elderly" practitioners and state legislatures.[19]

Aggregated data, however, tell only part of the story. A look at state-specific data reveals a wide variance in the pass/fail rates on these examinations. In 1910, the fail rates reported by each state on their medical licensing examination ranged from 0 percent to 45 percent, with a mean and median fail rate of 18 percent and 16 percent, respectively. Similar data were reported for 1913—failure rates ranging from 1 percent to 43 percent, with mean and median fail rates of 16 percent and 14 percent. Thus, at the time of the Federation's founding, a significant variance existed in the standard that each state applied to its licensing examination. Twenty years later much of this wide variance in the range of pass rates among the states disappeared. In 1929, 44 of 51 boards reported a failure rate of 12 percent or lower; by 1932, this rose to 47 of 51.

Perhaps more significant was the preponderance of boards now reporting no failures at all on their state examinations. Whereas this was uncommon in 1910, by 1932, this was now the case for approximately half of all state medical boards.[20] (See tables 3.2 and 3.3.) Setting aside any differences in test content, this variability in the standard applied to physician candidates for licensure would continue to hinder efforts toward greater uniformity nationally.

State medical boards focused considerable time and attention on their licensing examinations during the Federation's early years. Over time these examinations became an accepted part of the medical licensure process even for those who might earlier have questioned their value or criticized them as duplicative of testing within the context of medical school.

Table 3.2. Failure Rates Reported by States on Their Medical Licensing Examination

	1910	*1913*	*1927*	*1929*	*1932*
0–5%	7[a]	7	32	37	42
6–10%	9	12	9	6	2
11–15%	7	9	4	3	3
16–20%	5	4	2	0	2
21–30%	12	15	2	2	0
>31%	7	4	1	3	1

[a] number of states reporting a rate falling in that range

Source: Adapted from "State Board Statistics," *Journal of the American Medical Association* 56 (1911): 1568-1569; 62 (1914): 1646–1647; 90 (1928): 1202–1203; 94 (1930): 1310–1311; 100 (1933): 1242–1243.

If the comments of George Blumer, Dean of the Yale School of Medicine, are indicative, even the medical education community acknowledged the value of this independent assessment. At a 1917 AMA-sponsored Congress on Medical Education, Blumer proclaimed, "Without the safeguard of licensing examinations the public would be even less well protected than they are at present."[21] While the need for medical licensing examinations was no longer seriously questioned, increasingly the focus of conversation turned to the content and construct of these examinations.

Joint annual meetings of the Federation membership and the AAMC provided opportunities for both the licensing and medical education communities to engage directly in conversations about their respective assessment roles. Echoing comments made even today, both sides recognized the need to examine students and physicians less for their capacity for rote memorization and more for their ability to apply their "critical faculty." State medical board leaders such as Bierring admitted the tendency on the part of licensing boards toward examinations heavy in the recitation of medical facts and definitions. Blumer, Bierring, and others urged state medical boards to invigorate their examinations with content that not only assessed the "technical language of medicine" but also attempted to address the physician's ability to interpret and express in graphic form and to "reason from facts." The most important trend evidenced in medical licensing examinations during the first decades of the Federation involved the use of practical examinations.[22]

Table 3.3. States Reporting No Failing Candidates on Medical Licensing Examination

Year	*1910*	*1913...*	*1927*	*1928*	*1929*	*1930*	*1931*	*1932*
# of States	2	0	16	18	22	27	27	26

Source: Adapted from "State Board Statistics," *Journal of the American Medical Association* 56 (1911): 1568–1569; 62 (1914): 1646–1647; 90 (1928): 1202–1203; 94 (1930): 1310–1311; 100 (1933): 1242–1243.

For some time, the state medical boards had suspected that their written examinations were inadequate to genuinely "test the fitness" of a physician to practice medicine. Even a more robust written examination along the lines espoused by Blumer, Bierring and others was recognized as insufficient by itself as the focus remained wholly cognitive. The disquiet felt by many stemmed from a recognition that even when written examinations went beyond recall and understanding to demand a genuine application of medical principles, they were still operating solely in the cognitive domain. For many educators and state boards, modern medicine increasingly called for a "hands-on" clinical assessment. A 1917 survey by Walter Bowers, secretary of the Massachusetts State Board of Medical Examiners, underscored what many state medical boards had already begun to address. Bowers's survey revealed that sixteen boards were already administering a *practical* examination in addition to their written exam. Additionally, even those boards not administering a practical examination expressed themselves as being strongly in favor of such an exam.[23]

How were these practical examinations administered? Hospitals and medical school facilities were utilized by nine of these sixteen boards with the remainder conducted at board or state offices. This practical component varied considerably among boards to include laboratory work, use of medical instruments, examinations using mannequins as well as examinations using live human subjects. For example, Minnesota's candidates spent one day in written examinations followed by one half-day in laboratory work with the remainder of that day spent performing a bedside examination. The written examination contained three major topics (medicine, surgery and obstetrics-gynecology) and several minor topics (materia medica, therapeutics, medical jurisprudence, preventive medicine, anatomy, physiology, etc.). The urinalysis involved effectively using a microscope, reagents and several samples with blank forms for reporting findings; four specimens for microscopic work as part of a histology and pathology examination; and six gross specimens, such as lesions of the small intestine, brain hemorrhage, and so on. The afternoon was then given over to physical diagnosis of a patient at the nearby University Hospital followed by an interview and discussion of the case with two state board examiners. Massachusetts conducted one of the more ambitious practical examinations with the candidate passing between a series of examiners in various rooms and assessing obstetrics (mannequins; living subjects for pelvic exams), anatomy (dissections), physiology (sphygmomanometer), surgery (cadavers or living subjects), pathology (microscopic and gross specimens), toxicology (poison and reagents), theory and practice (examination of living subjects).[24]

Perhaps the greatest impetus spurring state medical boards to think more seriously about the content and construct of their licensing examinations was the establishment of the National Board of Medical Examiners (NBME) in 1915. The National Board's founder, William Rodman, had long advocated for a voluntary national examining board as a means to foster uniformity and physician mobility by authoring an examination that could be commonly recognized as representing a high standard that all state medical boards could accept for licensure qualification. Using his 1915 AMA Presidential Address as a platform, Rodman outlined the parameters for the board, including governance drawn from several branches of the armed forces, the U.S. Public Health Service, the Federation, the AAMC, the American College of Physicians and the AMA. The eligibility criteria for sitting the National Board's examination would represent a standard equal to, or higher than, that mandated by any of the state medical boards. Its candidates were restricted to high school graduates with two years of premedical college work (including chemistry and biology), graduation from a so-called Class A medical school and successful completion of one year of a hospital internship. The exhaustive examination lasted six days, covering not only cognitive knowledge but also practical aspects of medicine, including laboratory work and a bedside examination of patients. Subsequent results from the first administration in 1916 reflected the rigor of the National Board standard when only half of the thirty-two applicants were deemed to have met the educational prerequisites to sit the exam and only five of the ten candidates who appeared for the examination passed.[25]

The Federation dedicated much of its 1916 annual meeting to the topic of the recently constituted National Board. The meeting transcripts reflected tough questions and strong opinions coming from those on both sides of the matter. Objections to the National Board on the part of some state board secretaries in attendance took three primary forms: legal, administrative and speculative. Some questioned the legality of a state board "delegating" its authority in the matter of examinations to an independent body and cited opinions from their respective states' attorney general. Others questioned the NBME governance structure, citing an insufficient number of representatives from the state medical boards. Another common theme involved questioning whether a voluntary national board, lacking any genuine compulsory powers, would be able to gain a sufficient number of state medical boards to recognize its examination and thus make good on its stated goals.[26]

Supportive state board members and Rodman addressed these concerns and presented a persuasive case for the National Board. In particular, Pennsylvania Board President John Baldy spoke forcefully in addressing each of the concerns, characterizing many of them as "trivial criticisms" that lost sight of the larger picture. While acknowledging that some state statutes as currently written might prohibit recognizing the National Board's proposed examination, he made clear that seeking statutory relief was nothing new to state boards seeking higher standards for public protection. His colleague from Ohio, J. M. Howell, declared his political will in the matter, stating, "I for one will see the governor . . . and use all the influence . . . within me in favor of this national board." A determined John Baldy was even more adamant. "Pennsylvania is going to make the action legal if it is the only state in the Union that does so." He then pointed to the efforts of another voluntary national organization—the AAMC—as evidence of the effectiveness of such bodies and their ability to gain support despite a lack of compulsory power. Baldy and others made clear that the federal government's representation on the National Board governance represented a pragmatic reality stemming from the impending potential for U.S. involvement in the ongoing European conflict and the government's experience with examinations for military medical officers dating back to the nineteenth century. Ultimately, strong support from representatives of the Pennsylvania (Baldy), Iowa (Bierring), West Virginia (S. L. Jepson), Kentucky (H. H. Grant), Ohio (Howell), Louisiana (Isadore Dyer), Wisconsin (H. W. Abraham) and New Jersey (Alexander Marcy) state medical boards carried the day. It would seem that state boards concurred with Bierring's assessment that they were subscribing to a "pioneer movement" in medical regulation.[27] The Federation moved quickly to endorse the National Board. Soon thereafter Walter Bierring set forth the case plainly in a July 1916 editorial in the *Federation Bulletin:*

> The National Board and the Federation are working for a common purpose—to guarantee better trained physicians for this and future generations. Each has its own work but can do that work better with the cooperation of the other.

A number of early leaders within the licensing community became staunch advocates of the nascent NBME. Among the more important of these were John Baldy, Walter Bierring and Herbert Harlan (Maryland). The *Federation Bulletin* faithfully—and often extensively—reported National Board activities and the rapid progress by which state medical boards formally moved to recognize NBME diplomates. The National Board administered its first certifying exam in 1916 and within a year twelve state medical boards had formally recognized this credential as meeting their medical licensing examination requirements. Steady progress continued with twenty recognizing boards by 1920 and thirty-one boards by 1925. Further evidence of Federation and state board support for the NBME was evidenced by the many members of the licensing community who subsequently served as members of the National Board.[28] This trend continued throughout the era of the NBME certifying examination and continued with later examination programs like the Federation Licensing Examination (FLEX) in the 1960s and the United States Medical Licensing Examination (USMLE) in the 1990s.

As editor of the *Bulletin* and also a member of the NBME, Walter Bierring wrote forcefully and often on the necessity of state boards moving to recognize this credential. Once the National Board moved from concept to reality, Bierring urged boards to act. "This board is now clearly established as a permanent institution . . . state boards should . . . [have] their individual regulation or registration laws so altered as to permit the recognition of the National Board certificate." Even a decade later, Bierring could not refrain from correcting state board colleagues who had, in his opinion, "fallen into an error" by criticizing the National Board as a "presumptuous" de facto licensing entity.[29]

ADMINISTRATIVE PROCEDURES AND RECORD KEEPING

The modern state medical boards that came into existence starting in the 1870s were still finding their way as state regulatory agencies in the first decades of the twentieth century. Important social science theorists of that time, such as Max Weber, and management engineers like Frederick W. Taylor, developed and popularized concepts for a more "scientific" approach to effective management and administration. In keeping with the progressive nature of the times, state medical boards sought to incorporate appropriate best practices of their own. Still, boards were on a learning curve as they sought to identify the necessary administrative and record-keeping procedures to operate efficiently. This would prove particularly challenging for boards situated in heavily populated states with a large number of licensees and often insufficient resources. Not surprisingly, many boards looked to the Federation to disseminate best practices among its membership and help foster standardization wherever possible.

For many state medical boards, keeping track of the physical location of their licensees was among the most fundamental challenges they faced. To address this situation, the state boards advocated increasingly for annual registration of their physician licensees. The specifics may have varied somewhat among jurisdictions but what this ordinarily required was for each licensed physician to file a registration form or affidavit with pertinent information (e.g., name, address, nature of practice, license number) and pay a small registration fee on an annual basis. In many instances, this filing took place at the county clerk's office rather than with the board. Such lists would then be reported, or made available, to the state medical board as a means of accomplishing several goals: deriving an accurate number and list of actively practicing physicians; producing a directory of licensed physicians; and assisting the board in coordinating its efforts with local authorities in prosecuting unlicensed practitioners.[30]

A 1926 survey of annual registration requirements by the AMA's Bureau of Legal Medicine and Legislation underscored the limited success that state medical boards were experiencing in these efforts. Only thirteen states indicated that annual registration was required, either under their medical practice act or as part of a state-imposed occupational tax. The annual fees collected were usually modest ($1–2) when designated specifically for the administration and enforcement of the state's MPA and significantly higher ($5–25) when collected as an occupational tax directly routed to the state's general revenue. The diversion of potential operating revenue from state medical boards into the state's general revenue fund was a commonplace, if not frustrating, reality for state boards then as it is now. What is more surprising is the small number of states conducting annual registration given that nearly half of the professional societies responding to the survey and an overwhelming majority of state boards agreed that annual registration was "advantageous" and in the best interests of both the public and the profession. Perhaps the best explanation for this disconnect is derived from the survey comments coming from state medical societies. In several instances (Indiana, Rhode Island and Wyoming), it is clear that opposition to the annual registration of physicians stemmed from two related concerns: (1) a reluctance to impose any additional financial burden on licensed physicians; and (2) a presumption that any revenue derived from annual registration would likely be routed into the general coffers of the state rather than to the board for enforcement efforts under the state's medical practice act—specifically, efforts and resources that would target unlicensed practitioners.[31]

Regardless of whether annual registration of physicians was taking place, record keeping presented a different matter and challenge for many state boards. So common were these administrative issues that the Federation organized a Special Committee on State Board Records and Office Details headed by the executive directors of the California and Ohio boards, Charles Pinkham and Herbert Platter. The subsequent committee report provided recommendations and guidelines to state medical boards covering record maintenance both for licensees and for tracking board revenues and expenditures.[32]

The committee's report discussed at length the licensure application, examination records and a "record card" for each applicant/licensee. The report built upon earlier work by the Federation's Committee on Uniform Reciprocity Application Forms to highlight key identity elements that each board should be capturing as part of its licensure application.

Specifically, these were to include name, date and place of birth, address, educational background (preliminary, premedical and medical), license status in other states, criminal convictions, and, of critical importance to both identity verification and medical discipline, a detailed physical description, including a photograph. The report also encouraged boards to take the necessary steps, statutorily or otherwise, so that misstatements in any attached affidavits or false answers on the license application could be actionable, that is, the basis for sanction or prosecution by the board.[33]

The report made clear that the nineteenth-century practice of maintaining a registry book or ledger was inadequate to the needs of all but the smallest jurisdictions and even then no longer sufficient in a modern administrative setting. The report encouraged boards to use vertical files (color-coded by profession) with 4×6–inch record cards as the best organizing system. While not formally part of the report, coding systems for tracking licenses such as that utilized in California were reported within the pages of the *Federation Bulletin*. Also proffered were sample forms for licensee records that served as templates upon which boards might draw for their own use.[34]

The report also dealt with record keeping for licensing examinations, a subject covered in depth several times in the 1920s by Pinkham. The recommended administrative procedures were designed to not only protect the board against accusations of favoritism by disgruntled failing examinees but to reduce the potential for examinee fraud involving the use of an impostor to sit for an examination on the licensure candidate's behalf. The Federation's report encouraged boards to adopt detailed administrative procedures that "blinded" the identity of the candidate during grading of their licensing examination yet allowed for the results to be matched appropriately and accurately with the individual's record card within their license application file. Multiple duplicate photographs submitted as part of the license application included one to be utilized on-site during check-in prior to testing as a means of assuring that the candidate who was presenting in-person for the examination matched the photograph attached to the license application. Additional suggested protocols included having the examinee write his name, address, some biographical elements (e.g., place of birth, medical school) and signature on a sheet of paper supplied on-site. This was then placed into a sealed envelope for possible later comparison with information and signature on the license application. Pinkham's extensive and detailed writings on board administrative procedures and safeguards were prompted by his board's experience in a highly publicized case of an impostor named Philip Dyment. The case included the revelation that Dyment secured his medical license originally in Georgia through an impostor paid to sit that board's licensing examination on his behalf.[35]

Administrative procedures to safeguard the issuance of "duplicate certificates" (i.e., licenses) were also critical. Physicians were commonly required to register their certificate with the county in which they resided. Boards periodically received requests to replace certificates that had been lost, stolen or destroyed. While most states had provisions in place for issuance of a duplicate that included a written affidavit with a signature setting forth the physician's credentials and circumstances under which the certificate was lost, only nine required a certified photograph as part of their administrative process. This simple security measure—the required photograph—provided at least some assistance in the ongoing battle of medical boards to ferret out impostors. These limited measures were hardly foolproof, however, as evidenced by the cases presented periodically by Pinkham in the pages of the *Federation Bulletin*.[36]

LICENSE RECIPROCITY OR ENDORSEMENT

The Dyment case and others like it underscored not only the importance of appropriate administrative safeguards as a part of the medical licensure process but it also prompted state medical boards to continue thinking broadly about interstate endorsement and license reciprocity. At the time of the Federation's founding, reciprocal agreements between state medical boards seemed to present a viable solution to the nettlesome problem of expeditiously licensing physicians relocating from one state to another. Specifically, the problem facing boards was how to implement an appropriately thorough licensing process without duplicating the verification efforts previously performed by staff at another state board, or placing an unnecessary burden, such as reexamination, upon the physician. Reciprocal agreements between state boards flourished in the early years of the twentieth century after the establishment of the American Confederation. In 1912, such agreements were still viewed favorably enough that the Federation's original bylaws incorporated the reciprocity standards set forth by the American Confederation. However, by the 1920s reservations concerning the use of such agreements were increasingly being expressed.

The shift away from formally drafted reciprocity agreements between states stemmed from several factors. David Strickler, secretary of the Colorado State Board of Medical Examiners and Federation president from 1917 to 1924, summarized these factors in a 1920 address before the American Institute for Homeopathy. Strickler and others acknowledged that such agreements penalized the physician emigrating from a state that did not have a reciprocity agreement with the state medical board in the new jurisdiction where he sought to relocate. Two physicians from the same graduating class of a medical school might present a comparable record yet one would enjoy an expedited process for licensure, and the other would not, simply by virtue of the formal agreement, or lack thereof, between his home state and the new one. Said Strickler, "Each applicant should be treated on the basis of his qualifications, considered solely and alone." Additionally, reciprocity agreements were increasingly deemed an inadequate mechanism for dealing with applicants possessing questionable moral character. Some feared that state boards utilizing such agreements generally were not doing enough to investigate the physician's practice record and "standing in the community."[37]

Even the language of the discussion had begun to shift. The term "reciprocity" fell into disfavor in the 1920s with its implication of a written (or even informal) agreement between two or more state boards. Instead, speakers began using the term "endorsement" as one that was more reflective of a state board's decision to *endorse* the credentials of an applicant previously licensed in another state rather than reciprocating in the issuance of a license to a physician already licensed in another jurisdiction.[38]

In 1920, the Federation formed a committee to develop a "modified form of application for reciprocity or interstate licensure." The subsequent committee report brought forward an "endorsement blank" to serve as a template for all boards to utilize as a means of standardizing the information elicited from physicians and those being asked to verify key credentials. The multiple forms included those to be completed by the physician and one to be completed by the secretary of the state medical board issuing the original medical license. The proposed forms posed multiple questions intended to address the physician's record and moral character. The form to be completed by the state board issuing the original license sought both factual information and a statement that the physician was licensed in good standing.[39]

A 1922 survey of eighteen southern states by K. P. Bonner, secretary of the North Carolina Board of Medical Examiners, underscored the challenges inherent to administering an equitable process for reciprocity or endorsement in the South. Sixteen of the eighteen boards had some "fixed" process for reciprocal agreements. However, little consensus existed beyond the use of such agreements. Some boards adhered strictly to an examination requirement; others accepted candidates based upon a medical diploma and license from an originating state; others required both licensure examination and medical diploma. The details varied depending upon the specific agreement in place with a given state. The requirement for "practical experience" varied widely as well. Depending upon the state, upward of five years of experience after licensure was required under these agreements. Several responding boards indicated they were rethinking the entire premise behind such agreements.[40]

Such variations in requirements were not peculiar to the South. Connecticut state law provided for "reciprocal registry" but its state board declined to utilize this privilege. Massachusetts, while possessing similar legislative scope, was only slightly more accommodating to physicians seeking to relocate, as it restricted this privilege to physicians having at least fifteen years of experience in practice. Rhode Island offered reciprocal registry but only to the still relatively small number of physicians who had taken and passed the National Board examination. Boards such as those of New Hampshire, New Jersey, North Dakota, and Ohio had special policies in place, or exemptions to the standard policy, for "border physicians," that is, those residing nearby but on the other side of the state line.[41]

In retrospect, a certain irony can be found in the early success of the license reciprocity/endorsement movement. Whereas in 1904, twenty-seven states had "reciprocal relations" with other states, by 1922 the number had risen sharply, to forty-four states.[42] Thus, state boards were moving aggressively to develop procedures to facilitate licensing physicians seeking to relocate from another jurisdiction. However, the rapid pace by which the state boards developed broad remedies to facilitate the portability of a medical license seemed to be matched equally by an array of complicating factors. One of these was the discrepancy in the quality of the medical education behind the credential presented by physicians for licensure. The closure and/or consolidation of many medical schools before and after the issuance of Flexner's 1910 report reflected a slow but steady increase in the quality of U.S. medical education. Yet this sea change in medical education could not account for the vast number of previously licensed physicians whose educational credentials from inferior schools predated this shift. What these physicians lacked in the way of a credential suitable for a license by endorsement through their medical diploma, they might make up for in political influence in resisting the other viable option, licensure by endorsement through examination. More distressing was the experience of state boards in dealing with issues of moral character presented by a minority of prospective licensure endorsement applicants. The practical experience of boards investigating the background of candidates soon taught them the numerous ways that dishonest candidates could circumvent the system. Impostors sitting exams, frauds assuming the identity of licensed physicians and frequent relocations one step ahead of local authorities provided every board with cautionary tales. Administrative procedures calling for personal appearances before the board, "advance filing" of the endorsement licensure application and duplicate photographs became commonplace not through gratuitous bureaucracy but as real mechanisms for combating deception.[43] The lesson being absorbed by state boards in the 1920s was clear: There was more to fear from the small number of practitioners with poor character and good education than the more numerous physicians with a lesser education but solid moral character.

DISCIPLINE

Perusing the early editions of the *Federation Bulletin* reminds today's readers of the significant challenge facing state medical boards as they sought to regulate the practice of medicine in their state. The June 1918 issue offers typical examples of the news items carried in the *Bulletin* alerting its readership to criminal convictions of physicians and subsequent actions taken by the board against such individuals. A Michigan board revoked one physician's license after conviction for "criminal abortion"; an Ohio physician was fined for prescribing violations that included the "illegal selling of morphine"; an Illinois practitioner was fined for "practicing medicine without a license"; and an Oklahoma physician was jailed during World War I for violations under the federal Espionage and Sedition Acts of 1917–1918: the physician in question had encouraged military-age males to resist the military draft and had even gone so far as to assist draftees in failing the vision test portion of their physical examination.[44]

Dedicating a portion of the *Federation Bulletin* to these news items served its practical purpose of alerting state medical boards. Everyone involved in medical regulation, however, recognized that these laudable efforts were insufficient. The Federation's leadership publicly wondered just how much might be "safely published" in the pages of the *Bulletin* without exposing the organization to a potentially damaging libel suit. In 1917, Federation President David Strickler spoke of the need for state medical boards to "obtain reliable information" about their prospective and current licensees. What most frustrated leaders such as Strickler was the knowledge that information on physicians of "questionable character" existed but was too often inaccessible, buried in the records of another state.[45]

What was needed was a "central bureau" that might act as a clearinghouse for information about practitioners of questionable character and outright frauds. In February 1918, the Federation pledged to support such an initiative on behalf of its member boards. Anxious to proceed on this front, the Federation first explored housing such a bureau itself. Unfortunately, limited resources and a prospective cost in excess of $3,000 annually left the Federation convinced that it was not yet able to undertake such an initiative. Instead, the Federation formulated an arrangement with the Biographical Department of the AMA. The extensive records already in place with the department—gleaned from news clipping bureaus, state medical boards, medical schools, medical journals, and so on—provided the necessary infrastructure for an expanded repository. The Federation urged all its member boards to make routine, systematic reports to the AMA Biographical Department on frauds, impostors, criminal convictions and "all official actions" taken by the boards. Particularly important was providing the department with photographic copies of applications and a photograph of the physician. Thus, the onus fell upon state medical boards to make timely reports and routinely query the AMA department when circumstances behind a specific application warranted such action.[46]

The success of this de facto central bureau of disciplinary actions depended ultimately upon diligent reporting by state medical boards. Success stories soon appeared. A testimonial from Francis Shepardson of the Illinois Department of Registration and Education touted that state medical board's satisfaction with this resource. The case of Philip Dyment, mentioned earlier, was successfully pursued, in part, due to the photographic material forwarded to the Biographical Department.[47] (For a relatively contemporary case of a medical impostor, consult Robert Derbyshire's *Medical Licensure and Discipline in the United States*.)

If availability and dissemination of information was one challenge facing state boards in their disciplinary function, another challenge arose at a more fundamental level. For most state boards, the early emphasis of their work centered on the licensing function. Specifically, this meant assuring the qualifications of the prospective licensee. In most instances, this stemmed directly from legislative failure to codify the disciplinary function of the board. For example, in Virginia the state board did not receive authority to revoke a license until after 1910, nearly twenty-five years beyond the board's creation. It was only later in the twentieth century that the disciplinary and regulatory functions of the boards came increasingly to the forefront. In the first decades of the twentieth century, as state boards assumed a more active disciplinary role, they repeatedly faced disinterest, noncooperation, and sometimes even opposition, from both local courts and the public. Texas's experience is instructive. In 1908, the newly unified Texas Board of Medical Examiners began moving vigorously against "advertising" physicians—in the late nineteenth and early- to mid-twentieth centuries physicians were banned from advertising their services—who subsequently attempted to bury the board under an avalanche of writs of mandamus. The board sought financial assistance from the state's attorney general, only to be informed that the costs of unsuccessful suits (whether initiated by the board or not) would be collected from the board's funds.[48]

This lack of support can be seen in boards' experiences with pursuing cases involving illegal practitioners. A 1919 survey showed that only fourteen states saw any significant activity in prosecuting such cases, with most of these centered in Illinois, California, Pennsylvania, Indiana and Ohio. The situation seemed little improved several years later if a 1922 summary of actions taken against medical "advertising offices" in the Detroit area is any indication. In that instance, seventeen offices of unlicensed and non-physician practitioners advertising their services as physicians were closed with a handful of criminal convictions. In some states, legislative barriers limited prosecution in these cases. Until 1921 North Carolina's medical practice act contained a "fee and reward" clause such that the board had to prove not only the unlicensed practice of medicine but that the individual had received compensation for his or her services. For boards, dogged persistence was necessary to interest the average local prosecutor to collaborate in prosecuting and shutting down unlicensed practitioners. Additionally, little additional support seemed forthcoming from the public in these matters. For much of the public, the practice of medicine meant an individual skilled in using a scalpel or in administering drugs. Absent either of those, both the public and local prosecutors often refused to categorize behaviors that involved "treating" patients as the practice of medicine. Similarly, garnering support for enforcement under their medical practice acts (MPA) often proved difficult for state boards.[49]

State boards began looking more critically at their disciplinary and enforcement functions, starting with their MPA. For many boards, legislation in this area was wholly "piecemeal," with the result that too often a state's medical practice act was, in effect, little more than a disparate amalgamation of individual laws rather than a single piece of overarching legislation. The result sometimes was legislation that was largely "unenforceable," with physician misconduct handled at the local level by county or state medical societies, when it was addressed at all. Such was the situation in the Oklahoma Territory in the early twentieth century where, despite the existence of a board of health to register physicians, little monitoring of medical practice took place. The board added individuals to its registry on an "honor" system with the result that quacks and fakes found refuge as readily as duly educated physicians. Yet even long-established boards, such as that in North Carolina, did not benefit from updated legislation that clearly defined the practice of medicine until 1921. In other instances (e.g., California), the state medical board spent much of its early energy defending its legal status as the entity authorized to regulate the medical profession.[50]

While interstate variations in qualifications for medical licensure were still greater than many wished, the disciplinary arena did see considerable uniformity develop in key areas. One of these was the actionable bases for revocation of a medical license. A 1926 review of state statutes revealed striking commonalities among states. Routinely listed in most states' statutes were habitual intemperance, convictions for crimes involving "moral turpitude," criminal abortion, false or deceptive advertising, aiding and abetting an unlicensed practitioner, fraud and unprofessional conduct. Revocations for violation under federal narcotic laws (i.e., the Harrison Act of 1914) were also becoming more common in the 1920s. Two states had no provisions under the law for their state board to revoke a medical license, yet the medical boards in both acted upon individual licenses, citing their board rules as if the legal statutory underpinning existed.[51]

Noticeably absent from the bases for action was incompetence on the part of the physician. The legacy of the inexact nature of medical science fostered wide latitude for "good judgment" and the *art* of medicine. This was further reflected in the actionable bases listed in most medical practice acts, most of which centered upon exclusionary measures (e.g., unlicensed practitioners), normative standards (e.g., deceptive advertising), and criminal convictions. The term "unprofessional conduct" entered most statutory language but appears to have seldom, if ever, been used in a manner that addressed questions about the physician's technical competence.[52] The modern concept of standard of care was decades away from any meaningful use by state boards.

Of necessity, state medical boards in the 1920s were learning the importance of their procedural processes for medical discipline. Some state boards grew savvier in structuring their meetings along more legalistic lines for dealing with the resolution of disciplinary matters. Some took appropriate measures that allowed for "degrees of punishment" such as reprimand, probation and suspension rather than universal recourse to a draconian revocation. Procedural safeguards for due process were implemented which not only ensured fairness and equity for the licensee but provided a solid defense for the board's action should it be tested within the court system. The California board offers one example of the success of such measures. In a review of ten years of disciplinary data covering 1918–1928, Board President Percy Phillips noted that only seven of the board's 198 actions were reversed by a court. This success in the court system stemmed from the significant financial and human resources of the California board that afforded it legal and investigative units divided into northern and southern districts for the entire state.[53]

Developing appropriate investigative mechanisms proved critical for most state medical boards grappling with the persistent problem of individuals seeking a medical license by fraudulent means. Illustrative cases appeared often in the pages of *JAMA* and the *Federation Bulletin*. These profiles usually showcased particularly brazen or imaginative cases of individual fraud. While individual cases of fraud and/or the use of impostors continued to plague the medical regulatory system, far more troubling to the state medical boards, the medical profession and the public were the "diploma mills" still operating during the 1920s. In the late nineteenth century, efforts to gain some measure of oversight and protection of the public against outright fraud led most states to require that medical colleges be "chartered" with a specified agency or department of the state government. Mere acquisition of the requisite charter, however, proved inadequate without routine periodic state audit of their operations to ensure that they reflected those of a bona fide institution operating in good faith. Questionable medical schools operated throughout the country. Some of the more notable ones were the Pacific Medical College (California), Oriental University (Washington, D.C.) and the Kansas City College of Medicine and Surgery (Missouri).[54] The operations of the latter, in particular, led to major investigations in Missouri, Arkansas and Connecticut, including harsh criticism of the medical and eclectic boards in these states.

The Federation established a special committee in 1920 charged with summarizing relevant state laws and reporting specifics on the institutions in question. The Federation tapped Francis Shepardson (Illinois) and members of the North Carolina and New Jersey medical boards for the committee. Shepardson chaired the committee by virtue of his long involvement in medical education issues and his state's earlier successful intervention against a series of diploma mills operating in Illinois in the 1880s and 1890s. However, events nationally soon outpaced the committee's efforts.[55]

In California, the Pacific Medical College reflected a common practice of these institutions in granting a medical diploma without required attendance and "simply on paying a specified fee." Though the medical school successfully gained a charter in California, it was never recognized by the state medical board and its graduates were never eligible for licensure in that state. The school's dubious practices were exposed and its charter revoked. The California board went so far as to deny and/or rescind any reciprocal licensure agreement with other states that still listed the school as an approved institution. The Oriental University, based in Washington, D.C., engaged in similar practices though the primary audience for its diplomas was Europeans seeking to burnish their résumés and credentials. So blatant was the sale of diplomas in this instance that apparently no state board in the U.S. licensed individuals holding this school's medical diploma.[56]

The Kansas City College of Medicine and Surgery proved by far the most egregious offender among the diploma mills. An exposé series on the school by Harry Brundidge appeared in the *St. Louis Star* starting in 1923. A number of the degree holders were traced to Connecticut as licensees of that state's Eclectic Board of Medical Examiners. A subsequent investigation by the Connecticut Commissioner of Health resulted in revoked licenses for 175 physicians licensed by that board. The eclectic board's standing with the public proved irreparably damaged by revelations that advance copies of their licensing examination were delivered to the school to prepare candidates. The governor and state legislature soon embarked on a "vigorous housecleaning" that included replacing the entire eclectic board and establishing a new three-person lay board. The latter board was designed to act as a "coarse sieve" through which all medical licensure applicants were funneled before presentation to the respective boards of healing arts in that state, such as medicine, osteopathy, homeopathy, and so on. While embarrassing in the short term, the actions taken in Connecticut proved effective in remedying a situation which had led one critic to earlier label the state "an asylum to practice medicine [for those] . . . graduated from discredited medical schools."[57]

The repercussions for the Missouri board proved even more severe, stemming in part from a seemingly minor 1921 change in the language of that state's Medical Practice Act. Where previously the language in the Act required licensees to hold a medical diploma from a "reputable" medical school, a revision to the statute removed this term and substituted "legally chartered." As a legally chartered institution in Missouri, the Kansas City College—despite glaring deficiencies in facilities and faculty—now had a basis for its "graduates" to pursue a license within that state and elsewhere. After revelations appeared in the *St. Louis Star*, the state board acted quickly, issuing citations for nearly fifty physicians to appear and show cause why their medical license should not be revoked. More sensational news soon followed with evidence of extortion by one of the school's officials claiming "influence" with a member of the state medical board sufficient to keep a Kansas City College graduate's name from appearing before the board during its investigation. The implicated board member was later removed from the board. In 1925, the Missouri governor asked the entire medical board to resign; only three members were retained on the newly constituted board. These individuals had been diligent in pursuing the investigation, once launched, and securing the governor's attention regarding the activities of the board member in question.[58]

A 1923 investigation launched by the board into broader issues of medical education and licensure in the state subsequently expanded to address the questions raised about the board's administrative processes that had proven deficient in handling the diploma mill scandal. Case Western Reserve's Frederick Waite authored the widely circulated report, observing that the marked improvements in medical education in recent years and the prescribing allowances for physicians provided for under the Harrison Narcotic Act of 1914 and the Volstead Act of 1919 made the medical diploma a "highly prized" credential. Accordingly, unethical and criminal elements gravitated toward fraudulent and spurious credentials as a revenue stream. Waite's report identified a number of substandard schools in Missouri, Illinois and Massachusetts, in addition to the gross violations occurring at the Kansas City College. In tracing the subsequent holders of these medical diplomas, Waite turned an unsparing eye on a few state medical boards, especially the eclectic boards in Arkansas and Connecticut. Waite attributed much of the failure of the licensing system in those states to their examination processes—specifically, inadequate proctoring of prospective licensees during the licensing examination; frequent repetition of questions on the examination over time; and overly "generous" and inconsistent scoring of examinations.[59]

The Federation used this unfolding drama to advocate for specific practices. The Federation regretfully noted the continued practice of the Arkansas Eclectic Board in licensing graduates of the discredited Kansas City College, even after the school's exposure as well as the indictment of G. A. Munch, former secretary of the then dissolved Florida Eclectic Board, for mail fraud in issuing back-dated licenses. For some unscrupulous individuals, appointment to a medical board was a "plum" worthy of any politicking required to obtain the appointment. In response, the Federation renewed its call for a single board of medical examiners in each state and the discontinuance of multiple boards representing specific schools of medicine. The Federation also encouraged all states to reconsider their practices for appointment to state boards. Specifically cited were practices such as excluding medical educators from state board appointments, structuring board representation along geographical lines within the state, or blatant political appointments without regard to qualifications.[60]

The diploma mill scandals of the mid-1920s were hardly a unique phenomenon. The activities of John Buchanan more than forty years earlier involving multiple real and bogus schools in Philadelphia culminated in his arrest in 1880 on multiple counts of mail fraud and forgery. This came, however, after his sale of an estimated 30,000 diplomas and widespread criticism from multiple quarters at the ineptitude of Pennsylvania authorities in shutting down Buchanan's operation.[61] The 1920s diploma mill redux underscored the need for continued vigilance on the part of state medical boards and other state agencies. Requiring educational institutions to hold a state charter represented a reasonable, but woefully inadequate, starting point. Mandating accreditation through reputable accrediting bodies offered even greater potential assurances for quality. Elsewhere in the field of medical education, the Federation and state medical boards enjoyed the fruits of reform measures starting in 1906.

STATE BOARDS AND MEDICAL EDUCATION

In 1855, Nathan S. Davis, founder of the American Medical Association, stated that "the union of . . . teaching and licensing in the same hands is wrong in principle, and liable to great abuse in practice."[62] Davis's lament was understandable. The nineteenth-century practice in some states of treating the medical diploma as an ersatz license to practice medicine had encouraged unscrupulous individuals to treat medical education in strictly commercial terms. Davis recognized state-based licensure as a valuable means toward accomplishing two complementary goals: (1) improving medical education using state licensing boards as an independent quality assurance mechanism, and (2) establishing high professional standards for the practice of medicine.

As noted earlier, the medical licensing community's interest and activities in medical education date back to the nineteenth century. State medical boards had made significant progress in mandating higher standards for medical education that were consistent with the internally driven reforms of progressive medical schools committed to a model of academic medicine as the template for medical education in the United States. Still, much work remained to be done in the first decade of the twentieth century. Flexner's 1910 report and assessment on the quality of medical education in the United States and Canada devoted an entire chapter to state medical boards and their role in facilitating quality medical education. Clearly, voluntary and professional organizations such as the AAMC and the AMA Council on Medical Education played pivotal roles in fostering quality medical education. Yet Flexner was unequivocal in his recognition of the contribution of state medical boards, characterizing them as "the instruments through which the reconstruction of medical education will be largely effected." Flexner and others recognized that state medical boards alone possessed the necessary legal authority to secure higher standards for medical education and deny licensure to graduates from those substandard schools either unwilling or unable to implement such standards. In this manner, the boards' licensure requirements specifying standards for preliminary and medical education facilitated a rising educational tide. Flexner recognized what medical boards had long known: the licensing examination was the great "lever . . . [by] which the entire field may be lifted." Furthermore, limiting access to the examination "only after a fair presumption of intellectual fitness . . . has been established" served a similar salutary function. Flexner felt boards were clearly within their rights to "refuse to entertain the applicant's petition . . . [when] medical education rests upon no preliminary training or was received under conditions that forbade thorough or conscientious instruction." The medical licensing community must have been gratified by Flexner's surprisingly strong assertion that improvement in medical education would derive "from control of all schools through the state boards."[63]

From the time of its founding, the Federation spent considerable energy on the topic of medical education. This continued the work of the Federation's predecessor organizations and enabled the Federation and state board representatives to remain in close contact with the medical education community, especially the AAMC and the AMA Council on Medical Education. In 1916, the Federation established a Committee on the Standardization of Medical Colleges led by Beverly Harrison, John Baldy and two members of the New York and Illinois boards, Henry Minton and Enos Spindel. The committee's recommendations built upon the momentum already evident from state medical boards in establishing clear educational requirements. In the span of a single generation, state medical boards assisted in transforming medical education through mandated higher standards as part of the requirements for medical licensure. In 1904, only ten states required a high school diploma as a requirement for obtaining a medical license; no state yet required college course work. By 1929, forty-three states mandated one to two years of college course work in addition to the high school diploma. Additionally, fourteen states now required a one-year hospital internship after graduation from medical school and prior to sitting a licensing examination. Three years later the number requiring the internship year rose to eighteen states.[64]

The committee reports and their recommendations issued by the Federation in 1916, 1918 and 1923 reflected the trends evidenced by the statistics mentioned above. The 1918 report recommended that state medical boards adopt two years of college work as a preliminary educational standard for medical licensure, though formal adoption of this recommendation by the Federation's membership did not occur until 1921. More broadly, the committee report noted the ongoing classification of medical schools (Categories A, B, C) by the AMA Council on Medical Education beginning in 1906. The report articulated the important differences in ranking schools based upon an educational "ideal" and the "minimum standard" environment within which state medical boards operated. As the committee noted, from a licensing perspective the minimum standard devolved into a single clear differentiation between approved and unapproved medical schools. This was an important distinction between the objectives of the educational and licensing communities. Well-intentioned but inadequately informed state legislators could inadvertently err by applying the educational ideal (i.e., recognizing only Class A medical schools) rather than focusing on the minimum acceptable standard. The committee report provided state medical boards with a "suggestive" list of approved medical colleges which the Federation updated periodically.[65]

By virtually every measure, the complementary efforts of the Federation and its state medical boards along with the AAMC and the AMA Council on Medical Education wrought major improvements in the quality of the medical education in the United States. Admittedly, much of the earlier impetus for medical education reform came from the more progressive schools themselves. Indeed, historian Kenneth Ludmerer argued this persuasively in his excellent review of U.S. medical education, *Learning to Heal*. Yet the reality was that many of the proprietary schools (Class C schools) were not receptive environments for reform; it was only through the "regularizing influence" of the AAMC and the AMA working in concert with the statutory mandate of state medical boards that the reform movement achieved its greatest fruition. The number of Class C (or after 1928, "nondescript") medical schools dropped markedly, from twenty-three in 1913 to six in 1932. Included in this handful were virtual medical diploma mill institutions whose graduates were all but unlicenseable in the vast majority of states. Class A schools that once accounted for little more than half of all the medical school graduates in 1918 accounted for 87 percent of all graduates by 1929. Where once only thirty-one medical schools were recognized by all state boards (1914), seventy schools enjoyed such recognition by 1927.[66] It also warrants mention that the state boards' focus on bringing inferior and proprietary medical schools up to minimum standards had something of a moral imperative to it. Unlike fifty years earlier, the education and training of a physician *did matter* in terms of patient outcomes. The knowledge, training and likely effectiveness of the physician educated at Johns Hopkins were markedly different from the physician graduated from the Georgia College of Eclectic Medicine and Surgery (an institution labeled "disgraceful" in Flexner's report). The public protection function envisioned for state medical boards clearly necessitated their involvement in medical education even if that role was largely one as the regulatory hammer extracting the last few rusty nails from the planks of medical education.

Toward the end of the 1920s, the conversational emphasis between the medical education and licensing communities had shifted toward avoiding "duplication" of efforts in overseeing medical education and avoiding overly detailed and inelastic state requirements that hampered curricular changes. Fred Zappfe, secretary of the AAMC, noted that even well-intended standards could prove counterproductive at times. As an example, he pointed to educational experiments involving a four-quarter system that allowed for the potential truncation of the curriculum into thirty-six months (three calendar years) that technically violated the law or board requirements in many states. Another example pointed to the wide variance among the states in content coverage on their licensing examination and the preparation efforts of some medical schools that were a "detriment . . . [to] good teaching." In a telling example, the Pennsylvania medical board informed the Tufts medical school in 1914 that it would no longer examine its graduates for licensure if the school continued admitting students "on condition." This despite the fact that Tufts was rated as a Class A school by the AMA Council on Medical Education in 1913.

Ludmerer has described these and other "constraints" as reflective of an overzealous inflexibility on the part of state boards eager to deliver the coup de grace on proprietary medical schools.[67]

The point expressed by Zappfe, and shared by many others, was that the same hyper-vigilance and specificity necessary to foster improvements in medical education during the earlier years of the twentieth century was now less critical. Identifying the appropriate accrediting body to set standards seemed now the more appropriate means for ensuring quality. The Federation agreed, as evidenced by a 1929 resolution adopted by its membership, calling for revisions to their Medical Practice Acts that "conform[ed] as far as possible with the principles" of the AAMC.[68] In hindsight, the success enjoyed by the Federation and state medical boards in the area of medical education might have been predicted. The interests of the medical profession and the medical licensing community coalesced and complemented one another in medical education. Higher standards served the physicians' long-term self-interest for a burgeoning profession and the public's more immediate need for protection against charlatans and unscrupulous practitioners. Consensus, however, was not always so easily achieved in other areas.

POSTWAR AMERICA, PROFESSIONAL TENSIONS AND BASIC SCIENCE LAWS

In the late nineteenth century, professional identity and economic self-interest were two of the most significant pressures acting upon the medical profession. Physicians understood the former as an appropriate concern for a profession still formalizing amidst rapid advances in the medical sciences. Critics, among both the public and other practitioners, pointed to the latter as the primary factor motivating physicians feeling threatened by competition arising at home and abroad. Despite the growing authority vested in the profession, these tensions spilled over into the medical licensing community.[69]

In the years after World War I, increasing numbers of "foreign graduates" presented themselves before state medical boards for licensure. Wartime disruptions had precluded many physicians who might otherwise have desired immigration to the United States from doing so. Adverse postwar conditions, particularly in Germany and elsewhere in Central and Eastern Europe, now served to encourage ostensibly qualified professionals with sufficient means to consider starting anew overseas. However, the atmosphere in 1920s America was markedly different from that preceding the war. Where once European medical schools were routinely perceived as superior to their American counterparts, the sentiment on this side of the Atlantic had since changed markedly. The significant changes in U.S. medical education already under way in the first decade of the twentieth century meant that fewer Americans started with a presumption of inferiority when comparing U.S. institutions to their European counterparts. Just as important, a heightened sensitivity to political radicalism characterized postwar America in the 1920s. In 1921, the U.S. Congress passed the Emergency Quota Act, effectively limiting the number of immigrants and establishing quotas based upon nationality. Given the political climate it was not surprising that these quotas disadvantaged many immigrants, including physicians, from Central and Eastern Europe, Asia and the Pacific.[70]

Neither the Federation nor the state medical board community proved immune to the sentiments prevailing in postwar America. Early in the 1920s, language such as "alien invasion" and "influx of undesirable foreign applicants" crept into editorial pieces in the *Federation Bulletin*. Others noted the increasing number of foreign physicians (a category that almost routinely excluded Canadians) examined by state medical boards—fewer than one hundred annually between 1917 and 1920 and then jumping sharply to more than five hundred per year in 1924 and 1925.[71]

Almost simultaneously state legislatures began amending their medical practice acts to include U.S. citizenship as a requirement for medical licensure. By 1926, eleven states had established this requirement: Arizona, Arkansas, Florida, Illinois, Indiana, Kansas, Kentucky, Mississippi, South Dakota, Tennessee, and Wyoming. Ten other states required naturalization papers to have been filed and five more required a declaration of intent to have been filed. In other instances, state medical boards (Michigan, New York) might require a year's work in a U.S. medical school or direct the candidate to a hospital internship year (Pennsylvania).[72]

More significant tensions within the medical profession arose from the continuing and burgeoning number of individuals treating patients in some form or fashion other than what was deemed traditional or regular. Here the passions grew more heated as the stakes, including a growing general population that increasingly sought and needed health care, seemed even higher. Just as the AMA had argued against cooperation with homeopathic and later eclectic physicians in the 1800s, physicians who were members of state medical boards now cast a wary eye toward osteopathic physicians, chiropractors, Christian Scientists and "drugless healers." Mainstream physicians found fault with these groups on two bases: (1) allegedly inadequate education and training for the practices they utilized, and (2) a tendency to stray outside their system to include treatment options (e.g., administration of drugs) that fell clearly under the statutory definition of the practice of medicine—a realm traditionally inhabited solely by allopathic (M.D.) physicians. In 1917, the Federation identified this tension as the single "most important problem" facing state boards.[73]

This was not the first time the medical profession confronted tensions resulting from competing "schools" of medicine. In the late nineteenth century, physicians were often differentiated as homeopathic, eclectic or "regular." A number of states maintained separate boards for the three classifications of physicians. However, by the 1920s the allopathic profession had largely integrated and subsumed the homeopathic and eclectic physicians under the commonly shared mantle of M.D., in part because the educational reforms of the early twentieth century had resulted in the closure of most schools teaching narrower philosophies of medicine. In the 1920s, the animosity directed toward osteopathic physicians, chiropractors and others was noteworthy only for the relentless nature of the attacks. The vehemence behind these attacks seemed little changed from the verbally aggressive tone struck two decades earlier by the president of the Texas Medical Association, who proclaimed a fervent desire to slay osteopathy "with the jaw bone of an ass." Physicians routinely referred to these practitioners in disparaging terms such as "cults," with some of the harshest language reserved for the chiropractic community and Christian Scientists.[74]

Osteopathic medicine traced its origins to the experiences in the 1860s of Andrew Taylor Still, an allopathic physician and largely self-taught bone setter who watched helplessly as the best medications of the day could not save three of his children suffering from meningitis. Still later sought "the opinions of the most learned" (including a fellow physician trained in Edinburgh, Scotland) and formulated after many years of study and application a new approach to medical practice that he called osteopathy. Still postulated that diseases were caused in part by mechanical interference with nerve and blood supply and misalignment of bones and muscles. In 1892, he formalized his philosophy through the founding of his own medical school, the American School of Osteopathy, in Kirksville, Missouri, where both manual manipulative treatment and a holistic approach to medical care—which included traditional practices in medicine, surgery and obstetrics and initially a sparing use of medications—would eventually be taught. While osteopathic physicians trained in the United States are today able to practice unencumbered in all fifty states and have significantly integrated with their allopathic counterparts, so much so that one in every five medical students is an osteopathic medical student, a considerable professional and legislative battle for recognition and acceptance resides behind these accomplishments.[75]

During the late nineteenth and early twentieth centuries, osteopathic physicians (D.O., Doctor of Osteopathy, later Doctor of Osteopathic

Medicine) encountered significant opposition within the medical profession while managing to achieve considerable success in gaining professional independence, if not the recognition they sought. In large part, this stemmed from the ready willingness of the osteopathic profession to embrace broader therapeutic offerings as a supplement to the traditional osteopathic manipulative treatment they practiced as a means of distinguishing from chiropractors focused almost exclusively on spinal manipulation. Vermont was the first state to license osteopaths in 1896, with fourteen more states doing so by 1901: California, Connecticut, Illinois, Iowa, Indiana, Kansas, Michigan, Missouri, Montana, Nebraska, North Dakota, South Dakota, Tennessee, and Wisconsin.[76] Extending state licensing privileges to osteopathic physicians, however, did not always mean the general unrestricted medical practice they desired to prescribe medications, deliver babies, and perform surgeries. Many states, such as Illinois, Maryland, and Ohio, initially issued limited licenses that restricted the scope of practice of osteopathic physicians. In 1903, Michigan became the first state to extend "unlimited practice rights" to osteopathic physicians. By 1929, fifteen states enacted similar laws. Such progress, however, was offset by setbacks such as Army Surgeon General William Gorgas's staunch opposition to commissioning osteopathic physicians in the Army and Navy Medical Corps during World War I, an uncompromising position that set the tone for the military's position for decades, until the Vietnam War.[77]

Approximately seventeen states provided for a separate osteopathic medical board during that same time period. The osteopathic experience in states where a single composite board had members representing multiple "systems" varied markedly. In some instances, the board modified its licensing examinations accordingly for osteopathic candidates (e.g., dropping materia medica questions); in other cases, such as Iowa, the results were much different. There the board was empowered to accredit osteopathic medical schools with the result that none received accreditation.[78]

There were reasonable individuals on both sides, however, who were willing to seek appropriate accommodations and curb the inflammatory language. Federation President David Strickler, a self-described "sectarian" physician who graduated from a homeopathic medical school, addressed the AMA's Congress on Medical Education in 1917 sounding a conciliatory tone. Strickler acknowledged that the true intent of many individuals pushing for a single state medical examining board was really to "eliminate the sectarian" physician. Strickler voiced a surprising willingness to make room within the profession for those willing to ensure adequate education and training for the practitioner and condemned the "vindictive spirit" of many within the profession. "I personally believe that no school of healing can attain any definite standing in a large territory without some basic element of truth underlying it." Strickler did not deviate from this willingness to consider the possibility of the efficacy of other systems and treatment modalities.[79]

Several years later, and growing exasperated with the entrenched attitudes on both sides, Strickler issued a pragmatic call for a "clinical study of [those] systems of healing" that already enjoyed public support and / or recognition. According to Strickler, both the medical profession and the public badly needed education on the "fundamental facts" where they were known and answers to basic questions concerning the scientific underpinnings of the various systems of healing. State medical boards were caught squarely in the middle of these turf battles. Strickler acknowledged that "there are truths in some of the cults which the medical men will not see." He urged the state board members to set aside narrow professional interests and demonstrate a "broader spirit" and "readiness to accept the good [within any system], irrespective of its origin." The AMA, the American Osteopathic Association (founded in 1897), the American Institute of Homeopathy and the AMA Council on Education all supported this proposal.[80] Before such a progressive proposal could gain sufficient traction, however, independent initiatives in Wisconsin and Connecticut channeled discussions in a new, and unexpected, direction.

In 1920, a Sheboygan, Wisconsin physician commenced a campaign designed to revise medical licensure in that state. Specifically, he proposed an examination in the basic sciences for anyone practicing the healing arts in that state. The impetus for this proposal stemmed from an earlier state law allowing chiropractors to practice provided they did not hold themselves out as a licensed physician. A subsequent influx of chiropractors into the state and turf wars between Wisconsin's physicians and chiropractors created a contentious environment leading to the first basic science law in 1925. Until their demise nearly sixty years later, independent boards assessing candidates in the basic sciences would appear in twenty-three states and administer 150,000 examinations.[81]

As the Wisconsin legislation proved a model for much of the rest of the country, explaining the details of its statute serves a broad illustrative purpose. Wisconsin's law sought to protect the public against "fraud, ignorance or lack of skill" by individuals professing to "treat the sick," whether those individuals were allopathic or osteopathic physicians, chiropractors, homeopaths, and so on. The ostensible intent was to ensure patient protection and adequate knowledge by practitioners, not to render any specific mode of treatment or system unlawful. Wisconsin established a basic sciences board to test candidates in four areas: anatomy, physiology, pathology and diagnosis. The board would be composed of laymen, none with an affiliation or vocation related to one of the healing arts. The board would have access to "technical aid" in overseeing the construction of an examination in these four subjects. Anyone engaging in treating the sick would first have to pass the basic science examination and present this credential to the respective licensing board (e.g., medical, chiropractic). The licensing board could then, at its discretion, accept this credential in lieu of further examination in these basic sciences as part of its licensing requirements.[82]

This model soon spread elsewhere. Connecticut enacted a similar law later in the same year, though primarily in response to the diploma mill scandal that tainted that state's eclectic board. Washington and Nebraska followed suit in 1927; Minnesota and the District of Columbia in 1928; Arkansas in 1929; and Oregon, Iowa and Arizona in the early 1930s. The subject matter covered by these basic science boards was largely the same, though some variance occurred with a few states adding hygiene, bacteriology and chemistry. The composition of these boards usually followed the Wisconsin model, with three to five members often drawn from university faculty. When membership drew from the respective fields of practice, as in Minnesota, they usually placed an equal number of representatives for physicians, osteopaths and chiropractors.[83]

The Federation's leadership appears to have struggled in identifying an appropriate response to this trend. In 1926, the Federation expressed the opinion that the basic science boards might provide a beneficial service as a "sifting agency" removing the chaff (inadequately trained practitioners) before forwarding the wheat to the respective licensing board within each state. Two years later, however, an editorial in the *Federation Bulletin* sounded a doubtful tone in characterizing the basic science movement as a "distinct advantage to the cultist" that did not "further the higher standards of medical licensure." It is not entirely clear what prompted this changed tone. One possibility is the "inconsistencies" among the various basic science laws that appeared lax in the expectations for non-physicians taking these exams. Perhaps more important, the changed tone may have stemmed from the fact that basic science boards arose primarily in states where multiple boards already existed, representing different fields in the practice of the healing arts. It seems possible that the Federation may have come to view basic science boards as a mechanism that would make permanent this division of licensing boards within these states—a reality inconsistent with the organization's long-standing position that the public in each state was best served by a single board of medicine. Additionally, pass/fail statistics on the basic science boards seemed in actuality to indicate that rather than providing any advantage these examinations represented a significant hurdle to the non-M.D. physicians taking them. Between 1927 and 1932, allopathic physicians posted an 89 percent pass rate on these examinations; "other practitioners" (i.e., osteopathic physicians and chiropractors) experienced a far lower pass rate of

51 percent.[84] Unfortunately, data from this time period do not differentiate between the performance of osteopathic physicians and chiropractors so it is not possible to determine to what extent, if any, the performance of the latter group had an effect upon the overall figure.[85] Regardless, far from advantaging the interests of these other practitioners, the basic science laws appeared to set a minimum standard that many struggled to meet. Perhaps even more important, the introduction of basic science examinations in multiple states added yet another variable into the licensing system. The persistence of these examinations for decades to come meant that state medical boards were saddled with an unevenly adopted requirement that did little to foster the uniformity in standards that more progressive state board leaders sought.

As the 1920s drew to a close, the Federation's newly elected president, Herbert M. Platter, longtime secretary of the Ohio State Medical Board, looked back on more than a decade of notable collective efforts by his state board brethren. Yet rather than rest on the laurels of legitimate accomplishments by offering self-congratulatory platitudes, Platter delivered a stark message to the assembled representatives from the nation's state medical boards. Despite the many achievements by the state boards on behalf of the public within their states, Platter viewed the licensing landscape as one lacking sufficient uniformity to warrant continuance under its current construct. Platter lamented the tendency to view legislation as a solution to every licensure problem, the counterproductive regional variations hindering physician mobility and even the de facto "rotation system" by which the Federation put forth its prospective elected leadership. Platter stated plainly that "we are at a parting of the ways . . . we must present a united front . . . or we should quit deluding ourselves and fooling the public and profession and embrace the British system of licensure." The next several decades would test not only the resolve of the state medical boards but the viability of the entire state-based system for medical licensure in the United States.

NOTES

1. "Constitution and By-Laws of the Federation," 90.
2. Ibid., 92; Harrison, "Unconstitutionality of Indorsement," 481.
3. "Constitution and By-Laws of the Federation," 90; James Duncan to Charles Cook, FSMB Archives.
4. "Constitution and By-Laws of the Federation," 90.
5. Ibid., 91–92.
6. James Duncan to Charles Cook, FSMB Archives.
7. "For a Higher Standard in Medicine," *Harpers Weekly*, July 12, 1913.
8. "Now for a House of Doctors," *New York Times*, July 14, 1913.

9. "A Short History of the National Institutes of Health," National Institutes of Health, accessed on January 13, 2012, http://history.nih.gov/exhibits/history/index.html; John Milton Cooper, *The Warrior and the Priest: Woodrow Wilson and Theodore Roosevelt* (Cambridge: Belknap Press, 1983), 79–80.

10. George Matson, "Financial Report of Secretary-Treasurer," February 25, 1913, FSMB Archives, Euless, Texas; "Federation of State Medical Boards: Executive Session," *Federation Bulletin* 2 (February 1917): 252; "Report of Committee," *Federation Bulletin* 15 (April 1929): 71.

11. David Strickler, "President's Address," *Federation Bulletin* 2 (February 1917): 245–46.

12. Samuel L. Baker, "Physician Licensure Laws in the United States, 1865–1915," *Journal of the History of Medicine and the Allied Sciences* 39 (1984): 175–77; Hamowy, "Early Development of Medical Licensing Laws," 115–18; Anita Ernst Watson, *Reflection, Recollection and Change: The Nevada State Board of Medical* Examiners (Reno: University of Nevada Oral History Program, 1996), 91; Pat Ireland Nixon, *A History of Texas Medical Association, 1853–1953* (Austin: University of Texas Press, 1953), 236.

13. *General Laws of the State of Texas Passed at the Session of the Thirteenth Legislature* (Austin: John Cardwell State Printer, 1873), 74–75; "Medical Legislation," *JAMA* 30 (February 14, 1885): 182; "The Texas Medical Law," *JAMA* 22 (April 21, 1894): 598.

14. "Medical Education and State Boards of Registration," *JAMA* 47 (October 27, 1906): 1410–11; Baker, "Physician Licensure Laws," 187.

15. Ira Carleton Chase, ed., *Texas State Journal of Medicine*, vol. 3 (Fort Worth: State Medical Association of Texas, 1908), 67; W. B. Russ, "The Danger and Injustice of Special Legislation for Medical Sects," *Federation Bulletin* 5 (June 1919): 139.

16. Walter Bierring, "Present Non-Uniformity of Medical Licensure," *Federation Bulletin* 1 (October 1915): 93.

17. "State Board Statistics for 1910," *JAMA* 56 (March 27, 1911): 1562; "State Board Statistics for 1913," *JAMA* 62 (May 23, 1914): 1658; Baker, "Physician Licensure Laws," 188–89; Hamowy, "Early Development of Licensing Laws," 113.

18. "Medical Licensure Statistics for 1932," *JAMA* 100 (April 22, 1933): 1246; Barbara Barzansky, "Abraham Flexner and the Era of Medical Education Reform," *Academic Medicine* 85 (September supplement 2010): S519–20.

19. "An Abstract of Various Views in Medical Licensure," *St. Louis Medical Review* 55 (February 9, 1907): 141; Walter Bowers, "Practice Examinations by State Licensing Boards," *Federation Bulletin* 2 (March 1917): 304; Nixon, *History of Texas Medical Association*, 265.

20. "State Board Statistics for 1910," *JAMA* 56 (May 27, 1911): 1568–69; "State Board Statistics for 1913," *JAMA* 62 (May 23, 1914): 1646–47; "State Board Statistics for 1929," *JAMA* 94 (April 26, 1930): 1310–11; "Medical Licensure Statistics for 1932," *JAMA* 100 (April 22, 1933): 1242–43.

21. George Blumer, "On the Desirability of Changing the Type of Written Examinations," *Federation Bulletin* 5 (June 1919): 128.

22. Ibid., 128–129; Walter Bierring, "Examinations: Written Versus Practical," *Federation Bulletin* 11 (July 1925): 156.

23. Bowers, "Practical Examinations," 303.

24. Ibid., 306; "The Practical License Examination in Minnesota," *Federation Bulletin* 2 (July 1916): 84.

25. John P. Hubbard and Edithe J. Levit, *The National Board of Medical Examiners: The First Seventy Years* (Philadelphia: National Board of Medical Examiners, 1985), 6, 8–9, 163–68; Walter Bierring, "The National Board of Medical Examiners," *Modern Medicine* 1 (July 1919): 247.

26. "Discussion on the National Board of Medical Examiners," *Federation Bulletin* 2 (April 1916): 6–9.

27. Ibid., 8–15; Sohn, "19th Century Academic Examinations for Physicians," 472–73.

28. The authors' comparison of leadership rosters for NBME and FSMB from 1915 to 1985 identified thirty-two individuals who served on both the Federation executive committee/board of directors and as a member of the National Board during that period.

29. "New Fees of the National Board," *Federation Bulletin* 2 (June 1916): 51; "National Board of Medical Examiners," *Federation Bulletin* 6 (April 1920): 75; "National Board of Medical Examiners," *Federation Bulletin* 11 (March 1925): 54; "Reciprocity and the National Board of Medical Examiners," *Federation Bulletin* 11 (October 1925): 217.

30. David Strickler, "Annual Registration of Physicians," *Federation Bulletin* 5 (October 1919): 230–32.

31. "Annual Registration of Physicians: A Survey by the Bureau of Legal Medicine and Legislation," *American Medical Association Bulletin*, November 1926.

32. Charles Pinkham, Herbert Platter and Alexander Macalister, "State Board Records and Office Details: Report of the Committee," *Federation Bulletin* 9 (May 1923): 107–108.

33. Ibid., 109.

34. Ibid., 110–11; Charles Pinkham, "Applicant's Record Card," *Federation Bulletin* 9 (January 1923): 13–15.

35. McCready and Harris, *Quackery to Quality Assurance*, 7; Pinkham, Platter, and Macalister, "State Board Records," 114–16; Charles Pinkham, "Safeguards Against Imposition in State Board Examinations," *Federation Bulletin* 7 (August 1921): 178–79; "Secured Licenses by Fraud," *Federation Bulletin* 5 (October 1919): 223.

36. Charles Pinkham, "Safeguarding State Board Records," *Federation Bulletin* 13 (July 1927): 203–205.

37. David Strickler, "Licensure on Credentials," *Federation Bulletin* 6 (September 1920): 234–35.

38. Ibid., 232; Byron U. Richards, "Uniform Endorsement Certificates," *Federation Bulletin* 7 (May 1921): 118; K. P. Bonner, "Reciprocity Problems in the South, with Particular Reference to Special State Licensure Requirements," *Federation Bulletin* 8 (April 1922): 80; T. J. Crowe, "Why Reciprocity?" *Federation Bulletin* 10 (June 1924): 144; G.M. Williamson, "Interstate Endorsement Versus Reciprocity," *Federation Bulletin* 13 (July 1927): 209.

39. Richards, "Uniform Endorsement Certificates," 118–19.

40. K. P. Bonner, "Reciprocity Problems in the South," 80–81.

41. T. J. Crowe, "Why Reciprocity?" 145–46.

42. Arthur Bevan, "Report of the Council on Medical Education and Hospitals to the House of Delegates of the American Medical Association," *Federation Bulletin* 8 (July 1922): 164.

43. T. J. Crowe, "Why Reciprocity?" 149–50; K. P. Bonner, "Reciprocity Problems in the South," 81–82; George M. Williamson, "Interstate Endorsement," 214–15.

44. "News Items," *Federation Bulletin* 4 (June 1918): 128–29.

45. David Strickler, "How Can We Best Obtain Reliable Information?" *Federation Bulletin* 3 (November 1917): 229, 234.

46. David Strickler, "Cooperation for Prevention of Medical Frauds," *Federation Bulletin* 4 (March 1918): 56–58.

47. "Central Bureau of Information," *Federation Bulletin* 5 (April 1919): 77; "Our Central Bureau of Information," *Federation Bulletin* 5 (October 1919): 218; "Board of Medical Examiners," *Journal of California and Western Medicine* 22 (September 1924): 477.

48. Swope, Mayo, et al., *Virginia Board of Medicine*, 9; Nixon, *History of Texas Medical Association*, 264–65.

49. "Activity of State Licensing Boards During 1919," *Federation Bulletin* 5 (December 1919): 265–266; "The Quack Situation in Detroit," *Federation Bulletin* 8 (June 1922): 125–27; Proctor and Long, *North Carolina Board of Medical Examiners*, 11; Herbert M. Platter, "Enforcement of the Medical Practice Act," *Federation Bulletin* 9 (March 1923): 67.

50. Green, "Oklahoma Medical Board History," 531–32; Apperson, *Protecting the Public*, 37; McCready and Harris, *Quackery to Quality Assurance*, 8.

51. K. P. B. Bonner, "Revocation of License," *Federation Bulletin* 12 (July 1926): 157–59; Percy T. Phillips, "Discipline of the Licensed Practitioner," *Federation Bulletin* 15 (April 1929): 103; Green, "Oklahoma Medical Board History," 533.

52. Carl Ameringer, *State Medical Boards and the Politics of Public Protection* (Baltimore: Johns Hopkins University Press, 1999), 18.

53. Bonner, "Revocation," 160; Phillips, "Discipline," 103; Charles Pinkham, "Problems of Enforcement of the Medical Act," *Federation Bulletin* 7 (January 1921): 15.

54. "Carl Elfes, Alias Maximilian R. Schneller," *Federation Bulletin* 14 (January 1928): 16–17; "Series of Chartered Diploma Mills," *JAMA* 87 (August 21, 1926): 594.

55. "Series of Diploma Mills," 594; "A Study of Diploma Mills," *Federation Bulletin* 6 (May 1920): 102.

56. "Pacific Medical College," *Federation Bulletin* 6 (August 1920): 202; McCready and Harris, *Quackery to Quality Assurance,* 14–15; "The Oriental University: A Fake," *Federation Bulletin* 7 (February 1921): 36.

57. Brock, *Charlatan,* 88; "Investigation of Diploma Mill Activities in Connecticut," *Federation Bulletin* 10 (April 1924): 78; "Medical License Investigation in Connecticut," *Federation Bulletin* 10 (July 1924): 159, 164; Robert L. Rowley "Medical Legislation in Connecticut," *Federation Bulletin* 12 (May 1926): 112–13.

58. "Medical Licensure in Missouri," *Federation Bulletin* 9 (April 1923): 75; "Missouri Investigation," *Federation Bulletin* 11 (February 1925): 35–36; "The Missouri Licensure Scandal," *Federation Bulletin* 11 (October 1925): 228–31.

59. Frederick C. Waite, "Some Types of Fraudulent Medical Diplomas and the Uses Made of Them," *Federation Bulletin* 12 (May–June 1926): 114, 130–34; Frederick C. Waite, "Recent Licensing of Graduates of Inefficient Medical Schools," *Federation Bulletin* 12 (September 1926): 225–27.

60. "A Single Board of Examiners," *Federation Bulletin* 11 (July 1925): 146; Watson, *Reflection, Recollection and Change,* 55; "Closing the Back Doors to Medical Licensure," *JAMA* 89 (August 20, 1927): 625; "Qualifications of State Board Examiners," *Federation Bulletin* 9 (November 1923): 242.

61. "Eclecticism vs. Allopathy," *Medical Tribune* 6 (October 15, 1880): 504; "History of the Philadelphia Fraudulent Medical Colleges," *Medical Record* (June 26, 1880): 726–27; "History of Buchanan's Diploma Mill," *Medical Gazette* (July 24, 1880): 457–58.

62. Nathan S. Davis, *History of the American Medical Association, from Its Organization up to 1855* (Philadelphia: Lippincott, Grambo, 1855), 35.

63. Abraham Flexner, *Medical Education in the United States and Canada: A Report to the Carnegie Foundation for the Advancement of Teaching,* Bulletin No 4 (New York: Carnegie Foundation, 1910), 169, 173.

64. "Committee on Standardization of Colleges," *Federation Bulletin* 2 (October 1916): 147; "State Board Statistics for 1927," *JAMA* 90 (April 14, 1928): 1212; "State Board Statistics for 1929," *JAMA* 94 (April 26, 1930): 1318; "Medical Licensure Statistics for 1932," *JAMA* 100 (April 22, 1933): 1249.

65. "Report of the Committee on Classification and Standardization of Medical Colleges," *Federation Bulletin* 3 (May 1917): 38; "Standards of the Federation," *Federation Bulletin* 4 (April 1918): 75; Donald G. Kassebaum, "Origin of the LCME, the AAMC-AMA Partnership for Accreditation," *Academic Medicine* 67 (February 1992): 85; "Timelines AMA History," American Medical Association, accessed January 13, 2012, http://www.ama-assn.org/ama/pub/about-ama/our-history/timelines-ama-history/1900–1920.shtml

66. Ludmerer, *Learning to Heal,* 88, 234, 327fn; "State Board Statistics 1913," *JAMA,* 1651; "State Board Statistics 1927," *JAMA,* 1205; "State Board Statistics 1929," *JAMA,* 1316; "Licensure Statistics 1932," *JAMA,* 1243.

67. Ludmerer, *Learning to Heal,* 251–53; Fred C. Zappfe, "Revision of Medical School Regulations as Related to Licensure," *Federation Bulletin* 14 (March 1928): 85, 90.

68. Hugh Cabot, "The Relation of the Federation of State Medical Boards to Medical Schools," *Federation Bulletin* 15 (April 1929): 77; "Federation of State Medical Boards and the Association of American Medical Colleges," *Journal of the Association of American Medi-*

cal Colleges 6 (May 1931): 190; "Federation of State Medical Boards," *Journal of the Association of American Medical Colleges* 4 (April 1929): 167; Stevens, *American Medicine and Public Interest*, 169.

69. Starr, *Social Transformation*, 143–44.

70. Derbyshire, *Medical Licensure and Discipline*, 134–35; Norton, Katzman, et al., *People and Nation*, 686–87.

71. "Citizenship as a Requirement for Licensure," *Federation Bulletin* 9 (October 1923): 217; "Foreign Medical Graduates," *Federation Bulletin* 12 (April 1926): 74; "State Board Statistics 1929," *JAMA*, 1307.

72. "Licensing of Foreign Physicians," *Federation Bulletin* 12 (August 1926): 170.

73. "The Problem of Medical Cults," *Federation Bulletin* 3 (June 1917): 57.

74. Rothstein, *American Physicians*, 305–10; Starr, *Social Transformation*, 107–109; Nixon, *History of Texas Medical Association*, 237.

75. Joel D. Howell, "The Paradox of Osteopathy," *New England Journal of Medicine* 341 (November 4, 1999): 1465–68; Norman Gevitz, *The DOs: Osteopathic Medicine in America*, 2nd ed. (Baltimore: Johns Hopkins University Press, 2004), 17; Andrew Taylor Still, *Philosophy of Osteopathy* (1899; repr. American Academy of Osteopathy, 1986), 14; Apperson, *Protecting the Public*, 49–50.

76. Howell, "Paradox of Osteopathy," 1466; Gevitz, *The DOs*, 46–48.

77. "Ohio Medical Practice Act," Federation Bulletin 2 (December 1916): 201; "History of Osteopathic Medicine in Maryland," Maryland Association of Osteopathic Physicians, accessed January 13, 2012, http://www.maops.com/about.html; "History," Illinois Osteopathic Medical Society, accessed January 13, 2012, http://www.ioms.org/about/history.htm; "Osteopathic Medicine – A Brief History," Missouri Association of Osteopathic Physicians and Surgeons, accessed January 13, 2012, http://www.maops.org/displaycommon.cfm?an=1&subarticlenbr=22; Norman Gevitz, "The Sword and the Scalpel—The Osteopathic 'War' to Enter the Military Medical Corps: 1916–1966," *Journal of the American Osteopathic Association* 98, no. 5 (May 1998): 280.

78. "Important Dates in Osteopathic History," American Osteopathic Association, accessed January 13, 2012, http://history.osteopathic.org/timeline.shtml; "Years States Passed Unlimited Practice Laws," American Osteopathic Association, accessed January 13, 2012, http://history.osteopathic.org/laws.shtml; Gevitz, *The DOs*, 55–56.

79. David Strickler, "The Problem of Medical Cults," *Federation Bulletin* 3 (June 1917): 71.

80. "President Strickler's Statement," *Federation Bulletin* 10 (May 1924): 113–14.

81. "A New Method of Medical Licensure – The Basic Science Laws of Wisconsin, Connecticut, Washington and Minnesota," *California and Western Medicine* 27 (October 1927): 525; Norman Gevitz, "A Coarse Sieve: Basic Science Boards and Medical Licensure in the United States," *Journal of the History of Medicine and Allied Sciences* 43 (1988): 36; Leo P. Clements, "The Basic Science Laws," *Academic Medicine* 18 (March 1943): 105.

82. Michael Guyer, "Wisconsin State Board of Examiners in the Basic Sciences," *Federation Bulletin* 12 (April 1926): 84–85.

83. "Value of Basic Science (Qualifying Certificate) Laws: As Proved by Experience," *California and Western Medicine* 46 (January 1937): 4; "New Basic Science Laws," *Federation Bulletin* 13 (September 1927): 258.

84. "Examining Boards for the Basic Sciences," *Federation Bulletin* 12 9 (May 1926): 98; "Basic Science Boards," *Federation Bulletin* 14 (July 1928): 194; Derbyshire, *Medical Licensure and Discipline*, 120–21; "Medical Licensure Statistics 1932," *JAMA*, 1250.

85. Norman Gevitz's *The DOs: Osteopathic Medicine in America* provides data from 1942 to 1953 detailing the performance of osteopathic physicians and chiropractors on the basic science exams. Those data show a consistently lower pass rate for chiropractors (30–38 percent) at a time when osteopathic performance improved from a 50 percent to 80 percent pass rate.

Chapter 4

Stasis and Resurgence, 1930–1959

> Will this Federation . . . justify the hopes of those who labored . . . to bring it into being?
>
> —Charles H. Cook, Federation Presidential Address, 1913

In 1959, as the Cold War between the United States and the Soviet Union heated up in places like Vietnam and Cuba, a New York publisher issued a modestly titled work called *Modern Organization Theory.* The book's editor, Mason Haire, contributed to this compilation with an influential essay of his own entitled "Biological Models and Empirical Histories in the Growth of Organizations."[1] As the title implied, Haire theorized that organizations were akin to living organisms in that each passed through predictable stages or life cycles starting with birth and growth before transitioning to maturation and ultimately decline. While Haire was among the first to propose a biological metaphor for a theory of organizational life cycles, a host of later business writers and sociologists have updated and refined the model and more recently applied it to the nonprofit sector.[2]

In the same year that the Haire essay appeared, the Federation of State Medical Boards and the state board community basked in the success of its fourth Examination Institute, a major initiative for collective improvement of the nation's medical licensing examinations. This iteration of the Examination Institute culminated a decade that witnessed a resurgent Federation emerging from an extended period of tempered growth and achievement. By the end of the 1950s, the organization had partnered with others in successfully addressing a major issue that historically had vexed state boards—assessing the preparedness of international (then known as foreign) medical graduates for licensure—and achieving a long-sought goal with the drafting and adoption of a model Medical Practice Act.

It is almost certain that no one at the Federation in 1959 heard of Haire's theorized model; but if they had, there would likely have been satisfaction that the organization appeared to have reversed course in such a way that the model's ominous predictive outcome seemed less likely. As we will see, the Federation experienced a period in the 1930s and 1940s during which the organization seemed to have lost its earlier vibrancy. For a host of reasons, the vigor and excitement one sensed from the Federation's early years seemed to have softened into predictable patterns and comfortable routines reflected in everything from the *Federation Bulletin* to the selected discussion topics at the annual meeting. That the organization successfully renewed itself was testament to the efforts of a new generation of Federation leadership that emerged in the 1950s and reflected the excitement generated by major organizational initiatives like the Examination Institutes and a model Medical Practice Act.

The 1930s opened with the cautionary words of outgoing Federation President Herbert Platter still hanging in the air. Platter used his presidential address to signal a belief that something was amiss with the Federation and the American medical licensing community, warning the assembled state board representatives that a "parting of the ways" was imminent. He challenged the licensing community to exert concerted, collective action to meet the challenges facing them or else seek a more centralized regulatory model less vulnerable to the impulses and vagaries of individual states and their legislatures.[3] Platter's challenge and his observations on the state of regulatory affairs seem prescient in hindsight, considering the history of the Federation over the two decades following his speech.

This era of the Federation's history opened auspiciously enough. In 1930, the Federation and its member state boards rose to the challenge posed by Platter. State medical boards had worked in complementary fashion with the AAMC and the AMA Council on Medical Education to support significant improvements and reform in medical education in the decades after the turn of the century; in particular, state boards had provided the statutory leverage needed to shut down the remaining proprietary schools. So successful were these efforts that in 1928 the Council on Medical Education discontinued its classification system for medical schools that had been in place since 1906. In the same year that Platter warned of the need for collective effort to resolve long-standing issues, the Federation's member boards adopted a resolution encouraging all states to conform to the AAMC's principles and standards for medical education; in essence, the Federation and its member boards acknowledged their willingness to defer oversight for the quality of U.S. medical schools to the AAMC.[4] This resolution marked a notable early achievement by the Federation. In particular, it demonstrated that a state-based system for medical regulation could achieve consensus toward a common standard without sacrificing the very autonomy of the individual state boards. In retrospect, this achievement stands out all the more prominently when measured against the relative paucity of comparable achievements over the next two decades.

It would be inaccurate to characterize this period of Federation history from the early 1930s to the early 1950s as empty or without interest or significance in its own right. Doing so unnecessarily denigrates the contributions of the many individuals from that period who volunteered their time and energy to serve the organization. In reviewing the extant records, however, it is difficult to escape a gnawing sense that the Federation had entered a subtle, but distinct, period of diminished activity and lesser returns on the invested labor of its members. The evidence for this prolonged torpor can be seen in numerous small indicators.

A PERIOD OF STASIS, 1931–1951: INDICATORS AND CONTRIBUTING FACTORS

Perhaps the most surprising indicator of such relative passivity was the absence of special committee activity over a protracted period of time. Prior to this time period, the Federation had made extensive use of special committees to address a variety of topics and issues. The committees, composed of individual members from state medical boards, benefited the Federation in multiple ways. First, these committees served a utilitarian function. Because the Federation had essentially no permanent staff in its earliest days, with the exception of the ever-willing Bierring, these committees allowed the organization to draw upon the expertise of its membership in researching and developing policy matters. Second, these committees fostered relationships and a collective sense of purpose among the organization's geographically dispersed member boards. Third, these committee reports, and the Federation as a whole, benefited from the gravitas of a document derived from representatives of the medical licensing community drawn from across the country. Previously, such final reports and periodic updates from Federation special committees had been quite commonplace from the organization's inception in 1912 and throughout the 1920s. Yet after the Federation's participation on a committee dealing with medical education in 1934, no further special committees were formed until 1946, when it established a committee seeking to "better integrate" the activities of basic science boards and medical licensing boards. No special committees of lasting importance were then constituted until the 1950s with the Special Committee on Uniform Licensure Laws (1952) and the Special Committee on Examination Institutes (1956).[5]

Symptoms of organizational malaise could also be found in the content of the Federation's annual meetings and its monthly *Bulletin*. The Federation's annual February gathering of its membership in Chicago provided the sole opportunity for bringing together a quorum of the organization's member boards. Medical boards have historically been underfunded state agencies with board member travel frequently considered a nonessential function and expense. Additionally, the Federation's resources were inadequate to supplement the limited travel budget of its members. Thus, the Federation held its annual business meeting in conjunction with the largest gathering of medical professionals in the country—the annual meeting of the AMA in Chicago. The Federation's business meeting culminated a program interwoven with medical professionals and educators as part of the AMA's Congress on Medical Education and Licensure, drawing attendees from the AMA, the AAMC and the Federation's state medical board representatives. The annual Congress offered a rich program with natural points of mutual interest for physicians, medical educators and state board members. As the 1930s and 1940s progressed, however, the Federation's portion of the program reflected an increasingly narrow range of interests. This is not to say that there was no diversity in the annual meeting program, as a number of timely issues periodically made their way into the program. However, a small number of topics, or variations upon them, came steadily to dominate the content of these meetings. A review of the annual meeting programs from that time period shows that the single most frequently recurring topic involved international medical graduates (IMGs). Assessing the credentials and qualifications of international medical graduates presented state boards with one of their most significant challenges. The other topics consistently appearing on the Federation's program included licensing examinations, disciplinary procedures, basic science boards and their examinations, medical legislation, the certifying examination of the National Board of Medical Examiners, licensure endorsement and presentations on state-specific experiences from member boards. Unquestionably these topics were all relevant for state boards but increasingly, as the years passed, the topics acquired a certain staleness stemming from attendees' prolonged familiarity with the subjects. Presenters inherited the unenviable task of trying to impart a new twist on a recurring list of thorny issues.

A similar narrowing of focus can be seen in the *Federation Bulletin*, which continued to be the primary communication tool linking the Federation to its membership nationally. With the passage of time, specific content and features reappeared in the pages of the *Bulletin* on a consistent timetable. The January issue could be counted upon to present the program for the February annual meeting. The minutes from the business meeting appeared in March or April. Papers and presentations from the meeting appeared throughout the remainder of the year in subsequent issues. The summer issues invariably carried aggregate statistical data on the examinations of the NBME and the state basic science board exams. Summaries of legislation impacting medical regulation appeared routinely in the fall issues. Undoubtedly, many longtime readers of the *Bulletin* benefited from this familiar publication schedule, knowing almost exactly when these updated topics would next be appearing. However, this familiarity in the *Bulletin*'s schedule seemed to spill over into its content as well. Admittedly, the content repertoire of the *Bulletin* remained relevant to a state medical board audience. The "News Items" and "Medico Legal Abstracts" continued to offer short informational pieces on state board happenings as well as legislative and judicial matters. Longer articles on issues unique to licensing boards also continued to appear regularly. But as the 1930s and 1940s unfolded, the *Bulletin* devoted increasingly more space to medical education and issues more broadly relevant to the medical profession as a whole compared to the more specialized issues surrounding licensure and discipline. Articles written by the leadership of the AMA Council on Medical Education and the AAMC were regular features of *Bulletin* content. In some ways this was to be expected and certainly not inappropriate. The Federation depended upon financial assistance from the AMA in printing the *Bulletin* and its annual meeting took place in conjunction with the larger meetings of the AMA's Congress on Medical Education and Licensure. The result of these influences can be seen retrospectively in the *Bulletin*. Issues impacting medical education and the medical profession were clearly relevant to medical boards but they appeared with such disproportionate frequency in the *Bulletin* that one senses a developing insufficiency in focusing on the issues and problems unique to the medical licensing community.

There were other small but telling indicators as well. Over the course of nearly a century of publication, the *Bulletin* occasionally carried presidential addresses or historical articles looking back at the Federation's past. These articles presented rich, detailed material on the first two decades of the organization; yet almost invariably these pieces devoted little or no space to the period of the 1930s and 1940s. The retrospective silence hovering over these years seems a tacit acknowledgment of fewer tangible accomplishments comparable to those witnessed by the organization in earlier and later periods.[6]

Perhaps most telling of all was the lack of progress in certain key areas that characterized these two decades. Despite years of discussion and general agreement that a uniform Medical Practice Act would facilitate license portability and strengthen America's state-based regulatory system, no progress had been made. To the contrary, the burgeoning number of basic science boards that began appearing in the 1920s added an additional barrier to license portability and undermined the Federation's stance in support of a single medical examining board in each state. Yet despite strong consensus, the Federation and individual state medical boards had little success in reversing basic science board legislation. There was also a strong general agreement that state boards needed a better means for evaluating the qualifications of international medical graduates; yet despite this consensus, no solutions gained traction during the 1930s and 1940s.

This list of indicators does not, however, explain the reasons behind the organizational torpor affecting the Federation. The more critical question is, "What caused this?" Here one can only speculate, but four factors seem to have been at work. One of the more obvious explanations involves the impact of national and international events on the Federation and this country's medical regulatory system, specifically the Great Depression and World War II. The October 1929 stock market crash soon sent the United States spiraling into the worst economic depression of its history. Like most of America, the Federation was not spared from the economic shock waves generated by the Great Depression. The Federation's aspirations for organizational growth depended heavily upon increasing its financial resources. At that time, the Federation lacked a revenue-generating product or saleable service for its membership. Thus, the Federation relied upon member dues as its primary means for revenue to conduct its work. As the nation did not emerge fully from the Great Depression until 1939–1940, the Federation had little choice but to keep its annual dues static. Set at $25 at the time of the organization's founding, the annual dues were not increased until 1950, when they witnessed a modest rise to $35. That occasionally member boards were in arrears on these relatively low dues underscored the depth of the economic burden falling upon all the states. It is probably not coincidental that the organization achieved its most significant achievements in the 1950s when the annual dues were increased markedly: first to $100 in 1956 and then to $200 two years later. It appears that these increases provided the Federation with sufficient funds to sustain major initiatives on behalf of its membership.[7]

Even as the country regained its economic footing in the early 1940s, the United States' entry into the European and Pacific theaters of World War II meant that national and international events continued to shape the issues facing the Federation and state medical boards. Now workforce issues such as physician preparedness for active duty military service and later their reintegration into the civilian sector moved to the forefront, while the more traditional issues that the Federation and its membership had grappled with previously such as disciplinary processes and licensing examinations temporarily ceded the center stage. Similarly, issues such as physician preparedness were viewed predominantly as matters for the federal government, not the states. It is possible that these events tempered the Federation's sense for urgency in making progress on its traditional issues concerning medical licensure. Once the organizational momentum waned, it proved difficult to recapture, especially during an era when the magnitude of events like the Depression and World War II seemed to require federal, rather than state-based, solutions.

A second related factor may have been at work as well. The scale and complexity of the problems confronting the nation in the 1930s and 1940s seemed beyond the ability of individual states to address. Consequently, this era saw a tremendous expansion in the scope and role of the federal government in everything from social services (e.g., the Social Security Act, 1935) to economic stimulation through jobs programs (e.g., the Works Progress Administration, 1935).[8] To some Americans, the urgency of the national situation served to legitimize the appropriateness for a large-scale federal response to certain issues. The public's perception of voluntary associations and state government as being inadequate to address large-scale sociopolitical issues had been cemented with the failures of the Hoover administration in addressing immediate relief for the economy in the early 1930s. Even in failed initiatives, such as the push for national health insurance in the 1930s and again in the immediate postwar era, attention turned first toward the federal government as the appropriate responder to drive reform.[9] This trend toward seeking national solutions may have seemed antithetical to the state-based system of medical licensure. Indeed, it seems possible that the Federation leadership may have slipped unconsciously into a reactive mode in which they ceded the initiative for addressing regulatory problems to larger professional organizations and the federal government.

In other instances, decisions were made consciously to defer to national solutions. Such appears to have been the case with the relationship of medical licensure to the growing trend for specialization in medicine. Surgery, ophthalmology and otolaryngology were among the first medical fields to carve out a distinct niche for physician specialists. The question soon arose about how best to ensure that individuals holding themselves out as specialists were indeed qualified and competent within the narrower field of medicine they had embraced. The unrestricted license issued by state medical boards allowing a physician to practice medicine and surgery provided the broad baseline establishing minimally acceptable competence—an ideal formulation in the late nineteenth century when the general practitioner held sway. But with increasing specialization, did boards have an obligation to consider a higher tier license distinctly framed for the specialist? Clearly some legislators and physicians thought so. An unsuccessful 1913 bill in the Illinois legislature sought to restrict all surgery to those physicians specifically licensed as surgeons. In 1929, similar legislation failed in New Jersey by one vote that would have created a supplementary board of surgical examiners with licensing responsibility for virtually all general surgeons and related surgical areas. In 1930, the New York Academy of Medicine went on record favoring a state license issued by specialty.[10]

State medical boards and the Federation seemed less enthusiastic about the prospects for the issuance of specialty licenses. It is unclear whether this stemmed from reluctance on the part of the boards to take on added responsibilities or from an even greater reluctance to avoid the inevitable discord such a move would trigger within the profession. Federation President Harold Rypins called for state boards to "make haste slowly" on this issue and urged that they look to postgraduate training as the best solution for establishing appropriate standards. Federation Secretary-Treasurer Walter Bierring offered similar counsel and cited his perhaps overly optimistic belief that, despite the evident educational trend toward greater specialization, the majority of physicians would still fall into the category of general practitioner. He speculated that fewer than 15 percent of patients would require specialists' services. Thus, the Federation and state boards collectively eschewed a state-regulatory solution and instead opted to relinquish the field to a national solution predicated upon voluntary specialty boards that would set standards for certifying specialists. The Federation formally embraced this approach in 1934 with its support for, and representation on, the Advisory Board for Medical Specialties (later the American Board of Medical Specialties), which would standardize the rapidly growing number of specialty boards.[11]

A third explanatory factor for the organizational torpor affecting the Federation in the 1930s and 1940s falls under the broad heading of leadership. Here there are two salient points to be made. In 1924, the Federation revised its bylaws to accommodate the annual selection of a president-elect for the organization. Prior to that time, the Federation had been guided by physicians Charles Cook (1913–1916) and David Strickler (1916–1924), both of whom served multiyear tenures as president. In shifting to a time-specific tenure for elected leadership (one year of service as president), the Federation broadened the base of its participants in leadership. Undoubtedly, this contributed to a greater sense of inclusion by state medical boards and a stronger collective vested interest in the outcome for initiatives involving the Federation. This may have been offset, however, by some loss of continuity in senior leadership responsible for long-range planning and multiyear initiatives. The energy and early vibrancy of the organization may have arisen in part from the very continuity in senior leadership provided by the extended tenures of Cook and Strickler. Absent multiyear tenures and permanent staff, a gradual shift in mind-set may have developed in which organizational planning oriented itself around the short-term tenures of elected presidents serving a single year in office. As the 1930s and 1940s progressed, a burgeoning number of individuals had moved through the position of president, each with his own perspective on priorities, each with subtle (or not so subtle) areas of preferred emphasis for the Federation. There is another important point to be made about leadership—the potential for complacency. As will be discussed more fully in the next chapter, it was not unusual for physicians of this era to enjoy extremely long tenures on their respective state medical boards. Many of the Federation's early leaders fall into this category. For some individuals, a long tenure on their respective state boards may have fostered an understandably high degree of self-confidence and assurance arising from having firsthand experience with many of the immediate issues facing the medical licensing community. The "confident" state board member, with his long tenure in service, was no longer easily shocked or surprised by the issues and challenges confronting him. Without realizing it, the confident and unshakeable board member may have transitioned unawares into complacency over time. After all, when one already knows the landscape intimately (medical licensure) and the schedule for moving through it remains predictable and constant (selection to the Federation executive board, followed by running for president-elect, then serving as president), some degree of complacency can be expected. It seems likely that these elements contributed to a leadership cycle during the 1930s and 1940s that lacked the dynamism seen earlier.

A final factor behind the stasis characterizing the Federation during this era may well have been an internal one, located in the biological metaphor applied to organizational growth by Mason Haire. If there is an element of truth to this metaphor, then all business organizations—including the Federation—are constantly engaged in activities that either hasten them toward a theoretically inevitable decline or seek to reinvigorate the organization in ways that maintain a prolonged period of growth and maturation. By the end of the 1940s, the life cycle phase within which the Federation operated was wholly unclear. It seemed the organization passed rapidly from "inception" to a *limited* maturity beyond which it could not grow without major organizational changes. To all outward appearances the organization had entered its adulthood with "formalized" operating procedures and organizational roles and activities.[12] The Federation had achieved a degree of efficiency within the limitations of the staffing and finances available to it. As some organizational theorists have noted, however, the same formalization trend promoting efficiency could also manifest itself as an emergent culture or "influence" fostering bureaucratic rigidity and contributing to "ineffectiveness and decline."[13] The unspoken question then was this: Had the Federation drifted into a period of limited maturity leading inexorably toward decline or was it in the midst of a prolonged adolescence with a subsequent upward trajectory of growth and maturation still before it? By the mid-1950s it was clear that further growth—indeed, genuine renewal—remained before the Federation.

A MODEL MEDICAL PRACTICE ACT

One of the first major accomplishments of the Federation in its 1950s resurgence occurred in what initially seemed an unlikely area—the development of a model Medical Practice Act. This long-sought goal had been languishing for decades as an outstanding issue on the agendas of the Federation and the nation's state medical boards. The Federation's success in drafting the essentials for a model Medical Practice Act (MPA) signaled a new burst of energy characterizing the resurgent organization. To fully appreciate the significance of this accomplishment, it is necessary to understand some of what preceded it.

The wave of medical licensing laws passed in the United States during the last quarter of the nineteenth century reflected state-specific attempts to address fundamental problems stemming from the unregulated practice of medicine. These laws reflected a growing concern for ensuring some measure of minimal qualifications to practice medicine. Yet as these laws were being enacted, medico-political realities at the state and local level led to inevitable variations in legislation. These variations included everything from qualifications for practice to the content of the licensing examination; from the selection and composition of the state medical board to the disciplinary powers vested in that board. In some instances, the legislation evolved in piecemeal fashion over time from an accretion of laws, each one covering some narrow aspect of medical regulation. More commonly, these laws attempted to deal broadly with the full parameters of medical licensure. Generally speaking, this legislation was referred to as a state's Medical Practice Act.

As these laws spread to all states and territories, physicians and medical regulators recognized the need and desirability for some measure of national uniformity or commonality in the standards for medical licensure. The medical profession's efforts in this regard first began with a 1910 conference convened by the AMA Committee on Medical Legislation. This conference typified most early efforts to bring greater legislative consistency to the practice acts in place across the country. The AMA committee reached consensus on the need for model legislation that might serve as a template for all states. However, little in the way of tangible outcomes resulted from the conference.[14]

The Federation experienced a similar lack of early success in addressing this topic despite the centrality of the issue to much of the work of medical regulation. The Federation's original constitution identified the main objective of the organizations as striving for "uniform standards of medical licensure." That variations in standards for licensure existed was an uncontested fact and stemmed as much from state-specific exigencies and legislative prerogatives as they did from a disinterest on the part of state boards to find and codify common standards. Proceedings from the Federation's second annual meeting in 1914 reported on an extensive discussion of the need for greater uniformity in states' medical practice acts. Despite disagreements over various processes for selecting the membership of a state medical board and the viability of implementing certain educational requirements for licensure, a retrospective reading of the discussion shows more areas of consensus than one might have anticipated—investing the board with adequate resources (e.g., permanent staff, funding) and sufficient disciplinary powers, including suspension and revocation of a license; mitigating "political" influences, and so on. [15]

Despite these areas of consensus, very little in the way of legislative progress would be made for decades. One reason for this may be inferred from the seemingly innocuous comment of one board's secretary. Walter Bowers, a member of the Massachusetts board, stated, "I am a believer in men more than in measures." In his expanded comments, Bowers called for delegating the details of board administration to strong, "qualified" members, providing them with a wide latitude and broad discretionary power in carrying out that administration, and resisting overly detailed protocols that might tie the board's hands as it grappled with changing "conditions" in medical education, training and practice. If Bowers's comments are reflective of his colleagues' views, then state board members cast an inherently wary eye toward lawmakers seeking a legislative "fix" as the final solution to any and all problems. For at least some state board members, the desire for greater uniformity in medical regulatory legislation did not outweigh concerns that overly prescriptive laws might restrict their discretionary authority. Additionally, state medical boards recognized that turning to the legislatures to resolve outstanding issues required a willingness to distinguish between what was legislatively "practical" as opposed to what was theoretically possible. For some professionals, an unwillingness to accept less than the ideal legislative measure meant a preference for informal ad hoc solutions rather than risk a statutory outcome worse than the original problem. Such sentiments, when combined with an acknowledged understanding that success in this area would come only after a protracted period of "discussion and study,"[16] resulted in little progress for decades.

In 1952, Federation President John McCann, of the Ohio Medical Board, established a Special Committee to Draft a Uniform Medical Practice Act. The committee was charged with making a "comprehensive study" of all medical practice acts with the intent of identifying those "essential or basic requirements" that should be present in all iterations of such legislation. Chaired by the Kentucky board's Bruce Underwood, the eight-man committee drew assistance from AMA legal staff to review all medical practice acts and undertook extensive surveys of state board members and medical educators to inform their labors. At the February 1954 Federation annual meeting, the committee shared preliminary findings. The committee determined that the shared commonalities of all boards could be counted upon one hand: the existence of a state agency overseeing medical practice; requiring graduation from an approved medical school (applicable to U.S. graduates); passing a qualifying examination; and some methodology for revocation of a license. Beyond these areas, little statutory uniformity existed. Variance in the requirements for licensure (e.g., internship, citizenship); content for examinations; the basis for selection to the board; and bases for revocation of licenses proved the norm.[17]

Despite the litany of variances, the committee remained hopeful. The legislative staff who assisted with the research concluded that the true "extent of the lack of uniformity" was not widely known or fully appreciated simply because the state boards had so "ably administered" within the allowable scope of the laws under which they operated. In essence, the boards' able administration had already wrought "a large measure of practical uniformity." Buoyed perhaps by this acknowledgment and the labor already invested in the initiative, the committee pushed on. They sought to complete their work with recommendations presented at a forthcoming Federation annual meeting and requested that the Federation prepare to receive a document that could serve as a "guide" to inform each state's medical practice act. The committee was gradually coming to the realization that while a "uniform" Medical Practice Act might be impractical, it was still possible to identify the "essentials" of such a document that could serve as a template to a modern Medical Practice Act.[18]

With a growing sense for what was practical and achievable, the committee finished its work. Their efforts bore fruit when, in 1956, the Federation released *A Guide to the Essentials of a Modern Medical Practice Act*. The modestly titled volume culminated several years of concerted committee effort and more than forty years of discussion. The report distilled a series of recommendations that addressed five core areas: the definition of the practice of medicine; eligibility standards for licensure; licensing examinations; licensure endorsement; and the bases for probation, suspension, or revocation of a license.[19]

Since its initial publication in 1956, the *Essentials of a Modern Medical Practice Act* has passed through thirteen updated editions, with the most recent in 2012. The purpose behind the *Essentials* has been twofold: (1) to guide states seeking to revise or write anew their Medical Practice Act and (2) to encourage the use of consistent standards, language and definitions in the states' medical practice acts. The success of the document has been significant, in part because of the Federation's decision to convene periodic special committees of state board members and staff charged with revisiting and updating the *Essentials.* Accordingly, the *Essentials* has become a living document frequently referenced by state boards as a template and tool in drafting their state statutes or board's rules. Tim Miller, former executive director for the Arizona Medical Board, speaks glowingly of the *Essentials'* practical utility. In his experience, not only did the *Essentials* alleviate the need for his board to "reinvent the wheel" in crafting language anew but it "built credibility with legislators" when proposed changes carried the imprimatur derived from model language developed by a national organization representing all state medical boards.[20]

Perhaps the greatest testament to the *Essentials'* utility comes from a comparison of the original recommendations constituting the document to its most recent edition. For example, one finds that the definition for the practice of medicine contained in the original *Essentials* remains at the core of the current definition which has been updated for twenty-first-century realities, such as telemedicine and Internet prescribing.[21] Additional definitions have been added to the *Essentials* for key terms (e.g., competence, remediation and impairment), reflecting the dynamic nature of medicine and the challenge this can pose to medical regulators attempting to stay abreast of rapid changes in the field.

The original five core sections from the 1956 *Essentials* have been updated where appropriate. For example, the section on standards for licensure originally dealing solely with U.S. graduates has been expanded to include international medical graduates; the endorsement section acknowledges outsourced services such as those provided by credentials verification organizations; and the disciplinary section broadens the suggested range of actions open to state boards as well as the bases for such actions. Elsewhere, entirely new sections have been added to the *Essentials*, for example, resident/limited licenses for physicians; compulsory reporting requirements; physician impairment; and license renewal. A section on the structure and composition of state boards was also added. This led the Federation to develop a separate companion document in 1989, *Elements of a Modern State Medical Board.* This document fulfilled a request from the U.S. Department of Health and Human Services for a document that might provide a "blueprint" for creating and maintaining "properly organized and effectively empowered" state medical boards.[22]

By virtually any standard one might apply, the *Essentials* document has proven an invaluable resource and a sturdy workhorse for state medical boards. Whether being used to revise statutory language or as leverage against balky legislators, *Essentials* has proved to be perhaps the single most successful policy document of the Federation. Like all Federation policy documents, it represents the "latest thinking from national experts," according to David Henderson, executive director for the North Carolina Medical Board, and offers a model for best practices in medical regulation.

STATE MEDICAL BOARDS AND INTERNATIONAL MEDICAL GRADUATES

During the 1953–1954 academic training year more than 5,000 international medical graduates (IMGs)[23] held intern or resident positions in the United States. This international cohort accounted for nearly a quarter of all medical interns and residents.[24] For many years, state medical boards, hospitals and graduate medical educators struggled with how best to evaluate and assess the credentials and preparedness of international medical graduates, both those immigrating to the United States for the purpose of relocation and practice and those seeking only to obtain additional training. In the mid-1950s, the Federation engaged in a series of collaborative discussions and initiatives designed to alleviate these concerns. The Federation's contributions to success in this area came only after many years of difficult, even contentious, dialogue at the intersection of sometimes conflicting interests among the licensing community, the medical profession and international medical graduates.

To fully appreciate the landscape of medical licensure in the 1950s and the position of international graduates, it is necessary to first look back at developments over the preceding decades. By the early 1930s, historical concerns for the quality of U.S. medical education had largely disappeared under the standards set by the AAMC, the AMA Council on Medical Education and individual state medical boards. Immigration quotas set by the federal government in the 1920s had slowed the pace of entry by IMGs into the United States, though fundamental questions about the nature and extent of their education remained unanswered in any systematic fashion. Instead, in the 1930s two unrelated issues drew the attention of the medical profession and the licensing community: the number of U.S. citizens attending European medical schools and a surge in restrictive legislation linking citizenship as a requirement for a medical license.

A steady cohort of Americans had long sought medical education in Europe. This proved particularly true in the late nineteenth and early twentieth centuries when American medical education still struggled to achieve some measure of uniform quality among its schools. An estimated 1,000 Americans attended European medical schools in 1922. However, by the 1930s the reduced number of American medical schools had seen significant improvements in quality, removing one impetus to American student emigration for medical education. Yet somewhat surprisingly, the early 1930s saw a marked and unexpected increase in the number of Americans studying in European medical schools. From well below 1,000 individuals in the 1930–1931 academic year, the number nearly doubled to 1,900 by 1932–1933. Some of the reasons for this trend were related by former Federation President Harold Rypins (New York). Rypins chaired a multi-organizational committee studying the issue with representatives from the Federation, the AAMC, the AMA Council on Medical Education and Hospitals, the NBME and the New York Board of Regents. The committee's research and Rypins's separate demographic analysis of licensure candidates in New York found that American students unsuccessful in matriculating to U.S. schools had increasingly been drawn to European schools with dual-track curricula for the medical degree. One track offered a less clinically oriented pathway leading to the professional degree (M.D.); the other track, including additional clinical work, a hospital internship, and a more rigorous "practical examination," was designed for those students seeking to practice in that country. American students had been disproportionately entering the former track and then returning to the United States intending to sit for a state licensing examination.[25]

In December 1932, the committee's representatives endorsed a pair of resolutions for presentation to their respective organizations. The first resolution recommended that no American student matriculating at a European school subsequent to academic year 1932–1933 should be admitted to a state medical licensing examination (or the NBME certifying examination) without first presenting the state board with a certificate from the AAMC or the AMA Council on Medical Education attesting to having met the premedical education requirements set by these two institutions. The second resolution dealt with the curriculum from medical schools outside the United States. It called for a minimum medical course of four academic years and required the graduate to obtain either (a) a license to practice medicine in the country where the medical school was located, or (b) receive the M.D. degree after an additional year of study at a U.S. or Canadian medical school approved by the Federation, the AAMC and the AMA Council on Medical Education. A slightly modified resolution to this effect was adopted by the Federation's member boards and the NBME in spring 1933.[26] These resolutions and the deepening world economic depression combined to curtail much of this American student exodus. Later, international events related to the war in Europe created a different problem—émigré and refugee physicians entering the United States and confronting restrictive U.S. licensing laws.

In 1938, the AMA House of Delegates adopted a resolution requiring all international graduates seeking a medical license in the United States to have "full citizenship." It also called upon the Federation to encourage its member boards to push for adoption of the necessary rules and/or legislation to enact the resolution.[27] Within months several boards (Alabama, Iowa, West Virginia, and Wisconsin) responded by implementing requirements for full citizenship as a condition of medical licensure.[28] This AMA resolution, and the subsequent adoption of restrictive board rules and/or legislation, marked the continuation of a trend that began in the 1920s. However, not all states enacted such draconian measures. The New Jersey board's examination remained open to international graduates with the caveat that those passing would receive a license valid for six years, during which time the physician had to achieve citizenship status or see the license annulled. A contemporaneous ruling by the New York State Supreme Court ensured international graduates' access to that state's licensing examination. Such instances, however, were contrary to the overall trend. By mid-1939, all but four states and the District of Columbia required either full citizenship or "first papers" to have been taken out as a condition for licensure.[29]

The situation confronting émigré and refugee physicians seeking to practice in the United States on the eve of World War II resembled a perfect storm of obstacles. Federal law had imposed quotas on the number of allowable immigrants since 1924; subsequent citizenship requirements such as those imposed for a medical license raised separate state-specific hurdles. Additionally, the economic conditions of 1930s America left medical professional groups staunchly opposed to measures that would increase physician numbers and potential competition. Lingering "nativist" biases rounded out this mix of powerful oppositional forces confronting these physicians.[30]

Perhaps the most telling explication of this opposition can be seen in a 1939 article by the secretary of the Michigan board and future Federation president, J. Earl McIntyre. In reviewing the status of citizenship initiatives and medical licensure, the secretary acknowledged an "economic aspect" presented by émigré and refugee physicians but asserted it was "not the function and duty" of the state medical board to concern itself with such a matter. Instead, the boards' responsibilities rested upon maintaining "standards of the [public] health." But McIntyre then proffered vague "tests" of fitness based upon "ethical standards," "morality," and "respect" for the U.S. "system and operation of government"—all of which culminated in the assertion that "the alien who can meet these tests must be the exception" and his request that all states adopt legislation mandating citizenship as a condition for licensure. One might reasonably question whether such comments should be construed as representative of most state boards' sentiments. While not conclusive, two other pieces of evidence seem relevant here. In most states, the restrictions on licensure (e.g., citizenship requirement, acquisition of first papers, use of approved school lists) emanated not from state statutes but as regulations established by the board itself. Additionally, the comments of state board representatives reacting to a presentation on refugee physicians at the 1940 AMA Congress on Medical Education and Licensure are revealing. The clear majority of comments were unsympathetic to the émigré and refugee physicians and unyielding to requests asking for "liberalization" of state board regulations.[31] Such sentiments are not surprising given the cultural milieu and sociopolitical norms of the era. Discriminatory practices based upon race, ethnicity and religion were embedded into state law and local codes throughout much of the country, as evidenced by the long-entrenched Jim Crow–era segregation in the South. A segment of the public increasingly resonated to those voices associating immigrants with political radicalism. The sentiments of individual state board members toward immigrant physicians were understandably influenced by these broader social attitudes and at times appear to have perpetuated them.

The *Harvard Law Review* weighed in later that year with its own assessment of the national situation. The *Review* labeled restrictions applied to international medical graduates as falling into two categories: citizenship requirements and licensure prerequisites that were "difficult or impossible" for refugees to meet. The article openly questioned the "connection between competence and citizenship," specifically citing the "rationalization" proffered earlier that year by the Michigan secretary. The author's final assessment was even more damning: the constitutionality of such measures was not only questionable but seemed "more clearly inspired by a desire to protect the 'rights' of American physicians." Somewhat ironically, the author's review of the legal profession's restrictions relative to citizenship lacked comparable vigor, declaring the matter a "question for legislative determination" and listing practical considerations that rendered citizenship requirements as largely superfluous measures.[32]

While the overall sentiment of state boards appears to have run strongly in one direction, there were individual members of state boards whose views ran counter to the trend. Walter Bierring, of Iowa, signaled a change in his own earlier beliefs when he acknowledged that the circumstances prompting the flight of refugee physicians from Europe had prompted him to rethink his earlier stance. In 1940, he acknowledged that he now viewed the overall situation in a "different light" than he had previously and urged his colleagues to a "more charitable interpretation of the citizenship clause." The Colorado board's Nolie Mumey, himself a beneficiary of European postgraduate training obtained years earlier, helped signal a change in that board's attitude toward international physicians and worked on an individual basis to help relocate refugee physicians. As a longtime member of the New York board, Harold Rypins's support for émigré and refugee physicians helped them maintain access to that state's medical licensing examination. Philip St. Leger Moncure (Virginia) helped reverse his board's policy in favor of licensing refugee physicians. As a hospital surgery chief, Moncure saw these internationally trained physicians as potentially valuable resources to fill internship positions that might otherwise go unfilled and as potential candidates for practice in rural areas of the state.[33] Such a hope was not misplaced. Subsequently, IMGs demonstrated a willingness to provide primary care in designated underserved and rural areas—a trend that continues to this day, linked to specific visa rules and incentives, though with regional variations.[34]

The 1941 report on émigré physicians by the National Committee for Resettlement of Foreign Physicians provided a factual basis for objective discussion of the topic and reflected a shift in attitude already under way near the end of 1941. The report reviewed the legal status of citizenship statutes and regulations and advocated that all states adopt New York's model, which required only first papers before licensure and then a ten-year period to attain citizenship or see the license revoked. The report acknowledged the lack of any definitive legal precedent striking down the linkage of citizenship with medical licensure but cited the rulings of multiple state attorneys general (Illinois, South Dakota, Texas, Utah) as to their unconstitutionality. With the United States' entry into World War II in December 1941, wartime exigencies soon created a different set of priorities. Securing adequate physician numbers for wartime needs undoubtedly helped those seeking to curb the more restrictive elements of medical licensure for international medical graduates. Later, in the aftermath of the war, state medical boards were again confronted by physician refugees, now categorized as "displaced" physicians. The medical profession evinced a noticeably different tone at this point, if the report of the AMA's Committee on Displaced Physicians is any indication. The report encouraged the Federation and state medical boards to give "special study" to the circumstances of these physicians, accept the certificate of the United Nations' International Refugee Organization when conventional evidence of credentials was not available, and frame appropriate "special regulations" such as limited licenses for practices in state hospitals.[35]

The wartime disruptions of travel and education meant that, émigré and refugee physicians aside, the number of international medical graduates voluntarily seeking additional medical training in the United States had diminished. This reality did not last long. In 1948, as a measure to encourage international goodwill in the postwar world, the U.S. Congress passed the Information and Educational Exchange Act, which permitted the granting of visas for educational purposes. However, the legislation did not stipulate requirements. In theory, anyone who wanted to be educated in this country could apply. At the same time, American hospitals were expanding at the height of the baby boom after the return of hundreds of thousands of veterans. However, there were not enough U.S. medical school graduates to fill all the internship and residency positions available at these hospitals. A substantial number of U.S. graduates chose other paths (e.g., military, research, public health service) and bypassed hospital training. By 1953, international graduates accounted for an estimated 5,500 interns and residents in the United States. Two years later the number was documented at slightly more than 6,000. Additionally, many of these internships were merely service positions, not formally structured educational opportunities for learning. Of the 7,000 hospitals in the United States looking for interns, only 1,300 were said to have had approved education programs connected with them.[36]

State medical boards were now facing an unprecedented number of international medical graduates. For those boards that did not unilaterally preclude international graduates from licensure, these physicians presented significant challenges in terms of both verification of credentials and drawing reasonable, informed conclusions as to the preparedness of the individual to treat patients safely. Additionally, by 1949, an increasing number of state boards (27) were licensing interns and/or residents. Thus, issues of access to, and qualification for, internship and residency positions were ones fully within the domain of state boards. These same boards and other interested organizations increasingly looked to the Federation to see if guidance toward a national solution would be forthcoming. In early 1949, discussions began in earnest with the meeting of an informally constituted Committee on Foreign Medical Credentials. Representatives from the Federation as well as the Illinois, Minnesota, New York and Wisconsin state medical boards were in attendance, along with fourteen other organizations, institutions and foundations, including observers from the U.S. State Department. Reflecting the slow shift in tone toward a more receptive understanding of international medical graduates, the committee condemned administrative and statutory restrictions that resulted in "complete exclusion" of these physicians. But the committee also affirmed the responsibility of state medical boards to obtain adequate information about the quality of these physicians' medical schools and thus the education they had received. The group recommended a multi-organizational pooling of resources to investigate and gather information supporting a list of medical schools "comparable" to U.S. schools. Formal standards to ensure comparability of U.S. schools had been set in 1942 with the establishment of the Liaison Committee on Medical Education (LCME), the sole accrediting authority for medical school programs in the United States issuing the M.D. degree. As a joint initiative of the AMA Council on Medical Education and the AAMC, the LCME formalized the joint inspection process of medical schools that were already being conducted by these two organizations for several decades.[37]

Acting as de facto accrediting agencies, the AMA Council on Medical Education and Hospitals and AAMC had long provided the evaluative and informational bases for determining "approved" medical schools in the United States—a listing that state medical boards had come to accept and rely upon. Now the two organizations prepared to expand their periodic surveys and evaluation of medical schools to those outside of the United States. A preliminary listing of approved international schools appeared in early 1950 with the vast majority of listed schools located in the United Kingdom, Scandinavia (Sweden, Norway and Denmark) and the Netherlands. By 1951, an updated listing named forty-nine schools. As for the schools not listed, the Federation quickly addressed the question of how state boards should deal with these schools' graduates in a February 1951 resolution. The resolution called for all graduates of schools not on the approved list to complete two years of additional medical education in the United States or Canada before being allowed to sit for a medical licensing examination.[38]

Rather than proving to be a definitive solution, the insufficiency of these measures soon became apparent. Within a few years, it was clear that a mechanism for assessment predicated upon a list of approved schools was inadequate for the large number of international graduates seeking graduate training and/or medical licensure in the United States. There were simply too many physicians presenting themselves from schools for which information was lacking. At an April 1954 conference with twenty-two participating organizations, a Federation proposal presented the group with a strategic change in course: evaluative efforts should shift from evaluating schools and back to evaluating *individual candidates*. This shift was consistent with a unique approach to individual assessment of international medical graduates being utilized by the Michigan medical board at the time. An "oral screening board" composed of medical educators from the states' two medical schools conducted oral examinations in basic and clinical sciences. Passing candidates received a temporary license to begin serving an internship in an approved hospital. Failing candidates for whom English seemed to be the source of difficulty were provided access to language courses. Word of this system soon spread throughout the medical licensing community such that several other states requested

Michigan's assistance in reviewing prospective international candidates.[39] The suggested proposal by the Federation in 1954 built upon the Michigan experience to utilize a "central screening agency" to evaluate credentials and assess preparedness before allowing the physicians to begin an internship and then sit for a licensing examination. The Federation returned with a formal proposal for a "joint commission" that was accepted in principle by the AMA Council on Medical Education, the American Hospital Association and the AAMC. Soon thereafter the four organizations established a "Cooperating Committee" on Graduates of Foreign Medical Schools. The Cooperating Committee recommended that a separate organization be established to receive applications from international graduates, verify their credentials and administer a preliminary examination. Passage of this preliminary examination would allow the physician to enter into an internship and subsequently sit for a state board licensing examination.[40] In 1956, the resulting organization was established: the Educational Commission for Foreign Medical Graduates (ECFMG).

The stated purposes of the organization were twofold: (1) to provide international graduates with "an opportunity to establish their qualifications for . . . advanced medical training" in the U.S., and (2) to provide state medical boards and hospitals with evidence of a physician's preparedness to begin an internship or residency. The ECFMG[41] soon engaged the National Board of Medical Examiners to develop the preliminary examination in basic and clinical sciences that, along with the verification of credentials, formed the basis for issuance of an ECFMG certificate. Since 1958, more than 300,000 physicians have gained ECFMG certification qualifying them to enter into graduate medical education in the United States.[42]

The subsequent value and efficacy of the ECFMG has been reflected in the decision of all state medical boards to require its certification as a standard requirement of all international medical graduates seeking licensure. The Federation's collaborative role leading to the creation of the ECFMG offered a second major success for the organization in the 1950s. With a growing sense of momentum building around the organization, the Federation in 1956 tackled perhaps its biggest challenge—bringing some measure of uniformity to the nation's medical licensing examinations.

EXAMINATION INSTITUTES—COLLECTIVE IMPROVEMENT IN ASSESSMENT

In 1956, the Federation embarked upon perhaps its most ambitious initiative to date. State board members had long been keenly aware of growing deficiencies in their examinations. Critics pointed specifically to several problems. These included examination content that varied widely between jurisdictions, outdated test items oriented too heavily around factual knowledge and recall, and the inevitable differences in scoring leading to the application of an uneven standard for minimum performance. Even sympathetic medical educators lamented state licensing examinations as too often duplicative of their educational testing and out of step with curricular innovations. The Federation's leadership understood that all of these factors diminished the prospects for meaningful progress on licensure by endorsement initiatives as they undermined the potential for licensing examinations to serve as the common standard upon which all endorsements might rest. Indeed, the recommendations forming the basis for the 1956 *Guide to the Essentials of a Modern Medical Practice Act* explicitly identified examination standards as the "prerequisite to nationwide . . . endorsement."[43]

Sensing that these criticisms could no longer be discounted, and inspired by recent collaborative initiatives in medical education, Federation President McKinley Crabb urged state medical boards to undertake a major collective effort to improve their examinations. In February 1956, Stiles Ezell, secretary of the New York State Board of Medical Examiners, picked up the gauntlet thrown down by Crabb when he introduced a resolution calling for the Federation to establish a five-member "permanent committee . . . to develop and activate examination institutes in the major branches of medicine . . . for the purpose of creating uniformity in content and quality" of medical licensing examinations. With the approval of the resolution in that same year, the Federation selected Ezell to chair a Permanent Committee on Examinations which included Sam Poindexter (Idaho), Frank Peterson (Iowa), Andrew Gehret (Delaware) and Harold Jervey (South Carolina).[44]

The Permanent Committee developed a proposal modeled upon the AAMC's experience using teaching "institutes," each of which was oriented around a specific subject matter. These national gatherings (1951–1953) had resulted in an evolving document that set forth the educational objectives for teaching in U.S. undergraduate medical education. The Federation sought to duplicate this model and apply it to the construct and content of the nation's medical licensing examinations. Each one in the series of institutes would draw upon individual members of state medical boards selected from across the country to identify the major concepts and content for assessment in a given subject area routinely included on the nation's medical licensing examinations (e.g., obstetrics and gynecology). At the first planning meeting of the Permanent Committee for the Examination Institute, the following objectives were identified for the institutes:

1. Promotion of uniformity in licensing examinations
2. Establishment of equivalent levels in examinations
3. Improvement in the quality of examinations
4. Creation of a rational basis for endorsement
5. Placement of licensure in a definite relation to modern medical education
6. Assistance for state boards in assessing international medical graduates

In setting forth the objectives behind the institutes, the Federation and the Permanent Committee made clear that the endeavor was not intended to "challenge or criticize" the work of the National Board of Medical Examiners. The latter, however, had recently decided in 1954 against admitting international medical graduates to its certification program; thus, the assessment of this sizable cohort fell squarely upon the shoulders of the Educational Commission for Foreign Medical Graduates (ECFMG) and state medical boards. A supportive National Board acknowledged the institutes as necessary exercises in self-improvement for state boards.[45]

The objectives set forth by the Permanent Committee were important, but perhaps the most critical idea to come from the planning session was the concept of "fitness to practice" or "fitness testing." Here the committee explicitly acknowledged, and attempted to delineate, a clear distinction from the "educational testing" conducted by medical educators. With the disappearance of unapproved medical schools in the United States, state boards had far less need to worry about testing in the domains inhabited by medical educators (e.g., basic medical sciences). State medical boards could instead focus on the clinical application of medical knowledge with patient-centered questions that posed a problem requiring the licensure candidate to demonstrate the ability to transfer theoretical knowledge into diagnosis, treatment and patient management. Fitness testing represented a significant philosophical shift in the written questions utilized by most boards. Previously, they had attempted to assess fitness through practical examinations—an increasingly expensive and less utilized methodology—with written examinations focused predominantly upon factual medical knowledge.[46]

The Permanent Committee proposed convening a series of institutes over a three-year span and covering the following major areas: Anatomy; Physiology; Pharmacology; Biochemistry; Bacteriology; Pathology; Hygiene and Public Health; Surgery; Obstetrics and Gynecology; and Internal Medicine. State medical boards were encouraged to allocate funds to support member participation with the goal that each institute would convene a minimum of twenty participating members from across the country. The committee would draft a "master plan" for each institute, identifying the objectives for each session with the goal of a final report outlining the content areas and construct for an appropriate examination in each area. Each institute participant would then return to his respective board charged with carrying on the work of revising his or her board's examination to align with the content outline developed through the institute. Through this method, the Federation hoped to jump start a collective "self-improvement" initiative that would raise the quality of licensing examinations nationwide using trained, thoughtful individual state board examiners.[47]

The first institute took place in 1957. The Federation prefaced its work by setting forth what the institutes did not represent, an attempt to infringe upon individual state's autonomy. The Federation sought to work within its "advisory capacity" by assisting state medical boards in coordinating dialogue to eliminate the "instability and variations" within their examinations that hindered efforts at licensure by endorsement. The work of this first institute was representative of all that followed. Attendees were led through a series of questions designed to elicit how testing oriented toward fitness to practice should manifest itself in the construction and outline for examination content covering, for example, obstetrics and gynecology. Attendees were asked to consider where these licensure candidates fell on the educational continuum as a means for identifying appropriate content coverage, bridging the gap between assessment being conducted for medical students and interns as opposed to the "highly specialized" knowledge and skill set being assessed by the specialty certification boards. In this regard, the attendees sought to identify the inherent level of "responsibility" vested in the physician by virtue of the medical license; having done this, the attendees then attempted to outline the corresponding parameters for testing in that clinical area.[48]

The inaugural 1957 Institute on Obstetrics and Gynecology proved successful. Its attendees concluded that it was possible for a licensing examination to "confront the candidate with a [patient-centered] problem situation involving the use of responsibility and judgment . . . which requires evidence of a methodical approach and a logical conclusion." Subsequent institutes on anatomy, bacteriology, pathology, and surgery followed in 1958. Permanent Committee Chair Stiles Ezell soon realized that the institutes posed perhaps their most significant challenge to the individual state board examiner. These physicians were required to not only think deeply about the construct of their examinations but to view them as *dynamic* instruments requiring boards to maintain some degree of currency in both medical knowledge and the emerging science of assessment. This posed a considerable practical challenge. In essence, Ezell confronted state boards collectively with a responsibility for "self-improvement" that would justify their continued assessment role in medical regulation. This would provide the best recourse for silencing critics who questioned the utility of state board exams. According to Ezell, the changing times and a modern regulatory system required that state medical boards offer "more logical reasons for existing and more stimulating purposes than self-perpetuation."[49]

The Federation conducted nine institute workshops by the end of the 1950s. The organization's leadership remained cautiously optimistic that their labors in this area might rapidly bear fruit. Certainly the expectations were high. The *Federation Bulletin* stated bluntly that "if there is not a marked improvement in examination construct [by next year], there may . . . not be any at all."[50] As it turned out, by the 1960s a variety of factors forced the state medical board community to make difficult decisions about their continued role in the assessment arena.

Yet, this cautionary note did not alter the importance of much that had transpired with the Federation during the 1950s. The organization had succeeded in reversing course from a protracted period of lesser accomplishments in the 1930s and 1940s that threatened to leave the Federation irrelevant in the rapidly changing landscape of medical regulation. The major initiatives of the 1950s (Examination Institutes, a model Medical Practice Act, establishment of the ECFMG) signaled a reengaged and resurgent Federation. These initiatives demonstrated the ability of the Federation to coordinate dialogue among the nation's state medical boards, assist them in reaching consensus on major issues and then help implement changes that benefited the entire state-based system of licensure. While much work remained to be done on a multitude of fronts (e.g., disciplinary databases, greater uniformity in licensing examinations), the Federation leadership could enter the 1960s appropriately optimistic for the organization's future. Rather than the decline theorized by social scientists as the norm in their biological model for organizations, the achievements of the Federation in the 1950s signaled growth, rather than decline, as the immediate future direction of the organization.

NOTES

1. Mason Haire, "Biological Models and Empirical Histories in the Growth of Organizations," in *Modern Organization Theory*, ed. Mason Haire (New York: John Wiley, 1959), 272–306.
2. See Richard L. Daft, *Organizational Theory and Design* (Mason, Ohio: Cengage Learning, 2007) and Judith Sharken Simon, *The Five Life Stages of Nonprofit Organizations* (St. Paul, Minnesota: Amherst Wilder Foundation, 2001)
3. Herbert Platter, "President's Address," *Federation Bulletin* 15 (March 1929): 74.
4. Ludmerer, *Learning to Heal*, 257; "Federation of State Medical Boards of the United States: Executive Session, February 18, 1930," *Federation Bulletin* 16 (March 1930): 83.

5. "Federation of State Medical Boards: Executive Session, February 12, 1946," *Federation Bulletin* 32 (March 1946): 71; "Federation of State Medical Boards of the United States: February 10–12, 1952," *Federation Bulletin* 38 (March 1952): 75; "Report of the Resolutions Committee," *Federation Bulletin* 43 (March 1956): 82.

6. See Walter Bierring, "Medical Licensure after Forty Years," *Federation Bulletin* 43 (April 1956): 101–13; Baker, "The Federation: Its Origin, History and Obligations," 72–90; and various articles from the 1987 issues of the *Federation Bulletin*.

7. "Report of the Executive Committee," *Federation Bulletin* 36 (March 1950): 68; "Report of Secretary-Editor and Treasurer," *Federation Bulletin* 43 (March 1956): 72; "Report of the Secretary, Treasurer, Editor," *Federation Bulletin* 45 (April 1958): 116.

8. Norton, Katzman, et al., *People and Nation*, 748.

9. Peter Dobkin Hall, "Historical Perspectives on Nonprofit Organizations in the United States," in *The Jossey Bass Handbook of Nonprofit Leadership and Management*, ed. David O. Renz (San Francisco: John Wiley & Sons, 2010), 17; Starr, *The Social Transformation*, 280, 286; Stevens, *American Medicine and the Public Interest*, 268.

10. "Should Specialists Be Licensed?" *Federation Bulletin* 16 (December 1930): 356; Stevens, *American Medicine and the Public Interest*, 90, 165.

11. Shryock, *Medicine Licensing*, 68; Ameringer, *State Boards and Politics of Public Protection*, 141fn; Harold Rypins, "The Licensure of Specialists," *Federation Bulletin* 17 (November 1931): 336; Walter Bierring, "Consistency Versus Chaos in Medical Education and Licensure," *Federation Bulletin* 22 (November 1936): 336–37; "Advisory Board for Boards Certifying Specialists," *Federation Bulletin* 20 (May 1934): 132.

12. Oliver P. Roche, *Corporate Governance and Organization Life Cycle* (Amherst, New York: Cambria Press, 2009), 15; Robert C. Andringa, *The Nonprofit Board Answer Book: A Practical Guide for Board Members and Chief Executives* (San Francisco: John Wiley & Sons, 2007), 280–82.

13. James P. Walsh and Robert D. Dewar, "Formalization and the Organizational Life Cycle," *Journal of Management Studies* 24 (May 1987): 215.

14. "A Guide to the Essentials of a Modern Medical Practice Act," *JAMA* 161 (May 26, 1956): 381.

15. "Constitution and By-Laws of the Federation," 90–93; "Discussion on a Model Medical Practice Act," *Federation Bulletin* 1 (April 1915): 5–12.

16. "Discussion on a Model Medical Practice Act," *Federation Bulletin* 1 (April 1915): 5–6; Charles Pinkham, "Eligibility for a License: An Essential Principle of a Medical Practice Act," *Federation Bulletin* 11 (August 1925): 178; "Guide to Essentials of Medical Practice Act," *JAMA* 381.

17. Dale Breaden, "A Guide to the Essentials of a Modern Medical Practice Act: A Goal Long Sought," *Federation Bulletin* 74 (October 1987): 310; "Essentials of a Modern Medical Practice Act," *Federation Bulletin* 40 (June 1954): 162–64.

18. "Essentials of Modern Medical Practice Act," 167–68.

19. Breaden, "Guide to the Essentials," 310.

20. Timothy Miller, J.D., interview by David Johnson, March 18, 2011, Euless, Texas.

21. The 1956 *Essentials* defined the practice of medicine as diagnosing, treating or correcting (or attempting thereof), or holding oneself out as being able to diagnose, treat or correct any and all human conditions, ailments, disease, injuries, or infirmities (whether physical of mental) by any means, methods, devices or instrumentalities.

22. *A Guide to the Essentials of a Modern Medical Practice Act* (Euless, Texas: Federation of State Medical Boards, 2010), 3, 11–12, 14; *Elements of a Modern State Medical and Osteopathic Board* (Euless, Texas: Federation of State Medical Boards, 2009), 1, 3.

23. State boards of this era and earlier routinely used the phrase "foreign physicians." The authors of this text have chosen to use the more modern terminology "international medical graduate" or IMG throughout this narrative.

24. James E. McCormack and Arthur Feraru, "Alien Interns and Residents in the United States," *JAMA* 158 (August 13, 1955): 1357.

25. Donald E. Melnick, "From Defending the Walls to Improving Global Medical Education: Fifty Years of Collaboration between the ECFMG and the NBME," *Academic Medicine* 81 (December 2006 Supplement): S31; Harold Rypins, "Report of the Committee on Foreign Medical Students," *Federation Bulletin* 19 (November 1933): 339; "Licensure of Foreign Medical Graduates," *Federation Bulletin* 19 (April 1933): 98.

26. "European Medical Graduates," *Federation Bulletin* 19 (January 1933): 2; "Committee on Foreign Medical Students," *Federation Bulletin*, 337.

27. "Full Citizenship Requirement for Licensure," *Federation Bulletin* 24 (August 1938): 227.

28. See "News Items," in *Federation Bulletin* 24 (October 1938): 312; (November 1938): 348; (February 1939): 57.

29. "Thirty-Four Aliens Pass State Examinations," *Federation Bulletin* 25 (January 1939): 25; "Citizenship as a Condition Precedent to Medical Licensure in the United States," *JAMA* 113 (October 14, 1939): 1496–97.

30. A 1939 article is typical of the era. In presenting statistics on immigrant physicians, Europeans were categorized by "racial stock" and included a subcategory for those individuals identifying themselves as Jewish. See "Immigration of Alien Immigrant Physicians," *JAMA*, February 25, 1939.

31. J. Earl McIntyre, "Citizenship and Medical Licensure," *Federation Bulletin* 25 (March 1939): 77–78, 83; David L. Edsall, "The Émigré Physician in American Medicine," *JAMA* 114 (March 23, 1940): 1068; Joseph M. Pratt and Irving Graef, "The Refugee Physician," *Federation Bulletin* 26 (April 1940): 109–13.

32. "Refugees and the Professions," *Harvard Law Review* 53 (1939): 112.

33. "Refugee Physician," 109; Eric D. Kohler, "Relicensing Central European Refugee Physicians in the United States, 1933–1945," *Simon Wiesenthal Center Annual* 6 (1989): 6, 12–13.

34. L .G. Hart and S. M. Skillman, "International Medical Graduate Physicians in the United States: Changes since 1981," *Health Affairs* (July-August 2007): 1159–69; M. J. Thompson and A. Hagopian, "Do International Medical Graduates 'Fill the Gap' in Rural Primary Care in the United States? A National Study," *Journal of Rural Health* 25, no. 2 (Spring 2009): 124–34.

35. David L. Edsall and Tracy J. Putnam, "The Émigré Physician in America, 1941: A Report of the National Committee for Resettlement of Foreign Physicians," *Federation Bulletin* 28 (January 1942): 15, 19, 21; Alexander Manlius Burgess, "Resettlement of the Displaced Physician in the United States," *Federation Bulletin* 36 (June 1950): 170–71.

36. James McCormack and Arthur Feraru, "Alien Interns and Residents in the United States," *JAMA* 158 (August 13, 1955): 1357; James E. McCormack and Arthur Feraru, "Alien Interns and Residents in the United States, 1955–1956," *Federation Bulletin* 43 (July 1956): 201; Willard C. Rappleye, "Foreign Medical Graduates," *Federation Bulletin* 48 (November 1961), 322–23.

37. J. Earl McIntyre, "Licensure of Hospital Resident Physicians," *Federation Bulletin* 35 (October 1949): 299, 301; "Licensure of Foreign Medical Graduates," *Federation Bulletin* 35 (April 1949): 100–103; Kassebaum, "Origin of the LCME," 85–87.

38. "Foreign Medical Schools," *Federation Bulletin* 36 (February 1950): 45; "Executive Session," *Federation Bulletin* 37 (March 1951): 71.

39. For a detailed discussion of Michigan's screening board, see Elmer W. Schnoor, "Today Is Not Yesterday: The Problem of the Foreign Medical School Graduate," *Federation Bulletin* 41 (April 1955): 118–21.

40. Walter Bierring, "Evaluation of Foreign Medical Graduates," *Federation Bulletin* 40 (December 1954): 355–56; E. C Swanson, "Communications," *Federation Bulletin* 70 (December 1983): 371–73; "Report of the Cooperating Committee on Graduates of Foreign Medical Schools," *Federation Bulletin* 40 (December 1954): 367, 369–70.

41. To minimize confusion, reference has been omitted to ECFMG's prior names, such as "Evaluation Service for Foreign Medical Graduates" and "Educational Council for Foreign Medical Graduates."

42. James A. Hallock, "Celebrating 50 Years of Experience: An ECFMG Perspective," *Academic Medicine* 81 (December 2006 Supplement): 58–59; Hubbard and Levit, *National Board of Medical Examiners*, 53.

43. Stiles Ezell, "Examination Institutes, 1958," *Federation Bulletin* 45 (May 1958): 136–37; Dean F. Smiley, "The Relation of Medical Education to Licensure," *Federation Bulletin* 43 (March 1956): 95–96; S. M. Poindexter, "Application of the Institute Idea to the Licensure Examination," *Federation Bulletin* 44 (August 1957): 221–22; Bruce Underwood, "Report of Committee to Draft a Uniform Medical Practice Act," *Federation Bulletin* 40 (December 1954): 362.

44. "Resolution No. 3," *Federation Bulletin* 43 (March 1956): 82; "The Permanent Committee," *Federation Bulletin* 43 (September 1956): 271.

45. Smiley, "Relation of Medical Education to Licensure," 95–96; "Program of the Permanent Committee," *Federation Bulletin* 43 (December 1956): 355; "On Improving Licensing Examinations," *Federation Bulletin* 43 (September 1956): 257–58.

46. "Preliminary Statement of Permanent Committee," *Federation Bulletin* 43 (November 1956): 324–26; William A. Sodeman, "General Concept of Fitness Testing," *Federation Bulletin* (June 1963): 160–64.

47. "Preliminary Statement," *Federation Bulletin*, 324–32; "Program of the Permanent Committee," *Federation Bulletin*, 356–57.

48. Joseph J. Combs, "Reevaluation of the Purposes of the Licensing Examination," *Federation Bulletin* 44 (May 1957): 122; Poindexter, "Application of the Institute Idea," *Federation Bulletin*, 221–24; A. M. Gehret, "The First Examination Institute," *Federation Bulletin* 45 (March 1958): 80–84.

49. "The 1958 Institutes," *Federation Bulletin* 45 (April 1958): 101; "Examination Institutes: 1958," *Federation Bulletin* 45 (May 1958): 135–39.

50. "A New Era in Licensure," *Federation Bulletin* 46 (August 1959): 177; "Objectives for 1959," *Federation Bulletin* 45 (December 1958): 338.

Nineteenth-century America saw the rise of alternative medical philosophies that often resulted in state medical boards constituted along sectarian lines. Seen above is A. T. Still, an allopathic physician who founded osteopathic medicine.

Photograph courtesy of the Museum of Osteopathic Medicine (SM), Kirksville, MO.

Dr. John Rauch's pioneering work (1877–1893) on the Illinois Board of Health reflected the late-nineteenth-century focus of state boards on assessing physician knowledge.
Photograph courtesy of the U.S. National Library of Medicine.

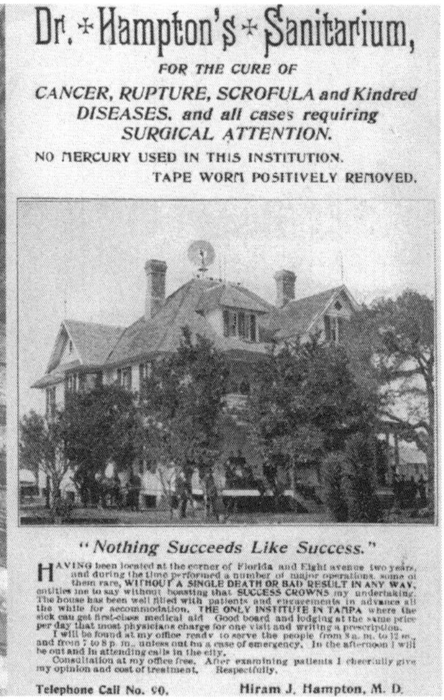

Dr. Hiram Hampton (Florida Eclectic Medical Board) enjoyed a successful practice in early-twentieth-century Tampa offering a wide range of treatments reflective of the still largely unregulated claims made by practitioners.

Images courtesy of the State Archives of Florida and Special & Digital Collections, Tampa Library, University of South Florida.

Drs. George Matson (left) and Beverly Drake Harrison (right) represented the National and American Confederations at the critical February 25, 1911, meeting that led to the founding of the Federation of State Medical Boards. Abraham Flexner and representatives from the AMA and the AAMC helped mediate the negotiations.

Matson photograph courtesy of the Ohio State Medical Association.

Massachusetts's Charles Cook (left) and Colorado's David Strickler (right) guided the Federation as its first presidents from 1912 to 1925.

Photographs from the FSMB Archives.

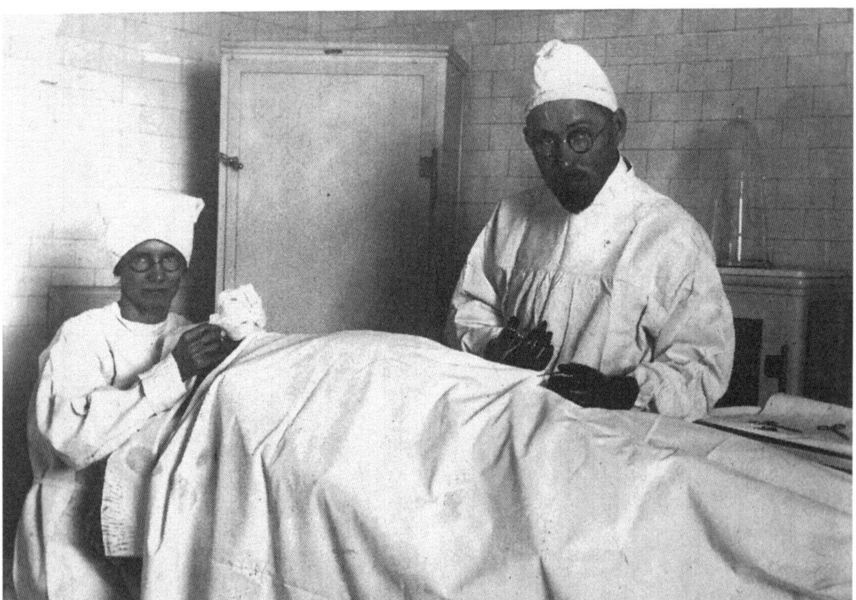

State medical boards faced many challenges from unscrupulous and questionably trained physicians. The Kansas State Medical Board ultimately revoked the license of John R. Brinkley, the infamous "Goat Gland" doctor, seen here performing surgery with his wife assisting.

Photograph courtesy of the Kansas State Historical Society.

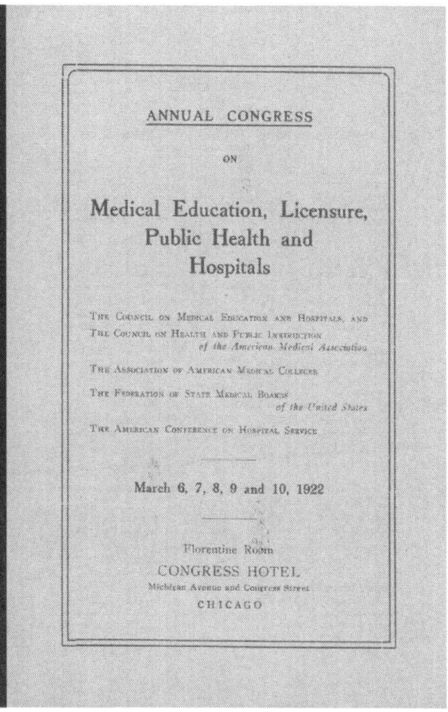

ANNUAL CONGRESS

ON

Medical Education, Licensure, Public Health and Hospitals

The Council on Medical Education and Hospitals, and
The Council on Health and Public Instruction
of the American Medical Association

The Association of American Medical Colleges

The Federation of State Medical Boards
of the United States

The American Conference on Hospital Service

March 6, 7, 8, 9 and 10, 1922

Florentine Room
CONGRESS HOTEL
Michigan Avenue and Congress Street
CHICAGO

Dr. Walter Bierring (Iowa Medical Board) served as Federation secretary-treasurer from 1915 to 1961, providing continuity and an important liaison with organizations such as those at the Annual Congress on Medical Education and Licensure. From 1913 to 1981, the Federation convened state medical boards annually in Chicago at the Congress and Palmer House Hotels.

Bierring photo courtesy of the U.S. National Library of Medicine.

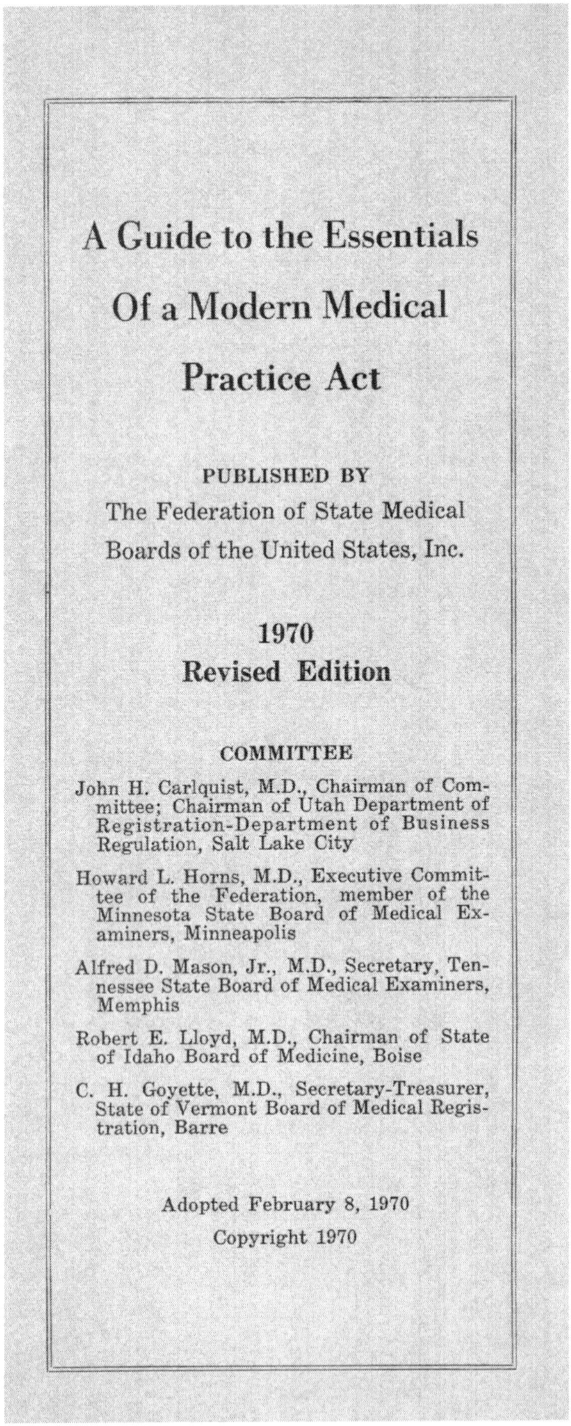

A Guide to the Essentials

Of a Modern Medical

Practice Act

PUBLISHED BY

The Federation of State Medical

Boards of the United States, Inc.

1970

Revised Edition

COMMITTEE

John H. Carlquist, M.D., Chairman of Committee; Chairman of Utah Department of Registration-Department of Business Regulation, Salt Lake City

Howard L. Horns, M.D., Executive Committee of the Federation, member of the Minnesota State Board of Medical Examiners, Minneapolis

Alfred D. Mason, Jr., M.D., Secretary, Tennessee State Board of Medical Examiners, Memphis

Robert E. Lloyd, M.D., Chairman of State of Idaho Board of Medicine, Boise

C. H. Goyette, M.D., Secretary-Treasurer, State of Vermont Board of Medical Registration, Barre

Adopted February 8, 1970

Copyright 1970

The Federation's greatest successes have come as a policy and assessment resource for state medical boards. The licensing community achieved a long-sought goal in 1956 with the adoption of the Essentials of a Modern Medical Practice Act. Now in its 12th edition.

Image courtesy of the FSMB Archives.

In 1968, FSMB introduced the Federation Licensing Examination (FLEX). This nationally administered medical licensing examination closed the era of state examinations. Dr. Fred Merchant (Ohio Medical Board) is seen here exhibiting at the June 1970 AMA convention.
Photo courtesy of the FSMB Archives.

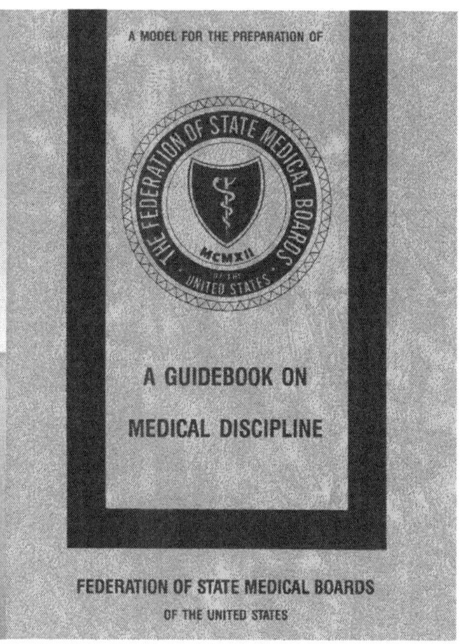

Dr. Robert Derbyshire (New Mexico Medical Board) typified the new generation of Federation leadership in the 1960s. Derbyshire published widely on medical licensure and discipline. In the 1960s, the Federation supported the emerging shift toward a more robust disciplinary role for state medical boards through the production of model practices and guidebooks.
Images courtesy of the FSMB Archives.

Dr. Bryant Galusha served as the Federation's chief executive officer from 1984 to 1989, building on the efforts of predecessors (Drs. McKinley Crabb, Harold Jervey) and laying the foundation for his successors: James Winn, James Thompson, Barbara Schneidman, and Humayun Chaudhry.
Image courtesy of the FSMB Archives.

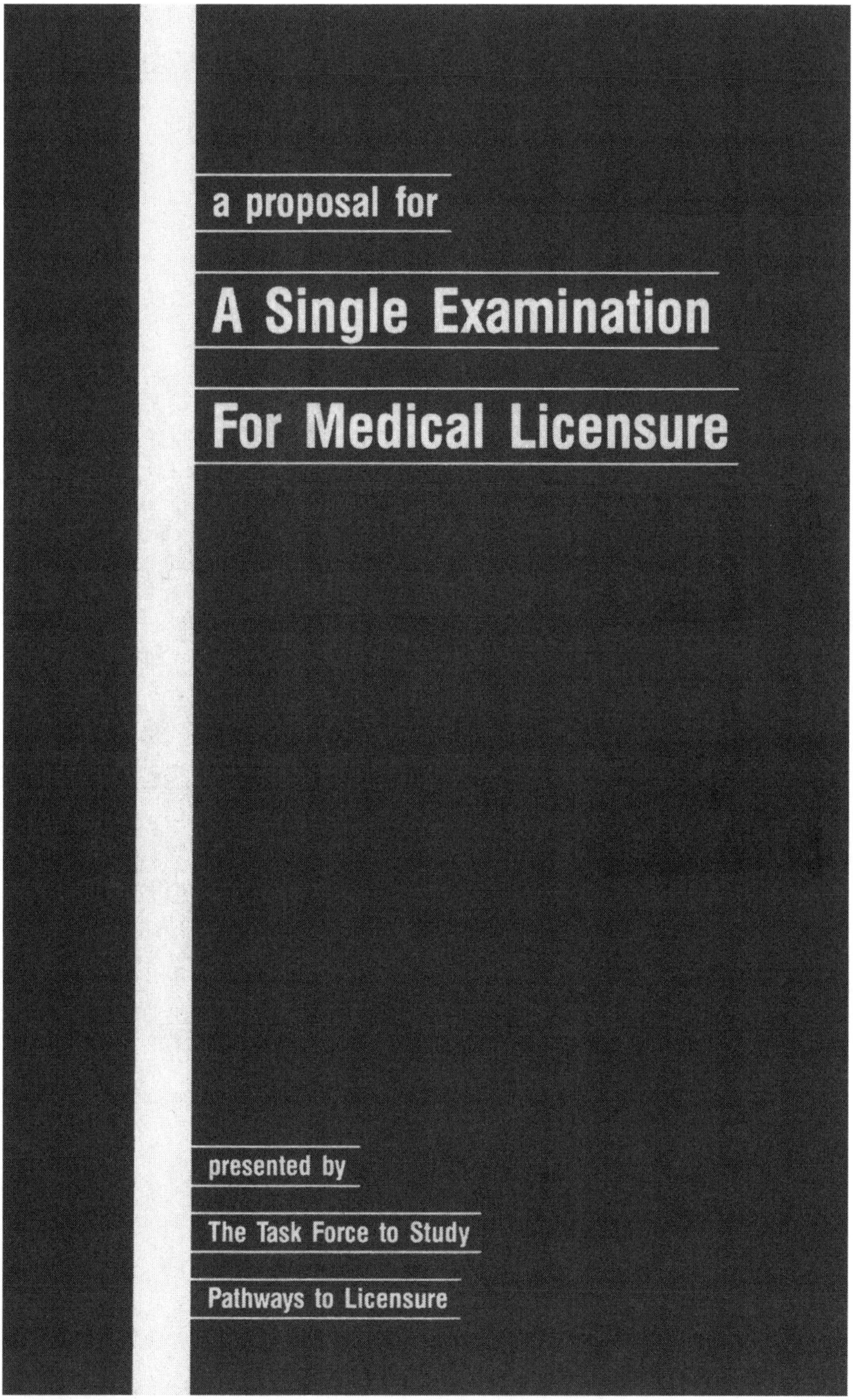

A 1989 task force recommended a single examination pathway for medical licensure that later culminated in the establishment of the United States Medical Licensing Examination® (USMLE®), a joint program of the FSMB and the National Board of Medical Examiners.

Image courtesy of the National Board of Medical Examiners.

The Federation's annual meeting convenes representatives from all the state medical boards in a House of Delegates that sets official policy for the organization. Pictured above is the 2010 meeting in Chicago.

Photo courtesy of the FSMB Archives.

Chapter 5

Walter Bierring and the Federation's Early Leadership

An institution is the lengthened shadow of one man.

—Ralph Waldo Emerson, *Self-Reliance,* 1841

As the year 1959 drew to a close, Walter L. Bierring, ninety-one years old and secretary-treasurer of the Federation as well as editor of its monthly *Bulletin* since 1915, had reached a decision. Plagued by failing health, he resolved to inform the Federation's executive committee of his intention to relinquish his duties effective with the organization's February 1960 meeting. After forty-six years, time and tide could no longer be stemmed. Bierring's resignation marked the final passing of a generation of early leadership at the Federation. In many ways, Bierring was akin to the "last leaf" memorialized by Oliver Wendell Holmes in his nostalgic ode to an elderly Revolutionary War soldier from his childhood. Bierring provided one of the last human links to the early era of medical regulation and leadership unique to the first decades of the twentieth century. This chapter considers Bierring's remarkable career and enduring legacy as well as that of other major leaders of the Federation and the American medical licensing community of that era.

In contemplating the evolution of America's state-based system of medical licensure from its modern origins in the late nineteenth century through the first half of the twentieth century, three distinctive features emerge as a generalized portrait of these physician medical regulators and the system they created. One of the more striking aspects was the longevity of service on the part of physicians like Bierring and his colleagues. Appointments to a state medical board, whether solely through the discretion of the governor or in concert with a state medical society, appear not to have been constrained by term limits in those days.[1] Walter Bierring's long tenure on Iowa's state medical board and then later as health commissioner were hardly unique. Nor was this tenured longevity a regional phenomenon. A few examples suffice to demonstrate the tenure of some of the key voices among state medical boards. Henry Fitzhugh served twenty-five years on the Maryland medical board—an impressive tenure and almost unprecedented by today's standards but one that pales next to that of many of his contemporaries of that era. Roy Harrison (Louisiana), Arthur McCormack (Kentucky), George Williamson (North Dakota), Thomas Crowe (Texas), William Scott Nay (Vermont), Charles Pinkham (California) and Beverly Drake Harrison (Michigan) all spent more than three decades on their respective state medical boards. Amazingly, Maine's Adam Leighton and Ohio's Herbert Platter enjoyed even longer tenures (forty years) on their boards.[2] The positive results of such extensive service were unmistakable. A generation of leaders, both at the state level and within the Federation, possessed a deep, intimate knowledge of the issues, problems and complexities faced by medical boards across the country. The relationships cultivated by these men in decades of service created a strong and tangible network of contacts at all levels, from local and regional to national, upon which they might draw for assistance. For example, a medical board seeking expertise in regulatory statutes had only to turn to the Michigan board's Beverly Harrison, a successful veteran of numerous contests with that state's legislature. A board struggling to establish administrative and procedural protocols for investigations and discipline knew that the California board secretary, Charles Pinkham, was perhaps the preeminent authority on such matters. Consequently, the relationships acquired through these long tenures and yearly gatherings at the Federation's business meeting proved invaluable. They provided the Federation and the individual state medical boards with a knowledge base and institutional memory that, while not quantifiable in the literal sense, returned dividends many times over.

Still, such longevity on the part of so many figures at the state and national level could represent a mixed blessing. It seems that many of these leaders were forceful, strong-willed individuals who by necessity had become adept at navigating the professional and political issues within their state. The resulting mix of professional success, firm convictions and long tenure could easily produce an element of rectitude within these leaders. This may have been at the heart of some of the criticism stemming from both within and outside the medical licensing community. As one critic noted, the combination of long tenure, influence with state legislators and "professional prestige" created decision-makers whose edicts carried a de facto "force of law" they did not always enjoy by the formal authority of their position.[3]

Robert Derbyshire, a former Federation president (1965–1966) and physician member of the New Mexico Medical Board, drafted one of the more insightful critiques of state medical boards in his 1969 book, *Medical Licensure and Discipline in the United States*. Derbyshire drew upon first-hand knowledge and acquaintance with the elder statesmen of medical licensing in the 1950s and the norms of this medical regulatory system. Derbyshire rightfully acknowledged the mixed blessing of long tenures for so many members of medical boards when he considered the two major functions of a board—licensing and discipline. For Derbyshire, the very longevity of its members that served state boards so well in working through disciplinary matters could also be a deficit when these same board members were required to examine young physician candidates who understandably were better versed in the latest medical knowledge—a situation ripe for criticism from younger physicians interacting with the licensing system for the first time.[4]

A second feature of the state-based licensure system was the apparent lack of diversity (by modern standards) in the leadership of the medical regulatory community at the time. Women and minorities were mostly absent from leadership positions within much of American society. Women constituted only 5 percent of all allopathic medical school graduates in 1905, and this figure rose to as high as 12 percent in 1949 before dipping to 7 percent in 1965. As one might expect, such relatively low numbers translated into an absence of women on medical boards. In some states, this absence persisted until fairly recently. For example, Louisiana did not have a female member on its medical board until 1992. A perusal of the Federation's officers and executive committee members over its first half century found solely male membership. As late as 1968, only one woman was serving on a state medical board (New Hampshire) in the United States.[5] According to Susan Behrens (Wisconsin), the first woman elected president of the Federation in 1989, only a handful of women joined her in a caucus of female members from state medical boards during a Federation annual meeting in the early 1980s. This contrasts markedly with the situation today, when a perusal of the 2011 *Federation Handbook* reveals that women constitute approximately 40 percent of state boards' membership. There was a similar paucity of racial and ethnic minorities. In his seminal 1910 report about undergraduate medical education, Abraham Flexner evaluated seven historically black medical schools, of which only two (Meharry and Howard) are still in existence. These seven schools produced only 1,253 graduates between 1908 and 1910. Another estimate placed the number of African-American physicians in the United States at fewer than 4,000 throughout the entire interwar period. Ironically, it may well have been the effectiveness of state medical boards in driving the remaining proprietary medical schools out of existence by 1930 that exacerbated such numbers. Setting aside questions of quality and effectiveness for the moment, these schools had provided a significant opportunity for women and minorities to access a medical education stretching back many years. In an 1890 *Report on Medical Education, Medical Colleges and the Regulation of the Practice of Medicine* by the Illinois Board of Health, it appears that at least one-third of all schools identified as open to both genders were homeopathic, eclectic or physio-medical schools. In the years after the Flexner Report, all but one of the extant women's medical colleges shut their doors along with several historically black medical schools.[6] In essence, the pool of prospective physicians that might have diversified medical boards shrank markedly.

Such small numbers and the multiple sociopolitical and cultural constraints characterizing all aspects of American society prior to the burgeoning Civil Rights movement of the 1950s greatly reduced the potential for African-American physicians to access positions of authority in medical regulation. Though definitive data are lacking for all state boards, it seems reasonable to accept not only Derbyshire's characterization of the typical medical board member (middle-aged, white male) but also that the mid-twentieth-century demographic reality he described was an extension of a pattern dating back to the modern origins of the medical licensure system in the late nineteenth century.

One other feature marked this early generation of leaders, though it was as often inferred as made explicit by word or action. State medical board and Federation leadership sometimes struggled to maintain an appropriate distance and distinction between their professional interests as physicians and their public protection role as members of state boards. That many of these men also held leadership positions within their professional societies further complicated matters; especially as the issues they confronted sometimes overlapped both the public and professional domains where the interests of each were not always in harmony. The challenges this posed were considerable. The deference generally shown physicians and the prestige enjoyed by the profession likely fostered a tendency to view the medical regulatory landscape through a professional rather than a public lens. Given this reality, the tendency on the part of some leaders to see the best interests of the profession as synonymous with the public interest becomes understandable. In part this tendency can be attributed to the paternalism inherent in the physician–patient relationship of the day. This paternalism manifested itself in multiple ways, starting with the fundamental issue of assessing physicians' qualifications for licensure. After all, who was better positioned than another physician to make this judgment? Such was clearly the view of Federation President Herbert Platter, who deemed it "the business of medical men to pass on [physicians'] qualifications," not the public.[7]

In the first half of the twentieth century, the notion of a lay role in medical regulation remained years away from acceptance.

In the first decades of the twentieth century, the very notion of *who* should be practicing medicine was contested ground where physicians, sitting as members of state medical boards, often saw their professional interests overridden. Most were adamant in their view that the successful inroads of the "irregular" practitioner or cultist stemmed from legislative persistence, deception and an uninformed public. While the "thinking public" might be extolled for its wisdom in recognizing and supporting the terrain staked out by the medical profession, distain for the willfully stubborn was equally clear—there would always be a "group that obstinately refuses to be saved."[8] That the public needed saving was an assumption apparently unquestioned by many physicians.

Federation and state board leaders were engaged in a balancing act of professional identify and public responsibility, neither of which could be ignored entirely in any given instance. However, the wide latitude of self-regulation bestowed upon the profession left its individual physicians particularly vulnerable to criticism when, as members of a state medical board, a decision or statement adhered too closely to professional, rather than public, interests. Any number of examples may be cited but one is characteristic. In the post–World War II era, the Minnesota medical board operated under a state law denying non–U.S. citizen physicians access to their licensing examination. When a displaced physician from Poland relocated to a small Minnesota town lacking a doctor, the medical board, hands tied by state law, denied the application for licensure. Undeterred, the town and the physician pushed ahead, gaining newspaper coverage and a meeting with the governor. The medical board knew immediately that public sentiment in the case sided with the refugee physician. Though legally in the right and sympathetic to the physician, the board witnessed firsthand how "safeguards . . . surround[ing] licensure" which were once acceptable to the public in the abstract, now struck a different chord in the reality of this particular situation—protectionism. This charge of protectionism was perhaps the most dogged criticism of the medical profession over much of this time period. The profession's vocal opposition to "socialized medicine" and state boards' unwillingness to consider a role for irregular practitioners, whom some termed "quacks" and "cults," lent credence to critics who questioned the ability of state board members to act with public rather than professional interests foremost in their mind. The Federation's leadership at the time might characterize the pursuit and prosecution of "irregular" practitioners as a "distasteful task" but this distaste was belied by the frequency and passion of the many articles and news items running in the *Bulletin* that covered the legal and legislative battles against chiropractors, osteopathic physicians and Christian Scientists in the first two decades of the Federation's existence.[9]

Federation President Harold Rypins might argue that state medical boards were unwise not to bear in mind the "interests of the medical profession" when making decisions with overall best interests of all parties in mind. Partisan critics, however, pounced on such statements to bolster their charges against the profession. Doing so, however, conveniently overlooks the definitive qualifier that Rypins and many other conscientious state board members applied as the standard for their decision-making. As Rypins sagely observed, a different standard must be applied:

> At times the point of view of the medical profession does not entirely coincide with the wisest public policy and on such occasions it is the duty of the state boards, after carefully considering the medical profession's point of view, to weigh with equal care the effect of their decisions upon the public, *and in case of doubt, to resolve the doubt in favor of the public.* [Italics added]

That such a distinction could seldom be cleanly achieved was the challenge faced by the Federation and a generation of state board leadership. That so many were willing to serve in what was becoming an increasingly thankless public service role speaks well for these individuals and their profession. Criticism comes easily to many, particularly in hindsight, when the sociopolitical and cultural norms of society have shifted. Suffice it to say that this generation of leadership genuinely believed that state medical boards could effectively serve both the public and the profession simultaneously.[10]

As noted in chapter 2, the Federation drew its earliest leadership from its two predecessor organizations, the National Confederation and the American Confederation. Consequently, during its early years the Federation enjoyed the luxury of leaders deeply versed in the issues inherent to medical regulation and familiar with the challenges of managing a national organization. Charles Cook, who served as Federation president from 1913 to 1916, led a contingent of National Confederation leaders who were shifted into positions as Federation officers and executive committee members at the time of its founding. Others included physicians Arthur Brown (Louisiana), P. H. Tatman (Arkansas), George Matson (Ohio), James Duncan (Ohio), and Charles Tuttle (Connecticut). Cook's tenure was marked by a mixture of pragmatism and aspiration. Some of Cook's extant correspondence reflects this balance, sometimes tempering his colleagues' enthusiasm for the "ideal"—whether in examinations, license reciprocity or the idea for a state board "bulletin"—with "practical" considerations. In this regard, Cook demonstrated an admirable ability to weigh issues as "abstract question[s]" without losing sight of the real-world ramifications of proposed solutions.[11] His private comments on the issue of license reciprocity reflect sensitivity to this balance of philosophy and pragmatism. Despite his overall strategic support for reciprocity initiatives, Cook evinced a savvy tactical awareness for contemporary legislation and case law in various states. Cook remained cognizant of these on-the-ground realities as factors that could not be ignored when pursuing larger strategic goals.

As Federation president, Cook moved cautiously to put the organization's best foot forward. This was especially true in his attempts to ensure positive impressions of the new organization. For example, Cook believed that the greatest value derived from careful, deliberative processes. The Federation was better served by the firm imprint resulting from a carefully chosen step than the churned ground of hasty actions and backtracking from untenable positions reached too quickly and without sufficient consideration. In the only one of his presidential addresses that survives, Cook assessed the prospects for greater uniformity in standards in state legislation, setting forth a two-stage approach: first having state medical boards reach a reasonable consensus on the "essentials" of a medical practice act and then mobilizing the profession and the public in a concerted legislative push. Ever the realist, he acknowledged and expected that the first stage alone would require several years of concerted effort by a special committee and outreach to all medical boards. Anything less, such as a rushed effort lacking consensus, would end as similar efforts had before with an "embalmed" document sitting idle and forgotten once the parties returned to their respective states.[12] A modern echo of this reasonable approach can be found in the words of Humayun Chaudhry, the Federation's current president and CEO, who has remarked publicly on the value of the Federation embarking on an "iterative" and "methodical" timeline, rather than a "shock to the system," for the advancement of its Maintenance of Licensure (MOL) initiative on behalf of state medical boards. (See chapter 8 for a detailed discussion.)

Cook also recognized the value of strong relationships with other organizations; he maneuvered (sometimes behind the scenes) to place individuals with collaborative temperaments as Federation representatives to organizations like the National Board of Medical Examiners. In an era when much of the business of governance was already hindered by the limited communication tools available, time lost in repairing the damage wrought by insufficiently tactful representatives was a luxury the Federation could not afford. A similar sensitivity to perceptions can be seen in Cook's concern for the Federation's relationship with the American Medical Association. During his tenure previously with the National Confederation, Cook heard the criticism leveled by some against the organization as one too closely linked to the AMA and specifically to its influential Council on Medical Education. In private correspondence with

Bierring from 1916, Cook cautioned that "great care must be exercised in managing the affairs of the Federation lest the feeling get a foothold that the Federation was too much under the control of the AMA, simply an appendance of the latter."[13]

Cook had particular interest in the Federation's *Bulletin* and its annual meeting program. Much of the success behind both stemmed from his strong grasp of the major issues, national and local, confronting state medical boards. Cook felt strongly that issues of *national* import were the appropriate content focus for both forums. In fact, he was not averse to proffering friendly advice to the editor of the *Federation Bulletin* encouraging that article submissions of narrowly local interest be declined, even when the submission in question originated with one of his colleagues on the Massachusetts board.[14]

A 1920 resolution adopted by the Federation membership memorialized his contributions this way:

> Dr. Cook accepted the office of President of the Federation at a time when there was lack of cooperation between the various boards of this country and allied organizations, and by his tact and perseverance succeeded in developing an earnest, aggressive and moral organization which has accomplished much good in elevating the standards of medical education and practice in this Union.[15]

Several contemporaries ably assisted Cook during his tenure. Among these was George H. Matson, secretary of the Ohio board beginning in 1906 and later active in the National Confederation. Matson was also a key negotiator in the talks that merged the National and American Confederations. Walter Bierring later characterized Matson as "instrumental in bringing about the union of the two confederations." His critical role is perhaps evidenced by his selection in 1912 as the first elected secretary-treasurer of the Federation. Matson appears to have been a quietly effective force, characterized as "modest and unassuming in his bearing, so that only those intimate with him know of his personal work and absolute reliability."[16]

Ironically enough, one of the more influential early leaders behind the Federation was not even a member of a state medical board. Nathan P. Colwell, longtime secretary of the AMA Council on Medical Education, was a charter "Fellow" of the Federation and a "potent influence" in the formulation of Federation policy, particularly in the area of standards for medical education. The practice of the licensing board organizations (first the National and American Confederations, then later the Federation) to meet in conjunction with the AMA and the AAMC in an Annual Congress on Medical Education and Licensure brought Colwell into early contact with colleagues in the medical licensing community. Colwell was held in such high regard that he was asked to assist in drawing up the Federation's constitution and bylaws. He was even credited, according to one source, with proposing the revised new name for the merged organization of the two confederations—the Federation of State Medical Boards of the United States. With the first issue of the *Federation Bulletin* in April 1915, he acted as a managing editor and continued in this service until his retirement a few years later. Colwell's long tenure as secretary of the AMA Council on Medical Education uniquely positioned him to provide input into Federation policy in this area, and even earlier with the National Confederation. In 1932, the Federation presented Colwell with a testimonial expressing the organization's appreciation for "his eminent services in the field of medical education and to the cause of medical licensure"—a fitting tribute for one of the eighteen original charter Fellows of the Federation.[17]

Among the leaders from the American Confederation, only Beverly Drake Harrison took a major leadership role within the Federation. One contemporary called him the "Father of Medical Legislation," an endearment that seems a not-unreasonable claim considering his early and long-standing efforts in that arena, both in Michigan and nationally. In the legislative act creating it, the Michigan board had authority to inspect and recognize (or refuse recognition to) U.S. medical schools as part of its decision-making powers for granting a license to practice medicine in that state. In 1903, the Michigan Board set standards for both premedical and medical education as part of its licensing requirements, which included graduation from a recognized medical college. In addition, the board required candidates meeting the educational requirements to pass a satisfactory examination before the board. In the words of one contemporary medical regulator, Michigan at that time "had a more advanced and practical method of recognizing and listing colleges than any other state." Its licensure standards "served as a model for other states, as well as national organizations concerned with medical education and licensure." Harrison and the Michigan Board were also on the forefront of medical license reciprocity, as evidenced by their signing one of the earliest reciprocity agreements with the Wisconsin Board in 1901. Harrison organized, and served as secretary for, the American Confederation of Reciprocating Examining and Licensing Boards. In this regard, the greatest contribution of the American Confederation was the adoption and promotion of principles involving reciprocal relations between states. Harrison served as a "committee of one," representing the American Confederation during negotiations leading to the founding of the Federation. After the merger, Harrison served as a member, and later chairman, of the Federation's Committee on Standardization of Medical Schools, continuing his long-standing work and interest in medical education and its relationship to medical licensure.[18]

The contributions of many others could be listed here. John Baldy parlayed his position on the Pennsylvania board with his physical proximity to the National Board offices in Philadelphia to provide a solid, long-term connection between the medical licensing community and the medical assessment organization that was founded in 1915. The New York board's Otto Huffman served as the first editor for Federation publications and secured valuable publicity for the organization with timely pieces that appeared in the *New York Times* in 1912.[19] Iowa board member Bierring joined the Federation in 1915 and, based upon extant correspondence, quickly became a confidante of President Cook.

Cook's successor, David Strickler (Colorado) provided an energetic element to the Federation. During his eight years as Federation president, the longest tenure of any elective president in the Federation's history, Strickler presided over a wealth of activity. Strickler's leadership relied heavily upon seeking direct input from the Federation's constituent state boards. In this way, he kept a finger on the pulse of the state medical boards and the issues drawing the bulk of their attention. For Strickler, these issues were license reciprocity / endorsement; annual registration; prosecution of illegal practitioners, and others. Several times during his tenure, Strickler dedicated his presidential address at the Federation's annual meeting to presenting the findings of his outreach efforts. In each instance, he blended recognition for the good work of individual boards with acknowledged missteps when collective action on the part of the medical licensing community failed to materialize. Thus, Strickler might laud boards for their successes in helping to secure higher standards for medical education and then call them to account for failure to report consistently to a central bureau housing information on medical frauds and impostors.[20]

Perhaps the most striking aspect of Strickler's tenure was his concern for the interrelationship of medical boards, the medical profession, the public and the various medical disciplines. As a self-described "sectarian," Strickler understood the fallout from the long history of tension marking the integration of homeopathic and eclectic physicians into the profession. The same public who had witnessed this earlier infighting within the profession turned a wary eye to the animus being expressed now against osteopaths, naturopaths and chiropractors. Strickler acknowledged that while the profession might tout legislation designed to curb unqualified practitioners as being "ostensibly in the interest of public health," a portion of the public saw this as little more than a rationalized economic attack on practitioners not yet incorporated into the fold. Strickler believed that these battles were inevitable no-win situations for state medical boards that only fueled further skepticism on the part of the public, making it even more difficult for boards to secure convictions against the most egregious medical offenders (i.e., outright frauds and charlatans). His conciliatory tone is striking for the time. Early in his tenure as Federation president, he asserted a belief that "no school of healing can attain any definite standing . . . without some basic element of truth underlying it." Strickler saw a counterproductive circle unfolding. He believed that too many within the profession and from their seats on state medical boards evinced a "vindictive spirit" more concerned with stamping out "medical heresy" than establishing fair and equitable educational standards for health practitioners. The profession needed a "more tolerant attitude" and willingness to explore therapeutic value "irrespective of its origin." Strickler's assessment found fault with the public, too. Their collective failure to appreciate the need for reasonable educational standards for those who would treat the sick and acquittal of "the most ignorant and blatant quacks" frustrated Strickler greatly. So much so that he once uncharacteristically observed, "Barnum certainly knew the American public"—a glancing reference to the legendary circus showman and scam artist.[21]

More characteristic of Strickler's approach was his suggested proposal for the creation of an independent commission composed of "capable scientists" to study the clinical results from various systems of healing which had gained public support. He recognized that the Federation lacked the resources for such an undertaking and, more importantly, even if these were readily available, such an effort must be conducted by impartial educators in order to avoid immediate protests of bias by adherents of the systems being examined. He appealed to the influential Carnegie Foundation and its president, Henry Pritchett, who had selected Flexner for the nationwide survey of medical schools, to support the effort but without success. Still, the magnanimity shown by Strickler and his willingness to open such a contentious area to insight with impartial evaluators spoke well for his leadership and that of others within the state board community. Cook and Strickler proved fortunate choices as the Federation's only two presidents during the organization's first twelve years. Looking back many years later, Bierring attributed the successes of the Federation's early period to the "good judgment and executive ability" of these thoughtful men.[22]

After Strickler stepped down as president in 1924, the office transitioned into an elective one limited to a single one-year term, a practice that still exists today but under a different title, chair of the Federation's board of directors. A succession of elective presidents transitioned through the office over the next thirty years, but two physician-leaders stand out, in particular—Charles Pinkham (California) and Harold Rypins (New York).

As secretary of the California board for thirty years and later Federation president from 1930 to 1931, Pinkham was among the more energetic physician regulators of his day. He published often and extensively within the pages of the *Federation Bulletin* on an impressive array of topics associated with licensure, in particular the disciplinary role of state medical boards. With the considerable resources of the investigative divisions of the California state medical board at his disposal, Pinkham vigorously tackled "quack specialists," diploma mills such as the Pacific Medical College, and physician impostors and frauds relying upon bogus credentials. He cooperated with federal authorities in campaigns that shut down the operation of a Pacific coast "abortion ring" and a nationwide group he colorfully labeled as "eyesight swindlers."[23] Though the titles of some of his articles bordered on the sensationalistic, Pinkham's writing arose from a deep concern and genuine outrage that patients, as well as members of the medical profession, were being victimized by unscrupulous individuals exploiting vulnerable areas of the medical regulatory system. Pinkham's thoughtful analyses of state boards' administrative procedures, first as chair of a Federation Special Committee on State Board Records and later through his own work in California, identified the licensing system's weak points while offering specific recommendations for closing these gaps. For example, detailed procedures requiring an applicant's photograph, handwriting sample and signature were proffered as a deterrent to "substitutes" sitting the licensing examination. Pinkham's detailed narrative expositions on the techniques used by physician impostors provided other boards with not merely cautionary tales but a roadmap for implementation of procedures to forestall these deceptions.[24]

Like his predecessor Charles Pinkham, Harold Rypins viewed the Federation and its role as primarily one of leadership—providing inspiration, assistance and resources to individual state medical boards. Both men understood well that the singular chorus of a united Federation membership carried greater weight than the multiple state board voices sounding similar but unharmonized notes. In his presidential address, Rypins expounded on the Federation's twofold role in leadership: first, assisting state boards in reaching consensus decisions, and then fostering implementation once policy had been set. He commended the assembled state boards on their collective wisdom in "voluntary withdrawal" from U.S. medical education oversight, leaving the field to the AAMC and the AMA Council on Medical Education. For Rypins, this voluntary withdrawal was not an abdication. The Federation still had to see the mission completed by urging its member boards "to use their legal authority to eliminate the grad[uate]s of low-standard medical schools from their examinations." At the time of his 1932 presidential address, Rypins was already deeply involved in an extensive survey effort, running from 1930 to 1935, of U.S. and Canadian medical schools being conducted by the AMA Council on Medical Education and the AAMC. In that capacity he served on multiple inspection site visits on behalf of the Federation. Rypins understood from firsthand experience that direct oversight of U.S. medical education had passed irrevocably into the hands of these organizations. State medical boards had provided a valuable function in this area previously but no longer. Finishing the job by tending to the remaining legislative details meant that the Federation could move to a more forward-looking, aspirational leadership role. With disciplinary and legislative matters as major concerns for state medical boards, the Federation must "anticipate and lead the way." Here Rypins could speak from direct experience. His experience in helping draft the 1926 New York Medical Practice Act underscored for Rypins the role of thoughtful medical regulatory leadership. Despite Rypins's accomplishments, he was perhaps best known to several generations of medical students as the author of *Medical State Board Examinations*, which passed through multiple editions under his guidance. After his death, Walter Bierring and a group of coeditors brought out the fifth through eighth editions of Rypins's text.[25]

THE CONTRIBUTIONS OF WALTER BIERRING

Over the course of its history, many gifted leaders served the Federation of State Medical Boards and the larger state medical board community. Some were recognized during their lifetime through the establishment of namesake events at the Federation's annual meeting. For instance, the Federation introduced the Platter Luncheon to commemorate the longtime secretary of the Ohio medical board, Herbert Platter. The Federation added the Galusha Lecture to its annual meeting program in honor of Bryant Galusha, former chair of the North Carolina medical board and the Federation's chief executive officer from 1984 to 1989. Other leaders created their own legacy by so immersing themselves in Federation activities as to be almost synonymous with them. This would include Ray Casterline, long-serving editor of the Federation *Bulletin*, and Frederick Merchant, the stalwart force behind what became the Federation Licensing Examination (FLEX). But in the long history of the Federation, one man stands tallest in nurturing and sustaining the organization through its first half century—Walter L. Bierring. In considering Bierring's long, multifaceted career, one feels a mixture of awe and humility: an awe that stems from the sheer length and breadth of the man's many interests and activities; and a sense of humility that arises almost involuntarily when contemplating our own efforts compared with those of the energetic Iowan whose pace rarely slackened over ninety-two years.

When writing about this remarkable man's life and work, one quickly realizes that his varied interests and career impacted many organizations. While today he is best known for his long association with the Federation, during his lifetime many groups and organizations rightfully claimed Bierring as one of their own. In order to do full justice to Bierring's legacy, any biographical sketch must touch upon all aspects of his long career. This seems only fair. The Federation may rightly claim pride, but not exclusivity, in honoring the man considered by most as integral to the organization's first half century.

In many ways, Bierring's life and career offer the classic American success story. Born in Davenport, Iowa, in 1868 to immigrant Danish parents, Bierring's childhood closely resembled that of many Midwestern youth: immigrant family connections with Europe, a first job hawking the city newspaper and a fondness for the fledgling American pastime, baseball. It seems that the young Bierring possessed a mild entrepreneurial streak, as evidenced by his enrollment in a local business college and a talent for penmanship which he cultivated as a means for underwriting his school costs. The beautiful penmanship evident in his signature allowed him to earn extra money ornamenting scrolls and writing elaborately flourished renditions of people's names. Despite the many activities and roles he assumed over his lifetime, Bierring must have enjoyed this simple artistry. Over the many years that he served as president of Alpha Omega Alpha, the national honor society for medical students, residents, scientists and physicians, he insisted upon personally signing the certificate of each new member of AΩA with his beautiful and distinctive signature.[26]

An early turning point in Bierring's life occurred at the age of fourteen. A portion of one foot was crushed when Bierring was caught standing too close to a moving train. A period of extensive treatment by two local physicians followed. This proved important as they later encouraged their young patient to consider a career in medicine. The young man was less fortunate in regard to the injured limb. Years later a cancerous growth necessitated amputation of first the foot, in 1902, and then four years later the entire leg just above the knee. These setbacks did little to slow Bierring down, however. Instead, they appear to have strengthened his character with an affinity for hard work and mental activity. Bierring himself appeared to understand and appreciate the impact of the injury upon his character. When asked later in life what he might have done with two good legs, he responded, "I wouldn't have done as well."[27]

In 1889, Bierring matriculated at the State University of Iowa College of Medicine. His talents and intellect then quickly brought him to the attention of the school's faculty, particularly Thomas MacBride and Lawrence Littig. By the end of his first year, Bierring was acting as an assistant demonstrator for anatomy. After his second year, he worked directly with

MacBride in the nascent field of bacteriology. It was Littig, however, who proved most influential, providing a professional model for Bierring. The young faculty member mentored Bierring with an eye to placing him at the head of a newly created department of pathology and bacteriology. Upon graduation, Bierring replicated Littig's educational experience by immediately embarking upon a two-year course of study in Europe preparatory to his return to the faculty at Iowa City. Bierring was hardly alone in such educational excursions, as an estimated 15,000 American physicians continued their studies in Germany between 1870 and 1914.[28]

Bierring's facility with languages ably assisted him from 1892 to 1894, starting first at the University of Heidelberg, then moving on to the University of Vienna and finally, the Pasteur Institute in Paris. Many years later, he spoke glowingly of this European training when he enjoyed the opportunity to learn firsthand from Louis Pasteur, Theodore Billroth and others. He embraced the scientific research shedding first light on the underlying mechanisms of disease that were making possible true therapeutics in medicine. Bierring eagerly returned to Europe, in 1896 and again in 1901, to continue studies for short periods in London, Paris, Prague, Berlin and Vienna. Upon his return in 1894 from his first foray to Europe, Bierring took up his faculty position and applied the principles he learned in Paris. This included his preparing the first diphtheria antitoxin west of New York City.[29]

These were exciting times for young physicians interested in medical research and study in Europe. Medicine had entered a new era, focused increasingly on scientific inquiry, and moving rapidly to build upon the recent successes in identifying the source of contagion with commensurate diagnostic and treatment options. Thus, in 1895 the German physicist Wilhelm Röntgen, baffled by the mysterious light rays he elicited while studying luminescence by cathode ray tubes, applied a mathematical symbol to an unknown quantity: X-rays. At the Prussian institute eventually named for Robert Koch (who isolated the organisms that cause anthrax, tuberculosis and cholera, and who is credited with definitively proving the germ theory of disease) it was still not clear in the 1890s as to the precise method by which bacteria caused disease or the method by which antitoxins of the type Bierring prepared actually worked. Though bacteria were first observed in 1676 by Dutch scientist van Leeuwenhoek using a single-lens microscope of his own design, it wasn't until 1909 that German scientist Paul Ehrlich developed the world's first antibiotic, a chemotherapeutic agent he called Salvarsan 606 (arsphenamine) that he termed a "magic bullet" against syphilis because it neutralized, or poisoned, the infecting agent without harming the patient. Ehrlich's pioneering work, and Koch's revolutionary elucidation of the "postulates" required for infectious disease transmission, would ultimately save many thousands of lives and usher in a race to find a chemical cure for each of the world's major infectious diseases.[30]

Bierring had been exposed to some of the best minds in medicine and cherished his educational and training experiences in America and abroad. Undoubtedly, they cultivated in Bierring a more "worldly and cosmopolitan" outlook than may have been the case for many of his contemporaries, whose background and experiences lacked the broad exposure to other cultures that Bierring enjoyed. At a time before the Internet shrank the world to a flat global village, Bierring embraced the growing interconnectedness of modern life that demanded more than "simplistic solutions" and provincial worldviews. One senses this worldly outlook was also behind his innate empathy for the hurdles facing international medical graduates, based in part upon his own experiences in Europe.[31]

In retrospect, one perceives the seed of a positive attribute frequently ascribed to Bierring later in life—his patience and willingness to assist younger colleagues. Several writers commented upon this quality, including one identified only as "E.R.C.W." in the *British Medical Journal,* who cited Bierring's "relationship with young colleagues to whom he devoted time and trouble unstintedly."[32] Younger physicians and colleagues just entering the field of medical regulation frequently commented upon Bierring's generosity and the sincerity of his interest in their careers. As one writer stated, Bierring seemed "genuinely happy to see me" despite the many demands upon his time and person coming from so many quarters. This nurturing of younger colleagues is perhaps best exemplified in a story shared by a Davenport, Iowa, physician. A fire that destroyed one of the medical buildings also claimed this future physician's pathological specimen collection integral to his Master's thesis. Having had the opportunity to review the student's collection recently, Bierring, unprompted, went before the faculty committee vouching for the quality of the lost collection.[33] It would seem that the mentoring from older physicians that Bierring benefited from, first as a patient and later as a student (both in the United States and abroad), was repaid many times over as his career progressed.

One also sees the early signs of a quality of intellectual curiosity that persisted with Bierring throughout his life. A Bierring bibliography published in 1957 by the Iowa State Medical Society listed 194 separate published monographs. The writings cover a broad range of topics: medicine, health policy, licensing, and others. Though trained in general medicine during the nineteenth century, he closely followed developments in more specialized areas, such as geriatrics, as they unfolded in the twentieth century. In this regard, it was apt that he quoted Pasteur, who said, "chance favors only the mind that is prepared."[34] Perhaps just as important, Bierring represented a mind not only prepared to take advantage of opportunities but one *receptive* and eager to act upon those opportunities.

Upon his return to the United States in 1894, Bierring commenced what one writer described as the first of several careers—medical educator. He remained on the faculty at the University of Iowa College of Medicine until 1910, first as a professor of pathology and bacteriology (1894–1903) and then as a professor in the theory and practice of medicine (1903–1910). He held a similar position at Drake University's School of Medicine, in Des Moines, from 1910 to 1914. Bierring's tenure at the University of Iowa ended prematurely and unexpectedly. The 1910 issuance of Flexner's widely anticipated report on medical education in the United States carried a stinging assessment of many medical schools, particularly a number of those in the western part of the country. Flexner's preliminary report on the Iowa College's clinical instruction sent University of Iowa officials scrambling to salvage the medical school and the funding stream that flowed from the Carnegie Foundation. The price for salvaging the school of medicine turned out to be the forced resignation of Bierring, then serving as hospital director and vice dean, from his leadership positions. Institutional politics, personal relationships and Bierring's part-time position and private practice combined to make him the easiest target for assuaging external criticism.[35]

Bierring quickly transitioned onto the faculty of Drake University's School of Medicine. Ironically, the ripple effects of the Flexnerian "revolution" in medical education followed him there, as well. Drake had fared even worse than the state university in Flexner's final report, with the clinical instruction described as inadequate and funding characterized as insufficient for first-class instruction. By 1913, political and economic forces combined to close the school through a merger with the University of Iowa College of Medicine.[36] With the merger, Bierring's first career as a medical educator came to a close.

During the next twenty years, from 1913 through 1933, Bierring maintained a busy practice in Des Moines while his professional interests expanded into public health and medical regulation. Almost simultaneous to the door closing on his career as a medical educator, another opened for him as the first president of the newly reorganized Iowa State Board of Health and Medical Examiners. He served in this capacity from 1913 until 1921. It was during this time that Bierring first became actively involved with the Federation. Indeed, as a regular attendee of the AMA's annual meetings since 1899, Bierring was well positioned to observe the nascent FSMB even before its birth. Recall that both of the FSMB's predecessor organizations met in conjunction with the annual meeting of the AMA and discussions leading to their merger were common talk and speculation in the years prior to the Federation's establishment. Bierring joined the FSMB executive committee in 1913 and two years later assumed the position of secretary-editor (Federation *Bulletin*)—a position he subsequently, and remarkably, held for nearly fifty years.[37]

Bierring's career blended long service, as the appointed health commissioner for the state of Iowa from 1933 to 1953, with a burgeoning role as "medical statesman." He was an early advocate and staunch supporter of the National Board of Medical Examiners and its program of voluntary certification. Beginning in 1916 he spent twenty-seven years as a member of the NBME, including a two-year term as its president, in 1931, while still employed by the Federation. His twin interests in assessment and licensing paid dividends internationally when he joined a National Board delegation visiting Europe in 1918. Bierring assisted the delegation in securing reciprocal relations between the National Board and Britain's Conjoint and Triple Qualification Boards. When one adds to this list his long participation with the AMA (serving as its president, from 1934 to 1935), his early involvement with the American Board of Internal Medicine and the American Board of Preventive Medicine (holder of certificate #1 for both boards), and his presidency of Alpha Omega Alpha, it is difficult to imagine how one lifetime contained enough hours for this whirlwind of activity. Clearly, Bierring reflects a bygone generation of joiners and activists whose days were filled with social, civic and professional duties.[38]

On occasion, this medical statesman role placed Bierring directly in a national spotlight. President Franklin Roosevelt's proposed Economic Security Bill brought Bierring into a national political dialogue touching upon compulsory employment taxes to support an economic safety net for the aged and national health insurance. As a member of the medical advisory committee to the President's Council on Economic Security, Bierring was drawn into the intense dialogue around proposals that would include old age compulsory contributions to social insurance and national health insurance. Though the final legislation (renamed the Social Security Act) dropped all reference to national health insurance in the face of strong opposition from the AMA, legislators used committee hearings, such as those in which Bierring testified, to demonstrate clearly both the need for removal of this issue from the final bill and their own personal disposition on the issue.[39] The exchange between Bierring and Robert Doughton, chairman of the powerful U.S. House Ways and Means Committee and Democratic Congressman from North Carolina, is telling. Though the bulk of Bierring's testimony and comments dealt with public health issues addressed in Title VI of the final bill, the chairman also sought a clear statement from Bierring on Title VIII, dealing with employment taxes funding benefits to the aged, dependent children, and so on. The chairman queried Bierring about the legislation and any potential for it leading to the "regimentation" of medicine and infringement upon the physician's "right to charge fees and to enjoy an individual practice."

> *Chairman Doughton*: Is there any such apprehension in your mind?
>
> *Dr. Bierring*: No, sir.
>
> *Chairman Doughton*: You . . . are opposed to any interference with the traditional ethical practice of the medical profession as it is known today, are you not?
>
> *Dr. Bierring*: I am, sir; yes, sir.
>
> *Chairman Doughton*: I just want that as a matter of record because . . . legislation of this sort should not be made an entering wedge toward possible regimentation. I wanted to get your view point.
>
> *Dr. Bierring*: I do not think there is any fear of that, because this is entirely within the line of preventive medicine.
>
> *Chairman Doughton*: We are going to find it necessary to use quite a number of medical men in connection with it, in the supervision of crippled and needy children, and it was in connection with that I was first apprised that the medical men throughout the country were of the impression there are possibilities in this bill which may lead to regimentation of the medical profession, ultimately engulfing them all.
>
> *Dr. Bierring*: I am sure there is not, in Title VIII.[40]

Bierring's testimony and comments are not surprising given that he was called to testify based upon his position as the AMA president. Whether they reflected his personal beliefs, as well, is less certain.[41]

Bierring's contributions to the Federation were numerous but some were so obvious that they might easily be passed over without adequately appreciating their significance. One can marvel at the length of Bierring's tenure in doing the business of the Federation and in doing so miss just how critical his role proved. Those unacquainted with the Federation's history might observe the organization today—nearly 200 employees; offices in Texas and Washington, D.C.; multimillion-dollar annual budgets—and fail to appreciate that none of this existed during Bierring's tenure with the organization. It is important to remember that the organization possessed little in the way of funds and lacked a dedicated office and staff. Its work as a national organization involved members dispersed around the country, in an era when telegrams, first-class mail and expensive long-distance telephone calls were the height of business communications technology. Indeed, much of the work of the organization during the period 1915–1961 took place at Bierring's home in Des Moines. With no independent income stream beyond the modest membership dues assigned to each member board, the Federation received critical financial assistance from the AMA for many years. Here, too, the quiet diplomacy of Bierring proved critical to maintaining and protecting this important financial relationship.

Additionally, the interpersonal relationships that Bierring cultivated throughout the house of medicine over his many years of service proved invaluable to sustaining the Federation during much of its first half-century. Indeed, it is the personal aspects of Bierring that strike the reader perusing the many tributes at the time of his retirement from Federation activities and later upon his death. As a leader, he evinced the qualities (modest, self-effacing, and understated) identified in recent years by business consultant Jim Collins, in *Good to Great,* as the characteristics of CEOs at the most successful Fortune 500 companies. These leadership qualities were evident very early to Bierring's contemporaries and deemed, by at least one, as critical to the ultimate success of the Federation. In a 1916 letter, Federation President Charles Cook stated unequivocally his belief that Bierring was the key to the organization's future success:

> The future of the Federation, as I see it, is today largely in your hands. You are the one above all others, holding an official position in it, who knows its past history, the pitfalls to be avoided, the problems to be solved, the lines of work to be taken up, the danger of its being over-shadowed by other organizations, etc.[42]

With so much that was unavailable to the Federation in its first half-century—full-time staff, permanent home office, strong revenue stream—intangibles such as leadership were all the more critical to sustaining the organization. In this regard, Bierring stands foremost among the early Federation leadership. Yet simply stating that Bierring's leadership proved critical to the organization's success does little to explain how and why he proved so effective. Here it is important to identify those qualities in Bierring which so resonated with others that often their positive impression of the man extended to a favorable disposition toward the organization. Robert Derbyshire, the author of *Medical Licensure and Discipline in the United States* and an acquaintance of Bierring, offered a pithy assessment of the man and his leadership. Derbyshire described Bierring as a "quiet diplomat" who led the Federation with an "iron hand in a velvet glove." What is most striking in reading others' assessment of Bierring is the extent to which the velvet overshadowed the iron. Observers of Bierring commented favorably upon the man's temperament, describing him as a "wise counselor" exhibiting "careful and knowledgeable judgment" while avoiding "hasty decisions." His personal style combined grace, charm, and intelligence with a penchant for what the business and management literature today would describe as consensus building and facilitation. This trait exhibited itself in behaviors that one contemporary described as "always constructive, never destructive."[43]

Another aspect of Bierring's leadership was his consistent willingness to share credit and recognize the contributions of others. While Bierring may have been the heart of the organization during its first half-century, he would never have acknowledged such an accolade without recognizing the contributions of the many early leaders in the history of the Federation. Indeed, over the years, he wrote glowingly of the contributions of his many colleagues and contemporaries in the early history of the Federation, penning a series of laudatory articles about the Federation's early leaders and their service to the Federation and medical licensure.[44]

Perhaps most critical to Bierring's success on behalf of the Federation was his flexibility and receptiveness to new ideas. In an undated newspaper interview, Bierring once responded to a question about his longevity by stating, "I think we inherit certain characteristics and some of us just wear better than others. One thing is important though—the ability to adjust yourself to live with your limitations." While it is clear that Bierring had the physical aspects of life in mind, his response holds equally true for his mental outlook. Bierring's colleagues commented often upon his brilliant memory, intelligence and adaptability to advances in medicine and the changing landscape of medical regulation. His memory dazzled audiences at the Federation's annual meeting when this gifted speaker offered introductions and recognized honored guests and members of the audience with unscripted comments and remarks that displayed an impressive memory of people and events (both major and minor) spanning more than a half-century.[45]

Criticisms of Bierring and his leadership in medical regulation are virtually nonexistent. This is particularly surprising given the breadth of his involvement over many decades with multiple organizations, some of which, such as the Federation and the AMA, have had politicized processes for electing their leadership. Such political realms seldom see individual success without triggering at least some resentment or opposition. Yet this seems largely absent from contemporary views of Bierring. Even those criticisms acknowledging the man's flaws were often little more than compliments in disguise, as evidenced by the colleague who stated, "he was too kind and too generous to his friends." Or in other instances, the criticism was tempered by the saving grace of his personality and temperament. Thus, a perceived tendency very late in life to adhere to the status quo was offset by his gentlemanly manner of conducting business. Indeed, one writer characterized Bierring as handling the Federation much like a "gentlemen's club" in the old-fashioned sense of collegial working relationships. In hindsight, such a description is also apt as a reflection of the lack of diversity in both medicine and the Federation at the time. In this regard, Bierring undoubtedly carried the views and perhaps an element of the paternalism so characteristic of many Americans, and of the house of medicine in particular, in those days. Perhaps the harshest implied criticism is found in Eric Kohler's 1989 assessment of state medical boards' reluctance to license European refugee physicians fleeing Nazi Germany and occupied Europe. Kohler looked closely at the role of various leaders in medical regulation (Bierring, Charles Pinkham, Harold Rypins, and Herbert Platter) in dealing with refugee physicians. Bierring's tenure as AMA president coincided with that organization's campaign discouraging the licensing of international medical graduates.[46]

Ultimately, such criticisms tend to fade into the background when one considers the entire body of work encompassing Bierring's career. The many laudatory descriptions ("a living legend") and fond nicknames ("Sir Walter") come close to capturing the essence of the man and his contributions. That he was able to accept these honors and accolades without succumbing to hubris and a sense of his own "infallibility" is greatly to his credit.[47] Perhaps his greatest contribution to the Federation may simply have been that of the steady hand on the tiller over a prolonged period of time. His stabilizing influence was not lost upon the succession of the Federation's elected presidents whom he assisted over many decades. In 1934, G. M. Williamson noted that "so long as he [Bierring] consents to remain . . . the work of a president is very easy." A later Federation president, Earle Johnson, acknowledged that Bierring "had made the Federation what it is today." More than thirty years after his death, a later Iowa board member, Hormoz Rassekh, invoked the "spirit" of Bierring in his inaugural address as the Federation's elected president. Rassekh cited the qualities of inclusiveness and teamwork that Bierring exemplified as the guiding philosophy for his tenure. It is not straining credibility too much to say that the organization might not have survived at all had it not been for the efforts of Bierring. Perhaps former FSMB President Harold Jervey said it best: "the most fitting and lasting tribute to Dr. Bierring is the Federation itself. This is his true testimonial . . . he has laid the foundation and it is up to us to build and carry on."[48]

NOTES

1. Derbyshire, *Medical Licensure and Discipline,* 41.
2. Walter Bierring, "Nestors in Medical Licensure Service, Part I," *Federation Bulletin* 44 (December 1957): 356–60, 363–64; Walter Bierring, "Nestors in Medical Licensure Service, Part II," *Federation Bulletin* 45 (January 1958): 16–18, 20–24; Walter L. Bierring, "Dr. Beverly Drake Harrison: An Appreciation," *Federation Bulletin* 10 (December 1924): 307–10.
3. Kohler, "Relicensing Central European Refugee Physicians," 8.
4. Derbyshire, *Medical Licensure and Discipline,* 42.

5. "Women in Medicine History," American Medical Association, accessed January 13, 2012, http://www.ama-assn.org/ama/pub/about-ama/our-people/member-groups-sections/women-physicians-congress/statistics-history/women-medicine-history.shtml; "First Woman on Louisiana Board," *Federation NewsLine* (January 1993); Derbyshire, *Medical Licensure and Discipline*, 44.

6. Louis W. Sullivan and Ilana Suez-Mittman, "The State of Diversity in the Health Professions a Century After Flexner," *Academic Medicine* 85 (February 2010): 247; John H. Rauch, *Report on Medical Education, Medical Colleges and the Regulation of the Practice of Medicine in the United States and Canada, 1765–1890* (Springfield: H. W. Rokker, Printer and Binder, 1890), 159–160; Duffy, *Humors to Medical Science*, 308; Ludmerer, *Learning to Heal*, 245–48.

7. Herbert M. Platter, "President's Address," *Federation Bulletin* 16 (March 1930): 79.

8. Charles Pinkham, "President's Address," *Federation Bulletin* 17 (March 1931): 53.

9. Earle Johnson, "Presidential Address," *Federation Bulletin* 35 (March 1949): 69–70; J. W. Bowers, "Address of the President," *Federation Bulletin* 24 (March 1938): 74; Platter, "President's Address," 78.

10. Harold Rypins, "President's Address," *Federation Bulletin* 18 (February 1932): 43; Charles L. Shafer, "The Role of a State Board Today," *Federation Bulletin* 38 (March 1952): 78.

11. Matson,"Report of the FSMB Secretary," 25 February 1913, FSMB Archives; Charles H. Cook to James A. Duncan, 20 June 1911, FSMB Archives, Euless, Texas.

12. Charles Cook, "The President's Address," *Quarterly of the Federation of State Medical Boards* 1 (April 1914): 212.

13. Charles Cook to Walter Bierring, April 26, 1916, and June 8, 1916, FSMB Archives, Euless, Texas.

14. Charles Cook to Walter Bierring, June 21, 1916, FSMB Archives, Euless, Texas.

15. "Dr. Charles H. Cook," *Federation Bulletin* 6 (January 1920): 6–8; "Report of the Committee on the Death of Dr. Cook," *Federation Bulletin* 6 (March 1920): 67.

16. "Dr. George H. Matson," *Federation Bulletin* 3 (September 1917): 154; "National Confederation of State Boards," *JAMA* 58 (February 10, 1912): 432–33.

17. "Nathan Porter Colwell, M.D., 1870–1936," *Federation Bulletin* 22 (January 1936): 1–2; "Dr. Colwell on the Editorial Staff," *Federation Bulletin* 4 (March 1918): 50; "Deaths - Nathan Porter Colwell," *JAMA* 106 (January 18, 1936): 231; Walter Bierring, "The First Decade of Federation Activities," *Federation Bulletin* 9 (March 1923): 60.

18. Bierring, "Nestors in Licensure, Part II," 22–24; Bierring, "Beverly Drake Harrison," 307–310. See also, "Beverly Drake Harrison," *The City of Detroit Michigan, 1801–1922* vol. 4 (Detroit: S. J. Clarke, 1922): 354–58; "Beverly Drake Harrison," *JAMA* 83 (December 13, 1924): 1940.

19. Otto Huffman, "Control of Healing: State Medical Boards Get Together to Raise Standards," *New York Times*, July 10, 1913.

20. David Strickler, "President's Address," *Federation Bulletin* 4 (February 1918): 30; David. Strickler, "President's Address," *Federation Bulletin* 5 (March 1919): 61; David Strickler, "Drifting," *Federation Bulletin* 8 (February 1922): 32.

21. David Strickler, "The Problem of Medical Cults," *Federation Bulletin* 3 (March 1917): 72; Strickler, "President's Address" from 1919, 60; David Strickler, "Coordination of Effort in Medical Licensure," *Federation Bulletin* 10 (March 1920): 55, 59.

22. Strickler, "President's Address" from 1918, 34; David A. Strickler, "The Truth in Healing," *Federation Bulletin* 9 (March 1923): 65; Bierring, "Nestors in Licensure, Part II," 17–18.

23. "After Thirty Years Service," *Federation Bulletin* 29 (April 1943): 98; Charles Pinkham, "The Pacific Coast Abortion Ring," *Federation Bulletin* 23 (February 1937): 36; Charles Pinkham, "Eyesight Swindlers," *Federation Bulletin* 15 (November 1929): 362; Charles Pinkham, "Eyesight Swindlers, Second Edition," *Federation Bulletin* 19 (February 1933): 46.

24. "State Board Records and Office Details," *Federation Bulletin* 9 (May 1923): 114; "Applicant's Record Card," *Federation Bulletin* 9 (January 1923): 13; "Safeguards Against Imposition in State Board Examinations," *Federation Bulletin* 7 (May 1921): 178; "Safeguarding State Board Records," *Federation Bulletin* 8 (July 1927): 198.

25. Harold Rypins, "The Place of the Federation," *Federation Bulletin* 18 (February 1932): 41–43; Bierring, "Nestors in Licensure, Part II," 19–20.

26. "Memorial Tributes: Walter Lawrence Bierring, M.D., 1868–1961," *Pharos* (July 1961): 185–186; "Walter Lawrence Bierring, M.D.," *West Virginia Medical Journal* 57 (August 1961): 287; Harold E. Jervey Jr., M.D., "Walter Lawrence Bierring (1868–1961)," *Federation Bulletin* 60 (April 1973): 128; Daniel J. Glomset, "Recollections of Walter Lawrence Bierring, M.D.," *Journal of the Iowa State Medical Society* 47 (August 1957): 478; "Walter Lawrence Bierring, President of the Alpha Omega Alpha," *Pharos* 6 (June 1943): 4.

27. "Bierring, 92, Dies; Famed Iowa Doctor," *Des Moines Register*, June 26, 1961.

28. Fred Sternagel, "The Pilot of Iowa's Public Health," *Journal of the Iowa State Medical Society* 47 (August 1957): 480; Lee Anderson and Lewis January, "Walter Bierring and the Flexner Revolution: At the University of Iowa College of Medicine," *Pharos* (Winter 1992): 9; Thomas N. Bonner, *American Doctors and German Universities: A Chapter in International Intellectual Relations, 1870–1914* (Lincoln: University of Nebraska Press, 1963), 23.

29. Anderson and January, "Bierring and the Flexner Revolution," 9–10; William B. Bean, "An Appreciation: Walter L. Bierring, M.D.," *Pharos* (October 1961): 226–27; Walter L. Bierring, "Medical Echoes," *Pharos* (April 1950): 2–5.

30. Strathern, *Medicine from Hippocrates to Gene Therapy*, 312–36.

31. Hormoz Rassekh, "In the Spirit of Walter Bierring," *Federation Bulletin* 80, no. 2 (Summer 1993): 75–76.

32. "Walter L. Bierring, M.D., Hon. F.R.C.P. Edin., F.A.C.P." *British Medical Journal* (August 12, 1961): 459.

33. J. Murray Kinsman, "Walter L. Bierring, M.D.," *Federation Bulletin* 48 (October 1961): 302; Gordon F. Harkness, "Walter L. Bierring, M.D.," *Federation Bulletin* 48 (October 1961): 297.

34. Walter L. Bierring, "Chance Favors Only the Mind Which Is Prepared," *Pharos* (October 1958): 39.

35. Derbyshire, *Medical Licensure and Discipline*, 46; Anderson and January, "Bierring and the Flexner Revolution," 9–12. See also Lee Anderson, *Internal Medicine and the Structures of Modern Medical Science: The University of Iowa, 1870–1990* (Ames: Iowa State University Press, 1996), and Susan C. Lawrence, "Iowa Physicians: Legitimacy, Institutions, and the Practice of Medicine. Part Two: Putting Science into Practice, 1887–1928," *Annals of Iowa* 62 (Winter 2004).

36. Flexner, *Medical Education in United States*, 222; "Drake University and Medical Education," *JAMA* 55 (April 23, 1910): 1381; D. S. Fairchild, "The History of Medicine in Iowa—Part 5: The Iowa College of Physicians and Surgeons of Des Moines and the Medical Department of Drake University," *Journal of the Iowa State Medical Society*, 1927.

37. Walter L. Bierring, "Medical Licensure in Iowa, 1886–1961," *Federation Bulletin* 48 (March 1961): 71; "Career Spans Progress from Leeches to Missiles," *AMA News*, July 13, 1959; Walter L. Bierring, "The First Decade of Federation Activities," *Federation Bulletin* 9 (March 1923): 58–59.

38. Derbyshire, *Medical Licensure*, 46–48.

39. "Social Security History: 1935 Administration Economic Security," accessed on January 13, 2012, http://www.ssa.gov/history/fdrbill.html; "Universal Coverage: The Elusive Quest for National Health Insurance," Timothy G. Ferris review of Rick Mayes's *Conversations in Medicine and Society* in *JAMA* 294 (September 28, 2005): 1556–57.

40. *Economic Security Act: Hearings before the Committee on Ways and Means, House of Representatives* (Washington, D.C.: U.S. Government Printing Office, 1935), 649.

41. For a more detailed look at this New Deal era attempt at national health insurance, see also Daniel S. Hirschfield, *The Lost Reform: The Campaign for Compulsory Health Insurance in the United States from 1932–1943* (Cambridge: Harvard University Press, 1970), and Jaap Kooijman, "'Just Forget About It': FDR's Ambivalence Toward National Health Insurance," in Robert Garson, ed., *The Roosevelt Years: New Perspectives on American History 1933–1945* (Edinburgh: Edinburgh University Press, 1999).

42. Cook to Bierring, 26 April 1916, FSMB Archives.

43. Derbyshire, *Medical Licensure and Discipline*, 48; D. G. Gill, "Walter L. Bierring, M.D.," *Federation Bulletin* 48 (October 1961): 295; C.L. Wilbar Jr., "Walter L. Bierring, M.D.," *Federation Bulletin* 48 (October 1961): 313; Lee Forrest Hill, "Walter L. Bierring, M.D.," *Federation Bulletin* 48 (October 1961): 299.

44. Bierring, "Nestors in Licensure, Part I," 363–64; Bierring, "Nestors in Licensure, Part II," 22–24.

45. F. J. L. Blasingame, "Walter L. Bierring, M.D.," *Federation Bulletin* 48 (October 1961): 293.

46. Kohler, "Relicensing Central European Refugee Physicians," 8.

47. G. M. Williamson, "Address of the President," *Federation Bulletin* 20 (March 1934): 74; Earle Johnson, "Presidential Address," *Federation Bulletin* 35 (March 1949): 67; William B. Bean, "Walter L. Bierring, M.D.," *Federation Bulletin* 48 (October 1961): 290; George Packer Berry, "Walter L. Bierring, M.D.," *Federation Bulletin* 48 (October 1961): 291; K. D. Graves, "Walter L. Bierring, M.D.," *Federation Bulletin* 48 (October 1961): 296.

48. Rassekh, "Spirit of Walter Bierring," 77; Harold Jervey, "Walter L. Bierring, M.D," *Federation Bulletin* 48 (October 1961): 278.

Chapter 6

The Push for Public Accountability, 1961–1979

> To become a real force for good, the Federation must have strong and imaginative leadership.
>
> —Robert Derbyshire, 1969

In January 1961, America's then oldest serving president, Dwight Eisenhower, relinquished office to the youngest man ever elected to serve in that capacity, John F. Kennedy. In one of the more famous lines from any presidential inaugural address, Kennedy acknowledged both the literal and symbolic transfer of power when he proclaimed the passing of a torch to a new generation of Americans. In the world of clinical medicine that summer, a new generation of American physicians, led by thirty-seven-year-old William Kannel of Boston, would publish what many would acknowledge as one of the most influential medical studies of the twentieth century. Following a six-year analysis of 5,209 residents of the town of Framingham, Massachusetts, Kannel and his colleagues postulated that hypertension and high serum cholesterol levels were "risk factors" (the first time such a term was used) for arteriosclerotic cardiovascular disease and that controlling elevations of blood pressure and cholesterol levels could lessen the burden of heart disease. The findings would lead to a revolutionary shift in the focus of physicians and scientists for years to come on the diagnosis and treatment of these factors to prevent heart disease and stroke, limit morbidity and prolong life.[1]

For the Federation and state medical boards, 1961 represented a similar dawning of a transformational era. On June 24, 1961, Walter Bierring passed away at the age of ninety-two after enough contributions to medical regulation and the profession to fill several lifetimes. His death marked the end of one era and the beginning of another for the Federation. A new generation of leaders moved to the forefront to grapple with the increasingly complex questions confronting the Federation and state medical boards. McKinley Crabb (Texas), Robert Derbyshire (New Mexico), Andrew Gehret (Delaware), Leo Heywood (Nebraska), Harold Jervey (South Carolina), Frederick Merchant (Ohio), and Lall Montgomery (Indiana) left a lasting positive imprint on the Federation that can be traced to this era.

Several issues emerged in the 1960s that tested the Federation's resolve and its willingness to embrace change. One involved the Federation's continuing efforts to coordinate state medical boards in reorienting their licensing examinations toward a determination of "fitness for practice" that clearly distinguished this testing from assessment in the educational arena. New ways of testing were poised to replace essay questions and factual-recall questions that measured knowledge but not always how that knowledge was actually used in the practice of medicine. The Federation and the state medical board community were now confronted with heightened standards and growing sophistication in assessment that seemed to necessitate the use of professional testing agencies for examination development and construction. Yet, the traditional primary function of the state medical boards had been to examine candidates for licensure. The changing landscape of assessment left some state board veterans wondering whether delegating this task signaled a fundamental change in the role of state medical boards; some even wondered if relinquishing this traditional role signaled a coming obsolescence.[2] The medical licensing community soon addressed these issues directly with the introduction of the Federation Licensing Examination (FLEX).

A second major issue confronting state medical boards and the profession beginning in the 1960s involved its disciplinary role. Historically, state boards operated predominantly as gatekeepers monitoring entrance into the licensed practice of medicine. Much of their disciplinary effort up to that time tended to be exclusionary in nature, often focusing on unlicensed practitioners and defending the physicians' statutory scope of practice against incursions by other health professions. The release of a 1961 report by the AMA Committee on Medical Discipline foreshadowed a growing criticism of the medical profession and state boards for failures both real and perceived in the realm of discipline. Criticism of the former emphasized the profession's role seeking to limit, localize and veil the outcomes of the relatively few disciplinary measures taken against physicians. State medical boards were criticized for their seeming unwillingness to pursue disciplinary matters, particularly into realms that addressed physician competence and the quality of care delivered to patients.[3]

The impact of this emerging focus on the disciplinary function of state medical boards would ultimately touch upon an array of other issues. Some related directly to this function, such as the addition of public members to state medical boards beginning in the 1960s or the introduction of continuing medical education (CME) requirements for physicians in the 1970s. Others appeared initially tangential to state boards' disciplinary role (e.g., oversight of limited practitioners such as physician assistants) but upon closer inspection revealed a growing awareness that guiding medicine's ship of state involved not only the physician but other allied health professions as well. Collectively these issues represented the beginnings of a paradigm shift in the 1960s and 1970s during which the autonomy of the medical profession and its self-regulatory model for licensure and discipline began giving way steadily to governmental and public interests. The "balance of power" was shifting from medicine's practitioners to its administrators, both governmental and corporate, in response to increasing public awareness of the regulatory system's deficiencies. Sensational accounts, such as Philip Wylie's *Generation of Vipers,* gained the public's attention as they presented a compelling indictment of the profession for failing to adequately police itself.[4] The degree of sovereignty long enjoyed by the medical profession began to erode as control of the regulatory and financial structures of medicine moved inexorably away from individual practitioners to a variety of third parties, such as hospitals, governmental agencies, and health care corporations.[5] This sea change under way in medicine required state medical boards to adapt to this new environment and expectations; and the Federation to develop a degree of nimbleness it had not previously demonstrated if it were to remain relevant on the national scene.

CHANGING EXPECTATIONS FOR STATE MEDICAL BOARDS AND THEIR DISCIPLINARY ROLE

In January 1960, the *Federation Bulletin* published one of the last editorials penned by Walter Bierring. A concerned Bierring was unequivocal in his observations on the contemporary state of disciplinary affairs.

> If a state cannot, or does not, for just cause, revoke a license or discipline a physician . . . a fatal weakness exists. If no machinery exists for investigations and hearings . . . discipline does not really exist. If there is nothing beyond what the state or county society can do, a license to practice becomes a potential license for abuse.[6]

Bierring's assessment reflected the grudging acknowledgment from within the profession, and growing concerns from the public, that the disciplinary framework used to regulate medicine remained too much of a hit-or-miss affair. This disciplinary framework involved not only state medical boards but the profession itself through the involvement of state and local medical societies. Bierring's comments portended the 1961 report of the AMA Medical Disciplinary Committee, whose findings marked the beginning of a fundamental shift in the role and function of state medical boards.

Several years earlier, in 1958, the AMA had appointed a Medical Disciplinary Committee to survey state medical boards and medical associations on the subject of physician discipline. The committee supplemented its survey work with personal interviews and a series of regional conferences. Federation representatives Harold Jervey (South Carolina) and Stiles Ezell (New York) served the committee as consultants. The committee's findings proved troubling. While they pointed to admirable efforts and adequate funding in some states (e.g., California, New York, Ohio, Oregon), the overall picture drawn by the report was disappointing. The committee found that, for a variety of reasons, relatively few state medical boards penalized unfit physicians and surgeons. Money was one obvious factor, as mounting an investigation into a disciplinary matter could be an expensive undertaking. One state board member confided that his board possessed "no budget for such purpose." More surprising was the lack of established procedures for disciplinary matters on the part of some boards. The committee's interviews with fifteen state board secretaries highlighted the fact that apparently only a minority of boards had formalized their rules and procedures governing investigations and hearings. Professional ethos compounded matters further. Those boards actively seeking to fulfill their disciplinary role were hampered by a professional culture in which physicians were reluctant to serve as complainants or witnesses lest they breach unwritten rules governing conduct. Boards often encountered physicians reluctant to report a colleague for fear of being sued or to avoid embarrassing a fellow professional. Some states rarely called a physician before the board; others did, but failed to issue penalties. Because the proper protocols for conducting a hearing were either absent or imprecise in addressing practices such as gathering or presenting evidence, state medical boards sometimes saw courts overturning their sanctions on technical grounds.[7]

One particularly discouraging finding from the committee's report was that physicians were looking to leadership on this topic not from the Federation or their state's medical board but from organized medicine. Many practicing doctors appear not to have known or fully appreciated the duties and obligations of state medical boards; in particular, that they were the only legally constituted entities charged with enforcing state law governing the practice of medicine. Their confusion was understandable as the medical profession had long attempted to utilize state and local associations as a mechanism for conflict resolution and for exercising some degree of oversight. So deeply ingrained was this bifurcated view of discipline that one of the fundamental questions the committee believed it important to answer was delineating where the "dividing line" ran between medical society and state medical board authority in disciplining physicians. Their recommendations reflected the profession's desire to retain some measure of control even when the final adjudicatory power fell clearly outside of organized medicine. For example, they called for state medical associations to work cooperatively with state boards in reviewing the disciplinary provisions of their state statutes and for the societies to use grievance committees as a means for bringing necessary actions against offenders. The value of such professional intercession remained questionable as everyone involved understood that expulsion from membership constituted the only real sanction available to a medical association, an ultimately toothless measure that neither threatened the physician's medical license nor protected the public.[8]

The most disconcerting aspect of the committee's report, however, stemmed from the portrait it drew of state medical boards and their willingness to fully assume a legitimate disciplinary function in regulating the practice of medicine. The report laid out the case that while limiting factors were clearly at work, "adequate mechanisms" did exist for the vast majority of state boards to carry out this function. The reason behind the infrequent application of these powers (i.e., the "failure" to act when "necessity arises") resided elsewhere. The comments attributed to state board members within the report revealed a deeply ingrained mind-set that perceived the disciplinary role in its most limited fashion. A "sizable number" of boards' responses to the survey reflected a belief that "discipline is . . . of secondary importance" or a subject to be avoided. During personal interviews, one board acknowledged that they had no budget for investigating disciplinary matters but insisted that "none is . . . needed." Despite the relative paucity of actions being taken against the nation's estimated 250,000 physicians (table 6.1), thirteen of the fifteen board members interviewed believed their board functioned adequately in handling discipline. Similarly, ten out of fifteen felt no statutory changes were needed in their state. Feedback at three out of four regional conferences with 24 state medical boards in attendance evinced a similar sense of complacency.[9]

In many ways the committee's report mirrored the findings of a contemporaneous but lesser known Federation survey of state boards taken in 1959–1960. Under the heading of "problems of discipline," Lall Montgomery (Indiana) explored state medical boards' definition, handling and scope of authority in resolving allegations of unprofessional conduct on the part of a physician. The survey results showed that only half (twenty-two) of the forty-one responding boards had a statutory definition for unprofessional conduct and a significant minority of boards (11:41) lacked statutory authority to revoke a license. Yet despite such apparent deficiencies in the statutory language, most boards (29:41) expressed satisfaction with their state's medical practice act as written. Similar to the later AMA report's findings, the Federation's survey reflected a strong preference among state medical boards (34:41) for a continued role by state medical society or association grievance committees to address matters not covered within the statute.[10]

The inference behind the AMA report's assessment of state medical boards' disciplinary activity was clear, and in many ways consistent with the findings of the earlier Federation survey: the greatest obstacle impeding state medical boards was a reluctance to fully embrace their disciplinary role. Such an inference was hardly surprising given the primary function assigned to state boards at the time of their establishment in the late nineteenth century which called for them to ensure that only adequately trained practitioners were licensed. To the extent that a disciplinary role was conceived for state medical boards, it remained largely an afterthought and as falling under the self-regulatory purview of the profession. The licensure role of state medical boards was not only paramount, it was their raison d'être, a consideration fully understood and embraced by the licensing community at the time and for decades afterward.[11] Nearly a century later, however, societal expectations—and to an extent those of the profession as well—had begun to shift. State medical boards and the Federation were now placed in a position that called for them to demonstrate their ability to recognize, and react appropriately to, this paradigm shift under way in regard to the primary function of state medical boards.

Having served as consultants to the AMA committee, the Federation's Harold Jervey and Stiles Ezell had monitored the progress of the committee and its report. Looking back, it seems clear that their written pronouncements and public statements in early 1961 reflected an attempt to not only prepare the licensing community for the stinging assessment that was forthcoming but to marshal that community behind the new imperative focusing on medical discipline. The Federation's leadership understood that a pendulum swing had occurred, resulting in greater public demand for a "more critical appraisal" of physician behaviors.[12]

As editor of the *Federation Bulletin*, Stiles Ezell used its pages to underscore the coming shift toward a disciplinary focus. He saw this shift as one that would proceed at an irregular pace among the states as it encountered localized pockets of acceptance and resistance inside the profession and the regulatory community. Within the near future, statutory limitations, financial constraints and insufficiently developed procedural guidelines would constrain progress. More important for Ezell was the necessity for a fundamental shift in *perspective* within the profession and among the state board community. Hastening a difficult transition to more effective discipline meant that the impetus for change should originate as much from the profession as the public.[13]

Federation President Harold Jervey embraced the cause in 1961, calling for "urgent action."[14] A strong states' rights advocate who was often opposed to the imposition of national standards, Jervey understood, nevertheless, that the lack of clear, uniform legal guidelines hampered state boards in their disciplining process. The term *discipline* itself was vague and often inconsistently defined. It ranged from a reprimand or probation on one end of the spectrum to suspension or revocation of a license on the other. Probation seldom included oversight or a formal program of rehabilitation, making it too often ineffective. Frequently, a physician disciplined in one state hurriedly crossed state lines intending to set up a practice in a new state before anyone was aware of his record in the prior one. There was little communication among the states or even within a state, between its agencies and the courts. Occasionally, physicians were convicted and incarcerated without notification to the state board with the result that the physician's license remained in good standing.

Jervey's 1961 presidential address to the Federation membership did not equivocate—there were problem physicians in practice and clear "deficiencies" in the disciplinary function inherent to the current construct of medical regulation. Jervey offered a personal estimate that 1–3 percent (2,500–7,000) of the nation's practicing physicians warranted punishment for serious offenses. If the scope was broadened to include ethical violations, he believed there were probably 15,000 to 20,000 doctors whose behavior should be corrected. In what may have been a bit of wishful thinking, Jervey expressed his belief that young, inexperienced physicians were more likely to err because they lacked an understanding of the canons of professionalism rather than through overt disregard for such standards.[15]

Jervey enumerated the many issues compounding the situation: a professional culture that left physicians reluctant to offer testimony or provide a deposition against a colleague accused of misconduct; systemic problems arising from inadequately developed procedural guidelines and poor record keeping; outdated statutory language that sometimes hampered boards; and inadequate financial resources for investigative staff. Jervey's survey of the state of disciplinary affairs did not spare his colleagues and contemporaries on state boards when he claimed "the attitude of too many leaves much to be desired." He condemned the "veiled secrecy" of some state medical board proceedings and proclaimed a professional imperative for all state board members to police their ranks. Jervey even called for more thoughtful appointments to state boards by insisting that board members would need a "flair for the judicial" to operate effectively in the emerging era of heightened expectations.[16]

Finally, Jervey clearly defined what he saw as the appropriate role for the Federation—to serve as a central repository for all disciplinary actions taken by state medical boards. This was not the first time Jervey had issued such a call. Two years earlier, Jervey lamented the lack of a central office that might facilitate communications with state medical boards and gather the necessary statistics and documents to support analysis for more complex initiatives. The timing for Jervey's proposal proved fortuitous. A Federation contingent led by Jervey, Louis Jones and McKinley Crabb soon commenced negotiations with the AMA to realize this proposal. In September 1962, the Federation announced that it had received an appropriation of $10,000 from the AMA to establish a central repository for all state board disciplinary actions. Several conditions were attached to this generous gift: (1) the Federation must establish a permanent central office; (2) the central office must maintain close communications with all state boards to obtain updated information on disciplinary actions taken; and (3) the Federation would prepare and forward a monthly report of all actions to the AMA.[17]

The ramifications of this largesse for the Federation are impossible to overstate. In one fell swoop, the organization gained the modicum of financial resources that had eluded it for half a century. The gift nearly doubled the Federation's modest budget and allowed the organization to function in a "business-like fashion" rather than as a virtual organization. Federation Secretary McKinley Crabb soon negotiated the lease of separate office space from the Texas medical board, which at that time maintained offices in Fort Worth. The establishment of a permanent office in Fort Worth, with Crabb as chief executive officer, meant that for the first time the Federation would not be solely reliant upon the good graces and personal work space of the organization's officers and executive committee who volunteered their time and effort.[18]

The era of the Federation as an all-volunteer agency had ended. With the establishment of its first national office, the Federation began immediately to collect statistics from state medical boards and circulate information among them, answering every question that came its way. In 1963 Remington-Rand set up a chaindex filing system at the Federation for tracking physicians who received disciplinary action from a state board. A monthly report naming physicians, their offense(s) and the actions taken by the state board was printed in the *Federation Bulletin.* A copy was sent to the AMA as well for its records. By 1966, Crabb reported that the Federation's office had received more than seven hundred reports of disciplinary actions during 1965, several hundred more than the prior year's total.[19] The increase stemmed from improved reporting on the part of state boards—an indication of just how seriously they were taking their commission in the disciplinary realm. The small Federation staff was attempting to expedite the clearance of licenses of doctors who moved from state to state. Reported information about doctors was collected at the Federation's central office and, in some cases, made available to hospitals and medical societies.

It would seem the Federation was now finding its proper role as leader, advocate and sometimes mediator on behalf of state medical boards, all the while protecting their role as the party responsible for the enforcement of medical discipline and the final arbiter of physician qualifications to practice within their jurisdiction. This transition to an emphasis upon the disciplinary function on the part of state medical boards occurred slowly, and to some critics far too slowly for their satisfaction. Considerable work needed to be done, including revised statutory language and the crafting of better procedural guidelines for resolving disciplinary matters.

The Federation attempted to assist state boards on both counts. As called for previously in the *Essentials of a Modern Medical Practice Act*, the state medical board was the appropriate designated authority for handling disciplinary matters involving physicians within each state. Doing this job adequately meant securing funds for the board's operations in carrying out investigations into complaints, hearings and the subsequent legal defense required when physicians appealed a board decision—a not uncommon occurrence. Just as important, it also required a commitment to enforcing the standards that the boards set for themselves. Beginning in the early 1960s, the Federation held workshops and circulated model guidelines for holding formal disciplinary hearings. All state board members needed to (re)acquire the basic concepts of due process and evidentiary rules and incorporate these into their rules and regulations. Boards were encouraged to establish protocols for implementing a complaint process and other measures such as utilizing a hearing officer acting as judge with the board as jury or dividing the board into separate panels charged with either an investigatory or adjudicatory function. Another recommended concept involved holding public hearings. Increasingly more common at Federation annual meetings were presentations such as those given by Howard Bobbitt (Oregon State Board of Medical Examiners) in 1962 on investigative procedures and the preparation of case materials.[20]

On the statutory side, there was considerable work remaining to be done. In 1956 the Federation had sent copies of its *Essentials* document to all state medical boards but progress in gaining greater statutory uniformity in the legislative arena continued slowly. There were more than ninety different grounds for the revocation or suspension of a license as stated in the various medical practice acts. Criminal abortion was the only punishable offense for physicians in all fifty states; narcotics use by physicians was close behind as a specific actionable basis for state boards in forty-seven states. Broadly defined behaviors such as "improper practice, incompetent practice, and unethical actions" appeared frequently but with a frustrating lack of precise definition. Updating or rewriting these statutes proved difficult. It required political astuteness and dogged determination on the part of the state medical board in working with the legislature. The process could take years. The Federation recognized the necessity of updated laws defining violations that warranted investigation and discipline and urged state board members to review and thoroughly understand the statutes that addressed these matters. Despite the seemingly slow pace, there were signs of change on the legal front that boded well for state medical boards. The Kansas Board of Healing Arts received a supportive ruling from that state's Supreme Court (*Kansas Board v. Foote*) when it upheld the board's decision to revoke a physician's license based upon "extreme incompetency." The court dismissed the plaintiff's argument challenging the revocation because state statute did not specifically list "incompetence" as a basis for revocation. The court rejected this contention and held that "extreme incompetence" constituted unprofessional conduct—a reasonable basis for action.[21]

With such divergent statutory language and sometimes uniquely local problems, each state had to go it alone, building up their own procedures and precedents, finding their way through the labyrinth of issues, particularly those surrounding allegations of unprofessional conduct. Indiana board member Lall Montgomery lamented that the disciplinary matters before the board seemed to require the wisdom of Solomon to differentiate the various overlapping legal, professional and social implications often inherent to each case. Undeterred, *Federation Bulletin* editor Stiles Ezell urged state boards to persevere in these endeavors; yet, he was also not above chastising fellow physicians about their priorities. Ezell pointed to intraprofessional squabbling over the ethics of allopathic physicians associating with osteopathic colleagues as an irrelevant distraction at a time when state boards needed to develop and maintain a singular focus on the important work of "eliminating fraud and deceit" among licensed practitioners.[22]

Despite the considerable attention being given to the state medical boards' role and function in disciplinary matters, progress came slowly in the 1960s and 1970s. This was true regardless of the metric used to measure progress, for example, the number of disciplinary actions taken by boards, the infusion of additional financial resources to bolster boards' efforts or legislative changes clarifying and/or strengthening medical boards' authority. Consequently, there was no shortage of critics; even some within the licensing community were unequivocal in their assessment that state boards were not yet performing adequately in their disciplinary role. Among the latter group, Robert Derbyshire (New Mexico) was the most prominent. Derbyshire published extensively on the topic of medical discipline, beginning in the 1960s with his book *Medical Licensure and Discipline in the United States,* which related the state of affairs at the decade's close.

Derbyshire reviewed the Federation's board action files for the period 1963–1969, when the U.S. physician population ranged from an estimated 250,000 (1960) to 320,000 (1970).[23] Unlike previously reported figures through the AMA (table 6.1), with its undefined "other" category that likely inflated the total number of actions, Derbyshire attempted to eliminate actions that might artificially inflate the national figure, such as actions rescinding a previous decision and reciprocal actions based upon action taken by another board.

The published data from *Medical Licensure and Discipline* set forth in tables 6.1 and 6.2 indicate the relatively small number of disciplinary actions being taken. Derbyshire used a similar methodology based upon the Federation's board action files in later publications to capture data for the period 1968–1972 and for the period 1974–1977. These revealed comparable national figures with the number of actions taken by boards at 1,033 during 1968–1972 and 1,768 during 1974–1977. Disciplinary actions taken by state boards during the period 1969–1978 provided an average national total of 362 actions annually. Figures such as these, while imperfect due to incomplete reporting and definitional issues, are helpful in providing a baseline for later comparisons, particularly those reflecting the surge in the reported number of actions taken by state medical boards beginning in the mid-1980s.[24]

Table 6.1. Disciplinary Actions Taken by State Medical Boards, 1960–1969

Year	*Revocation*	*Revocation with Stay*	*Suspension*	*Other*	*Total*
1960	70	—	—	—	554
1961	102	—	—	—	604
1962	72	53	66	276	467
1963	75	44	43	239	401
1964	83	57	42	225	407
1966	69	68	45	397	579
1967	61	64	47	176	348
1968	64	59	60	338	521
1969	58	53	33	386	530

Note: Data for 1960–1961 did not distinguish between license revocations and suspensions. Based upon later studies by other authors, it seems likely the "Other" category included letters of reprimand, probation, duplicate actions taken upon a previous action, and so on. No data appear to have been reported for 1965.

Source: Adapted from "Medical Disciplinary Reports" in *Journal of the American Medical Association* 194, no. 13 (December 27, 1965): 124; *Journal of the American Medical Association* 213, no. 4 (July 27, 1970): 589.

Table 6.2. Types of Disciplinary Actions Taken by State Medical Boards, 1963–1967

Probation	375
Revocation	374
Suspension	161
Reprimands	68
Total	938

Source: Robert Cushing Derbyshire, *Medical Licensure and Discipline in the United States* (Baltimore: Johns Hopkins University Press, 1969), 77. Reprinted with permission of Johns Hopkins University Press.

Narcotics violations and physician impairment stemming from substance abuse served as the cause/basis for half (51 percent) of all board actions taken in the 1963–1967 period described by Derbyshire (see table 6.3). This pattern continued for board actions taken during the 1968–1972 period, as well.[25] While some critics may have felt that state medical boards placed a disproportionate focus on physicians with substance abuse issues, physician impairment presented a significant challenge to state boards, particularly those seeking rehabilitation and recovery alternatives for their licensees. As early as 1958, Federation President C. J. Glaspel used his presidential address as a platform to warn state boards of the "danger" lurking in their midst in the form of physician impairment. Two years later, Federation board member John Fiorino signaled a shift toward a rehabilitative philosophy when he recommended that state boards seek out impaired physicians and counsel them to seek treatment as part of nonpunitive efforts to salvage individual careers.[26]

Table 6.3. Causes for Disciplinary Actions Taken by State Medical Boards, 1963–1967

Narcotics violations	440
Mental incompetence	94
Fraud and deceit in practice	74
Felony conviction	72
Abortion	71
Unprofessional conduct	68
Alcoholism	41
Moral turpitude	26
Other categories	52
Total	938

Note: Other categories included gross malpractice, fraudulent application, gross immorality, fee splitting, and gross misconduct.

Source: Robert Cushing Derbyshire, *Medical Licensure and Discipline in the United States* (Baltimore: Johns Hopkins University Press, 1969), 78. Reprinted with permission of Johns Hopkins University Press.

Significant progress toward a rehabilitation focus for impaired physicians came in 1969 when Florida passed legislation subsequently termed the "Sick Doctor Law." The legislation defined a sick physician as one "unable to practice medicine with reasonable skill and safety to patients" due to mental or physical conditions that included impairment from drugs and/or alcohol. Within several years, two dozen states adopted legislation modeled upon Florida's law. As physician impairment programs began to take root, state medical boards now had meaningful rehabilitative options available to them. Early results in the 1970s from the Florida, Michigan, Virginia and Colorado state boards proved hopeful as these boards could point to a growing number of physicians with reinstated licenses and those in active compliance with the terms of their probation. This was not entirely new territory for state boards as the Medical Board of California had extensive prior experience in this realm dating back to the 1940s. However, California's financial and staff resources for such initiatives were atypical of most state medical boards.[27]

After narcotics-related actions, the next most prevalent basis for a disciplinary action taken by state medical boards fell under the heading of mental incompetence. Here, too, state boards were seeking and gaining a rehabilitative focus. By 1966, approximately thirty-nine boards had authority to revoke or suspend a license based upon mental impairment. More important, boards were gaining latitude in using other measures such as probationary oversight for physicians either under active treatment or upon release to practice after treatment. Other categories reported by Derbyshire, such as fraud/deceit under the medical practice act, felony convictions and criminal abortion, provided firmer grounds for state board action. As clear-cut violations of state law, the boards sometimes had no discretionary latitude as some jurisdictions made a felony conviction an automatically revocable offense.[28]

While inarguably the numbers identified by Derbyshire remained small throughout the 1960s and into the 1970s (e.g., a total of 1,971 disciplinary actions taken by boards in 1963–1972), it is also clear in retrospect that many state boards were on the cusp of major changes. New York state offers one of the more telling examples with the 1975 establishment of its Office of Professional Medical Conduct (OPMC), responsible for investigating complaints, and its State Board for Professional Medical Conduct to oversee disciplinary proceedings. With multiple investigators scattered across the state through central and regional offices, the OPMC investigated more than 3,000 complaints in its first three years alone, resulting in 311 board actions.[29] Though the greatest surge in aggregate disciplinary actions would not come until the mid-1980s (as will be discussed in the next chapter), the pendulum had clearly begun to swing in the direction of a regulatory system in which state medical boards assumed a more active, and increasingly transparent, role in carrying out their disciplinary function.

Despite the scrutiny placed on state medical boards and their disciplinary role, they were hardly alone in the spotlight. A seminal case (*Darling v. Charleston Memorial Community Hospital*) established the responsibility of hospital administrators for ensuring the "competence" of their staff. Hospitals were in perhaps the best position to detect and address issues of physician competence through firsthand observation and peer review, though many critics questioned the efficacy of such measures. Meanwhile, medical societies seemed eager to shift the spotlight and any expectations for a true disciplinary role on their part. In 1969, the AMA discontinued receiving disciplinary actions from state societies, citing incomplete and/or absent reporting as the primary reason for its action and characterizing the endeavor as a "waste of time." Earlier in the 1950s, state medical societies had turned to grievance committees as a mechanism for professional self-regulation in response to public criticisms demanding greater accountability on the part of physicians.[30] These proved predictably unsuccessful as a long-term mechanism to address systemic problems in medical regulation and may even have reinforced negative perceptions of the profession, such as lack of transparency or shielding colleagues. Still, expectations remained highest for the medical licensing community. The lingering question was whether state medical boards could successfully realign their functions to meet changing expectations of their role. The Federation's Ezell echoed this question when he reflected back upon the rich heritage and role of the medical licensing community and then, looking into the future, offered the opinion that "stability" was no longer a given. The examining and licensing functions once so prominent in the state medical boards' conception of their function remained important; but they no longer commanded the center stage as they did in an earlier era. Discipline and a regulatory function had stepped from the shadows of an offstage chorus into central roles. To Ezell, state boards would have to accept "continuous evaluation," both in terms of their performance and their flexibility, as the price for maintaining any vestige of professional self-regulation within the state-based system for licensing and discipline.

THE PUSH FOR ACCOUNTABILITY

The push for more robust and transparent state board disciplinary processes represented only one aspect of a broader, overarching transformation under way in medical regulation beginning in the 1960s—a demand for greater public accountability through an expanded regulatory model blending multiple interests (e.g., public, professional, governmental). The government's historic decision to fund health care through Medicare (for those aged sixty-five and older and the disabled) and Medicaid (for the poor), enacted by the U.S. Congress and signed into law in 1965 by President Lyndon Johnson, signaled a fundamental shift in the economics of medicine that would also include heavy corporate investment in health care facilities and technologies. State medical boards were adapting to a changing environment characterized by new expectations for both their role and their measured performance. Just as the closed universe of state medical board discipline based upon "collegiality, informality and confidentiality" was being discarded for a system of accountability built upon transparent and legalistic processes, a similar shift was under way in state board composition and the expectations for physician licensees.[31]

No single factor accounts for this shift beginning in the 1960s. The steady erosion of the paternalistic role reserved for physicians in the doctor-patient relationship assuredly accounts for some of this change. While difficult to quantify, clearly a shift was under way in the dynamics of the physician-patient relationship. More important, however, this shift was emblematic of a broader societal trend seen elsewhere as an emerging public/consumer culture demanding accountability from both individuals and institutions traditionally vested with power. Evidence abounds of a growing advocacy movement, from Ralph Nader's *Unsafe at Any Speed,* a damning critique of safety standards within the American automotive industry, to Rachel Carson's environmental call to arms against the pesticide DDT in *Silent Spring*; from Betty Friedan's challenge to traditional gender roles in *The Feminine Mystique* to the 1971 release of the Pentagon Papers which detailed a systematic pattern of public deception by the U.S. government concerning its role and progress in the Vietnam War. All of these reflected an emerging culture within American society demanding greater transparency for those institutions wielding power and accountability of those holding positions of authority within them.

For state medical boards this call for accountability manifested itself most directly in the question of board composition and their physician members' willingness to hold their peers accountable to both disciplinary and competence standards. Some among the Federation's leadership responded positively, signaling the need for state boards to consider significant, meaningful changes. Thus, in 1970 Federation President Frederick Merchant echoed his colleague Stiles Ezell's earlier call for continuous evaluation within the licensing community by appointing an Ad Hoc Committee on Long-Range Organizational Planning for the Federation. The committee's charge called for identifying how the Federation could best address the many forces pushing for change in medical regulation. Merchant understood that self-evaluation was an important process but insufficient by itself, if there were not also a willingness to change and adapt to new circumstances. He insisted that the Federation embrace the possibility of substantive change as the only means for transforming critics' image of medical regulators as "gray haired" obstructionists.[32] And in an era of increasing federal involvement in health care, Merchant warned that state medical boards, despite their long history of integrity, would have to justify their continued existence with policies that were flexible, proactive and forward-looking.

Despite the clear call for change coming from leaders such as Merchant, one arena in which the Federation moved cautiously was the shift within the regulatory community toward including public members on state medical boards. Historically, medical boards had been the exclusive domain of physician members—a composition consistent with the paternalistic qualities of medicine as practiced throughout the first half of the twentieth century. Beginning in the 1960s, however, a growing chorus called for the addition of public (i.e., nonphysician) members on state boards. John Morton, from the New York medical board, acknowledged the impetus prompting the change. State medical boards were seen by some as entities too often protective of professional, rather than public, interests. Morton's editorial in the *Federation Bulletin* signaled a clear willingness to consider public members on state boards. He could identify no disadvantage to adding public members, provided that physicians remained in the majority. Later, Federation President Howard Horns urged state boards to give "serious thought" to adding public members to their board and cited his own board (Minnesota) as an early yet positive experience. Still, a formal position statement from the organization proved slower in coming.[33]

Earlier, the updated 1970 edition of the Federation's *Essentials of a Modern Medical Practice Act* reflected the traditional all-physician board construct while calling for the medical board's right to regulate the profession. By the mid-1980s, a revised *Essentials* implicitly reflected the infusion of public board members by calling for physicians to constitute a majority of every board's membership, *regardless of the board's composition*. With the publication of the *Elements of a Modern State Medical Board* in 1989, the Federation not only called for the inclusion of public members on state boards but recommended that they should constitute at least 25 percent of each board's membership.[34] Though the Federation had not moved with alacrity on this issue, when the formal position statement came it presented a standard that has since proved the norm nationally. The Federation's experience in this area reflects one of the fundamental challenges inherent to membership organizations—being neither too far in front nor lagging at the rear of one's membership. This balance required supporting the vision of those member boards seeking forward movement in key policies and initiatives, while simultaneously acknowledging the various local and regional realities contributing to the status quo in some states.

The push for public members stemmed from a mix of factors—some aspirational, some societal, and others wholly practical. One longtime member of the Washington medical board characterized the public members' role as that of "social conscience" for the board. These citizen members enhanced the board's credibility by virtue of their mere presence, conveying a transparency to medical board decision-making generally perceived as lacking in an earlier era.[35] Certainly, societal expectations had shifted over time, demanding a "patient perspective" as a part of an overall shift toward greater accountability to the public in the regulatory process. One public member of the Minnesota board hinted at this shift by acknowledging that boards had been hurt previously by their "too close" relationship with medical societies. Ultimately, strong practical considerations were at work as well. Unquestionably, public representation on medical boards served as a "buffer" against those questioning who would regulate the regulators—a much more difficult question to answer under the earlier predominant structure of physician-exclusive boards. Within the context of board discussions and decision-making, the presence of public members often resulted in transformative change. A physician member of the Connecticut board characterized this transformative aspect as the value of an intelligent layman's "being naive" on many aspects of medicine and health care. The public members' salutary naiveté forced the board to "distill" complicated medical issues into terms comprehensible to the general public.[36] In essence, the presence of public members appeared to foster greater emphasis on clearly communicating and articulating board decisions and their rationale.

The California board led the way in this movement, starting in 1961, as the first state board to include public members; later, a reorganized California board seated seven public members on its nineteen-member board. By 1976, public members comprised approximately 10 percent of all state medical boards nationally, with the percentage rising to 21 percent by 1996. By 1983, twenty-eight boards had public members; by 1999, all but three (not counting the U.S. territories) included public members that collectively comprised 24 percent of total state board membership nationally. This figure has remained constant to this day.[37]

The shift in state board demographics to include public members was part of a simultaneous transformation that saw state legislatures moving to shift and/or reorganize the operation of state boards within existing state agencies. State after state responded to criticisms of their medical board's performance by resituating the board within larger, umbrella agencies (e.g., the state's Department of Health) that utilized more formalized structures stressing public accountability. The "free hand" long accorded the medical profession in self-regulation was being altered in fundamental ways that traded a reduction in professional autonomy for greater transparency and sometimes additional resources in the disciplinary realm. According to a report from the U.S. Department of Health and Human Services, the number of state medical boards placed under an umbrella agency rose from sixteen in 1969 to thirty-one in 1986. California's Board of Medical Examiners offers one example, as it reorganized itself into the California Board of Medical Quality Assurance with seven public members and three divisions: Allied Health Professionals; Licensing; and Medical Quality. Placing multiple health providers under a single umbrella agency took hold in many states (e.g., Florida, Virginia, Nebraska, Illinois), sometimes with the establishment of a "Board of Health Professions" to manage policy development among their various health professions (including the medical board). Other state medical boards went through similar reorganizations, while many resisted major change but moved forward in a more incremental fashion.[38]

One underlying assumption behind reorganizing boards and adding public members to their roster was that this would translate into more vigorous oversight of the medical profession. Perhaps not surprisingly given the complexity and multifactorial nature of state board discipline, results from subsequent research have proven mixed. For example, a 1990 study examined the presence of public members on state medical boards with an eye toward the disciplinary measures taken by those boards. While there was no correlation between the presence of public members and the total number of disciplinary actions, the researchers did find a correlation between their presence and the seriousness of the disciplinary actions taken. On occasion, the news media have explored this relationship as part of the Federation's annual release of national disciplinary statistical data, sometimes commenting favorably upon the performance of all-physician boards. (See chapter 7 for a discussion of national disciplinary data banks.) A similarly mixed outcome appeared when looking at the implementation of board policies and application of standards for licensure. For example, one study looking at data from the mid-1980s found no correlation between the presence of public members on state medical boards and the likelihood of adopting reforms involving continuing medical education (CME) and licensure endorsement policies. However, a later study found an association between the presence of public members on state medical boards and consumer interests in licensing requirements (e.g., CME for physicians and number of years of residency training).[39]

Regardless of data results, the shift begun in the 1960s toward shared physician-public regulation of the profession is now an entrenched feature of the system. Any number of anecdotes might be related concerning the value of this new paradigm in regulation but perhaps one is most telling. A former president of the Virginia Board of Medicine deemed the presence of public members so critical that he lobbied his state legislature successfully to double the number of public members on the board. Apparently, the respect was mutual. A series of interviews with public board members conveyed a unanimous sense of collegiality with their physician colleagues. Far from "condescension," public members acknowledged a spirit of cooperation in which the greatest pitfall was "over-identification" with their physician co-members on the board.[40]

Almost simultaneous to the campaign for inclusion of public members on state medical boards, efforts at fostering accountability shifted the focus to physicians. In particular, interest centered upon the physicians' routine and periodic renewal of their medical license (i.e., relicensure) and the value of continuing medical education (CME) as a means for promoting continued competence of licensed practitioners. This represented a potentially significant change. State medical boards had historically treated the licensure renewal process as an administrative function, based upon an annual, biennial or triennial submission of a relicensing fee and updated information for a list of registered licensees within the state. Questions about ensuring competence were addressed explicitly and exclusively at the point of initial licensure. Afterward, a clean disciplinary record and timely submission of a renewal fee and forms meant that individual physicians could maintain their medical license indefinitely. Under this system, the onus for retaining currency of knowledge and adequate skills fell solely onto the physician as a professional responsibility. Opportunities for more formalized supplementary learning and education were not uncommon through the services of many state and local medical societies and extension programs through medical schools and universities.[41] Ultimately, however, responsibility in this realm fell to the individual physician as no state medical board prior to the 1970s mandated CME as part of its requirements for license renewal.

Signs of a coming shift toward legislatively mandated CME for physicians appeared first in the 1960s. A 1967 federal report on medical manpower directly challenged the "one-time" assessment inherent to state medical boards' licensure processes and called for state governments to consider linking license renewal with "acceptable performance" in CME or by an examination within the physician's specialty. A later report from the U.S. Department of Health, Education and Welfare (HEW)—renamed in 1979 the U.S. Department of Health and Human Services (DHHS)—commented upon the inadequacy of the states' license renewal processes to address "professional obsolescence." That physicians perceived value in more formally structured educational offerings was evident by the AMA's activities in this area. Beginning in 1964, the AMA began accrediting CME sponsors and then, in 1968, introduced its Physician's

Recognition Award (PRA) with an accompanying system of CME credits. Meeting this demand in the mid-1960s were more than 250 different CME providers offering 1,600 courses.[42] Similar work was progressing in the osteopathic medical profession, whose state osteopathic boards were not yet members of the Federation. In 1973, the American Osteopathic Association established its Council on Continuing Medical Education. That same year witnessed further momentum behind the concept of ongoing professional development as the National Board of Medical Examiners issued the report of its Committee on Goals and Priorities entitled *Evaluation in the Continuum of Medical Education*. This report articulated a clear continuum from undergraduate medical education to practice and continuing education and spoke of a need to "assure" continued competence as part of a license renewal process.[43]

Momentum in the area of continuing education had been building for many years. As early as the 1930s the AMA Council on Medical Education had speculated that at some future date the "public interest" would require physician participation in "continuation courses." In 1947, the American Academy of General Practice stepped forward to be the first to mandate a continuing education requirement as a condition for physicians maintaining membership in their organization. In the late 1960s the Oregon Medical Society became the first medical association to require CME as a condition for membership. The later expulsion of eleven physician members for failure to meet this requirement, in 1971, demonstrated their commitment to this standard. Similar conversations about "lifelong learning" were already taking place among the specialty certifying boards of the American Board of Medical Specialties (ABMS). In 1969, two of ABMS's member boards (Family Practice and Internal Medicine) developed recertification policies. Momentum continued such that by 1973, all ABMS member boards had adopted the principle of periodic recertification.[44]

Though the exact verbiage may have changed slightly over time, the profession had steadily moved to embrace, and then act upon, the concept of the physician-scholar as a "lifelong learner" within the context of the individual's medical practice. However, shifting CME from a voluntary basis in medical societies to a legislatively driven condition for licensure renewal proved challenging for many state medical boards. For example, the Virginia board embraced the concept as early as 1967 and began discussions with that state's medical society but implementation of a formal plan proved many years in coming.[45] In 1971, New Mexico became the first state in the United States to impose a CME requirement (150 credit hours every three years) as a mandatory condition for medical license renewal. Support from both the state's medical board and its medical society proved critical in navigating the bill successfully through the legislature.[46] Initially, progress with state boards pressing their legislature for, or implementing, CME requirements was slow. By 1975–1976, it appears that only Maryland and Arizona had joined New Mexico, while a handful of other states had legislation either pending or mired in committee.[47] However, little more than a decade later (1987), twenty-nine of the sixty-eight state medical and osteopathic licensing boards had CME requirements in place. By 1999, the number reached forty-seven and by 2011 all but five boards had mandatory CME. Additionally, as time passed, state boards and their respective legislatures incorporated specified content areas within the required CME hours. Today, nineteen boards require specified content in areas such as opioid prescribing, pain management, risk management, infection control, child abuse recognition, domestic violence, and other areas[48] (see table 6.4). All the while, the Federation supported state medical boards in their adoption of these requirements. Federation President P. T. Lamey addressed the state boards collectively at the organization's 1970 annual meeting and called for support of continuing medical education requirements, even making CME a central topic of that year's Bierring lecture. In his 1975 presidential address, Howard Horns spoke at length of the evolution in the education continuum, urging state medical boards to push harder for uniform standards by embracing those new ideas meriting consideration and eliminating the outmoded. Several years later, the Federation Ad Hoc Committee to Study Uniform Methods to Assess Physician Competence offered a mixed endorsement

Table 6.4. State Boards Requiring Continuing Medical Education (CME) for License Renewal

	1987	*1999*	*2010*
# non-requiring boards	40	21	6
# requiring boards	29	47	62
Avg CME hours/year[a]			
12–17 hours	4	6	4
20–25 hours	11	22	37
30–35 hours	1	1	3
40 hours	0	2	0
50 hours	13	16	18
Total # of state boards	69	69	68[b]

[a]Most state boards renew licenses every 2–3 years. Annual hours shown as average from the multiyear requirements, e.g., 150 hours every 3 years listed as 50 hours annually.

[b]Consolidation of Hawaii's allopathic and osteopathic boards into a single composite board reduced the total number of licensing boards in the United States to 68.

Source: Federation *Exchange*, 1987 and 1999–2000 editions. (Euless, Texas: Federation of State Medical Boards); "Continuing Medical Education Overview by State," Federation of State Medical Boards, at http://www.fsmb.org/grpol_keyissues.html.

of CME—and encouraged the FSMB to take no formal position on voluntary vs. mandated continuing education—but recommended educational programming based upon identified physician needs.[49] The next revision to the Federation's *Essentials of a Modern Medical Practice Act* (1985) explicitly called for state boards to require physicians to demonstrate their "continuing qualification" at the time of license renewal and specifically addressed the boards' authority to mandate CME.

By incorporating CME as a condition for license renewal, state medical boards had taken their first steps away from a system characterized by one state board leader as "lifelong licensure." If matriculation into medical school marked the start of an educational *continuum* for physicians, state medical boards increasingly recognized that they were the only entities statutorily positioned to oversee the postlicensure segment of the continuum on behalf of both the public and the profession. Indeed, as the philosophy behind much of CME began shifting away from evaluative markers predicated upon internal measures (satisfaction surveys; pre-/post-session tests) to external markers around physician performance in practice and patient outcomes, some among the licensing community looked hopefully to CME as a mechanism that might drive positive behavioral changes.[50] For example, in more recent years, opioid prescribing and pain management have been a particular focus of the licensing community as well as an area of increasing public and governmental interest. Some boards have mandated CME in this area; others have collaborated with CME providers to provide educational/remediation options when appropriate.[51] As will be discussed in the next chapter, the Federation's policy work emphasized this area starting in the 1990s and led to the application of grant funds creating an Online Prescriber Education Network (OPEN) providing state boards and physicians with free CME offerings.

Setting aside for the moment questions of the efficacy of CME across all medical and surgical specialties and the methodologies most likely to produce positive performance outcomes, much of the medical licensing community appeared to be arriving at a conclusion similar to that reached by the New Mexico board's Robert Derbyshire in 1971: it required "little faith" to be persuaded of the value of continuing education when applied and experienced by conscientious physicians. Demands for evidence demonstrating the efficacy of CME continued as the primary basis for opposition, however, even within the licensing community. Derbyshire, in particular, evinced a willingness to address these challengers head-on by citing numerous studies that, while providing no conclusive magic bullet rebuttal, spoke to the "favorable effects" of the continuing education process. More important, Derbyshire reminded his colleagues in the licensing community that mandatory continuing education tied to license renewal provided one of the best bulwarks against direct federal intervention in state-based licensure. Others, such as one member of the Maryland board, attempted to shift the tone of discourse by insisting that continuing education ultimately sought to remedy a generally acknowledged problem confronting all highly trained professionals—forestalling the *obsolescence* of knowledge and skills over time. Board members were advised to distinguish between knowledge deficits stemming from obsolescence as opposed to incompetence because more compelling arguments could be presented on the value of CME to address the former. Additionally, such an emphasis would reinforce the positive attributes of curiosity, initiative and integrity evinced by the self-directed educational and assessment activities that many (if not most) within the profession were already engaged in.[52]

Ultimately, dialogue around CME constituted one piece of a broader conversation about physician competence, an emerging theme of the accountability movement already transforming medical regulation. The Federation attempted to provide initial guidance to state boards through an Ad Hoc Committee to Study Uniform Methods to Assess Physician Competence formed in 1981. All parties in the dialogue understood that competence could not be assured solely by accumulation of continuing education credits. Thus, the committee looked broadly at other measures such as examinations, peer review, and patient satisfaction indices.[53] In retrospect, the complexity of the physician competence issue, a lack of consensus among state boards on even a CME approach to the issue and the pressures of other topics foreshadowed a relatively quiet end to the committee's substantial work. The issue of physician competence as a condition of license renewal would not be taken up again in any substantial form by the Federation for another two decades. However, as will be seen in chapter 8, significant progress toward assuring physician competence lay ahead under the mantle of Maintenance of Licensure.

FEDERAL OVERTURES

The push for greater accountability in medical regulation garnered federal interest beginning in the 1960s. For much of the decade, the federal government's strongest interests in health care were associated with the economic aspects of medicine; the state-based system of medical licensure and discipline received relatively little attention from federal authorities. Signals that the scope of federal interest in health care was changing were made explicit in a report by a national commission established under the Johnson administration. The charge to the commission called for making recommendations to government agencies and private entities for strengthening the health care workforce. In 1967, the National Advisory

Commission on Health Manpower released its report and state medical boards soon took notice as the report and its related studies gained broader dissemination.[54]

The report's findings rattled the medical licensing community with a series of assertions challenging the overall value and effectiveness of the system. The commission report asserted that state statutes constrained curricular innovations at medical schools and hampered needed developments in graduate medical education. The licensing system was characterized, in its then state, as a barrier to physician mobility and license portability; and its examinations were faulted as out of step with the nature of medical education. The report examined the health care workforce and cited state laws for their poor handling of the burgeoning role of allied health professionals and underutilization of osteopathic physicians. The report touched upon competence issues by lamenting the absence of broader utilization of continuing education to prevent "educational obsolescence."[55]

The medical licensing community was well aware of the issues underscored in the commission's report and many state boards were actively working to resolve them. In spotlighting issues such as license portability, physician competence, and the burgeoning role of allied health care professionals and osteopathic physicians, the report drew attention to areas in which state medical boards would have to demonstrate substantive progress or risk the threat of federal legislation—a concept that could not help but sharpen the focus of state medical boards and create an urgency to address them. The Federation now kept a closer watch on activities in Washington, D.C., to anticipate, and if necessary forestall, federal overreach into the state-based system of medical regulation. The wait was not long as the pace of federal legislation and initiatives related to health care quickened in the 1970s. The 1971 Health Manpower Training Act utilized capitation grants to increase federal support for training primary care medical providers, including, for the first time, physician assistants (PAs). More typically, however, federal legislative initiatives focused on the economics of health care delivery. That same year, President Richard Nixon announced a "new national health strategy" featuring health maintenance organizations and a proposal for national health insurance standards. Both political parties, Democratic and Republican, now spoke in terms of a health care "crisis" and the need for immediate action.[56]

From the perspective of state medical boards, the most significant proposed legislation appeared in 1974 with U.S. Senate Bill 3585 (S-3585), sponsored by Massachusetts Senator Edward Kennedy. This ambitious legislation proposed shifting the Department of Health, Education, and Welfare into the foreground with a role for it to influence the issuance of licenses to practice medicine. S-3585 proposed authorizing the HEW Secretary to develop and set the minimum standards for a national medical licensing examination and, subsequently, to create a nationally administered examination as a condition for relicensure every six years.[57]

In testimony before a Senate subcommittee on the bill, a physician undersecretary for the HEW called state licensure "anachronistic" and a "mess," saying states granted licenses too soon, too broadly, and for too long a time. Such strong language accompanying the bill prompted immediate reaction from the Federation. The Federation adopted an official position in opposition to the legislation, broadly disseminated its rebuttal document drafted by the organization's Long-Range Planning Committee and encouraged state medical boards to actively engage with their Congressional representatives on the bill.[58] A steady stream of editorials in the *Federation Bulletin* addressed multiple aspects of the pending legislation, keeping it prominent on the licensing community's radar.

The Federation acknowledged some of the salient points in the bill and the HEW undersecretary's criticism. For example, some states still did not require any graduate medical education before granting a license for independent practice, and those that did usually stipulated only one year of internship or training. Few within the medical education community were arguing the adequacy of medical school alone as preparation for independent practice and the Federation had been urging state boards to require a minimum of two years of graduate medical education. In this area, it was grudgingly acknowledged that some physicians were being licensed "too soon."[59]

Assertions that physicians were being licensed too broadly arose from the general, undifferentiated nature of the medical license—a model wholly consistent with the nature of medical practice at the time that modern medical licensing laws arose in the late nineteenth century. Within the increasingly specialized nature and practice of medicine beginning midway through the twentieth century, the appropriateness of the general license seemed antithetical to the realities of American medicine in the 1970s. This overlooked, however, the de facto realities that already served to limit the scope of individuals' practice, such as hospital privileging and individual physicians' decision to seek specialty board certification. This criticism also overlooked the significant practical obstacles behind any serious legislative effort at limiting a license by specialty or practice focus. Crafting the necessary statutory and/or regulatory definition for a specific medical field represented an exercise fraught with legal, professional and logistical difficulties stemming in part from the overlapping nature of most medical disciplines.[60]

Criticisms that the medical license was granted for too long ignored the transition already well under way within medical regulation, including continuing education requirements, specialty board certification and recertification, and professional expectations. Mandatory continuing education for physicians was already a condition of license renewal in some states; and in many others, it constituted a requirement for membership within the state's professional association. The medical specialty boards were already moving toward recertification requirements. The practical and environmental realities at work in the mid-1970s indicated that the days of a physician enjoying a "license for life" were numbered.[61] Though the transition to fully actualize competency elements within license renewal would require many years, the emerging trend was clear.

As was so often the case in the 1960s and 1970s, Derbyshire offered some of the more thoughtful observations on the state of medical regulation and this particular legislation. In writing about his testimony on the bill before the U.S. Senate, Derbyshire lamented the relative ignorance about medical licensure intimated through several aspects of the legislation. He reminded the Senate subcommittee that a nationally administered examination for medical licensure had been in place for six years (see next section on the Federation Licensing Examination, or FLEX) and was already producing excellent results. The FLEX provided a basis for uniform standards that made a federally developed examination superfluous. Derbyshire expressed support for licensure renewal incorporating continuing education but questioned the practicality of a nationally administered examination as a condition for license renewal. He cited the trends already under way in licensing and specialty board certification and respectfully pressed the committee on what they envisioned testing, the whole of the field of medicine or just the area of specialty? Derbyshire also questioned the underlying constitutionality of the legislation, citing the explicit language of the Tenth Amendment and the long history of precedent supporting the police powers interpretation that relegated medical licensure and discipline to the states.[62]

Ultimately, a modified form of the bill passed both the U.S. House and Senate, but (not surprisingly) without the sections on federal involvement in medical licensure. This did not, however, mark the end of federal interest in state-based licensing. A 1976 HEW report, entitled "A Proposal for Credentialing Health Manpower," suggested a nongovernmental national certifying body for health occupations responsible for apprising the federal government of those organizations approved to issue certificates. This proposed body would also be responsible for setting national standards for credentialing selected health occupations. The report further called for "improved licensure procedures," proficiency examinations based upon competency measures and requirements to support continued competence of health care practitioners. The Federation's board of directors responded officially to the HEW with its position on the major recommendations of the report. Where consistent with the policy and aims of the organization, the Federation expressed support for recommendations such as those to improve license procedures and support continuing competence measures. But the Federation strongly questioned the value of adding another certifying agency to the organizations already in place and providing the de facto national standards being sought by the HEW.[63] Other organizations such as the ABMS and the NBME weighed in as well, offering similar support in the areas cited by the Federation while also offering similar reservations about the construct and purview of a national certifying body.[64] Like the national aspects of the earlier proposed federal legislation, these proposals, too, did not come to fruition. However, in 1976 the federal government did involve itself directly in examinations through the Health Professional Educational Assistance Act, which necessitated "more stringent" screening of IMGs seeking to enter residency training in the United States. Specifically, the legislation led to the NBME's development of a visa qualifying examination for the ECFMG in order to meet the equivalency standard for examinations set by the HEW.[65]

For the Federation and state medical boards collectively, these federal legislative initiatives represented a cautionary tale about bringing one's house in order. The imperative to continue efforts toward achieving greater consistency and uniformity in standards was never clearer. In characteristically blunt fashion, Derbyshire urged state medical boards to forswear foot dragging and "capricious behavior" that obstructed progress toward needed reforms and warned that neither the public nor Congress would be dissuaded indefinitely. As it turned out, this period represented a peak in direct federal interest in state-based licensure. Within several years, unofficial signals from the HEW indicated a diminished sense of urgency on their part to address the "problem" of physician relicensure as they were no longer pursuing the topic as "energetically."[66] When federal interest focused again on the medical regulatory system in the 1990s, it would turn its attention instead to the disciplinary realm.

THE FEDERATION LICENSING EXAMINATION (FLEX): A NEW DIRECTION IN ASSESSMENT

Since 1957, the Federation had labored in joint effort with its state medical boards to improve the quality of the nation's state medical licensing examinations. An ongoing series of Examination Institutes assembled by the Federation drew together scores of state medical board members charged with identifying and outlining appropriate subject matter to assess a licensure candidate's "fitness to practice." The institutes promoted commonly agreed upon assessment objectives and allowed the participating state board members to review test questions and rate them as substandard, reasonably good or excellent, using straightforward criteria. For example, was the question centered upon a patient problem? Did it measure retained knowledge or show fitness? Could variations of the question be developed? Drawing upon their experiences and knowledge gained through the institutes, the state board members then returned to their respective states charged with incorporating the institutes' work into their licensing examinations.

Despite the initial enthusiasm for the institutes and their strong early attendance, by the early 1960s the logistical and assessment challenges inherent to a decentralized approach to state board examinations had become increasingly hard to ignore. For example, state board members sought to write high-quality, patient-centered clinical questions at a time when increasing specialization and fragmentation in medicine's clinical areas made creating current, relevant examination questions ever more challenging for state medical board members, most of whom were nonspecialist physicians trained many years earlier. Board members were required to distinguish between essential and nonessential content objectives for licensing exams, often in areas unrelated to their own practice, which meant they had to maintain some degree of familiarity with the changes in medicine and medical education. They were learning firsthand that the concept of "fitness" seemed far more complex than when first proposed.[67]

Another challenge stemmed from the pool of candidates that would be taking these examinations and the nature of the license being issued by the states. State medical boards were assessing potentially three distinct cohorts with their examinations: recent U.S. graduates; IMGs; and physicians entering their state after many years in practice elsewhere. The latter group posed a unique problem. Surveying this broad candidate pool and the scope of the license, a New York board member pondered how a state should examine a doctor who graduated two decades earlier. Should the board be assessing the physician on the curriculum encountered years earlier in medical school and training or what they believed the physician should know today? Should the physicians be held accountable for a degree of familiarity with the entire field of medicine or solely within their own specialty or practice focus? For any thoughtful examiner, questions such as these were inescapable when developing content for their state board examination.[68]

Perhaps the greatest challenge to the viability of the institutes stemmed from features of their original construction. When first proposed and developed, the institutes were seen as a mechanism that might cultivate a collective national group of examiners from within the medical licensing community. It quickly became apparent that the institutes were in some regards a massive exercise in faculty development, training a cadre of individual state medical board members to think creatively about the content and construct of their examinations. However, the institutes were ultimately a voluntary endeavor conducted without the ongoing assistance and resources of a professional testing agency. Thus, the task presented through the institutes was immense and called for board members to perform two roles simultaneously. They would serve as content experts developing and/or revising test items while also acting as de facto testing professionals crafting the measurement objectives and content outlines for their examinations. The sense of mission and higher purpose engendered by the introduction of the institutes lent a crusade-like quality to the endeavor. But faith alone, unsupported by adequate resources like access to a professional testing agency's expertise, proved insufficient.

One other aspect of the institutes' original construction in 1956 bears noting—the test items developed through the institutes appear to have been predominantly subjective, essay questions. While this was historically the most common assessment method of state boards along with oral and practical examinations, it represented an increasingly dated methodology at a time when professional testing agencies were moving to objective testing, such as multiple-choice questions. The National Board of Medical Examiners formally approved transitioning to an objective multiple-choice question format in 1954; the National Board of Osteopathic Medical Examiners did so as well for its licensure qualifying examination for osteopathic physicians in 1958. Sensing inadequacies in their examinations, some state medical boards were already looking to the NBME for assistance. As early as 1953, the Connecticut board sought the assistance of the NBME to develop and score questions for its licensing examination. Other states (New York, Massachusetts, Illinois, Virginia) were soon testing the waters as well. Some state boards drew upon the NBME's test item pool for individual questions to supplement their examinations; other boards utilized complete test forms from the NBME Part I and Part II examinations. By 1966, eight states were using NBME content (all objective items) to assess more than 3,000 physicians nationally.[69] The following year the number jumped to sixteen states assessing more than 4,500 candidates, which meant that more than half of all licensure applicants were being tested using at least some NBME material.[70]

All of these factors brought a key question to the forefront: Were the institutes sustainable under their board-driven format? In 1963 the Federation called upon George Miller, director of research in medical education at the University of Illinois, College of Medicine, to help work through the issues surrounding this question. His subsequent report in the *Federation Bulletin* (August 1964) proved a turning point. Miller's evaluation of multiple states' licensing examinations raised serious questions about the validity of their examinations. He covered the qualities of a good examination; the correlation between performance of a written examination and an objective, reliable rating of on-the-job performance; and setting standards of competence. Miller concluded that a good test is reliable, with repeatable results; it minimizes subjectivity in scoring; and it clearly separates the satisfactory candidate from the unsatisfactory one.[71] The inference was clear if not wholly made explicit. The state boards' examinations required major enhancements if they were to meet the evolving professional standards in testing. The current situation was unacceptable for a high-stakes examination such as that being conducted for medical licensure. Miller's work called for nothing less than a commitment to professional standards for assessment predicated upon an objective style format—a direction already undertaken by some state medical boards who had engaged the National Board of Medical Examiners for assistance in developing content for their examinations.

This transformation presented no easy task as the ongoing shift toward objective testing had already encountered resistance within the licensing community. In the 1950s, some state boards reacted negatively when the National Board discarded the essay test as a model for its examinations and began applying the foundational measures for educational testing: validity, reliability, objectivity and practicability. At the time, most state medical boards relied heavily upon subjective questions as the predominant feature of their examinations, an assessment focused on the *art* of medicine. Ten boards actually withdrew their recognition of the NBME certificate. However, the NBME quickly sought advice and counsel from the Federation's Walter Bierring who, along with NBME President John Hubbard and a newly constituted NBME Committee on State Board Relations, moved to reassure state medical boards of the value derived from this new testing format—especially the potential for statistical analysis of objective items to lead directly to improvement of examinations in all professional fields. While it took time, these efforts paid dividends as by 1966 the National Board had regained recognition for its certifying examination by all but four state boards nationally.[72]

Robert Derbyshire summarized the situation as it stood in 1965–1966. According to Derbyshire, the concept behind the institutes' creation was "excellent"; their goals were appropriately aspirational. They succeeded in identifying the appropriate assessment role for state boards with the concept of "fitness testing." Yet, the end result failed to meet the "lofty" goals of the institutes. In blunt fashion, Derbyshire acknowledged that the institutes' work appeared to have gained insufficient traction among state boards with the result that many "continued to ask the same dreary, unimaginative, archaic questions." The imperative was clear: Either the Federation must address substantive changes to the Examination Institutes or the institutes and the Federation itself risked regression into little more than a "debating society."[73] Furthermore, failure to achieve anything close to common standards for licensing examinations risked stalling progress on licensure by endorsement. Previously, in 1962, Examination Institutes Chairman Andrew Gehret (Delaware) reminded the medical licensing community that a nationally administered examination would eliminate questions about content and scoring standards and provide a uniform, rational basis for interstate endorsement.[74]

A reevaluation came swiftly with the original intent of saving the institutes as the primary vehicle for delivering quality examinations. At its 1965 annual meeting, the Federation adopted a resolution calling for the creation of a long-range examination development plan. All subject material covered by the state medical boards would be covered; permanent subcommittees would be appointed for each of the subjects. Most important of all, however, the resolution called upon the Federation to seek funding immediately for professional assistance in developing examinations from the subject matter provided by state boards. In this way, the boards would retain their autonomy by bringing aboard professional assistance to standardize and shape the content and outline of their examinations. The Federation would establish an examination center to house the project.[75]

The Federation then appointed Leo Heywood, of Nebraska, to chair the Examination Institute Committee. Joining him on the committee were Lall Montgomery, Arthur Wright (New York), Frederick Merchant (Ohio), and Ray Casterline (Oregon). The committee believed that a properly organized, funded and utilized examination development plan could contribute unity, solidarity and respect to state medical boards and the medical profession at large. They set to work, determined to have a workable plan within two years. But soon into their research, the committee concluded that the ambitious proposal was unrealistic. Securing funding and trained personnel seemed problematic, as did the time frame necessary to activate the plan. More important, the committee concluded that they would be "duplicating" the work of existing professional testing agencies and certifying bodies.[76]

During the course of its investigations, the committee concluded that one organization was best positioned to render the necessary assistance and meet all the needs of the state medical boards—the National Board of Medical Examiners.[77] The National Board possessed assessment experience dating back to 1916, a cadre of professional staff at its disposal and a large item pool derived from its NBME Parts certifying exam. The committee abandoned the idea of establishing an examination center within the Federation in favor of working directly with the National Board to develop an examination specifically for the Federation and to be utilized by state medical boards exclusively for licensure.[78]

In June 1967, the first meetings took place with the National Board. Rhett McMahon (Louisiana) and Kenneth Schnepp (Illinois) represented the Federation in these important talks and the following key points were soon agreed upon: a Federation Licensure Examination, to be abbreviated as FLEX, would be administered twice annually (June and December) beginning in 1968. The three-day examination would use objective multiple-choice questions to cover the basic and clinical sciences and assess clinical competence and fitness. Subcommittees drawn from state medical boards would work with the National Board to construct an overall examination blueprint, identify appropriate test material drawn from the Board's Parts item pool, and if necessary assist in revising or developing new questions. Determination of the passing level and the formula for converting raw scores to scaled scores would be made by a FLEX committee, with the scores to be reported uniformly from state to state.[79]

The scoring aspect was particularly important in light of research findings published by Derbyshire in 1965. Derbyshire had reviewed the failure rates for state board examinations over a ten-year period, from 1954 to 1964, and his findings provided strong evidence for an unacceptably wide variance in the scoring standard being applied to these examinations. He found three states that failed no candidates during the entire ten-year period. Two other states failed no one in nine out of ten years; four states failed no one in eight out of ten years.[80] The FLEX examination being contemplated offered an opportunity to remedy such inequities by applying a common standard for scoring all examinees.

The Federation and the National Board promptly worked out financial and other important details of the joint effort. The National Board would distribute and score the tests; the Federation would collect fees from candidates. The test questions would be selected by the FLEX committee, whose membership would be drawn directly from state medical boards. Institute Chairman Leo Heywood emphasized that the new test would not "duplicate any present service of the National Board" as the overall examination blueprint focused on medical school graduates and the concept of fitness to practice. An important corollary of this was that the FLEX would be open to both U.S. and international medical graduates, unlike the NBME's examination which was restricted to U.S. graduates.[81] The participating states would be responsible for test administration, including secure handling of the test materials before, during and after the examinations.

Each section of FLEX was constructed in an interdisciplinary format so that the examination would be presented as a comprehensive assessment of the basic and clinical sciences, rather than as a series of tests in individual disciplines. The FLEX subcommittee for the basic sciences selected items that required "fundamental knowledge which every physician should know how to use intelligently, either in carrying out diagnostic procedures or in planning therapy." For the clinical sciences, the subcommittee chose each test item to measure a physician's ability to apply medical knowledge in solving clinical problems.[82]

The clinical competence section of the FLEX reflected the kind of "practical" examination that state medical boards had once embraced. Here the FLEX was able to draw upon and utilize some of the more unique features that had appeared in the National Board's Part III examination. The clinical material presented to examinees included images (e.g., X-rays, electrocardiograms) requiring interpretation and motion pictures of carefully selected patients. Another intriguing feature of the FLEX was its assessment of the examinee's judgment in the "sequential management of patients." This format presented a patient scenario and required examinees to select diagnostic studies and prescribe therapies. in managing an unfolding case. Here the FLEX most directly confronted and addressed the goal of fitness testing set forth by the Federation's Examination Institutes in the 1950s.[83]

The first FLEX administration took place in June 1968 with eight participating state medical boards and 663 examinees. A large committee, including Federation members and representatives from the participating state medical boards, evaluated the results. They decided that the scoring for the FLEX should emphasize the practical aspects of the knowledge of medicine and developed a "weighted average" by assigning a greater weight to the clinical parts of the examination.[84] In weighting the preponderance of the score to the clinical science and clinical competence sections of the examinations, the examination provided a reasonable assessment for IMGs and physicians years removed from medical school. The Federation recommended a minimum passing score of seventy-five that state boards adopt as a common standard, the same passing score that state medical boards had commonly been using on their own examinations dating back nearly a century.

The Federation pushed vigorously for states to participate in FLEX as it was clear that the age of medical licensing examinations written and developed solely by state medical boards had passed. Developing high-quality examinations required a highly specialized professional organization that could keep up with the changes in medicine, technology and the science of testing. Concurrently, the National Board phased out its provision of licensing examination material for individual state boards beginning in 1970. The rapid acceptance of FLEX and participation by state boards signaled their support for this move. Eight boards participated in the first FLEX administration in 1968: Illinois, Maine, Nebraska, New Mexico, Ohio, Oregon, West Virginia and Wyoming. Almost half the state medical boards were using FLEX for licensure by 1970, only two years after its debut. By 1973, all but two state medical boards had adopted the FLEX. Full implementation came in 1979, when Texas and Florida joined the fold.[85]

Frederick Merchant became the FLEX's greatest champion. His yearly reports were consistently optimistic and expansive, noting that results were better each year. Merchant's enthusiasm was understandable as the FLEX represented a significant accomplishment not only in the history of the Federation but for medical licensure as well. The FLEX represented two major achievements in medical licensure in the United States: (1) a nationally administered examination designed specifically as a medical licensing examination on the threshold of minimally acceptable competence open to both U.S. and international graduates, and (2) the application of a *national* standard in scoring the medical licensing examination. The importance of the latter point cannot be sufficiently emphasized. One of the greatest barriers to license portability in the United States emanated from the state licensing examinations, specifically their variability in content, rigor and scoring. While the broad recognition of the NBME certificate by state boards had already done much to facilitate portability, the persistence of this variability among state-developed exams meant that every state board understandably viewed with some degree of skepticism the examination results presented by physicians licensed in another jurisdiction through these state exams.

For the Federation, the FLEX represented the potential for a modest but stable long-term revenue stream to supplement the organization's resources. The organization had sustained itself over the years through member dues from state boards and small yearly grants from the AMA. These annual revenues covered expenses only and contributed little toward building any financial reserves. The FLEX presented nothing akin to a financial windfall for the Federation as its pricing covered development and administrative costs with a small margin of excess revenue. However, the Federation could look long-term to its issuance of transcripts reporting FLEX scores as a small revenue stream that would grow over time.[86]

As the FLEX continued to build momentum, the Examination Institutes Committee met several times each year with the National Board to discuss FLEX results in detail, refine test content and review projections for future needs. As early as 1973, the committee made one major change when they opted to discontinue using motion-picture film clips of actual patients and replace them with theoretical patient management problems (PMP). The films, while a laudable attempt at fidelity, had never proven wholly satisfactory. Difficulties in finding patients with a simple diagnosis willing to be filmed and the opportunity for "irregularities" when the testing room darkened to show the film combined to dampen enthusiasm for the format.[87]

Even as state medical boards rapidly adopted the FLEX, developments within the broader educational, assessment and licensing communities threatened to outpace the Federation's collaboration with the National Board in this examination program. The educational continuum for medicine now commonly included graduate medical education (GME) as the vast majority of physicians entered GME for more specialized training and preparation prior to independent practice following their graduation from medical school. The accrediting body for U.S. allopathic medical school programs, the Liaison Committee on Medical Education (LCME), reflected this reality and stated unequivocally that their curriculum was insufficient for unsupervised practice without the benefit of additional graduate training. The trend toward specialization in practice had been accelerating for some time, leaving the general practitioner an increasingly less common feature of the medical landscape. For some this prompted questions about the basic nature of medical licensure in the United States. Was an undifferentiated license for the practice of medicine and surgery still the appropriate model for licensure?[88] The 1973 publication of a Goals and Priorities (GAP) report by a committee reporting to NBME's governance made explicit a number of questions and concerns afloat within the environment.

The GAP report spoke of an educational continuum with critical transitions occurring at the entrance into GME and the issuance of an unrestricted license to practice (table 6.5). The report recommended a single assessment (Qualifying Exam A) prior to entry into GME, followed by a later examination (Qualifying Exam B) at the conclusion of GME and before the issuance of an unrestricted license. The GAP report also envisioned, but with considerably less detail, the possibility of subsequent periodic assessment (Qualifying Exam C) to ensure continuing competence of licensed practitioners as part of either specialty recertification or relicensure.[89] Not surprisingly, the report generated considerable attention and discussion within the medical education and licensing communities.[90]

While supportive of some recommendations contained within the report—specifically, the concept behind the Qualifying A examination prior

Table 6.5. Proposed Assessment Continuum in GAP Report

Undergraduate Medical Education	A	Graduate Medical Education	B	Practice/ Continuing Education	C

Source: John Hubbard and Edithe Levit, *The National Board of Medical Examiners: The First Seventy Years* (Philadelphia: National Board of Medical Examiners, 1985), 113.

Used with permission from the National Board of Medical Examiners to entry into supervised practice under a limited/training license—the Federation reacted cautiously. The Federation saw the inherent merit of differentiating between two distinct licensing contexts (supervised practice within GME and independent practice) but feared undermining the substantial progress made in the adoption of the FLEX. In 1974, the Federation's board of directors endorsed the concept behind a comprehensive qualifying examination (i.e., Qualifying A); and the following year, the board avowed that it was the responsibility of state medical boards to oversee physicians engaged in GME. Then, in 1977, the Federation established an Ad Hoc Committee on Uniform Licensure which later recommended that FLEX be redesigned into two components (FLEX 1 and FLEX 2) with an examination blueprint designed explicitly to support the two distinct decision points appropriate for state boards to be exercising their judgment: practicing supervised medicine within the context of GME and assessing individuals seeking the independent practice of medicine. The committee report gained approval in 1980 from the Federation board and subsequently the organization's entire membership. Federation members from state medical boards were integral contributors to the task forces charged with guiding development and implementation of the revised FLEX—John Morton (New York), David Citron (North Carolina), Max Butler (Texas), Howard McQuarrie (Utah), John Clark (Utah) and Henry Cramblett (Ohio).[91]

Through the enhancements to the FLEX, the Federation demonstrated its ability to serve the interests of the medical licensing community while simultaneously staying abreast of developments within the broader licensing and educational environments. Additionally, the multiyear process leading to the introduction of a revised FLEX in 1985 deepened the already strong working relationship between the Federation and the National Board at both the governance and staff levels. This would prove important when both organizations later took an even larger step toward a single examination pathway to licensure.

The rapid adoption of the FLEX in the early 1970s had other implications as well. In 1973, the Federation created the FLEX Board as a permanent, separate entity with its own budget, replacing the Examination Institutes Committee. Its six state board members were elected at the Federation annual meeting. The growing number of FLEX examinees necessitated operational changes at the Federation's offices in Fort Worth. Previously, in 1962, Federation Secretary McKinley Crabb negotiated the lease of office space from the Texas Medical Board's offices at the old Medical Arts Building in Fort Worth. With FLEX volume growing steadily (approximately 87,000 registered examinees by 1976), Federation staff required more sophisticated office management systems to manage the influx of registrations. Earlier, the Federation acquired a state-of-the-art Remington Rand Kard Veyer filing system that produced duplicate computer punch cards for each candidate. The rapid adoption of FLEX soon pushed the capacity of the 90,000-card system and required the Federation to acquire another room for storage space.[92] Along with the disciplinary data being forwarded to the Federation by state medical boards, data from these FLEX registrations helped provide the origins for the organization's current licensure database, which contains more than 1.2 million records.

Though still relatively small in size, the Federation continued to evolve to take advantage of the opportunities arising from the organization's increasing profile nationally and the challenges presented by the multiple issues confronting state boards. The Federation's permanent standing committees (e.g., FLEX, Legislative Advisory, Public Relations) saw increased workloads, and new committees were added to address gaps in critical areas. For example, in 1970, the organization added an Editorial Committee to oversee the *Federation Bulletin* and a Long-Range Planning Committee to provide strategic guidance. Liaison activity with external organizations such as the NBME, ECFMG and the AMA Council on Medical Education continued with sometimes heightened urgency. In 1970, the Federation's board of directors instituted annual independent audits for organizational finances and realigned its fiscal year to coincide with the calendar year. Federation President John Morton, looking to the future technical needs of the Federation and state member boards, convened a symposium in 1975 on computerizing licensing data—a concept well ahead of its time for the vast majority of state boards in the mid-1970s but one, nonetheless, reflecting the long-term direction that Morton and others saw as inevitable in the disciplinary realm, in particular. All the while, the Federation's monitoring of the legislative landscape continued as evidenced by a revised third edition of the *Essentials* appearing in 1977.

Finally, one of the more important fundamental changes to the Federation's membership structure occurred in 1971 when the organization amended its bylaws to include independent state osteopathic medical boards as members. Because many of the earliest state laws limited the practice privileges of osteopathic physicians, any corresponding osteopathic board in that state had previously issued solely a limited or restricted license for the practice of medicine. Consequently, as these boards lacked the power to issue an unrestricted license to practice medicine they had previously been ineligible for membership in the Federation.

This change to the Federation bylaws reflected an ebbing tide in the long-standing professional tensions between allopathic and osteopathic physicians in the house of medicine. These tensions crested in California during the early 1960s when a merger between that state's allopathic and osteopathic medical associations soon brought osteopathic physicians under the purview of the medical board.[93] The state's simultaneous offer for osteopathic physicians to obtain an M.D. degree for $65 after completion of a seminar through the University of California College of Medicine in Irvine sparked controversy nationwide. Fortunately, mollifying actions soon followed as the AMA shifted away from the disparaging "cult" label assigned to osteopathy and, in 1966, U.S. Defense Secretary Robert McNamara announced the Johnson administration's decision to accept and recognize osteopathic physicians for full military services equivalent to those rendered by allopathic physicians.[94] Lieutenant General Ronald Blanck, an osteopathic internist who was among the first osteopathic physicians to serve in Vietnam, went on to serve as the thirty-ninth surgeon general of the United States Army from 1996 to 2000, overseeing 46,000 military personnel and 26,000 civilian employees worldwide.

Issues arising from allopathic-osteopathic relations reached the Federation directly in 1970 when a letter from a member of the Colorado board questioned whether osteopathic boards were eligible for Federation membership. As initial sentiment from the Federation's executive committee was favorable to admitting independent osteopathic boards, President Frederick Merchant promptly convened an ad hoc committee to study the matter. Chaired by Arthur Wright, the committee canvassed the Federation's member boards for input, met directly with the AOA Board of Trustees and gathered testimony through a series of open hearings at the Federation's 1971 annual meeting. Discussions at the hearings proved largely positive, though one member of the Maine board raised concerns that bringing osteopathic boards into membership might undercut the progress being made with the FLEX toward greater uniformity in licensing examinations; specifically cited was the continued option for osteopathic physicians to take the NBOME Parts examination. Despite any reservations that the inclusion of osteopathic boards would "indirectly endorse" a dual system of licensure based upon different exams, the committee's final report recommended revising the bylaws to admit osteopathic boards. The Federation's executive committee endorsed the recommendation and the organization's House of Delegates overwhelmingly accepted the revision.[95]

By the mid-1980s, the Federation's membership had expanded to include the osteopathic boards from Arizona, California, Florida, Michigan, Nevada, New Mexico, Oklahoma, Pennsylvania, Tennessee, Washington, and West Virginia. Some of the potential for expanding the Federation's membership was tempered in the 1980s and 1990s by the consolidation of the osteopathic boards in Hawaii, Maryland, Montana, and Nebraska into composite boards licensing both M.D. and D.O. physicians.[96] In retrospect, the Federation appears to have been fortunate in avoiding the extreme contentiousness that characterized much of the allopathic-osteopathic physician relationship in the decades prior to the 1971 bylaws revision. However, the concern raised by the Maine board member in 1971 regarding the persistence of two medical licensing examination pathways proved prescient as the topic reemerged as a major issue several decades later.

Throughout the 1960s and 1970s, the Federation steered a course between buffeting cross winds: professional versus public interests; the need for common standards against the preservation of a localized regulatory system; state boards' traditional activities versus shifting expectations for the role of the boards; and maintaining state-based medical regulation at a time of increased federal involvement in health care. As the 1970s drew to a close, the Federation could look back upon momentous changes impacting both the organization and its member boards. Beginning in the 1960s, state medical boards entered an era of heightened accountability in which public interests moved to the forefront in multiple areas. The composition of state medical boards changed irrevocably with the inclusion of public, nonphysician members. The boards' position within their state governments also changed as multiple states shifted their state medical boards into larger umbrella agencies licensing multiple professions—sometimes trading a measure of autonomy for access to greater resources such as investigative staff and in-house counsel. This manifested itself most clearly with the growing sophistication of the boards' disciplinary procedures as the primary focus of the boards shifted from their traditional licensing and examining function to a genuine disciplinary role regulating the practice of medicine. Heightened demands for accountability meant that even the traditional concept behind license renewal (i.e., a largely de facto administrative process) appeared to be misaligned when viewed through a continuing competence lens. State boards evinced a willingness to revisit their most fundamental historical function—the licensing examination—and relinquish some measure of control by adopting the FLEX as a means of fostering greater uniformity of standards. Progress often came more slowly than many would have preferred but, in retrospect, the magnitude of the changes under way nationally among state medical boards warranted perhaps measured steps rather than movement by leaps and bounds. This steady pace, with incremental progress on multiple fronts served state boards well as the national government assumed an increasingly direct role in health care delivery.

The Federation's role and function in these changes often proved central. Sometimes the organization acted as a catalyst to change; other times it traveled at its own measured pace seeking to move in concert with the majority of its member boards. In 1977, Federation Secretary-Treasurer Harold Jervey had such pressures in mind when he commented upon the increasing prominence of the Federation and the consequential demands upon it.

> The central office receives requests . . . for an ever widening variety of information and services . . . there is an ever increasing demand for the Federation to be represented . . . in Washington and at [national] meetings . . . the visibility and influence of the Federation has increased a thousandfold . . . and a unique opportunity exists for an even greater role.[97]

As it turned out, even more significant changes and opportunities lay ahead. The organization, supported by a handful of employees in the early 1970s, would soon increase to more than one hundred staff members. Opportunities in the guise of new assessment programs, a credentialing service and a computer database of board actions and licensee information were just beyond the horizon.

NOTES

1. "Framingham Heart Study," National Heart, Lung and Blood Institute, accessed January 17, 2012, http://www.framinghamheartstudy.org/about/history.html.
2. Walter L. Bierring, "A Third Point of View," *Federation Bulletin* (February 1960): 32–33.
3. Ameringer, *State Boards and Politics of Protection*, 3, 14–15, 21, 26.
4. Ibid., 1, 29.
5. Starr, *Social Transformation*, 7–8.
6. "The Status of Discipline in the Medical Profession," *Federation Bulletin* 47 (January 1960): 3–4.
7. "Report of the Medical Disciplinary Committee to the Board of Trustees," 1961 AMA House of Delegates Proceedings, American Medical Association, accessed on January 13, 2012, http://ama.nmtvault.com/jsp/browse.jsp, 55, 60, 63–64; "Discipline and the Doctor—The View from Atlanta," *JAMA* 172 (January 23, 1960): 121–22.
8. Ameringer, *State Boards and Politics of Protection*, 14; "Report of the Medical Disciplinary Committee," 1961 AMA House of Delegates, 56, 79–80.
9. "Report of the Medical Disciplinary Committee," 60, 64–66, 79.
10. Lall Montgomery, "Panel on Problems of Discipline: Unprofessional Conduct," *Federation Bulletin* 47 (September 1960): 306–9.
11. Ameringer, *State Boards and Politics of Protection*, 18–22.
12. Harold E. Jervey, "A Survey of Medical Discipline," *Federation Bulletin* 48 (April 1961): 84.
13. Stiles Ezell, "The Fate of Discipline," *Federation Bulletin* 48 (January 1961): 1–3.
14. Jervey, "Survey of Medical Discipline," 84.
15. Ibid., 85, 88.
16. Ibid., 88–92.
17. Ibid., 93; Harold Jervey, "The President's Page," *Federation Bulletin* 47 (June 1960): 209; "Again, Thanks to the AMA," *Federation Bulletin* 49 (September 1962): 234.
18. "Again, Thanks to AMA," 235.
19. "Report of the Secretary," *Federation Bulletin* (July 1966): 211.
20. "The Fate of Discipline," *Federation Bulletin* 48 (January 1961): 2; Howard L. Bobbitt, "Investigative Procedures and Preparation," *Federation Bulletin* 49 (September 1962): 240.

21. Leonard Larson, "Medicine's Role in Self-Discipline," *Federation Bulletin* 49 (June 1962): 151; William Smith, "Recent Cases and Tomorrow's Problems," *Federation Bulletin* 57 (December 1970): 379.

22. Lall Montgomery, "Unprofessional Conduct," *Federation Bulletin* 47 (September 1960): 310; "The Federation and Discipline," *Federation Bulletin* 48 (March 1961): 53.

23. James Sammons, "Health Manpower in the Medical Marketplace," *Health Affairs* 1, no. 4 (1982): 21.

24. Derbyshire, *Medical Licensure and Discipline*, 77; Robert Derbyshire, "Medical Ethics and Discipline," *JAMA* 228 (April 1, 1974): 61; Robert Derbyshire, "How Effective Is Medical Self-Regulation?" *Law and Human Behavior* 7, no. 2/3 (1983): 197; Ameringer, *State Boards and Politics of Protection*, 41.

25. Derbyshire, "Medical Ethics and Discipline," 59.

26. C. J. Glaspel, "Problems in Narcotic Addiction," *Federation Bulletin* 45 (July 1958): 200; John M. Fiorino, "Narcotic Addiction in Physicians," *Federation Bulletin* 47 (August 1960): 275, 279.

27. Robert Derbyshire, "Physician Competence," *New York State Journal of Medicine* (June 1979): 1030; Joseph Nesbitt, "The Sick Doctor Statute, a New Approach to an Old Problem," *Federation Bulletin* 57 (September 1970): 267; Louis E. Jones, "Experience with Probation in California," *Federation Bulletin* 45 (June 1958): 165–73.

28. Derbyshire, *Medical Licensure and Discipline*, 83–85.

29. Thaddeus Murawski, "Unscrupulous Physician: Our Success and Failure," *New York State Journal of Medicine* (June 1979): 1021–22.

30. Derbyshire, "*Medical Ethics and Discipline*," 59–60; Ameringer, *State Boards and Politics of Protection*, 29–30.

31. Carl F. Ameringer, "State Medical Boards and the New Corporate Order," *Journal of Medical Licensure and Discipline* 89, no. 2 (2003): 59–60.

32. Frederick Merchant, "Challenges to Medical Licensing Boards," *JAMA* 212 (June 15, 1970): 1949–51.

33. John H. Morton, "The Public on the Boards," *Federation Bulletin* 62 (June 1975): 184–85; Howard L. Horns, "Challenges to and Responsibilities of the Federation of State Medical Boards" *Federation Bulletin* 62 (March 1975): 81.

34. See revised (1970) and 4th edition (1985) of *A Guide to the Essentials of a Modern Medical Practice Act* (Fort Worth, Texas: Federation of State Medical Boards); *Elements of a Modern State Medical Board* (Fort Worth, Texas: Federation of State Medical Boards, 1989), 1.

35. Gregory Rockwell, "The Role and Function of the Public Member," *Federation Bulletin* 80, no. 1 (1993): 42; Andis Robeznieks, "Public Active on Medical Boards, but Not Always Tougher on Doctors," *AMedNews*, November 11, 2002.

36. Gwen Andrew and Harold Sauer, "Do Boards of Medicine Really Matter? The Future of Professional Regulation," *Federation Bulletin* 83, no. 4 (1996): 228–29; David McPhee, "The Public on the Boards . . . What Is the Role of the Consumer Members?" *Federation Bulletin* 65 (January 1978): 14; Linda Wasmer Andrews, "Public Members: The Voice of the Public," *Journal of Medical Licensure and Discipline* 88, no. 2 (2002): 70–71.

37. McCready and Harris, *From Quackery to Quality Assurance*, 28; Ameringer, *State Boards and Politics of Public Protection*, 48–49; Derbyshire, "How Effective Is Medical Self-Regulation?," 201; "Table 2—Membership: Composition, Terms," *1999–2000 Exchange: Volume 3: Licensing Boards, Structure and Disciplinary Functions* (Euless, Texas: Federation of State Medical Boards, 1999), 4–5; "State Board Composition Table," Federation of State Medical Boards, accessed on January 13, 2012, http://www.fsmb.org/grpol_keyissues.html.

38. Ameringer, *State Boards and Politics of Protection*, 62–64; Richard Kusserow, Elisabeth Handley, and Mark Yessian, "An Overview of State Medical Discipline," *JAMA* 257 (February 13, 1987): 822; Gregory W. Schroeder, "Board Reorganization, Umbrella Agencies, Super Boards: Pro's and Con's," *Federation Bulletin* 68 (October 1981): 292–99.

39. Elizabeth Graddy and Michael B. Nichol, "Structural Reforms and Licensing Board Performance," *American Politics Quarterly* 18 (July 1990): 376; Robeznieks, "Public Active on Medical Boards"; Andreas Broscheid and Paul Teske, "Public Members on Medical Licensing Boards and the Choice of Entry Barriers," *Public Choice* 114 (March 2003): 445; Elizabeth Graddy and Michael B. Nichol, "Public Members on Occupational Licensing Boards: Effects on Legislative Regulatory Reforms," *Southern Economic Journal* 55 (January 1989): 610.

40. Wasmer Andrews, "Public Members," 74.

41. Stephen Abrahamson, "Research in Continuing Medical Education: An Historical Review," *Mobius* 4 (October 1984): 11–12.

42. Robert Derbyshire, "Relicensure for Continued Practice," *Federation Bulletin* 59 (July 1972): 31–32; "Physician Relicensure? Not Yet!," *Federation Bulletin* 57 (February 1970): 53; "Study of the Need for Mandatory Continuing Education," *Federation Bulletin* 84, no. 1 (1997): 30; "Physician's Recognition Award and Credit System," American Medical Association, accessed January 13, 2012, http://www.ama-assn.org/ama/pub/education-careers/continuing-medical-education/physicians-recognition-award-credit-system.page; Abrahamson, "Research in Continuing Medical Education," 12.

43. *Handbook of the Council on Continuing Medical Education* (Chicago: American Osteopathic Association, 2009), 3; Hubbard and Levit, *National Board of Medical Examiners*, 110–13; *Evaluation in the Continuum of Medical Education* (Philadelphia: National Board of Medical Examiners, 1973), 38.

44. "Study of Need for Mandatory Continuing Medical Education," 29; "11 Doctors Expelled by Medical Society," *Federation Bulletin* 59 (February 1972): 78; *Golden Past, Brilliant Future—American Board of Medical Specialties: Celebrating 75 Years in Serving the Public Trust, 1933–2008* (Chicago: American Board of Medical Specialties, 2008), 12–13.

45. David Johnson, Dale Austin and James Thompson, "Role of State Medical Boards in Continuing Medical Education," *Journal of Continuing Education in the Health Professions* 25, no. 3 (Summer 2005): 184; Carroll H. Lippard, "The First Century: A History of the Virginia State Board of Medicine, 1884–1984" (unpublished TMs, 1984), 21 at FSMB Archives, Euless, Texas.

46. See Robert Derbyshire's "Relicensure for Continued Practice," *Federation Bulletin* (July 1972) for a detailed narrative charting the course of this historic legislation.

47. Robert Derbyshire, "Review of New Mexico Relicensure," *Federation Bulletin* 62 (October 1975): 300; "Recent Amendments to Arizona Medical Practice Act," *Federation Bulletin* 63 (July 1976): 219–20.

48. See 1987 and 1999 editions of *Exchange*, Sections 1–2 (Euless, Texas: Federation of State Medical Boards, 1987), 51, 59, 63, 86; "Continuing Medical Education Overview by State," Federation of State Medical Boards, accessed on January 12, 2012, http://www.fsmb.org/grpol_keyissues.html.

49. Gerald Dorman, "The Necessity for Change," *Federation Bulletin* 57 (March 1970): 72–75; Howard Horns, "Challenges to and Responsibilities of the Federation," 77; Howard McQuarrie and Dale Breaden, "Assessment of Physician Competence for Relicensure," *Federation Bulletin* 66 (December 1979): 358–60; Dan Nye, "Report of the Federation Committee to Assess Physician's Competence for Relicensure," *Federation Bulletin* 68 (August 1981): 249.

50. Derbyshire, "Relicensure for Continued Practice," 241; Linda Wasmer Andrews, "Maintenance of Competence: Boards Look for Ways to Teach Old Docs New Tricks," *Journal of Medical Licensure and Discipline* 87, no. 4 (2001): 143.

51. Anderson Spickard, David Dodd, et al., "Physicians Who Misprescribe Controlled Substances: A CME Alternative to Sanctions," *Journal of Medical Licensure and Discipline* 98, no. 1 (1998): 8; William Swiggart, James Pichert, et al., "Continuing Medical Education Courses on Proper Prescribing of Controlled Substances in the United States," *Journal of Medical Licensure and Discipline* 86, no. 1 (1999): 20.

52. Derbyshire, "Relicensure for Continued Practice," 236; "The Assurance of Quality Medical Care by the Medical Profession," *Federation Bulletin* 66 (June 1979): 173; Robert Derbyshire, "Let's Be Fair," *Federation Bulletin* 66 (December 1979): 366–67; Archie R. Cohen, "Preventing Obsolescence in Physicians," *Federation Bulletin* 58 (January 1971): 9; John F. Hubbard, "Self-Assessment Programs: Summation of Objectives," *Federation Bulletin* 58 (February 1971): 72.

53. Dan Nye, "Report of the Committee to Assess Physician Competence for Relicensure," *Federation Bulletin* 68 (February 1981): 244–49; Dan Nye, "Report of the Committee for Continued Study of Uniform Licensure and to Assess a Physician's Competence for Relicensure," *Federation Bulletin* 67 (July 1980): 217–20.

54. "Health Manpower Commission Study of Medical Licensure Indicates Need for Nationwide Federation-Backed Action," *Federation Bulletin* 57 (October 1970): 318.

55. Ibid., 319–20.

56. Starr, *Social Transformation*, 396–397; Stevens, *American Medical and the Public Interest*, 498–99.

57. John H. Morton, "S-3585, Prescription for a Nightmare," *Federation Bulletin* 61 (October 1974): 351–53.

58. Ray L. Casterline, "A Time for Action—The Development of a Federation Position Paper," *Federation Bulletin* 61 (October 1974): 325–26.

59. John H. Morton, "Too Soon," *Federation Bulletin* 63 (May 1976): 150–51.

60. John H. Morton, "Too Broadly," *Federation Bulletin* 63 (June 1976): 188–89.

61. John H. Morton, "State Licensure—A Mess?" *Federation Bulletin* (August 1976): 250–51.

62. Robert Derbyshire, "On Indentured Servitude and the Bureaucrats—Some Comments on S 3582," *Federation Bulletin* (September 1974): 295.

63. Liaison Committee on Medical Education (LCME); Liaison Committee on Graduate Medical Education (LCGME); Liaison Committee on Continuing Medical Education (LCCME); National Board of Medical Examiners (NBME); Federation of State Medical Boards (FSMB).

64. "Health Manpower Credentialing," *Federation Bulletin* 63 (November 1976): 341–46; "National Board of Medical Examiners Comments on 'A Proposal for Credentialing Health Manpower," *Federation Bulletin* 63 (November 1976): 346–49; "Response by the American Board of Medical Specialties (ABMS) to 'A Proposal for Credentialing Health Manpower,'" *Federation Bulletin* 63 (December 1976): 374–82.

65. Hubbard and Levit, *National Board of Medical Examiners*, 60–61.

66. Derbyshire, "Indentured Servitude," 297; Nye, "Report of Committee to Assess Physician Competence," 244–45.

67. "The Examination Institutes: Final Report," *Federation Bulletin* 48 (August 1961): 219–20.

68. "The Preventive Medicine Examination Institute," *Federation Bulletin* 47 (January 1960): 16.

69. "Evaluating the Institutes," *Federation Bulletin* 48 (January 1961): 4; Hubbard and Levit, *National Board of Medical Examiners*, 25, 28, 69–70; Betty Burnett, *In the Public Trust: The National Board of Osteopathic Medical Examiners, 1934–2009* (Chicago: National Board of Osteopathic Medical Examiners, 2010), 14.

70. Frederick Merchant, "Annual Report of the State Medical Board Relations to the National Board of Medical Examiners—1967," *Federation Bulletin* 55 (August 1968): 262.

71. George E. Miller, "Federation Institute 1964—Background," *Federation Bulletin* 51 (August 1964): 238–45.

72. Hubbard and Levit, *National Board of Medical Examiners*, 19–25, 27–29; Donald E. Melnick, "NBME Then and Now—1915 to 1990," in *Proceedings of the Seventy-Fifth Anniversary Invitational Conference, March 1990* (Philadelphia: National Board of Medical Examiners, 1991), 11–12.

73. "Step or Giant Stride?" *Federation Bulletin* 52 (March 1965): 77–78; "The Federation at the Crossroads," *Federation Bulletin* 53 (October 1966): 332.

74. "The Fiftieth Anniversary Program," *Federation Bulletin* 49 (March 1962): 50; "A Lawyer Speaks," *Federation Bulletin* 52 (May 1965): 144–45.

75. "Report of Examination Institute Committee," *Federation Bulletin* 52 (July 1965): 232.

76. Ibid., 233; "Step or Giant Stride," 79; "Annual Report of the Examination Institute Committee—1967," *Federation Bulletin* 55 (August 1968): 252.

77. Consult chapters 6 and 11 of *The National Board of Medical Examiners: The First Seventy Years* for a detailed description of the FLEX program from inception through its major revision in the 1980s.

78. "Report of Examination Institute Committee—1967," 252.

79. Ibid., 255–56; See also, Arthur Wright, Ray Casterline, and Kenneth Schnepp, "Analysis of FLEX, Part I, II, III," *Federation Bulletin* 56 (February 1969): 26–44.

80. Robert Derbyshire, "How to Obtain a License in One Easy Lesson," *Federation Bulletin* 52 (April 1965): 124–27.

81. "Report of Examination Institute Committee, 1967," *Federation Bulletin*, 257.

82. Hubbard and Levit, *National Board of Medical Examiners*, 71.

83. Ibid., 72; *FLEX: Description of Examination*, 3rd ed. (Fort Worth, Texas: Federation of State Medical Boards, 1973), page 1 insert.

84. Hubbard and Levit, *National Board of Medical Examiners*, 72.

85. John H. Morton, "F Is for Florida," *Federation Bulletin* 66 (July 1979): 205; Frederick Merchant, "Annual Report on Relations Between the Federation of State Medical Boards and the National Board of Medical Examiners," *Federation Bulletin* 57 (July 1970): 226; Ray L. Casterline, "Dates FLEX First Used in Participating Medical Licensing Jurisdictions," *Federation Bulletin* 61 (June 1974): 210.

86. "Federation News: Report of the Treasurer," *Federation Bulletin* 56 (August 1969): 233; "Report of the Treasurer," *Federation Bulletin* 57 (November 1970): 370.

87. Frederick T. Merchant, "Annual Report of the FLEX Board," *Federation Bull*etin 61 (May 1974): 164.

88. Hubbard and Levit, *National Board of Medical Examiners*, 112; John H. Morton, "Questions about the GAP Report," *Federation Bulletin* 60 (September 1973): 312–13.

89. Hubbard and Levit, *National Board of Medical Examiners*, 113.

90. For state board reaction, see John Morton's articles and editorials, "The State Medical Boards Approach the Gap," *Federation Bulletin* 61 (July 1974): 228–34; "What's Wrong with Qualifying B?" *Federation Bulletin* 62 (January 1975): 24–25; "Concerning a Comprehensive Qualifying Examination," *Federation Bulletin* 64 (May 1977): 154–56. See also chapter 10 of *The National Board of Medical Examiners: The First Seventy Years*.

91. Hubbard and Levit, *National Board of Medical Examiners*, 116, 119–20, 124–29.

92. "Again, Thanks to the AMA," *Federation Bulletin* 49 (September 1962): 235.

93. Interested readers should consult chapters 8–9 of Norman Gevitz's *The DOs: Osteopathic Medicine in America* for a detailed discussion of the California contretemps.

94. Howell, "Paradox of Osteopathy," 1466; Emil P. Lesho, "An Overview of Osteopathic Medicine," *Archives of Family Medicine* 8 (November/December 1999): 478; Gevitz, "Sword and scalpel," 283–85.

95. Ray Casterline, "Federation Membership Offered to Independent Boards of Osteopathic Examiners," *Federation Bulletin* 58 (September 1971): 348–56.

96. *1986 FSMB Handbook* (Fort Worth, Texas: Federation of State Medical Boards, 1986); "Maryland, Montana, Nebraska," *Federation Newsletter*, March 1982.

97. Harold Jervey, "The Federation Stands at a Crossroads," *Federation Bulletin* 64 (September 1977): 274.

Chapter 7

The Modern Federation Emerges, 1980–2001

The question is not whether we should act but how soon we can act.

—Bryant Galusha, 1989

On June 5, 1981, a brief report appeared in the Centers for Disease Control and Prevention's *Mortality and Morbidity Weekly Report* describing five cases of young men who did not know one another but who had contracted *Pneumocystis carinii* pneumonia at three different hospitals in Los Angeles, California. Two of the patients died but all five had laboratory-confirmed evidence of previous or current cytomegalovirus (CMV) infection and oral thrush suggesting, the report said, "the possibility of a cellular-immune dysfunction related to a common exposure that predisposes individuals to opportunistic infections." By 2009, the illness that these first cases described, Acquired Immune Deficiency Syndrome (AIDS), had claimed the lives of 30 million people worldwide. As the AIDS epidemic enters its fourth decade, however, there are signs of hope: Since 1999 the number of new infections has fallen 19 percent even though an estimated 33.3 million people now have the human immunodeficiency virus (HIV) that causes AIDS.[1]

Ominous developments in the world of medicine like AIDS, or the H1N1 pandemic of 2009, represent not merely challenges to physicians and health care providers but also to the medical regulatory systems that were intended to support the continuous delivery of quality health care services.

For example, a 1996 study of adult male patients with AIDS found those who were cared for by physicians with the most experience had a 31 percent lower risk of death than patients care for by physicians with the least experience.[2] Should medical regulatory authorities review the ability of physicians to continue to practice medicine in their area of practice, given the continued explosion and complexity of medical knowledge across all specialties? This and related questions would gain momentum as the new millennium approached. The ability to not only identify but to anticipate regulatory needs and craft responses to them requires strong and proactive state board leadership. During the 1980s and 1990s, Bryant Galusha and James Winn, the Federation's successive executive leaders, would be supported by forward thinking and support from the organization's governance that allowed the organization to grow and mature with a series of major initiatives that would help to promote quality health care nationwide while assisting the state boards in their mission to protect the public.

The first wave of organizational growth began in 1984 when Bryant Galusha assumed the duties of chief executive officer for the Federation. The organization remained small, with fewer than fifteen staff members, but its potential for growth and increased prominence were abundantly clear. Galusha's administrative background as medical director at a Charlotte (North Carolina) hospital, his earlier tenure on the North Carolina Medical Board, chairmanship of the Federation's Long-Range Planning Committee and relationships cultivated as a member of the National Board of Medical Examiners (NBME) offered a blend of superb skills and experiences perfectly suited to coordinate the many aspects of the Federation's diverse activities. These proved particularly important at a time when the Federation was poised for significant growth.

Stepping into his new role, Galusha identified two necessary goals for his tenure as the Federation's chief executive: To make the organization and its offices as efficient as possible and to educate the public on the work of the Federation and its member boards. Before he left the organization, he added one more ambitious goal—to pursue a single examination pathway for medical licensure.[3] By the end of the century, several efficiency initiatives had laid the groundwork for the enhancement and expansion of Federation services related to the collection and sharing of reliable information. These initiatives also opened communications with representatives of federal agencies, state legislatures, private advocacy groups and other organizations in the "house of medicine" (both national and international). They reflected as well a renewed responsiveness to the interests and demands of the public at large, providing new opportunities for the Federation to take a leadership role on a much larger stage; and with the advent of the United States Medical Licensing Examination (USMLE) the organization took a major step toward uniformity in medical licensure.

COMPUTERIZATION OF FLEX AND BOARD ACTION RECORDS

Galusha inherited a small cadre of experienced staff from his predecessor, Harold Jervey, and was determined to improve upon the daily operations of the Federation's offices. In particular, Galusha and the Federation's board of directors scrutinized the informational and data needs of the organization. Modernization of its operational procedures and data management constituted a primary concern if the Federation wished to fully perform its role in aggregating and disseminating information and data for use by state medical boards. Galusha's efforts accelerated the Federation's transition to a digital environment, a process that had commenced only several years earlier. This transition responded to a 1980 directive from the Federation's member boards, calling upon the organization to develop a "centralized computerized data base" in order to better serve the licensing community.[4]

The operational impetus for computerizing the Federation's records arose in the late 1970s. A backlog of nearly 100,000 hard-copy FLEX records prompted the organization's board of directors to establish a special task force to consider options for computerization of the Federation's operations in 1978. With this backlog of records and wholly manual processes for their maintenance, the task force recommended that the organization move rapidly to computerize its FLEX and board action records. To address the former, the Federation turned initially to the National Board of Medical Examiners who, as the assessment arm supporting the FLEX, then housed FLEX data electronically in addition to the hard-copy records located at the Federation's offices. The National Board's assistance took two forms. Their Psychometrics Department provided an "early vision" for the Federation's computer system while the NBME governance proposed absorbing a portion of the initial costs. Meanwhile, the Federation pursued funds from private foundations to subsidize the endeavor. Initial progress faltered when it became clear that private foundations could only distribute funds to 501(c)3 entities, such as foundations—or "friends of organizations"—under the U.S. Internal Revenue Code. The Federation, focused as it was on the advancement of the interests of a membership community and organized as a 501(c)6 entity in 1966, was ineligible to receive the funding it anticipated from the Robert Wood Johnson Foundation. This temporary setback had a positive long-term benefit, however, as it spurred the subsequent creation of the Federation's Education and Research Foundation.[5] By 1983, Federation staff had successfully addressed the backlogged FLEX records with the assistance of the NBME, while several computer terminal stations for Federation staff and additional funding support from the Educational Commission for Foreign Medical Graduates (ECFMG) helped expedite the transfer of records.[6]

The successful transfer of FLEX data into an electronic format represented only one-half of the major data sets housed by the Federation. In addition to functioning as the official repository for FLEX data, the Federation served as the national repository for disciplinary actions taken by all state medical boards. The organization now turned its attention to computerizing its board action data bank. The Federation had long been a conduit for communicating disciplinary actions among state medical boards. Prior to 1971 this meant publishing disciplinary actions taken by state medical boards in the pages of the *Federation Bulletin*—a helpful though not exhaustive listing of all actions. Then, in 1971, the Federation began disseminating this information through a monthly Disciplinary Action Report. All the while, the board action data bank existed as a massive file system consisting of thousands of index-card records. Querying these records as part of the more than 20,000 annual requests received by the Federation to search this data bank meant manually searching this massive card system, a time-consuming and labor-intensive process inherently vulnerable to human error.[7] Efficiency and quality assurance dictated that the Federation transition to a searchable, computerized database for all disciplinary actions.

Efficiency alone, however, did not serve as the primary driver of the Federation's efforts toward modernizing its board action data bank. The federal government's desire to detect and prevent fraud and abuse in the administration of its Medicare and Medicaid programs had prompted a closer look at the state-based system for medical licensure and discipline. Delayed and incomplete reporting by state medical boards had been an unfortunate reality that hampered the Federation's ability to provide a definitive national repository for disciplinary data or to demonstrate effective state-based protection of the public. Indeed, it was not until 1981 that the Federation could promote the fact that all of its state boards had provided disciplinary reports for that year. This reality had not gone unnoticed at the federal level. A 1984 report of the U.S. General Accounting Office (GAO), later the General Accountability Office, addressed the "undetected movement" of physicians seeking a license in another state after being sanctioned by the medical board in their home state. In 1985, Galusha addressed the situation directly and in forthright fashion with his colleagues in the state board community. The Federation had already committed itself to modernizing its disciplinary data bank. The Federation and its member boards would have to work together to address and resolve the reporting issues undermining the ability of a state-based system to collect, assimilate and distribute disciplinary data about physicians. Failure to do so, Galusha asserted, meant that a federal agency—likely the U.S. Department of Health and Human Services (HHS)—would seek enabling legislation to assume this role for itself in the public's interest.[8] Years later, similar concerns would help drive the Federation's interest in promoting state-based programs such as license portability, a uniform licensing application and expedited licensure for telemedicine.

The Federation moved quickly to address this situation by undertaking a multiyear project that involved coding and electronically entering the information from thousands of board actions already residing in hard copy at the Federation's offices. Simultaneously, the Federation's leadership embarked upon an outreach initiative to establish close contacts with key federal agencies, specifically the HHS, the Veterans Administration, Department of Defense and the GAO. These efforts soon paid off with a $225,000 federal grant from the Health Resources and Services Administration (HRSA), a division of HHS, to facilitate continued work toward computerization of the Federation's board action data bank as well as an additional grant supporting a FLEX task force to refine computerization of those records. During this period, Galusha and the organization's chief operational officer, Dale Breaden, developed invaluable contacts and relationships with Richard Kusserow, the Inspector General of Health and Human Services, key legislators such as U.S. Senator Claude Pepper of Florida, and the Congressional staff who had an interest in promoting quality health care for the nation.[9]

This progress paralleled the Federation's efforts to assure that all state boards were not only timely and accurately reporting their disciplinary actions to the Federation but also that they were able to rapidly query the organization's board action data bank as part of their licensing process. Galusha understood that computer technology was an enabler for progress but not the sole determinant. Ultimately, the efficacy of the state-based disciplinary system, he noted, rested upon "thorough, timely and conscientious reporting" by each state medical board. The Federation attempted to streamline the system further through the introduction of a standard form for reporting disciplinary actions, which most boards were utilizing by 1986. The "extensive modernization" embarked upon by the Federation was deemed critical because the board action data bank (with more than 16,000 actions) supported nearly 20,000 queries annually as part of the medical licensing and credentialing process. Federal grants allowed the Federation to conduct additional analyses to ensure that its coded "interpretation" of the actions reported by state boards accurately reflected the intent and action of those boards. Additionally, the organization moved rapidly to develop a prototype "ready access system" allowing boards to contact the Federation electronically to query the data bank. In 1988, the Georgia, Illinois, Ohio, and Texas medical boards piloted a prototype program that the Federation eventually introduced for all boards as the Direct Access System (DAS). This system represented an important advance in medical regulation by allowing all boards with a desktop computer and an online or telephone modem to remotely and quickly query the Federation's board action data bank on the physicians they were credentialing as part of their licensing process.[10]

The Federation's DAS rendered a critical service by further constraining an historical loophole by which a small number of errant and unscrupulous physicians exploited inadequate interstate communications and the lack of a proactive reporting feature within a national disciplinary data bank. As long as boards reported their actions on a timely basis and routinely queried the Federation, state-hopping physicians could no longer relocate with impunity from one jurisdiction to the next for a medical license in hopes of remaining one step ahead of the authorities. Admittedly, the mechanism was not perfect as the onus for timely reporting and querying still fell to the state boards. Nevertheless this represented a major advancement in the state-based system's safeguards that proved timely as events at the national level and the evolving discourse on physician discipline in the 1980s and 1990s increased the spotlight on the effectiveness of state boards' disciplinary efforts.

FURTHER FEDERATION ASSISTANCE TO STATE MEDICAL BOARDS IN THEIR DISCIPLINARY ROLE

Some level of scrutiny had always been the case for state medical boards in carrying out their historical function as the "gatekeeper" responsible for licensing and disciplining physicians within their state or territory. However, the gatekeeper terminology carried more pejorative connotations than praise to critics and historians who, reflecting on the earlier era of boards comprised exclusively of physicians, characterized them as inherently monopolistic and likely to shield professional interests. Any truth to such assertions grew weaker during the last half of the twentieth century as the medical profession witnessed steady erosion in its traditional power and authority as the exclusive voice of medical regulation.[11] Market forces and governmental agencies had shifted the dynamics of power, particularly for those operating under the impetus of the public accountability movement that reinvigorated state boards with public members and a heightened focus on disciplinary matters. The pendulum swing toward consumer interests and more extensive governmental oversight seemed to belie the notion of state medical boards being "captive" to the interests of the medical profession. Indeed, the history of state medical boards in recent decades appears to undercut much of the criticism arising from economic theorists equating virtually all efforts at professional licensing with a monopoly.[12] One legal scholar's assessment of the medical practice acts establishing state boards (dating to the nineteenth century when evidence of professional self-interest is easiest to demonstrate) determined that they were now being redrafted "clearly pursuant to the legislative authority . . . protect[ing] public health and safety."[13]

By the late 1970s and continuing forward, state medical boards continued to face an increasing number of questions concerning the performance of their disciplinary function. How many complaints were being investigated? How many actions were being taken annually against physicians? What kinds of cases were being prioritized? How was the board constituted to investigate and, if necessary, adjudicate cases? What resources had been dedicated to the investigative and disciplinary processes? This latter question was especially critical as boards seldom possessed the resources one would have expected for the task assigned to them. For example, the Virginia board did not gain funding for its first full-time investigative staff until 1976, when the board was already trying to process more than 5,000 complaints annually.[14]

As discussed in the previous chapter, beginning in the 1960s a transformation had commenced that shifted the primary emphasis of state boards toward their disciplinary function with a somewhat diminished emphasis on their traditional role in examining and licensing physicians. As this transformation continued into the 1980s, state boards and their disciplinary processes were increasingly scrutinized to see what progress had been achieved. Media assessments critical of state medical boards' performance in disciplinary matters, then as now, have invariably focused on the number and timeliness of actions being taken by boards. Similar critiques have come from other groups such as Public Citizen, a consumer advocacy group founded in 1971 by activist Ralph Nader.[15] The quantitative focus of such critiques is understandable and, in many ways, appropriate for a profession (medicine) defined in large part by its observance of evidence-based standards for clinical practice. At times, however, these critiques inadequately consider both the limited resources and legal constraints under which medical boards operate as state agencies. Specifically, this means affording both procedural and substantive due process to their physician licensees. While courts have been generally deferential to state boards in their licensing and disciplinary decisions, such deference cannot be presumed in the absence of sound judgment by a board in setting reasonable standards and demonstrating a "rational connection" between their decisions and the physician's ability and fitness to practice.[16] Such caveats notwithstanding, it is worth noting that state medical boards are also empowered to take summary action in egregious instances of physician misconduct that place the safety of the public in danger, even without initially requiring due process.

More nuanced academic studies of state medical boards' performance began appearing in the late 1970s that took into consideration characteristics such as board composition, structure and access to resources. These studies underscored the multifactorial complexity of the disciplinary system.[17] Some scholars questioned the validity of board criticism that focused on the number of actions being taken (especially when fewer actions could also mean better enforcement and preventative measures by a board) and placed the medical regulatory system's national figures within interprofessional and societal contexts. The national data showed rates of disciplinary actions for physicians similar to those seen in other professions (e.g., the legal profession) and comparable to felony conviction rates among the general public. A 1998 study cited the national data as suggestive of state medical boards' "increased . . . ability and resolve" to pursue disciplinary matters. Others, such as the director for the Office of the Inspector General, pointed rightfully to the undervaluing of the many "second-tier" actions taken by boards. These ranged from reprimands or censures to stipulated agreements, in which a physician might voluntarily surrender a license. The HHS characterized these actions as "significant" and dismissed the notion of critics characterizing these actions as somehow less consequential in their implications.[18] State medical boards were understandably heartened that federal agencies recognized the importance of all actions being taken by state boards and not solely those involving license suspension or revocation.

The breadth of work conducted by state boards as regulators of the practice of medicine grew markedly beginning in the 1980s. National data for this period derived from the Federation's Physician Data Center (table 7.1) underscore the growing emphasis given to this aspect of the boards' functioning. In 1980, there were 1,163 total actions taken by all state medi-

Table 7.1. Board Actions Reported to FSMB by Member Boards and Total Number of Physicians with a Board Action, 1980–2000

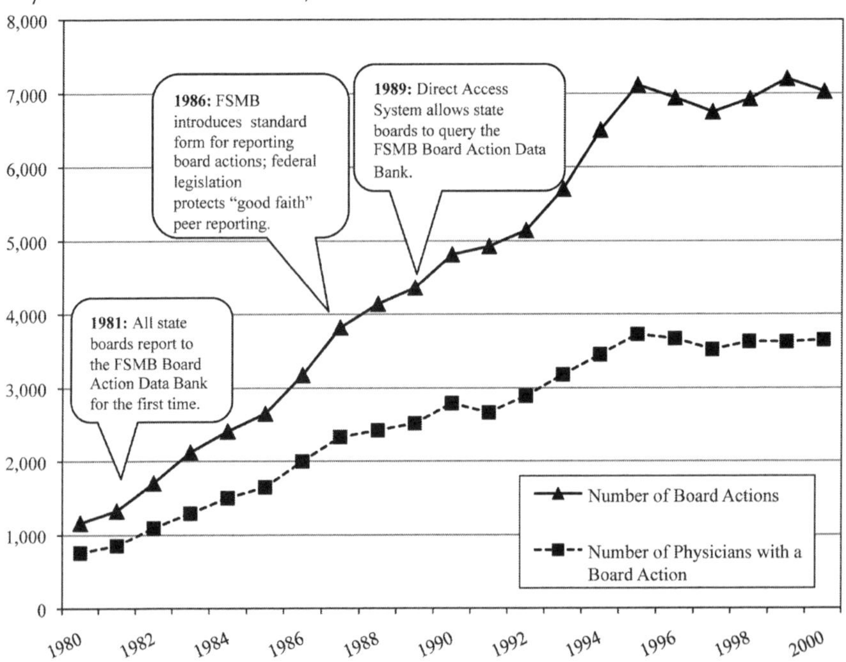

Note: Board action and physician counts reflect reportable actions from FSMB member boards; "notices" and "accusation actions" are excluded.

cal boards against 756 physicians; thirty years later, the annual figures exceeded 7,000 actions, involving 4,457 physicians. While the number of physicians disciplined by state boards remained small as a percentage of all active U.S. physicians (0.17 percent of the estimated 441,000 physicians in 1980 and 0.6 percent of the estimated 738,000 physicians in 2000), these figures represent a more than 300 percent increase in the number of disciplined physicians.[19] More important, as a reflection of the total body of disciplinary work engaged in by state boards across the country, this period witnessed a 600 percent increase in the total number of actions taken by state member boards.

Precisely what contributed to this increase is unclear but one might speculate concerning the impact of several factors. The Federation continued to assist boards in making their disciplinary practices a key point of emphasis. In 1986, all state boards received a copy of the Federation publication *A Model for the Preparation of a Guidebook on Medical Discipline*, along with a standardized form for reporting actions to the Federation's disciplinary data bank. Perhaps more important, however, was the introduction of the Federation's Disciplinary Alert Service in 1988, which facilitated state boards' ability to query the FSMB board action data bank and thus made it easier to (1) identify one of their licensees with an action taken in another jurisdiction, and (2) take a reciprocal action, if appropriate or necessary. Beyond this, there were national factors likely contributing to this upward trend in the national data, such as the 1986 Health Care Quality Improvement Act, which legally protected "good faith" peer reporting.[20] Ultimately, measures such as this and the generally greater emphasis that state boards placed upon their disciplinary functions appear to have contributed to creating a milieu in which state medical boards were responding in a positive and appropriate manner to public and professional expectations.

Even if one accepted that the number of disciplinary actions taken by a state board represents a reasonable quantitative basis for measuring that board's performance, such data have generally not been presented with sufficient explanatory and contextual information addressing the multiple factors impacting the data. State boards faced significant legislative, legal and sociological obstacles in their transition toward becoming more robust disciplinary bodies. Robert Derbyshire wrote extensively about state medical boards and their disciplinary processes beginning in the 1960s and continuing well into the 1980s. As recently as 1983, he noted, all but fifteen states lacked statutory language enabling the state board to suspend or revoke the license of one of their physicians as part of a reciprocal action based upon a similar sanction taken against that physician's license in another state, a practice that is routine today. In numerous states, the legal system itself presented an obstacle with ex parte stay orders (a decision made by a judge without a requirement for all of the parties to the controversy to be present) available to physicians seeking to contest a board ruling for suspension or revocation. Further compounding the challenge for state boards was the "curtain of silence" that long surrounded the profession for much of its history in the United States and which sometimes insulated errant physicians against outside scrutiny. This reality did not go unnoticed in a mid-1980s assessment of medical discipline by the Office of the Inspector General (OIG) of HHS. The report commented on the "strikingly few" actions then originating as complaints or reports from physicians' peers, hospitals or other health professionals.[21] When factors such as these are considered in conjunction with the paucity of resources generally allotted to state boards, the story that emerges from aggregate national disciplinary data in the 1980s and 1990s seems all the more impressive for the scope and volume of work undertaken by boards under challenging conditions.

The Federation's efforts to assist boards in their disciplinary role took many forms in the 1980s and 1990s. The aforementioned computerization and enhancements to the Federation's board action data bank represented a significant investment by the organization to close the communication loop among the Federation and state boards in alerting the latter to the actions taken against one of their licensees by another jurisdiction. The Federation provided procedural and statutory assistance through a series of publications such as the aforementioned *Model for the Preparation of a Guidebook on Medical Discipline*. This guidebook evolved from the work of the Federation's Legislative and Legal Advisory Committee, chaired by David Citron (North Carolina), and provided boards with a framework for constructing their own customized version of a disciplinary guidebook. Updated editions appeared into the 1990s as well as multiple updated and revised editions of the Federation's *Essentials of a Modern Medical Practice Act* that reflected best practices and trends in the disciplinary arena. Meanwhile, the Federation supported federal legislative efforts to assist state boards when appropriate, such as those sections of the 1986 Health Care Quality Improvement Act protecting good-faith peer reporting. The Federation also championed the adoption of mandatory reporting laws in states lacking this legislation and better enforcement in those states where the laws already existed.[22]

If state medical boards were once "little noticed instrumentalities" within state government, such a reality has long ceased to characterize medical regulation. Instead, high-profile cases of physician misconduct continue to arise periodically, sometimes capturing national media attention, and casting a spotlight on the role of state boards and their disciplinary processes. As a complaint-driven system, state board discipline is admittedly a "reactive" process. However, proactive features of state board discipline are not only possible but desirable, particularly as a means for addressing quality of care cases. A series of reports from the HHS Office of the Inspector General in the 1990s outlined the challenges to boards in attempting to address these types of cases. Inadequate funding and resource limitations (investigative, medical, legal) were clearly major stumbling blocks, but the OIG also deemed the commitment of boards to pursue such cases as being equally critical. The report *State Medical Boards and Quality-of-Care Cases: Promising Approaches* noted the proactive measures in multiple states to identify and address substandard practice, for example, the Ohio board's work to increase awareness of such requirements in its state; the Minnesota board's willingness to enforce its reporting requirement; North Carolina's random audit of pharmacy records; Wisconsin's prioritization scale for evaluating complaints; and several boards' creative use of physician committees and contract physicians/nurses to help prioritize complaints. The OIG reports acknowledged the value of these individual measures and encouraged boards to develop and adopt comprehensive programs that increased proactive oversight. Comparisons were made explicit to the possibilities this approach represented in an earlier OIG report noting the billing and practice audits that have long been utilized in Canadian provinces to identify deficiencies and, when appropriate, direct physicians to assessment and remediation programs. The underlying assumption behind these reports holds that addressing deficiencies before they metastasize into outsized quality of care cases reaching the board through formal complaint represents the ideal for medical regulators.[23]

Despite the potentially adverse publicity from high-profile disciplinary cases or the periodic exposé articles they might engender, such occurrences sometimes have a salutary effect. For example, such cases sometimes spotlight the lack of enabling legislation to assist boards in carrying out their mission. Similarly, such cases often draw attention to the limited resources usually available to state boards and the all-too-frequent practice of diverting funds from the board into the state's general coffers. In regard to the latter, recent scholarship has already confirmed what many suspected intuitively. Larger boards with greater autonomy and resources are those most likely to discipline physicians and to do so more frequently. Even critics of the disciplinary system have attributed the variance in state boards' performance in this realm as stemming—at least in part—from differences in funding and staffing levels. This sine qua non remains a frustrating reality for state medical boards that has sometimes been addressed most forcefully in the wake of high-profile disciplinary cases such as a recent one involving the Delaware pediatrician Earl Bradley. The 2009 investigation and subsequent conviction and sentencing of Bradley on multiple counts of rape and child exploitation spurred state legislators to pass a series of laws empowering the board to expedite license suspensions, obtain information from peer review panels and impose fines for failure to report unprofessional conduct.[24]

Undoubtedly, the public and media will continue to view board performance as correlative with the number of disciplinary actions taken. This remains an important metric but insufficient by itself to attest to a board's efficacy. Accordingly, in 2011 Federation Board Chair Janelle Rhyne (North Carolina) established a working group to examine state medical board metrics. Chaired by Kevin Bohnenblust, executive director for the Wyoming Board of Medicine, the group is considering better and more informative ways by which state boards can objectively and effectively measure their performance beyond the absolute number of board actions they take each year. Whatever is ultimately decided, it seems clear that unless a numerical focus also includes pressure on state legislators to remove legislative and fiscal impediments to adequate board resources, neither the public nor the media are likely to see further dramatic changes in the disciplinary data.

The medical disciplinary system appeared to reach critical mass in the 1980s when even those within the medical profession were acknowledging the need for greater enforcement of standards. *New England Journal of Medicine* editor Arnold Relman reflected this shift in view when he asserted that most state boards have been "too lax" rather than "too strict" in holding all physicians accountable to minimum professional standards.[25] Public frustration grew with every newspaper report exposing shortcomings in the disciplinary system, such as those in the *Detroit Free Press* and *Chicago Tribune* between 1982 and 1984. More direct federal interest and involvement in the disciplinary realm arose from an unrelated investigation into the sale of fraudulent credentials and medical diplomas. A 1982 U.S. Postal Service investigation into activities connected with two medical schools in the Dominican Republic (Universidad CETEC and Universidad CIFAS) led to their subsequent closure and federal wire fraud and conspiracy charges against several individuals. The fallout from this scandal overlapped with a pilot study started several years earlier by the OIG that checked the licensure status of physicians billing under Medicare and found fifteen individuals illegally billing Medicare despite a revoked or suspended license.[26] This prompted the OIG to begin an extensive investigation into the state-based system for medical licensure and discipline culminating in a major report in 1986.

The OIG report, *Medical Licensure and Discipline: An Overview*, drew a largely positive picture of state medical boards and their efforts. The report lauded boards for their achievement with the introduction of the FLEX examination in 1968 and cited multiple examples of innovative or best practices in disciplinary matters. Specifically cited were California's model disciplinary guidelines and the use of separate investigative and hearing panels in Colorado and Vermont. Positive statutory changes were duly noted, such as those in Massachusetts that precluded ex parte rulings during the appeal phase of a board's final decision and in Florida where the board was empowered to issue "cease and desist" orders against unlicensed practitioners.[27]

According to the OIG report, however, discipline remained a "festering" problem due in part to the disconnect between public expectations for improvement and state boards' capacity to perform their role at that level given their available resources. The report culminated in a series of recommendations that included better reporting from peer review organizations (PROs) and hospitals and requiring state boards to report their disciplinary actions to HHS so that physicians with revoked or suspended licenses could be excluded from legally billing Medicare and Medicaid for their services. These burgeoning conversational threads about state boards, disciplinary processes and their intersection with federal agencies soon coalesced in the form of federal legislation (PL-99-660) calling for a national database that would house information on disciplinary actions, adverse malpractice decisions and hospital privileging—the database known today as the National Practitioner Data Bank.[28]

The Federation appeared uniquely positioned to serve as the national repository envisioned by the federal legislation. The Federation's board action data bank contained over 16,000 board actions by 1988, housed within a modernized computer system on the verge of integrating remote searches by state member boards. However, the funds and manpower necessary to incorporate the malpractice and privileging components called for in the proposed federal database represented a scope of work too large for the organization to attempt singlehandedly. Thus, the Federation partnered with the American Medical Association in drafting a response to the federal government's request for a proposal on the new databank. The two organizations labored through the first half of 1987 to formulate the proposal, which was submitted in August of that year. The FSMB-AMA proposal called for joint operation of the data repository, with the Federation maintaining the disciplinary component and the AMA handling the malpractice and hospital-privileging component. A subsequent "best and final offer" to HHS on this Practitioner Adverse Credentialing Data Bank followed in October 1987.[29]

When federal funding for the proposed databank failed to materialize, HHS issued a new request for proposal (RFP) in 1988. The Federation and AMA noted the complexity and expanded scope in the new RFP for a National Practitioner Data Bank. Lingering concern by the Federation about providing "access" without relinquishing "ownership" of the disciplinary data it housed, as well as the new elements of complexity inherent to the revised RFP, led both organizations to decline further pursuit of the initiative. Though not reflected in the extant correspondence, anecdotal evidence suggests that joint FSMB-AMA operation of the data bank might well have encountered opposition within Washington, D.C., from those seeking a wholly independent entity to run the data bank—one insulated from any perceptions of protecting the interests of either physicians or state boards. Ultimately, a government contract to establish and run the National Practitioner Data Bank went to UNISYS, a global provider of information technology services.[30]

EXPANDING THE SCOPE OF SERVICES: THE FEDERATION AS INFORMATION AND DATA RESOURCE

The computerization efforts of the Federation in the 1980s reflected the organization's commitment to becoming an informational and data resource in service to the medical regulatory community. While much of the work during this time period involved developing the physical infrastructure and technical systems to facilitate this role, an equally significant effort went into a series of initiatives that broadened the scope of the Federation's services. Some of these, such as the All-Licensed Physicians (ALP) initiative and the Federation Credentials Verification Service (FCVS), represented large-scale efforts dependent in part upon the organization's nascent information technology (IT) infrastructure. Other initiatives undertaken at this time represented intensive (and often manual) information and data gathering for published documents intended for use by state medical boards.

One of the first of these initiatives resulted in the Federation's publication of its *Legislative and Regulatory Exchange*, or as it simply became known, the *Exchange*. By the 1970s, state medical boards, though acting as independent entities, looked increasingly to their sister boards and colleagues within the regulatory community for insight and shared knowledge concerning the many challenges facing them. This proved especially true in the legislative arena. In 1980, the Federation moved to facilitate better networking and information sharing among boards by assigning designated regional coordinators drawn from senior state board staff members.[31] The coordinators facilitated the collection of detailed information on changes in state laws and other data related to licensure. In 1983, the Federation released the first edition of the *Exchange* under the guidance of Dale Breaden. The publication quickly proved itself as an invaluable reference and resource for state boards. As its name implied, the *Exchange* facilitated information sharing among state boards by offering a document that quickly identified sister boards where similar legislative activities were under way.[32] The

Exchange moved through eleven editions between 1982 and 2000, starting as a slim single volume before growing into a three-volume set covering three hundred pages. Initially the *Exchange* focused exclusively on changes and developments in legislation, board rules and regulations. By 1986, the *Exchange* expanded into its three-volume format, with individual volumes dedicated to licensing requirements for allopathic and osteopathic physicians as well as a volume dedicated to detailed information on board composition and characteristics for each state.

In some ways, the *Exchange* may have suffered from its own success. Already a resource-intensive undertaking as a single-volume publication drawing upon regional coordinators, the expanded multivolume *Exchange* added significantly to the information and data acquisition required to sustain it. Each volume contained a state-by-state breakdown in tabular format covering an expanding set of information. The expansive informational and data elements being captured placed time demands beyond the capacity of state board staff volunteering their time to the project on top of their full-time state responsibilities. Federation staff soon absorbed the information/data acquisition task. Even then, however, the resource-heavy project—which continually generated requests for inclusion of new and additional informational elements—proved unsustainable in its then-current format. The Federation ultimately placed the *Exchange* on hiatus after the 2000 edition but began working in 2011, at Janelle Rhyne's suggestion, on a new, streamlined and Web-based version of the *Exchange* that will reorient it closer to its original design as a vehicle for communicating legislative activity.

The 1990s witnessed another major information/data initiative by the Federation—the development of a Self-Assessment Instrument (SAI) for state medical boards. The genesis for the SAI can be traced to the efforts of a Federation workgroup chaired by Melvin Sigel (Minnesota) in 1988. At that time, HRSA issued an RFP for a descriptive document outlining the key structural and functional elements for an effective state medical board. In fulfilling that RFP, the Federation's workgroup drafted the first edition of what became the *Elements of a Modern State Medical Board,* a companion piece to the Federation's *Essentials* document. As the workgroup progressed in drafting the *Elements,* they recognized that developing a template document for model board structure and function represented only a first step. Individual state boards urgently required an objective instrument for measuring their own performance longitudinally and in comparison to other boards of similar size and structure. An added incentive for such a tool emerged from the increasingly common practice of rating boards' effectiveness based solely upon the annual number of disciplinary actions taken by each board—a questionable practice that one writer referred to as counting the scalps on a lodge pole.[33]

The federal Agency for Health Care Policy and Research (later the Agency for Healthcare Research and Quality, or AHRQ) picked up the workgroup's recommendation for an assessment instrument and soon after contracted with the Federation to develop the SAI. An assessment task force, chaired by Gerald Bechamps (Virginia), spent eighteen months constructing the SAI. The result was an extensive (forty-two-page) questionnaire designed to be used by each state board to assess its overall performance in organizing and administering its affairs, licensing physicians, handling discipline, communicating with the profession and the public, dealing with legislative matters, addressing the problems of impaired physicians, and regulating allied health professionals. The questions elicited detailed, objective information and provided a basis for ongoing self-evaluation and improvement. First introduced in 1991, subsequent iterations of the SAI in 1992–1993 offered a computer-disk option for inputting data. The resulting executive analysis report of aggregated data represented input from a majority of the state boards.[34]

PROMOTING COLLABORATION AMONG INTERNATIONAL REGULATORY AUTHORITIES

When Walter Bierring served as the Federation's de facto executive officer and editor of the *Federation Bulletin*, he regularly published articles on medical regulation practices throughout the world. Having trained overseas himself, he often looked for opportunities to include speakers from the international medical community on the Federation's annual meeting program. In the late 1970s, Harold Jervey joined ECFMG's chief executive officer, Ray Casterline, in visiting several nations to present information about the FLEX to various international medical regulatory authorities. Hearing of the value of such exchanges, the Federation's board of directors in 1977 voted to explore and promote the establishment of an international association of medical licensing authorities from English-speaking countries; the Board reaffirmed its position in support of the initiative a year later. In 1983, Dale Breaden led a Federation contingent on a three-week trip through the Soviet Union and China, deepening the Federation's understanding of medical regulation internationally and sharing the organization's expertise and experiences. In 1987, another delegation led by former Federation Board Chair John Sage (Nebraska), visited Australia and New Zealand with the result that medical regulatory leaders from these nations have frequently attended Federation meetings ever since. Representatives of medical regulatory authorities in a number of Canadian provinces, meanwhile, have long been attending Federation meetings.[35]

In 1987, the Federation encouraged the federal government to formally support an international conference on medical regulation. The rationale was simple—the problems and issues faced by medical regulators were "not unique to any one nation," with all parties potentially benefiting from an exchange of ideas and best practices.[36] Further progress did not occur until the early 1990s, when the Federation turned to Margaret Wilson at HRSA's Bureau of Health Professions. The Federation had collaborated with Wilson on several initiatives previously, and benefited from her depth of knowledge about medical licensure and discipline. In 1993, the Federation received an RFP from HRSA for an international conference focusing on a research agenda for medical licensure/registration and discipline. Later that year, HRSA awarded the Federation a contract to plan and oversee what became known as the First International Conference on Medical Licensure/Registration and Discipline. According to Dale Breaden, "it was a logical extension of the Federation's vision [and a] clear recognition that . . . no nation can ignore the lessons to be learned through the sharing of experience, information, research, and insight with others around the world." The conference was set for May 1994 in Washington, D.C.

From the beginning, the Federation saw the conference as the start of a continuing dialogue leading to conferences in future years and a growing roster of participating countries. The meeting's Planning Committee was chaired by Gerald Bechamps, the Federation's president-elect, and included representatives from much of the Anglophone world—Australia, Canada, Ireland, New Zealand, South Africa and the United Kingdom.[37]

Among the key decisions made by the planning committee was that those countries with multiple licensing jurisdictions (e.g., Australia, Canada, and the United States) would have six funded representatives each and those with a single, national licensing system (e.g. Ireland, New Zealand, South Africa, and the United Kingdom) would have four, permitting a total of thirty-four funded participants. It was also decided that up to one hundred observers would be welcome, and sixty-five ultimately attended. At the meeting, Fitzhugh Mullan, then director of HRSA's Bureau of Health Professions, delivered an initial address followed by presentations and guest speakers from the New York Department of Health; the National Board of Medical Examiners; the Josiah Macy Jr. Foundation; the Johns Hopkins University School of Hygiene and Public Health; and the Educational Commission for Foreign Medical Graduates. In attendance were representatives from HRSA, the American Osteopathic Association, the National Council of State Boards of Nursing, Public Citizen's Health Research Group, and numerous observers from nonparticipating nations—Egypt, Israel, Mexico, and Taiwan.[38]

The conference examined the potential for research to inform a number of commonly shared issues: medical discipline; accreditation versus examination as the basis for medical regulation; physician impairment; physician competence; and others. Attendees had the opportunity to explore differing practices for fundamental features of the medical regulatory process. For example, countries such as Australia and the United Kingdom rely upon graduation from an accredited institution as their basis for adding someone to their register of physicians, while in the U.S. and Canada medical school graduates are independently assessed before being issued a license. The fundamentally different roles played by assessment in the participating countries led the conference attendees through a constructive dialogue that helped them self-identify strengths and weaknesses of their own and others' processes. Similar dialogue informed the discussion and potential for collaborative research in nearly a dozen other areas.[39] The success of the conference was borne out by its continuation in Melbourne (1996) and Cape Town (1998). These conferences culminated in a concerted multinational effort that in 2000 led to the creation of the International Association of Medical Regulatory Authorities (IAMRA),[40] as first envisioned by the Federation's board nearly a quarter century earlier.

FACILITATING LICENSURE ENDORSEMENT: THE SPECIAL PURPOSE EXAMINATION AND THE FEDERATION CREDENTIALS VERIFICATION SERVICE

The first and traditional function of state medical boards has been licensing, that is, reviewing the credentials and qualifications of a physician to assure minimum standards for the safe and effective practice of medicine before issuing a full, unrestricted medical license. This remained a labor-intensive yet critical task consuming a good deal of state boards' time and resources even as public expectations grew to demand greater board vigilance and activism in the disciplinary arena. A thorough vetting of credentials and qualifications at the point of initial licensure remained a given for all boards. But what about physicians already licensed in one state and relocating to another? How appropriate and efficient was it to rely upon a vetting process conducted potentially years earlier by a sister board in another state? This proved one of the more vexing challenges facing the state boards, dating back to their modern origins in the late nineteenth century. In many ways, the issue devolved into a practical question: Just what level of scrutiny and assessment was necessary in licensing a physician already licensed (and presumably in good standing) in another state? Direct assistance in answering this question and providing state boards with appropriate assessment tools arrived in the mid-1980s.

Like most state boards, the Medical Board of California had long been challenged by the need for "trusted" information on the current knowledge and abilities of physicians presenting themselves to the board for licensure by endorsement. Performance on a licensing examination taken years earlier, letters of reference and self-reported information/data on the practice of the physician applicant were helpful but insufficient. In 1985, the California board contacted the Federation to request assistance in assessing its licensure endorsement candidates. A subsequent survey of all state boards the following year underscored the widespread interest in, and need for, a cognitive assessment tool to assist the boards' licensing decisions for these candidates.[41]

The Federation moved quickly by partnering with the National Board to develop the Special Purpose Examination (SPEX). The SPEX provided the state board community with a single-day examination focusing on clinical knowledge and underlying basic science principles in the practice of medicine. Built initially upon the practice model design of the FLEX, the SPEX offered a comparable breadth of coverage. However, the SPEX eschewed the depth of coverage on FLEX for an examination geared toward assessing physicians who had already been in practice for five years or more. FLEX Committee Chair Henry Cramblett (Ohio) and his colleagues guided the early SPEX.[42]

State boards responded quickly and favorably to this new assessment as a valid, objective measurement tool intended to identify individuals unable to "demonstrate a reasonable cognitive foundation" for practice. Seventeen state medical boards directed 275 physicians to take the SPEX in 1988, the first year of its administration. By the early 1990s, forty state boards were directing 700–800 physicians to the SPEX annually.[43] While not a panacea for all the challenges posed by physicians relocating years after initial licensure or reentering practice after extended absence, the SPEX offered boards an important addition to the resources available to them in attempting to address physician competency. The SPEX today serves as one component of the broader initiative by the Federation and the National Board to address the post-licensure assessment needs of state medical boards. The Post-Licensure Assessment System (PLAS), jointly sponsored by the Federation and the National Board, also features collaborative arrangements with physician evaluation/remediation groups from California to New York to address clinical competence concerns.

While the SPEX provided assistance to state boards in assessing the cognitive knowledge of physicians licensed previously in other jurisdictions, much more needed to be done in order to facilitate licensure endorsement even when assessment issues did not exist. For more than a century, state medical boards balanced their legal responsibilities for licensure with the need for practical solutions to license portability problems posed by geographically mobile physicians—an issue more pressing now than ever due to advances in technology that enable delivery of health care electronically. The challenge for state boards was to achieve greater efficiency and timeliness through *centralized* processes without abdicating their constitutional role in a decentralized state-based system of licensure. For state medical boards, the solution resided in part with the Federation. A 1980 resolution passed by the Federation's House of Delegates called upon the organization to establish a "centralized" database, accessible by member boards and housing a "licensing profile" for all physicians.[44] The envisioned, comprehensive Federation database for all licensed physicians in the United States and its territories remains a work in progress but in the mid-1990s the Federation, under the supervision of its new chief executive officer, James R. Winn, took a major step in that direction—one that sought to relieve boards of the labor-intensive work of credentialing while bringing the organization closer to the envisioned comprehensive database serving state boards.

The immediate origins of the Federation Credentials Verification Service (FCVS) can be traced to the discussions arising from a conference on licensure endorsement held in conjunction with the April 1993 annual meeting of the Federation. The conference brought together senior staff from state boards across the country to address issues stemming from state-specific requirements and processes for licensing physicians by endorsement. The conference culminated with the attendees recommending a pair of feasibility studies—one to examine the prospects for establishing a national credentials repository serving state medical boards and the other to study minimally acceptable standards for credentialing, including forms and documentation. Newly installed Federation Board Chair Hormoz Rassekh used these requests as the impetus to form a Federation Ad Hoc Committee on Licensure by Endorsement in May 1993. Drawing upon the expertise of senior staff from the California, North Carolina and Ohio medical boards, the committee submitted its final report and recommendations to the Federation's House of Delegates in spring 1995. The committee's report acknowledged some of the systemic barriers to license portability, such as variations in graduate medical education requirements among the states. However, the committee report clearly articulated reasonable measures for mitigating such barriers. Specifically, the committee called for the acceptance of commonly recognized and static core credentials as defined in its report (e.g., identity; medical education and training; and licensing examination results) and called for the establishment of a centralized repository of verified credentials. Following the House of Delegates' adoption of the report, the Federation's board of directors moved quickly to authorize the implementation of a credentials repository and verification service—the FCVS.[45]

FCVS represented the logical culmination of nearly a century's frustration and the answer to many state boards' need for assistance in verifying physicians' credentials for licensure and/or licensure by endorsement. Two key concepts rest behind the premise of the FCVS: First, that there are a handful of core credentials for physicians that, once achieved, are largely static (e.g., identity and education) and second, that once these are verified directly with the originating primary source such as a medical school or hospital and placed in a permanent repository, it is unnecessary to duplicate this verification. Thus, the profile created by the FCVS contains core physician credentials and produces this for the state board along with a discrepancy report comparing the self-reported information from the physician with the results from the direct source verification. In the words of one state board executive director, the FCVS represented a "significant renovation" in licensure and a key element in creating a "rational" and sustainable state-based system for medical licensure.[46]

The FCVS was launched in September 1996 and a handful of state boards moved quickly to accept the FCVS profile. The Utah Physicians Licensing Board and Oklahoma State Board of Medical Licensure and Supervision were the first accepting boards. The State Medical Board of Ohio holds the distinction as the first board requiring all licensee applicants to utilize the service. Acceptance of this Federation service came rapidly, as evidenced by the twenty-six state boards accepting the FCVS packet of credentials by the end of 1996. Rapid acceptance translated directly into large volume as 12,000 physicians were utilizing the service by 1997.[47]

By the close of 2011, the FCVS had credentialed nearly 130,000 physicians. This represents a significant accomplishment when measured against the 850,000 actively licensed physicians in the United States. State medical and osteopathic boards have recognized the value of the service and sixty-seven of the sixty-nine licensing jurisdictions in the United States now accept the FCVS program to facilitate decision making about licensure; fourteen state boards require FCVS as part of their licensure process.[48] In 2009, the FCVS repositioned itself for further growth when the Federation's board of directors, under Board Chair Regina Benjamin (Alabama), authorized a significant investment to upgrade FCVS through a major rewrite of its software application and retooling of its operational processes. State boards contributed directly to the construct of the enhanced FCVS through the input of Administrators in Medicine (AIM), a body comprising executive directors and chief administrators of most state medical and osteopathic boards. The Federation launched this enhanced service in February 2011 with the FCVS already showing evidence of faster, more efficient verification of credentials and, following initial licensure, more expeditious generation and distribution of the physician's profile to state boards for subsequent or additional licensure. The service is now in the process of seeking certification status by the National Committee on Quality Assurance (NCQA) as an objective marker of its enhanced efficiency and quality.

EXPANDING THE SCOPE OF SERVICES—THE ALL-LICENSED PHYSICIANS INITIATIVE

In the 1990s, the presence of a personal computer and availability of Internet access were increasingly common features of American households. By decade's end, approximately half of all U.S. households had a home computer and 41 percent had Internet access.[49] With the explosion in readily available information and data on the internet covering virtually every facet of modern life (social, cultural, political and economic), public interest and demand for access grew correspondingly. As state medical boards and the Federation soon learned, balancing personal privacy and public transparency were not abstract concepts. Instead, these issues stood prominently at the center of the national movement calling for access to information about licensed physicians.

In November 1996, after several years of intense lobbying and legislative efforts by public advocates, the Massachusetts Board of Registration introduced its Physician Profiles Project. In doing so, Massachusetts became the first state to make a broad range of information on individual physicians available to the public, including education and training, disciplinary actions, and specialty certification. Massachusetts's citizens evinced a strong interest in such information, as seen by the nearly 16,000 physician profiles released to callers within the first month the board went live with the service.[50]

The experience of the Massachusetts board in offering physician profiles represented the start of a broader national trend. The following year saw physician profile initiatives carried out in Florida, Rhode Island and California, with seven more states enacting profile laws in 1998–1999. Independent of these legislative mandates, and during that same time period, fourteen state boards proactively chose to make physician profiles public, often through the Internet.[51]

This national movement for physician profiles also prompted the Federation to look closer at the completeness of its own physician database and the potential for further expansion to include other elements such as licensure information. At the end of 1996, the Federation's database housed all disciplinary actions taken by state boards, all FLEX examination scores and the beginnings of considerable additional information and data via the FCVS. If the Federation could partner with all its member boards to acquire and share licensure information, the organization might provide an additional service to state medical boards through a strengthened board action data bank and as a backup data repository in the event of a regional or national emergency interrupting the operations of a state board. Throughout 1997, Federation President James Winn and the board of directors conducted extensive discussions on the subject of physician profiles and reviewed detailed analyses performed by staff on the scope of the information publicly available. The board concluded that the absence of licensure information on individual physicians (e.g., license status, issuing state) in the Federation's database constituted an omission that had to be addressed immediately. While there were legitimate concerns about the ability of all state boards to participate by providing complete, timely and updated licensure files in an electronic format, these paled in comparison to the significant opportunities such reporting presented: (1) allowing the Federation to proactively alert every state board in which a physician held a license in the event of a disciplinary action taken by the board in another state; and (2) allowing the Federation to assist state boards temporarily with license verifications and disciplinary checks in the event of a natural or manmade disaster interrupting board operations.[52]

The Federation quickly organized staff in support of what became known as the All-Licensed Physicians (ALP) initiative. Extensive conversations commenced between staff at the Federation and state medical boards to coordinate the electronic file formats that would be used for transferring data. For some state boards, the greatest challenge to participation stemmed from resource limitations in both staffing and technical support. To alleviate the burden on state boards, the Federation offered to accept the licensure files in whatever electronic format the boards could provide, thus shifting much of the workload to its staff. Once state boards forwarded an electronic file of their licensees to the Federation, work began in earnest. Files containing thousands of records invariably brought with them errors and omissions. Federation staff first had to "scrub" the data to assure their integrity before attempting an en masse electronic matching of individual records to those contained in the organization's database. Even with such scrubbing efforts, a significant portion of records had to be individually researched and manually entered.

The first files containing individual boards' rosters of licensees arrived in mid-1998. The first state boards to provide files were those in California, Kansas, Louisiana, Massachusetts, Missouri, Nevada, Rhode Island, Texas and Wyoming. Before the end of 2000, all state boards had forwarded at least one complete file of all their licensees. Equally important, two dozen state boards were now forwarding updated licensure files on a regular basis (weekly, monthly or quarterly) to supplement the initial roster of all their licensees.[53] This meant that the ALP initiative could directly support the Federation's board action data bank by sending out an alert, within twenty-four hours, to all state boards where a physician was licensed, after receipt of a board action by any one of those state boards. The pairing of these two data elements—board action and licensure—working in concert as the Federation's Physician Data Center represented the culmination of coordinated information management.

Several years later, in 2006, Federation Board Chair J. William McCord (Tennessee Osteopathic) reflected on the accomplishment represented by this collaborative effort between the Federation and its membership. With more than 1 million physician records, the Federation's database contained biographical, licensure, disciplinary and examination history for an estimated 98 percent of all physicians (both M.D.s and D.O.s) in the United States.[54] McCord and the Federation's staff took pride in the significant progress that had been made in bolstering an already robust FSMB database, and perhaps even greater pride in the successful coordinated response that severely tested everyone during the prior year when Hurricane Katrina slammed into America's Gulf Coast region.

Causing $81 billion in property damage and the loss of 1,836 lives from the damage and subsequent flooding in 2005, Hurricane Katrina was one of the deadliest and certainly the costliest natural disasters in U.S. history. The storm placed 80 percent of New Orleans underwater and completely shut down the offices and website of the Louisiana State Board of Medical Examiners for six weeks, making it impossible for the board to carry out license verification activities. As an influx of physicians arrived to assist in the emergency, the Louisiana board had no means to verify the legitimate credentials of those presenting themselves to render medical service. Medical boards in surrounding states, particularly Texas and Mississippi, soon witnessed an influx of displaced Louisiana physicians seeking to practice but had no means to verify an individual physician's license in good standing from Louisiana. The Federation stepped forward on both counts with its Physician Data Center and FCVS by enabling use of the FSMB website and staff for free verifications of Louisiana physician and physician assistant licenses. The Louisiana board authorized the Federation to act temporarily as a "display agent" in a manner that met the verification standards of the Joint Commission on Accreditation of Healthcare Organizations (JCAHO), later the Joint Commission. The system performed particularly well because the Louisiana board had sent the Federation its most current and updated licensure files less than sixty days before Katrina struck, allowing the FSMB to effectively act as temporary surrogate for the board utilizing relatively current information.[55]

The Louisiana, Texas, and Mississippi boards utilized the Federation's resources to check disciplinary history and credentials on hundreds of physicians as they worked to accommodate both early responders hoping to assist and displaced physicians seeking to practice. These critical functions proved necessary, as evidenced by the experiences reported by both state board officials and the Federation's staff. The Louisiana board's president acknowledged that some individuals lacking valid credentials and qualifications attempted to exploit the situation under the guise of good Samaritans. Similarly, Federation staff were contacted by physicians who had been sanctioned in other states yet were interested in "helping" during the emergency, despite lacking a valid license to practice anywhere in the United States.[56] The Federation's ALP initiative demonstrated its regional and national value and rewarded the faith of the organization's leadership in responding to a unique emergency situation in the fall of 2005.

Even before Katrina, however, and in much quieter ways, the ALP proved its ongoing value in conjunction with the Federation's board action database. Together these two services constitute the foundation for the Federation's disciplinary alert service that has now become a routine part of all state boards' daily operations. Through timely reporting of licensure and disciplinary data about physicians and physician assistants to the Federation by state boards, the state-based system of medical licensure has essentially eliminated the undetected movement of a bad actor physician from one state to another. The Federation and its member boards worked collaboratively to close what had been a historical weakness in the licensing system. This same collaborative spirit can also be seen in the Federation's work, more than twenty years ago, to further the cause of license portability through a common examination system.

THE UNITED STATES MEDICAL LICENSING EXAMINATION (USMLE)

In the early 1980s, the examinations for licensure recognized and utilized by state medical and osteopathic boards were sometimes characterized as a "dual track" system serving relatively distinct yet sometimes overlapping cohorts of physicians. U.S. medical school programs awarding the M.D. degree graduated approximately 16,000 physicians annually throughout the decade of the 1980s.[57] A vast majority of these physicians opted to take the NBME certifying examination, a medical knowledge and skills assessment examination whose origins date back to 1916. Rather than assessing minimum qualifications for licensure, the NBME certifying examination was designed to be an exam of such high quality that state medical boards would not require further assessment of those who had successfully completed it. At that time, the NBME certifying examination was recognized and accepted by all state medical boards as meeting their statutory requirement for an examination prior to issuance of a license, with the only exceptions being the Texas and Louisiana boards. The other primary examination pathway involved the Federation's own FLEX examination, an assessment tool designed explicitly for use by state medical boards for initial licensure purposes for all qualified applicants and first administered in 1968. Because the NBME certifying examination was open solely to students and graduates of medical school programs accredited by the Liaison Committee on Medical Education (LCME), this meant the FLEX candidate pool drew heavily from the IMG community, especially during periods when international interest in U.S. training and practice opportunities peaked. For example, IMGs constituted nearly 60 percent of all candidates sitting the first administrations of the revised FLEX in 1985; this occurred at a time when IMGs accounted for only 21 percent of the licensed physician population. This upward trend continued, with IMGs constituting 60–75 percent of all FLEX examinees between 1986 and 1991.[58]

Despite contemporary references to a *dual* track system for medical licensing examinations, there remained a third option—the smaller but significant track for osteopathic physicians. Approximately 1,000 physicians graduated annually from U.S. osteopathic medical school programs accredited by the American Osteopathic Association's Council on Pre-doctoral Education (later the Commission on Osteopathic College Accreditation) during the early 1980s.[59] Their preferred examination sequence was the series of National Board of Osteopathic Medical Examiners (NBOME) Parts examinations.

In some ways, the landscape of medical licensing examinations seemed almost tranquil at the start of the decade of the 1980s. The U.S. medical education community benefited from an examination (NBME Parts) that complemented their curriculum and internal assessment of the students. The medical licensing community, meanwhile, had recourse not only to the NBME examination for U.S. graduates but possessed a national assessment tool (FLEX) designed to their specifications and directly engaging them in test development and policy through the FLEX Board, which oversaw the construct and operations of the examination. Earlier criticisms of the FLEX had been successfully addressed. For instance, the use of derivative items drawn from the pool of NBME Parts questions had been discontinued; a weighted scoring scale alleviated initial concerns about performance on the basic science section in light of the many examinees being well removed in time from their immediate coursework in that area. Questions about the failure rate on the exam subsided after Federation chief executive officer Bryant Galusha took and passed the FLEX examination alongside other licensure candidates for the North Carolina Medical Board. In many ways, the FLEX had exceeded the expectations of even its most hopeful proponents with its relatively rapid, unanimous adoption by all state medical boards.[60]

To all appearances, the medical regulatory community had been "moving in the right direction" with its examinations. As Galusha later recalled, there was a certain irony and paradox behind the shifting landscape starting in the mid-1980s. At a time when these examinations were stronger than ever and solidly based on the science of assessment, new pressures arose questioning the fundamental fairness of the licensing examination system.[61] They sprang from within the examinee community—especially among IMGs—and spread to the political arena. These pressures, along with the commitment of organizations such as the Federation, the National Board and the ECFMG, contributed to what became a much-lauded outcome—the introduction of the United States Medical Licensing Examination (USMLE). Following some initial interest in joining this unified effort, the osteopathic profession ultimately decided to maintain the distinctiveness of its philosophy and practice by opting to maintain a parallel pathway to licensure eligibility for its physicians through its new Comprehensive Osteopathic Medical Licensure Examination (COMLEX-USA), subsequently developed by the NBOME.

To understand the context within which the USMLE was introduced, it is helpful to consider the demographics of the examinee community in the 1980s. The first half of the decade witnessed a surge in the issuance of ECFMG certificates, a credential necessary for IMGs to enter U.S. residency training positions. Particularly noteworthy were the growing number of US-IMGs, that is, U.S. citizens who had been students/graduates of medical schools outside the United States or Canada. Between 1982 and 1989, US-IMGs comprised the largest nationality cohort gaining ECFMG certification. They continued to represent one of the largest cohorts receiving ECFMG certification over the next two decades, rising in some years to account for as much as 25 percent of all certificates issued.[62] This trend gained long-term momentum with the 1977–1978 establishment of several large Caribbean medical schools catering primarily to U.S. citizens: Ross University, St. Georges University and American University of the Caribbean.[63] As the number of IMG, and especially US-IMG, candidates grew, so too did their interest in testing-related issues. Invariably their focus centered upon the respective pass rates on the FLEX and NBME Parts examinations.

This focus on testing hardly seems surprising. By the late 1970s the increasing importance of standardized testing, including decisions based in part upon these scores, reflected a reality not lost upon examinees. The ubiquitous testing in the educational arena as well as the prevalence of certification and licensing in multiple professions resulted in some examinees pressing lawmakers for legislation to ensure what they viewed as fundamental fairness in assessment. A 1979 New York law, popularly labeled the "Truth in Testing" law, required full disclosure of content on postsecondary and professional school admission tests. Though not applicable to the FLEX or the NBME Parts examinations, both the Federation and National Board expressed grave concerns should the legislation be extended to the licensing arena. By the late 1980s, the New York legislature returned to this legislation with the intent of not only extending its coverage to certifying and licensing examinations but expanding the law to require disclosure of specific test development processes. Even a key administrator within New York's Department of Education acknowledged the "severe" potential implications behind aspects of the legislation, such as the creation of a "bias review committee" with de facto editorial authority over individual test items.[64]

One New York legislator appeared before the assembled state board community at the 1987 Federation annual meeting and defended the need for such legislation by claiming a "considerable unevenness" in medical licensure that hindered IMG candidates. He specifically pointed to the additional graduate medical education (GME) training often required of IMG candidates for licensure eligibility as opposed to that required of U.S. graduates and an IMG perception that the only licensing examination open to them (FLEX) presented a more difficult examination hurdle than the NBME Parts exam, as evidenced by the respective pass rates on the two exams. In that same year, IMGs secured a resolution at the AMA national meeting calling for the ability to sit for the NBME Parts exam. The National Board attempted to address this concern and defuse any negative perceptions by opening its certifying examination to IMGs in 1989. That such legislation originated in New York was hardly happenstance. At that time, nearly one-third of all IMGs in graduate medical education were training in New York state. Even when IMG figures dipped as a national percentage of all newly licensed physicians, as was seen in the early 1980s, New York continued to enjoy a high percentage of IMGs seeking licensure. For example, in 1981 nearly 40 percent of all newly licensed New York physicians were IMGs.[65]

This legislative activity went beyond New York. In 1986, the executive director of the Florida Medical Board reported similar political pressures. Members of the state legislature had asserted discrimination by the state medical board in its licensing of IMGs—this despite the fact that IMGs constituted nearly 40 percent of newly licensed Florida physicians during the preceding five years. Legislative critics pointed to the ECFMG's certifying examination (the Foreign Medical Graduates Examination in Medical Science, or FMGEMS) as an "additional and separate" examination hurdle demanded of IMGs—forgetting the underlying rationale for the examination, which was to verify that physicians graduated from a non-LCME-accredited medical school possessed the requisite knowledge of the basic medical and clinical sciences to enter GME training and provide direct patient care. These same critics claimed the standard necessary to pass the FMGEMS exceeded that demanded of U.S. students on the NBME Part I exam. Various draft legislative measures circulated in Florida during this time period. One sought to waive the requirement for IMGs to obtain ECFMG certification; another would have waived the FLEX Component 1 (the basic science component) exam as a requirement for licensure for a subset of IMGs.[66]

Similar concerns and activity were evident on a national level as well. In 1987, the U.S. House and Senate introduced companion legislative bills (HR3241 and S1868) designed to "promote nondiscrimination" in medical licensure and encourage license reciprocity. While the proposed legislation extended well beyond issues of formal assessment, they specifically stated that IMGs not be held to requirements (including examinations) that "materially differ" from those mandated of U.S. graduates. While these bills did not pass, they underscored the heightened interest of legislators to constituents' concerns for real and perceived issues of fairness.[67]

The Federation found this swirl of legislative proposals troubling on several levels. Despite the well-intentioned efforts of some legislators, these proposed measures carried provisions that by their very nature undermined the licensing examination process and thus weakened public protection. Providing legislators with clarifying information and suggested revisions to flawed bills proved challenging and largely frustrating. One Federation senior staff member stated that the legislation was often framed in such a way that voicing opposition felt akin to "arguing against motherhood and the flag."[68] Certainly, the Federation and the National Board had no difficulty explaining their test development and scoring practices for the FLEX and Parts exams and demonstrating their adherence to professional testing standards. But the question emerging before them was increasingly more philosophical: Was the dual track system for licensing examinations—one for graduates of U.S. medical schools and one for IMGs—itself the problem? Was it raising fundamental questions about fairness that neither organization would ever be able to address satisfactorily to skeptical examinees and legislators?

The salutary outcome from this legislative churning was a return to the long-held desire on the part of many within the medical regulatory community for a more uniform examination pathway. The original Examination Institutes created by the Federation in the 1950s identified one of their main objectives as "uniformity in licensing examinations." Many veterans within the state medical board community pointed rightfully, and with pride, to the introduction of the FLEX in 1968 and its adoption by all states as a landmark step toward a "national . . . standard" for medical licensing examinations. Indeed, as recently as 1981, state medical boards collectively reaffirmed that desire with a resolution passed by the Federation's House of Delegates calling for "one uniform pathway to licensure" and the "orderly withdrawal" of the NBME Parts exam. Though a 1982 resolution superseded this effort by deferring withdrawal of state board recognition of the NBME Parts exam until after the introduction of a revised FLEX exam in 1985, clearly there was strong interest among state boards for moving toward even greater uniformity in the licensing examinations.[69]

As the nature of the legislative and examinee discourse began to change in the mid-1980s, Federation and National Board chief executives, Bryant Galusha and Robert Volle, responded by lending their considerable influence to revisiting the old topic of examination uniformity. Volle addressed the assembled state medical boards in spring 1988, acknowledged the "political forces at work" and stressed that they presented a galvanizing opportunity for the two organizations to embrace a major improvement to the licensing examination system. Galusha and Volle announced the formation of a multistakeholder task force to study the feasibility of a "uniform examination pathway." This voluntary task force brought together representatives from their two organizations as well as others throughout the house of medicine for discussions on the feasibility of a uniform examination. Joining the Federation and the National Board on the task force were representatives from the Educational Commission for Foreign Medical Graduates, the American Medical Association, the Association of American Medical Colleges, the National Board of Osteopathic Medical Examiners, the Accreditation Council for Graduate Medical Education and the U.S. Department of Health and Human Services. Volle and others hoped the task force and its discussions might also serve to publicly clarify and correct misinformation that questioned the "purpose and fairness" of the examination system. The state board community rallied behind the initiative with the adoption of Federation House of Delegates Resolution 88–1, reaffirming a "commitment to . . . a uniform examination pathway."[70]

The Task Force to Study Pathways to Licensure began its landmark series of meetings in early 1988. In reflecting back on these meetings, Janet Carson, former legal counsel for the National Board, noted the fortuitous presence of many "thoughtful" leaders at the table—individuals who quickly demonstrated an appropriate "balance of principles and pragmatism." Given the significant ramifications of the topic, it seems somewhat surprising there were no set agendas for the first several meetings. Intuitively, Volle and Galusha understood the importance of not constraining the initial dialogue and letting the discourse unfold naturally as the task force worked toward the goal that many embraced conceptually, if only the practical considerations might be resolved.[71]

One of the major points of discussion for the task force concerned unintended consequences should a single examination pathway become a reality. If there was a single examination open to all examinees (M.D., D.O., and IMG), what inferences might some be tempted to draw from passing the exam? Would some infer an equivalency in medical education based upon a passing score? Would such an inference indirectly compromise the meaningfulness of U.S. accreditation systems for undergraduate and graduate medical education? The task force saw the potential for unwarranted inferences that might minimize the "significant differences" in medical education among such a heterogeneous examinee population. So strong were the task force's concerns in this area that their final proposal document identified one of their major principles as follows: "A single examination for medical licensure . . . should not ignore or obscure differences . . . in the quality of the medical education . . . or . . . diminish the importance of education and educational standards in the licensing process."[72]

Additionally, the task force acknowledged the "general level of satisfaction" with the quality of the FLEX and NBME Parts exams. Thus, its proposal sought to keep the best aspects of both examinations. The resulting USMLE Step examination sequence utilized a three-component structure similar to the NBME Parts with a role for state boards in setting eligibility criteria for Step 3, similar to the boards' involvement with the FLEX. Additionally, Steps 1 and 2 were intended to meet the examination requirements of both Public Law 94–484 and ECFMG certification. Thus, the need for a separate examination (FMGEMS) for IMGs disappeared. This new examination would not only provide a "common denominator" for state boards in making their licensing decisions, it would serve as a complementary assessment to U.S. medical school programs in their evaluation of student progress and to the ECFMG in evaluating the preparedness of IMGs to enter residency. The task force concluded its efforts by adopting *A Proposal for a Single Examination for Medical Licensure* in February 1989.[73]

Galusha proved especially persuasive with the licensing community in advancing the uniform pathway concept. While some had urged state boards to not let unfounded accusations concerning fairness go unchallenged, Galusha sounded a different note. The dual-track system with two examinations simply did not pass the "common sense" standard and carried implicitly negative connotations. While data could be presented demonstrating fairness, any assertion of a separate but equal pathway sounded an inherently "sour and discordant note" in the late 1980s.

According to Galusha, the fact that the Federation and the state medical board community could articulate a rational basis for the dual-track system did not "justify" its continued existence. The question before the assembled state boards was no longer if change should occur but rather how quickly it could be brought about.[74]

The state medical board community concurred and adopted the *Single Examination* document as an official Federation position paper in April 1989. The governing boards for the Federation and the National Board met jointly in January 1990 and approved a set of principles to guide the ensuing discussions. These culminated in 1991 with a formal agreement establishing the United States Medical Licensing Examination (USMLE). The presence of David Citron (North Carolina) proved invaluable during the negotiations. As a former member of the Federation's board, then serving on the NBME Executive Board, Citron along with Galusha drew upon their relationships among and between individuals within the two organizations to foster an agreement founded upon mutual trust and respect.[75] The two organizations rolled out the USMLE Step sequence between 1992 and 1994 while simultaneously phasing out the FLEX and NBME Parts exams. (Around this same time period, the NBOME introduced the COMLEX-USA to replace its NBOME Parts examination sequence.)

In providing a national assessment tool to medical licensing authorities, the Federation and the National Board constructed the program to accommodate and maximize state board involvement. Thus, state medical boards were asked to set eligibility requirements for USMLE Step 3 beyond the core programmatic requirements. More than thirty boards assumed responsibility for administering the Step 3 in its pre-1999 paper-and-pencil format. Even more important, current and former members of state boards were recruited to serve in governance and oversight capacities on the USMLE Composite Committee and the three Step Committees.[76] Additionally, other individuals have participated on USMLE test development committees, standard setting and task forces. Approximately 112 members of state medical boards have served the USMLE in some capacity over the past two decades. In recent years, state board involvement has been fostered by an annual workshop for state board members hosted in Philadelphia. Thirty-seven state boards have been represented at these workshop sessions since 2007. Among the state medical board community, Stephen Schabel (South Carolina) distinguished himself by not only serving on multiple committees but taking and passing all three USMLE Steps in the early 1990s as a demonstration of the reasonableness of the standard.

Since its establishment, the USMLE program has administered more than 1.5 million Step examinations as the primary examination pathway to medical licensure in the United States. Along the way it has steadily advanced the scope of assessment for medical licensure with the incorporation of new testing formats during the transition to computer-based testing in 1999 (e.g., Primum® Computer-based Case Simulations) and the introduction of a clinical skills assessment component for Step 2 in 2004.[77] After two successful decades, the USMLE is such an embedded, integral part of the medical licensing and educational system in the United States that it would be easy to miss the significance of the "landmark" accomplishment it represented for the Federation, the National Board and the medical licensing community. The USMLE remains the first and only medical licensing examination recognized in all fifty states and U.S. territories, and open to all individuals (U.S. or international graduate; M.D. or D.O.) seeking licensure in the United States. The USMLE proved a "unique model of collaboration" between two organizations that play differing yet complementary roles and a "win-win" outcome for all parties. In creating the basis for a common examination standard, the USMLE not only ensured "equity" for examinees—a key concern among some examinee cohorts in the late 1980s—but it also provided a long-term contribution to license portability for physicians and state medical boards.[78]

EDUCATIONAL OUTREACH AND POLICY DEVELOPMENT

As a membership association, the Federation successfully introduced or enhanced multiple services to state medical boards during the last two decades of the twentieth century: the USMLE, the FCVS, the SPEX, and a Federation Physician Data Center comprising board action and licensure data. These services, while critical to the primary function and support of state medical boards, hardly encompassed all the needs of state medical boards in a consumer-focused era of transparency and accountability. In order to fully perform its role in supporting state boards, the Federation committed additional resources to facilitate training of key state board staff members such as board attorneys and board investigative staff. The Federation's annual meeting—dating back to 1913—evolved during this time period into a major educational program. Finally, as the scope of issues confronting state medical boards grew in the consumer era, the Federation responded with a concomitant effort to assist boards through a strengthened focus on policy development.

Much of this transition began with the Federation's 1982 annual meeting. That year saw the Federation stepping out from the shadow of larger national organizations for the first time when it held its first annual meeting independent from the AMA's annual gathering. From the time of the Federation's first annual meeting in 1913, the organization benefited from the assistance and willingness of the AMA Council on Medical Education and the AAMC to share space on the program of its annual Congress on Medical Education and Licensure, held each February at the Palmer House Hotel in Chicago.[79] This annual Congress reserved time on its program for the business meeting of the Federation's annual meeting and included topics germane to the state medical board community. As one of the largest annual gatherings of physicians in the United States, the Congress represented an ideal vehicle for incorporating the Federation's annual meeting of state board representatives. Despite the convenient setting and cooperation of the AMA, by the 1980s the Federation desired an opportunity to hold its annual meeting independent of the Annual Congress and Chicago's frigid February weather. The Federation's first stand-alone annual meeting took place in May 1982 in New Orleans. Despite the Federation staff's inexperience in coordinating a national conference, not to mention fears for an attendance drop with a meeting held outside the context of a national AMA gathering, the annual meeting proved a success, with 275 attendees.[80] In some ways, the meeting marked a turning point in the Federation's growth and the beginning of a more cohesive identity for both the organization and state boards as members of a larger representative national body. The reception hosted by the Louisiana State Board of Medical Examiners for that year's annual meeting attendees symbolized a growing élan among state boards, energized by the prospect of an independent, national conference devoted solely to their specific needs and interests.

The Federation's multiday annual meeting has since grown to become the preeminent national gathering dedicated to the issues and topics confronting state medical boards. In seeking to better serve its member boards, the Federation discontinued using a single site for its annual meeting (Chicago) and adopted a rotating schedule for holding the meeting in a different region of the country each year, thus covering all regions of the country within a period of several years and ensuring closer proximity and ease of attendance for a different group of boards each year. The Federation's annual meeting now presents a wide-ranging educational program that has matured over the years into an annual gathering of more than five hundred attendees, featuring prominent speakers who have included the U.S. surgeon general, the assistant secretary of health, and the director of the Department of Homeland Security. The meeting has continuously evolved through the addition of new features, such as a public members' forum, introduced in 1989 by Susan Spaulding (Vermont), the first public member of a state board to serve as the Federation's elected board president.[81]

The success of the annual meeting as the Federation's principal educational offering spurred the organization's leadership to seek opportunities for additional expanded programming. Subsequently, the Federation introduced a series of separate workshops for board attorneys, board members and state board investigative staff. The latter began in 1993 as a joint initiative with AIM and grew into an annual series of workshops drawing dozens of investigative staff. The first of these workshops focused on the challenges inherent to investigating quality of care and sexual misconduct cases. The sessions, which continue to this day under the auspices of AIM, provide a unique opportunity for investigative staff to share information and exchange best practices while learning directly from experts in specialized topics unique to the investigative arena.[82] For many years, the Federation held a board members workshop in conjunction with the investigators workshop. These popular offerings gave state board members similar networking and informational exchange opportunities through timely topics identified with the assistance of the Federation's Advisory Council of State Board Executives, an advisory group comprising selected executive directors from state medical boards.

The workshop for board attorneys represents a more recent offering that evolved from a session that was long a feature of the Federation's annual meeting program. Because of the critical nature of the role played by the state board attorneys and limited time available on the annual meeting program, the decision to offer a separate educational workshop specifically for this group has proven to be a wise one. This stand-alone workshop has increased the number of board attorneys available to participate and has provided a valuable resource for networking and professional development.

Another major area in which the Federation supported its state member boards centered upon advocacy, legislative analysis and policy development. While the Federation has supported state boards with this kind of assistance throughout its history, the depth and breadth of the organization's advocacy and policy work intensified significantly in the 1980s and 1990s. The annual reports of the Federation's chief executive officers from this time period framed a multipronged approach to the organization's policy work: (1) monitoring legislative activities at both the state and federal level; (2) serving as a national voice on behalf of the state board community; and (3) developing model policy for adoption by state medical boards. As the Federation's staffing level expanded beginning in the 1980s, the organization matured into the role and responsibilities desired by state boards through the facilitation of a wide range of policy work.

This growing emphasis on policy proved timely as the state board community entered a consumer-focused era stressing accountability and transparency. The Federation's chief executive officers during this time period—Harold Jervey, Bryant Galusha, and James Winn—devoted considerable attention to their role as the organization's national voice advocating for state medical boards. This advocacy extended across multiple fronts, including public and legislative outreach, and media relations. Just as important, Federation leaders committed to establishing and maintaining good working relationships with key contacts at critical governmental agencies like the Department of Health and Human Services and its Health Resources and Services Administration and Office of the Inspector General. Cultivating these relationships as a mechanism for informing a broader audience on the work of the Federation and the state board community paid dividends on more than one occasion as evidenced by the multiple federal grants and contracts secured by the organization beginning in the 1980s. The organization's increased national presence also resulted in numerous instances in which a Federation representative offered testimony before the U.S. Congress, federal agencies and state legislatures.[83] In addition, Federation staff provided assistance to state boards by researching legal issues, filing amicus briefs and monitoring state and federal legislation. Key staff hires proved critical as well. The Federation bolstered its support of state boards in this arena through its hiring of former staff and members from several state medical boards. Since the 1980s, former executive directors and board members from the Arizona, North Carolina, South Carolina and Texas boards have served in senior staff positions within the Federation—a practice whereby the firsthand experience of individuals with service to, or on, state boards made its way directly to the Federation, thus helping to inform the organization's priorities and efforts.

Perhaps the most important service provided by the Federation in this regard was its work in developing model policy for the state board community. The mechanism for doing so remains the business meeting held at each year's Federation annual meeting when representatives from all sixty-nine licensing jurisdictions (representing all fifty states, fourteen independent osteopathic boards and five U.S. territories) convene as the Federation's House of Delegates.[84] Their actions in passing resolutions and adopting the reports of ad hoc and standing committees and task forces constitute the collective policies of the Federation. While their collective actions are not binding upon individual state boards, the resulting policies provide a framework and template upon which all boards can draw in formulating and customizing policy and laws to fit the circumstances and exigencies of their own state. The House of Delegates' actions also serve as a barometer, measuring the pulse of the medical regulatory environment, including major issues and emerging trends confronting state boards.

James Winn, the Federation's chief executive during this time period, the Federation's board of directors and the volunteer members of numerous special committees formed to develop model policy made a real difference in much of the organization's policy work. Winn recognized the unique potential of the Federation's special committees to foster greater uniformity in policy and standards in the state-based system for medical regulation. Looking back at the extensive policy work undertaken by the Federation in the 1990s, much of it fell primarily into three categories: licensure; professionalism; and the practice of medicine. In the area of licensure, two of the more important special committee initiatives centered upon licensure by endorsement and uniform standards and procedures. Chaired by Patrick Carone (New York) and N. Stacy Lankford (Indiana), respectively, these committee reports crafted model policy and recommendations that upon adoption in 1995 and 1998 presented state medical boards with a suggested common template for framing their own policies. The report on licensure by endorsement succinctly identified the recommended core documents that should be used to establish physician identity and credentials for practice, and called for the creation of a central repository to house them. As mentioned earlier, the recommendations of the committee led directly to the Federation's establishment of the FCVS in 1995. Additionally, this policy addressed circumstances under which physicians presenting themselves for licensure by endorsement should demonstrate current competence.[85] This recommendation presaged the significant work that unfolded a decade later when the Federation's House of Delegates adopted a policy in 2004 calling for state boards to assure the "ongoing competence of physicians seeking relicensure."[86]

The *Report of the Special Committee on Uniform Standards and Procedures* provided a complementary policy resource centered heavily, though not exclusively, on the disciplinary side of state board functions. The report offered suggested definitions for key terminology, such as complaint and investigation, and provided multiple recommendations: That all boards have the authority to take reciprocal actions; that they develop protocols on sharing of investigative information with sister boards; and that boards formalize their conflict of interest policy. The report's recommendation specifying "preponderance of evidence" as the appropriate evidentiary standard for boards appears to have fostered greater subsequent uniformity in this area. At the time of the committee report, twenty-three boards utilized a higher evidentiary standard ("clear and convincing" or "beyond a reasonable doubt"). This number has shrunk to twelve states (with none using "beyond a reasonable doubt" as the standard), thus making preponderance the evidentiary standard for most of the country.[87]

This same report called upon all state medical boards to bring physicians in graduate medical education under their oversight. The committee determined that the direct patient care provided by resident physicians, even in an ostensibly educational setting, as well as moonlighting opportunities that often had young physicians practicing outside their area of expertise, made it imperative that state boards provide independent oversight in this area. This policy also recommended that all state boards adopt three years of progressive GME as the minimum for issuance of a full, unrestricted license to all physicians, allopathic and osteopathic, whether educated in the U.S., Canada, or overseas. Admittedly, this recommended standard has not garnered the support hoped for by the committee as most jurisdictions today require only one to two years. However, forty-seven licensing authorities now issue resident physician permits or licenses, with forty-two of them empowered to take disciplinary action against a resident.[88]

Professionalism and ethics represented another area of extensive Federation policy work in the 1990s. The Federation and the state board community turned their attention to this area twice during the decade, the first time as part of a joint 1995 Federation and AMA report, *Ethics and Quality of Care*. Citing the medical profession's obligation to self-regulate, the report lamented the "infrequent" instances of physicians notifying state boards of colleagues' incompetence and/or behavior that threatened patient welfare. The report placed the onus squarely on state medical societies and individual physicians to disseminate reporting guidelines, participate meaningfully in peer review and cooperate with impaired physician programs. Several years later, in 2000, the Federation's Special Committee on Professional Conduct and Ethics provided a more board-centric report outlining contemporary issues that warranted fully developed board policies and revisions to each state's Medical Practice Act (MPA). The principal topics covered in the *Report on Professional Conduct and Ethics* reflected the changing nature of medical practice in the late twentieth century, such as business and contractual arrangements, Internet prescribing and office-based sales of health and non–health related goods. The report also built upon the language of the 1998 report of the Special Committee on Managed Care that addressed financial or business behaviors that compromised the physician-patient relationship, including failure to refer and failure to order appropriate or necessary diagnostics. The report urged state medical boards to broaden the language of their policies and state statutes to account for not merely managed care scenarios but to address any business or contractual conduct that "exploits the physician-patient relationship for personal gain."[89]

The rapid expansion of the Internet into most American homes, and the advent of online prescribing based solely upon an electronic questionnaire, lent urgency for state boards to clarify the acceptable parameters for such activity. The Federation weighed in on this issue several times, beginning in 1996 with *A Model Act to Regulate the Practice of Medicine Across State Lines* and again in 2002 with *Model Guidelines for the Appropriate Use of the Internet in Medical Practice*. In these policies, the Federation consistently identified the locus of practice as the state in which the patient resides and urged state medical and osteopathic boards to create a special category of license to facilitate legitimate telemedicine practices, ultimately adopted by eleven state boards. These important distinctions were designed to establish an appropriate physician-patient relationship and assure the patient's access to his or her state medical board and its resources, if necessary.[90]

Rounding out this decade-long focus on professionalism and ethics were reports on physician impairment and sexual boundary issues. The Ad Hoc Committee on Physician Impairment drafted a model program for state boards to consider in establishing, or working with, an impaired physician program (IPP). The proposal covered multiple types of impairment (chemical, mental, physical), criteria for treatment, planning for follow-up care and relapse management. The Federation had long viewed this as an area warranting state medical board involvement. As early as 1958, the Federation's annual meeting program featured a presentation on physicians addicted to narcotics, with the organization's executive committee recommending that boards consider probationary measures predicated upon active engagement in rehabilitation efforts. Following Florida's pioneering efforts in this arena back in the 1970s, the number of IPPs has grown steadily, from the nine states with legislatively mandated programs in 1990 to the current availability of IPPs in virtually every state.[91] The same ad hoc committee studied sexual boundary issues and chose to address the problem in a separate report, based upon the belief that most sexual boundary violations did not arise from impairment or addiction. The *Report on Sexual Boundary Issues* offered state boards definitions distinguishing sexual violations from less egregious improprieties while presenting guidelines for board investigations and hearings involving these cases. The report also took the issue beyond the narrower confines of psychotherapy settings that some boards had already addressed.[92] When taken in conjunction with the increasing number of disciplinary actions being taken by state boards against physicians for sexual boundary violations, the adoption of policies such as these provided demonstrable evidence that medical regulators in the late twentieth century placed their greatest priority upon public protection.[93]

The final area of major policy development by the Federation and its member boards beginning in the 1990s centered upon the practice of medicine. State medical boards faced the unenviable regulatory task of staying abreast of the changes in medicine in a manner that placed them neither too far in front nor lagging too far behind the realities of modern medical practice. For example, as complementary and alternative medicine (CAM) gained greater acceptance with the public, some physicians sought to incorporate aspects of CAM into their practice and others pondered how best to deal with patients requesting CAM treatments and therapies.[94] In 2002, the Federation House of Delegates issued its *Model Guidelines for the Use of Complementary and Alternative Therapies in Medical Practice* to help state boards navigate the developments in CAM. The document provided boards with suggested guidelines for policy to regulate their licensees' use of CAM in patient evaluation, treatment, documentation and the sale of goods from a physician's office. The *CAM Model Guidelines* provided boards with a template for balancing evidence-based medical practices while respecting patient autonomy.[95] Even more significant was the Federation's *Report of the Special Committee on Outpatient (Office-Based) Surgery,* which addressed the rapid expansion in the number of outpatient surgical procedures. By the mid-1990s, most surgical procedures in the United States were conducted in office and outpatient settings. Adverse outcomes arising from office-based procedures (including fatalities) led both the California and Florida medical boards to draft strong policy measures in 1994–1995. The Federation's report built upon these boards' experiences and outlined options for state boards to consider in addressing this issue: adopting Federation guidelines outlined in the report; developing state-specific guidelines; or mandating facility accreditation by a recognized accrediting body. Those boards choosing to develop their policy based upon the *Report on Outpatient Surgery* received guidance on administrative, clinical, and quality of cares issues and more.[96]

Another far-reaching policy initiative relative to the practice of medicine involved the Federation's *Model Guidelines for the Use of Controlled Substances for the Treatment of Pain*. These model guidelines reassured physicians and patients alike that state boards understood the needs and concerns of both parties, including patient fears of inadequate treatment for pain management and the physicians' concerns for responsibly prescribing medications to manage chronic and acute pain. The Federation and its Foundation for Education and Research later built upon this policy with the publication of *Responsible Opioid Prescribing*. This prescribing guide, authored by pain management specialist Scott Fishman, has since been disseminated to more than 160,000 physicians in twenty-two states. With the adoption by the federal government of Risk Evaluation and Mitigation Strategies (REMS) under the Food and Drug Administration Amendments Act (2007), the guide will be available in 2012 in Fishman's updated and revised version. The need for such resources grew in part from under-prescribing practices stemming from physician fears of prosecution and/or sanctions in the course of prescribing pain medications. These fears, while understandable, have been proven unfounded, as evidenced by data from state and national studies showing that legitimate and appropriate prescribing practices are not the basis for state board actions.[97] The Federation recently clarified its role in educating physicians about responsible opioid prescribing:

> The prescribing of medications that are FDA-approved for pain management, such as long-acting and extended release opioids, should involve a careful balance by physicians between the benefits of these medications to control suffering and the concerns associated with their use, abuse and diversion. The FSMB supports efforts that educate physicians about these concerns and which emphasize responsible and appropriate prescribing when a decision is made to use this class of drugs.

One other policy document covering the practice of medicine warrants mentioning—the *Report of the Special Committee on Evaluation of Quality of Care and Maintenance of Competence*. The report focused on what has been historically the most challenging category of cases for state boards to handle—those involving quality of care. The committee's report echoed the finding of a 1993 report from the HHS pointing to the need for adequate funding of state boards to handle such cases and a strong commitment by the individual state boards to address them. The report offered numerous recommendations, starting with enacting mandatory reporting requirements in those few states still lacking such provisions and providing boards with authority to penalize individuals and institutions failing to comply. The latter authority existed in fewer than two dozen states in 1995–1996. Furthermore, the committee recommended developing proactive mechanisms for identifying physicians providing substandard care; seeking subpoena authority for the board; creating multitrack systems for investigating and resolving quality of care cases; and other options.[98]

The last decades of the twentieth century saw major transformative changes at the Federation of State Medical Boards. The flagship services to state medical boards commonly associated with the Federation—the USMLE, FCVS, SPEX, Physician Data Center—were all established or significantly enhanced during this time period. The organization grew from little more than a dozen staff to more than one hundred permanent, full-time staff members as a direct result of the USMLE and FCVS programs. The Federation's Fort Worth offices lacked sufficient space to accommodate such growth. Consequently, in 1995 the organization purchased its current two-building complex near the Dallas-Fort Worth airport in Euless, Texas. Commensurate with this growth was a rapid modernization of equipment and work processes. Services that had once been wholly or primarily paper-driven, such as applications for the USMLE Step 3 exam or the FCVS, now moved to electronic, Web-based platforms. Educational programming once offered strictly as in-person meetings now began utilizing Internet-based platforms to reach the broadest possible state board audience.

In many ways, these changes symbolized the Federation's evolution. The Federation was no longer a small organization with a national membership. Instead, it had become a large national organization whose long history and major initiatives secured its position as the voice of the state medical and osteopathic board community. Nowhere was this more apparent than in the Federation's policy work. While neither the resolutions nor reports adopted by the Federation's House of Delegates were binding upon individual state boards, they represented a collective consensus and commitment to key principles and practices among the broader state board community and a forward-looking vision for the future of medical regulation at the brink of a new century. The topic for a September 2000 symposium convened by the Federation in the nation's capital perhaps captured this spirit best—medical licensure in the twenty-first century. After its modest beginnings, the Federation had finally grown into the role originally envisioned by its founders.

NOTES

1. "Epidemiologic Notes and Reports: Pneumocystis Pneumonia—Los Angeles," *Morbidity and Mortality Weekly Report*, June 5, 1981, accessed January 9, 2012, http://www.cdc.gov/mmwr/preview/mmwrhtml/june_5.htm; "UNAIDS Report on the Global Epidemic, 2010," United Nations, accessed on January 9, 2012, http://www.unaids.org/documents/20101123_GlobalReport_Chap1_em.pdf.

2. M. M. Kitahata, T. D. Koepsell, et. al., "Physicians' Experience with Acquired Immunodeficiency Syndrome as a Factor in Patients' Survival," *JAMA* 334, no. 11 (March 14, 1996): 701–6.

3. Bryant Galusha, interview by Betty Burnett, June 6, 2011, Charlotte, North Carolina, notes at FSMB Archives, Euless, Texas.

4. Leroy Buckler, "Medical Licensure in the 21st Century: Are We Ready?," *Federation Bulletin* 82, no. 4 (1995): 205.

5. John Rupel, "Report of the Special Task Force on Computerization of Federation Operations," *Federation Bulletin* 66 (September 1979): 268–69; Ray Casterline, "Computerization of Federation Operations," *Federation Bulletin* 66 (December 1979): 371; Harold Jervey, "Annual Report of the Executive Director-Secretary," *Federation Bulletin* 67 (May 1980): 151–52.

6. See Harold Jervey's "Report of the Executive Director-Secretary," in the June 1981, 1982 and 1983 *Federation Bulletin*.

7. Dale Breaden and Bryant Galusha, "Official 1985 Federation Summary of Reported Disciplinary Actions," *Federation Bulletin* 73 (October 1986): 300; Michael Sanford, "The Federation's Central Data Bank of Disciplinary Actions," *Federation Bulletin* 72 (December 1985): 355; Galusha interview by Betty Burnett, June 6, 2011.

8. Harold Jervey, "Report of the Executive Director-Secretary," *Federation Bulletin* 68 (June 1981): 170; Bryant Galusha, "Physician Disciplinary Reporting: Progress, Problems and Prospects," *Federation Bulletin* 74 (May 1987): 139; Bryant Galusha, "Report of the Executive Vice President," *Federation Bulletin* 72 (June 1985): 178.

9. Galusha, "Report of Vice President 1985," 179–81; Galusha, "Report of the Executive Vice President," *Federation Bulletin* 73 (June 1986): 208–10.

10. Galusha, "Report of Vice President 1985," 179; Galusha, "Report of Vice President 1986," 205–6; Galusha, "Physician Disciplinary Reporting," 141; *The Direct Access System for the Board Action Data Bank* (Euless, Texas: Federation of State Medical Boards, 1989); Bryant Galusha, "Report of the Executive Vice President," *Federation Bulletin* 76 (June 1989): 183.

11. Nadia Sawicki, "Character, Competence, and the Principles of Medical Discipline," *Journal of Health Care Law and Policy* 13 (2010): 3; Clark C. Havighurst, "The Doctor's Trust: Self-Regulation and the Law," *Health Affairs* 2, no. 3 (1983): 65.

12. For economic and ideological criticisms of licensing, see George J. Stigler, "The Theory of Economic Regulation," *Bell Journal of Economics and Management Science* 1 (1971): 3–21; Morris Kleiner, "Occupational Licensing," *Journal of Economic Perspectives* 14, no. 4 (2000): 189–202; Stanley J. Gross, *Of Foxes and Hen Houses: Licensing and the Health Professions* (Westport, Connecticut: Greenwood Press, 1984), and Harris Cohen, "On Professional Power and Conflict of Interest: State Licensing Boards on Trial," *Journal of Health Politics, Policy and Law* 5 (1980): 291–308.

13. Sawicki, "Character, Competence, and Medical Discipline," 6.

14. Lippard, "Virginia Board of Medicine," 23–26.

15. Cheryl Thompson, "D.C. Board Rarely Punishes Physicians," *Washington Post* (April 11, 2005); "Ranking of the Rate of State Medical Boards' Serious Disciplinary Actions, 2008–2010," Public Citizen Health Research Group, accessed on January 13, 2012, http://www.citizen.org/statemedicalboardsdisciplinaryactions.

16. Sawicki, "Character, Competence, and Medical Discipline," 9.

17. See Andrew Dolan and Nicole Urban, "Determinants of the Effectiveness of Medical Disciplinary Boards: 1960–1970," *Law and Human Behavior* 7, nos. 2–3 (1983); Elizabeth Graddy, Michael B. Nichol. "Structural Reforms and Licensing Board Performance," *American Politics Quarterly* 18 (July 1990); Darren Grant and Kelly Alfred, "Sanctions and Recidivism: An Evaluation of Physician Discipline by State Medical Boards," *Journal of Health Politics, Policy and Law* 32 (October 2007): 865–884; and Marc Law and Zeynep Hansen, "Medical Licensing Board Characteristics and Physician Discipline," *Journal of Health Politics, Policy and Law* 35, no. 1 (2010): 63–93.

18. Sawicki, "Character, Competence and Medical Discipline," 14; James Morrison and Peter Wickersham, "Physicians Disciplined by a State Medical Board," *JAMA* 279 (June 17, 1998): 1892; Richard Kusserow, Elisabeth Handley, and Mark Yessian, "An Overview of State Medical Discipline," *JAMA* 257 (February 13, 1987): 822.

19. Derek R. Smart, *Physician Characteristics and Distribution in the US* (Chicago: American Medical Association, 2011), 436.

20. Dale Breaden and Bryant Galusha, "State Medical Discipline: Defects and Hindrances," *JAMA* 257 (February 13, 1987): 829.

21. Robert Derbyshire, "How Effective Is Medical Self-Regulation?" *Law and Human Behavior* 7 (September 1983): 194–95, 198–99; Office of the Inspector General, *Medical Licensure and Discipline: An Overview* (Boston: Department of Health and Human Services, 1986), 15.

22. *A Model for the Preparation of a Guidebook on Medical Discipline* (Fort Worth, Texas: Federation of State Medical Boards, 1986); Breaden and Galusha, "State Medical Discipline: Defects and Hindrances," 829.

23. Office of the Inspector General, *State Medical Boards and Quality of Care Cases: Promising Approaches* (Washington, DC: Department of Health and Human Services, 1993), iv, 4–6; Office of the Inspector General, *Quality Assurance Activities of Medical Licensing Authorities in the United States and Canada* (Washington, DC: Department of Health and Human Services, 1991), C1–C6.

24. Law and Hansen, "Medical Licensing Board Characteristics and Physician Discipline," 63; Sydney Wolfe, "Public Access to Discipline Data," *Federation Bulletin* 79 (December 1992): 229; "Summary of 2010 Legislation," Delaware Board of Medical Licensure and Discipline, accessed on January 13, 2012, http://dpr.delaware.gov/boards/medical practice/index.shtml.

25. Arnold Relman, "Professional Regulation and State Medical Boards," *New England Journal of Medicine* 312, no. 12 (March 21, 1985): 785.

26. Kusserow, "Overview of State Medical Discipline," 821; David P. Cyr, "Fraudulent Medical Credentials: United States Postal Inspection Service Investigations," *Federation Bulletin* 73 (February 1986): 35–42; Kenneth Nelson, "Perspective of the United States Department of Health and Human Services," *Federation Bulletin* 73 (February 1986): 44.

27. Office of the Inspector General, *Medical Licensure and Discipline: An Overview*, 17, 24.

28. Ibid., 17–18; Kenneth Yohn, "FSMB—Protection of the Public a Primary Function," *Federation Bulletin* 75 (August 1988): 241–42.

29. American Medical Association and Federation of State Medical Boards, *Technical Proposal for the Establishment and Operation of the Practitioner Adverse Credentialing Data Bank*, August 14, 1987, FSMB Archives, Euless, Texas; American Medical Association, *Best and Final Offer for the Establishment and Operation of the Practitioner Adverse Credentialing Data Bank*, October 2, 1987, FSMB Archives, Euless, Texas.

30. Bryant Galusha, Internal Memorandum dated June 29, 1987, FSMB Archives, Euless, Texas; Bryant Galusha correspondence to James H. Sammons, July 29, 1988, FSMB Board of Directors Meeting, October 1988, FSMB Archives, Euless, Texas; Bryant Galusha, "Report of the Executive Vice President," *Federation Bulletin* 75 (July 1988): 207; William Jacott, "Public Law 99–660," *Federation Bulletin* 76 (May 1989): 131; Bryant Galusha, telephone interview by David Johnson, July 13, 2011.

31. The original regional coordinators were drawn from staff at the California, Utah, Nebraska, Kansas, Virginia, George, Maine and Pennsylvania boards.

32. Harold Jervey, "Report of the Executive Director-Secretary," *Federation Bulletin* 70 (June 1983): 180.

33. *Elements of a Modern State Medical Board: A Proposal* (Fort Worth, Texas: Federation of State Medical Boards, 1988), preface; "Federation Receives Federal Contract to Develop Self-Assessment Instrument for State Medical Boards," *FSMB NewsLetter* 36 (September 1990); Dale Breaden, "Scalps on Lodgepoles and the SAI," *Federation Bulletin* 79 (June 1992): 9.

34. "The SAI on Screen," *Federation Bulletin* 79 (December 1992): 203; "Federal Contract & Purchase Order for *SAI* Completed," *FSMB NewsLine*, October 1994.

35. Dale Breaden and Ester Smith, "A Report on the First International Conference on Medical Licensure/Registration and Discipline," *Federation Bulletin* 81, no. 4 (1994): 243–57.

36. Ibid., 244.

37. Ibid., 246–47.

38. Ibid., 248–49.

39. Ibid., 250.

40. Originally named the International Association of Medical Licensing Authorities, the group was renamed in 2002.

41. I. Kathryn Hill, "SPEX: The Federation's Special Purpose Examination," *Federation Bulletin* 75 (April 1989): 115.

42. Anthony LaDuca, D. Taylor, and Kathryn Hill, "The Design of a New Physician Licensure Examination," *Evaluation and the Health Professions* (1984): 115; Henry Cramblett, "Special Purpose Examination (SPEX)," *Federation Bulletin* 73 (June 1986): 78–79.

43. David Johnson, Gerard Dillon, and Thomas Henzel, "The Post Licensure Assessment System," *Federation Bulletin* 86, no. 3 (2000): 120.

44. Buckler, "Medical Licensure in the 21st Century," 205.

45. Ray Bumgarner, "A Rational Licensing System," *Federation Bulletin* 83, no. 4 (1996): 213–215; *Report of the Ad Hoc Committee for Licensure by Endorsement* (Euless, Texas: Federation of State Medical Boards, 1995): 4.

46. Bumgarner, "Rational Licensing System," 212, 216.

47. "Federation Credentials Verification Service Opens Its Doors," *FSMB NewsLine*, October–November 1996; Bumgarner, "Rational Licensing System," 215;

48. Aaron Young, Humayun Chaudhry, et al., "A Census of Actively Licensed Physicians in the United States, 2010," *Journal of Medical Regulation* 96, no. 4 (2010/2011): 11; "Licensing Boards Accepting FCVS Physician Information Profiles," Federation of State Medical Boards, accessed on January 13, 2012, http://www.fsmb.org/fcvs_physboards.html.

49. "Households with a Computer and Internet Use: 1984 to 2009," U.S. Census Bureau, accessed on January 13, 2012, http://www.census.gov/hhes/computer.

50. "Public Responds to Massachusetts Board Physician Profiles," *FSMB NewsLine*, March 1997.

51. "Report of the Special Committee on Physician Profiling," *Journal of Medical Licensure and Discipline* 87, no. 2 (2001): 55.

52. See FSMB Board of Directors agenda materials for February, April, July and October 1997, FSMB Archives, Euless, Texas.

53. "FSMB Disciplinary Alert Participation Grows," *FSMB BoardNet News* (December 8, 2000).

54. J. William McCord, "An Emphasis on Credentialing," *Journal of Medical Licensure and Discipline* 92, no. 3 (2006): 3.

55. *Responding in Times of Need: Katrina & Beyond* (Euless, Texas: Federation of State Medical Boards, 2006), 4–8; "FSMB, AIM Take Lead in Assisting Boards," *FSMB NewsLine* (February 2005).

56. *Responding in Times of Need*, 5.

57. Bryant Galusha, "The Single Examination for Medical Licensure," *Federation Bulletin* 76 (November 1989): 330; "FACTS: Applicants, Matriculants, Enrollment, Graduates, MD/PhD and Residency Applicants Data," Association of American Medical Colleges, accessed on January 13, 2012, https://www.aamc.org/data/facts.

58. John H. Morton, "On the Abuse of Examinations," *Federation Bulletin* 75 (September 1988): 282; Henry Cramblett, "Report on the Activities of the FLEX Board, 1985–1986," *Federation Bulletin* 73 (October 1986): 310–11; Marjorie Wilson, "Single Examination Route to Licensure: The ECFMG Perspective," *Federation Bulletin* 76 (December 1989): 355; "Reports of FLEX Board, 1986–1991," FSMB Archives, Euless, Texas.

59. "Trends in Osteopathic Medical School Applicants, Enrollment and Graduates, March 2011," American Association of Colleges of Osteopathic Medicine, accessed on January 13, 2012, http://www.aacom.org/data/Pages/default.aspx.

60. John Morton, "Medical Licensure Examinations and State Medical Boards, 1989: What Have They Been, Where Are They Going?" *Federation Bulletin* 76 (June 1989): 165–66; John Morton, "A FLEXible Leader," *Federation Bulletin* 76 (July 1989): 207.

61. Bryant Galusha, "Uniform Single Examination Pathway for Medical Licensure," *Federation Bulletin* 76 (September 1989): 266–68.

62. *2001 ECFMG Annual Report* (Philadelphia: Education Commission for Foreign Medical Graduates, 2002), 10; *2006 ECFMG Report Commemorative Edition* (Philadelphia: Education Commission for Foreign Medical Graduates, 2007), 29; "Standard ECFMG Certificates Issued, 1986–2010," Educational Commission for Foreign Medical Graduates, accessed on January 13, 2012, http://www.ecfmg.org/resources/data-certification.html

63. In August 2011, DeVry, Inc., announced its purchase of American University of the Caribbean for $235 million, one indicator of the size of the offshore medical education system catering to U.S. citizens. See DeVry, Inc., "DeVry Announces Acquisition of AUC," accessed

on January 17, 2012, at http://investors.devryinc.com/Investor-Relations/Press-Releases/default.aspx.

64. John Morton, "Truth in Testing," *Federation Bulletin* 74 (September 1987): 268; David Bower, "Test Disclosure and Bias Issues: The New York Experience," *Federation Bulletin* 74 (July 1987): 199–200.

65. Federation Board of Directors Meeting Agenda Materials, October 9, 1987, FSMB Archives, Euless, Texas; A. Sutnick, M. Friedman, and M. P. Wilson, "Influence of Candidates' Test Selection on Pass Rates on Examinations for Certification by the Educational Commission for Foreign Medical Graduates," *Academic Medicine* 68 (February 1993): 150–52; James H. Donovan, "Medical Licensure: Let's Play by the Same Rules," *Federation Bulletin* 76 (September 1989): 270–73.

66. Dorothy Faircloth, "Barriers to Needed Legislative Change," *Federation Bulletin* 74 (June 1987): 170–71, 175.

67. "Executive Vice President's Report," FSMB Board of Directors Meeting Agenda Materials, February 5, 1988, FSMB Archives, Euless, Texas.

68. I. Kathryn Hill, "A FLEX Perspective: The Federation's View," *Federation Bulletin* 75 (April 1988): 106.

69. Henry Cramblett, "Report on the Activities of the FLEX Board, 1985–1986," *Federation Bulletin* 73 (October 1986): 306; Galusha, "Single Examination Pathway for Licensure," 268.

70. Robert Volle, "Licensure Examinations—Today and Tomorrow," *Federation Bulletin* 76 (February 1989): 35, 39; "Federation News," *Federation Bulletin* 75 (October 1988): 319.

71. Janet Carson, telephone interview by David Johnson, August 15, 2011, Philadelphia, Pennsylvania, notes in possession of the author.

72. Task Force to Study Pathways to Licensure, *A Proposal for a Single Examination for Medical Licensure* (March 1989): 3.

73. Ibid., 1–2, 24–25, 34.

74. Galusha, "Single Examination for Medical Licensure," 330–32.

75. "Federation News," *Federation Bulletin* 76 (June 1989): 191; Donald E. Melnick, telephone interview by David Johnson, September 13, 2011, Philadelphia, Pennsylvania, Federation of State Medical Boards.

76. *2010–2011 FSMB Handbook* (Euless, Texas: Federation of State Medical Boards, 2010), 33–36.

77. See Daniel Klass et al., "Development of a Performance-based Test of Clinical Skills for the USMLE," *Federation Bulletin* 85, no. 3 (1998), and Richard Hawkins, "The Introduction of a Clinical Skills Assessment into the USMLE: A Description of USMLE Step 2 Clinical Skills (CS)," *Journal of Medical Licensure and Discipline* 91, no. 3 (2005); Gerry Dillon, Steve Clyman, et al., "The Introduction of Computer-based Case Simulations into the United States Medical Licensing Examination," *Academic Medicine* 77 (October 2002): S94–96.

78. Melnick interview, September 13, 2011; James R. Winn, videotaped interview by David Johnson, April 28, 2010, Chicago, Illinois; Donald E. Melnick, "Licensing Examinations in North America: Is External Audit Valuable?" *Medical Teacher* (2009): 213.

79. From 1913 to 1926, the Annual Congress and the Federation's annual meeting were held at the Congress Hotel in Chicago.

80. "An Auspicious Beginning," *Federation Newsletter*, June 1982.

81. "Public Members' Forum Planned for Annual Meeting," *FSMB NewsLetter*, September 1988.

82. "Federation Investigators' Workshop," *FSMB NewsLine*, December 1992; "Board Investigators Workshop," *FSMB NewsLine*, June 1993.

83. See the "Report of the Executive Vice President" in the *Federation Bulletin* (June 1985): 178–82; (July 1986): 206–10; (September 1987): 280–86; (July 1988): 207–10; (June 1989): 183–85.

84. Federation membership includes each of the fifty state boards licensing M.D.s and D.O.s; the fourteen states with separate boards licensing osteopathic physicians; the District

of Columbia and the following U.S. territories: Guam, Commonwealth of Northern Mariana Islands, Puerto Rico, and the U.S. Virgin Islands.

85. For example, inactive in medical practice for two years prior; no licensing or specialty board certification exams taken in the prior decade; lacking current hospital privileges.

86. Federation of State Medical Boards, *Public Policy Compendium 2011* (Euless, Texas: Federation of State Medical Boards, 2011), 16.

87. Federation of State Medical Boards, *Report of the Special Committee on Uniform Standards and Procedures* (Euless, Texas: Federation of State Medical Boards, 1998), 3; "Standard of Proof in the United States," FSMB, accessed on January 13, 2012, http://www.fsmb.org/grpol_keyissues.html.

88. *Report on Uniform Standards and Procedures, 4;* "State Specific Requirements for Initial Medical Licensure," FSMB, accessed on January 13, 2012 http://www.fsmb.org/usmle_eli-initial.html; "Resident Licensure and Postgraduate Training Programs," FSMB, accessed January 13, 2012, http://www.fsmb.org/grpol_keyissues.html.

89. *Ethics and Quality of Care: A Report of the AMA and FSMB*, 1; *Special Committee on Professional Conduct and Ethics* (Euless, Texas: Federation of State Medical Boards, 2000), 1, 4, 9–10.

90. See the Federation of State Medical Boards, *A Model Act to Regulate the Practice of Medicine Across State Lines* and *Model Guidelines for the Appropriate Use of the Internet in Medical Practice.*

91. "The Federation and Narcotic Addiction," *Federation Bulletin* 45 (February 1958): 36; R. Ikeda and C. Pelton, "Diversion Programs for Impaired Physicians," *Western Journal of Medicine* (May 1990): 617.

92. *Report on Sexual Boundary Issues* (Euless, Texas: Federation of State Medical Boards, 2006), 1–5; Glen Gabbard and Carol Nadelson, "Professional Boundaries in the Physician-Patient Relationship," *JAMA* 273 (May 10, 1995): 1445.

93. James Morrison and Peter Wickersham, "Physicians Disciplined by a State Medical Board," *JAMA* 279 (June 17, 1998): 1889; Christine Dehlendorf and Sidney Wolfe, "Physicians Disciplined for Sex-Related Offenses," *JAMA* 279 (June 17, 1998): 1883.

94. See the series of articles in the 1997 *Federation Bulletin* (volume 84, no. 3).

95. *Model Guidelines for the Use of Complementary and Alternative Therapies in Medical Practice* (Euless, Texas: Federation of State Medical Boards, 2002), 1, 3–6.

96. Linda Wasmer Andrews, "Office-based Surgery—The Doctor Is In, and More Boards Are Watching," *Journal of Medical Licensure and Discipline* 87, no. 3 (2001): 99–101; Thea Graves Pellman, "Office Based Surgery and Public Safety," *Journal of Medical Licensure and Discipline* 87, no. 2 (2001), 47–48; R*eport of the Special Committee on Outpatient (Office-Based) Surgery* (Euless, Texas: Federation of State Medical Boards, 2002), 1–4.

97. Jack Richard and Marcus Reidenberg, "The Risk of Disciplinary Action by State Medical Boards Against Physicians Prescribing Opioids," *Journal of Medical Licensure and Discipline* 91, no. 2 (2005): 14; Donald Goldenbaum et al., "Physicians Charged with Opioid Analgesic-Prescribing Offenses," *Pain Medicine* 9, no. 8 (September 2008): 737.

98. *Special Committee on Evaluation of Quality of Care and Maintenance of Competence* (Euless, Texas: Federation of State Medical Boards, 1998).

Chapter 8

A New Millennium, A Second Century

America, we have come so far. We have seen so much. But there is so much more to do.

—Barack H. Obama (2008)

The end of the twentieth century marked a period at the Federation that seemed to focus on the continuity of its operations, at least according to the comments of its elected leaders. "The Federation is continuing to address issues previously identified by state boards and the House of Delegates," said Alan Shumacher (California) in a 1999 message as the Federation's president (a position that would soon be renamed board chair). In a symposium marking the new millennium hosted by the Federation that year in Washington, D.C., Shumacher's successor noted with some understatement that "we have begun to change focus from licensing to discipline" and gingerly hinted at whether member boards should "link licensure to periodic assessment of competence" as he introduced a range of distinguished medical educators and speakers to help contemplate what the future might bring.[1]

Shumacher and his contemporaries echoed a theme of change and continuity in contemplating the landscape of medical regulation. "Each Federation year is a blending of old and new," he said, "the ongoing projects, studies, and initiatives begun by previous Federation boards and presidents at the direction of state boards and the House of Delegates blend smoothly with new challenges and opportunities as they present themselves." While he humbly acknowledged that he stood "upon the shoulders of my predecessors," and vowed to "continue to move forward to enhance the role of state medical boards and the Federation," he and his colleagues could be forgiven for not foreseeing the substantive and progressive changes that the coming years would bring, as the Federation became more adept at creating its own opportunities rather than simply waiting for them to present.[2]

During the next dozen years, in fact, the Federation would do far more than assert continuity and promote the status quo. It would create an electronic Disciplinary Alert Service to enable state boards and others to have ready access to board actions within twenty-four hours of their receipt at the Federation; add a clinical skills component involving live "patients" to its USMLE exam (in partnership with NBME and in collaboration with ECFMG); invigorate with capital dollars its FSMB Research and Education Foundation; adopt a historic framework for the ongoing clinical competence of physicians called Maintenance of Licensure (MOL); invest in a significant upgrade of its Federation Credentials Verification Service (FCVS); agree to a Comprehensive Review of the USMLE program (CRU) leading to significant examination enhancements in support of the medical licensing decision; renew its interest in global medical regulation, first proposed in 1977, as the Secretariat for the International Association of Medical Regulatory Authorities (IAMRA); establish a full-time presence in Washington, D.C., with an advocacy office; publish a comprehensive census of actively licensed physicians in the United States for the first time (2011) and begin a quest, still nascent, to collaborate with organizations across the full continuum of medical education on an "electronic portfolio" and "data commons," and joining with many of these organizations in an endeavor called the Coalition for Physician Accountability.

The Federation's special committees, task forces and working groups—proposed by the Federation's chair, empowered by its boards of directors, led by representatives of state boards and assisted by Federation staff—continued to examine timely issues that were deemed relevant to the state boards: physician profiling, telemedicine, physician reentry, physician impairment and member board metrics for public reporting, to name just a few. The talent and expertise increasingly brought to bear upon these issues by the medical licensing community in the new millennium were recognized tacitly in 2009 when President Barack Obama appointed Regina Benjamin (Alabama), immediate past chair of the Federation at the time and the first African-American woman elected to AMA's Board of Trustees in 1995, as the nation's eighteenth surgeon general.

This final chapter reviews several of the major areas the Federation and its state boards have focused their attention on since 2000—the establishment of an international organization to promote greater collaboration and data sharing across national boundaries; changes to the process by which international medical graduates will gain entry into graduate medical education training programs in years to come; the successful adoption of physician profiling by all state medical boards; the evolution and adoption of the Federation's MOL framework; the Federation's invitational summits across the continuum of medical education, training and licensure; and the changes envisioned for the USMLE program.

THE INTERNATIONAL ASSOCIATION OF MEDICAL REGULATORY AUTHORITIES (IAMRA)

The success of the first three international conferences on medical regulation in the 1990s, as discussed in the previous chapter, had led the Federation and its sister medical regulatory authorities around the world to recognize the value of international collaboration as an essential element in their role as protectors of the public. At a meeting of a special steering committee at the fourth biennial international conference, held in Oxford, England, in 2000, the readiness of international medical regulatory authorities to come together and promote greater understanding and relations in the area of medical licensure, registration and discipline led to the decision to create the International Association of Medical Licensing Authorities (IAMLA). The Federation's chief executive, James Winn, delivered the meeting's keynote address, "Medical Regulation: By and For Whom?," while Bruce Levy (Texas) addressed challenges related to "Internet medicine" during one of the meeting's sessions. Also attending on behalf of the Federation were Shumacher, President-Elect George Barrett (North Carolina), George Van Komen (Utah)—who would serve as the Federation's president from 2001 to 2002—and the Rev. Daniel Morrissey (New York). Winn and Gary Johnson, the executive director of the Federation of Medical Licensing Authorities of Canada (FMLAC), were duly elected cochairs of IAMLA's interim governing committee, which included representatives from the United Kingdom (Finlay Scott), Australia (Lloyd Toft), Ireland (Gerard Bury), New Zealand (Tony Baird), South Africa (Len Becker) and Sweden (Gunilla Hulth-Backlund). The new committee agreed to the Federation's offer to serve as secretariat for the new organization—a role greatly facilitated by administrative support from Federation staff members Patricia McCarty and later Roxanne Huff. The Federation's House of Delegates in April 2001 promptly adopted recommendations in support of the new organization and encouraged the Federation and its representatives to IAMLA to seek opportunities to share information with the international community on matters related to the education, training and licensure of physicians.[3]

Meeting in March 2002, IAMLA's interim governing committee approved the organization's draft constitution and bylaws and agreed to present the final documents to the leadership of their respective organizations for "final affirmation" before "distributing it to all known medical regulatory authorities in the world." Signaling an interest in charging ahead to leverage the benefits of collaboration between meetings, the committee also forwarded a questionnaire to assist in the development of a system for the international exchange of physician information and an invitation to other medical regulatory authorities to join IAMLA.[4] Following the departure of Winn from the Federation that same year, Dale Austin was named interim chief executive officer for the Federation and went on to serve as the United States' delegate to IAMLA while Gary Johnson became the new organization's first sole chair.

The first general meeting of IAMLA's membership was scheduled for June 15, 2002, to coincide with the fifth international meeting in Toronto. At this meeting—attended by representatives from Albania, Australia, Belgium, Canada (including representatives from Quebec, Manitoba, Nova Scotia, Saskatchewan, Newfoundland and Labrador, and the Medical Council of Canada), Denmark, Dominica, Egypt, India, Ireland, Namibia, New Zealand, Pakistan, South Africa, Sweden, the United Kingdom and the United States—the new organization adopted a name change, becoming the International Association of Medical Regulatory Authorities (IAMRA), in order to better assert that its members' roles went beyond medical licensure and registration to also include physician discipline, a particular concern in light of several notorious cases of physicians disciplined in one nation who left to practice in another with tragic consequences for patients in both jurisdictions.[5] Two years later, the leaders of Canada's Federation changed the name of their organization, ostensibly for similar reasons, to the Federation of Medical Regulatory Authorities of Canada (FMRAC).

The interim governing committee of IAMRA in 2002 agreed to establish a website containing information with links to each organization's web page to provide easy access to such information for its membership and agreed to organize three working groups: one for planning the sixth international meeting (in Dublin), one for the international exchange of information about physicians, and one for exploring the concept of an "international medical passport." The last of these efforts was ultimately abandoned when it soon became clear that the issue was more complex than it appeared, owing to international laws and the challenges inherent in modifying multiple national laws, a more daunting challenge than even the Federation was accustomed to with its member boards and their state laws. Still, even efforts such as this which did not achieve the original purpose could bear fruit in other ways. The passport concept gave way to an internal initiative among IAMRA members featuring an exchange of information on the licensing and examination processes of the member jurisdictions that supported ongoing bilateral and multilateral agreements facilitating physician movement internationally.[6] In accordance with its new bylaws, the voting delegates of IAMRA proceeded to elect a Management Committee (supplanting its governing committee), which now consisted of a chair, deputy chair and five members, with Lloyd Toft, president of the Australian Medical Council and the Medical Board of Queensland, elected as IAMRA's second chair, and the Federation's Dale Austin serving as deputy chair. Ossama Rasslan, then the secretary-general of the Egyptian Medical Syndicate, is the only member of the original Management Committee still serving IAMRA in that capacity in 2012.[7]

Alongside well-attended meetings in 2006 (Wellington) and 2008 (Cape Town), IAMRA's leadership smoothly transitioned from Toft to Thanyani Mariba (South Africa) but the latter's premature departure from his South African post led to John Hillery (chair of the Medical Council of Ireland) taking on the IAMRA chair's duties earlier than planned. Hillery, whose father was president of Ireland some years earlier, served diligently for nearly four years as IAMRA's chair. In 2010, Fleur-Ange Lefebvre (executive director of FMRAC) was elected chair and Philip Pigou (New Zealand) was elected chair-elect. Pigou is expected to take over duties from Lefebvre in 2012 at the organization's tenth meeting, in Ottawa. The 2014 meeting is expected to be held in London and will be hosted by the General Medical Council and its chief executive, Niall Dickson, a member of IAMRA's current Management Committee.[8]

The international conferences described here and the relationships cultivated through these forums represented a positive, collaborative trend. They also reflected a growing recognition of today's health care environment as a "shrinking" global village in which one country's problem physician could easily become another country's tragedy. Perhaps no better examples of this danger can be cited than the cases of Michael Swango and Jayant Patel.

James Stewart's *Blind Eye* provides a chilling account of Swango, a licensed U.S. physician who was alleged to have deliberately poisoned at least thirty-five people in America and abroad. Though Swango's behavior and performance had raised suspicions early in his medical education and training and throughout his professional career, he managed to successfully navigate the medical regulatory system, abetted by careless verification of credentials by employers and an uncanny ability to repeatedly switch jobs before definitive action was brought to bear. Swango moved through multiple hospitals in four states before leaving the United States to practice in Zimbabwe and later Zambia—feeling secure that he had moved beyond the reach of U.S. authorities. His career ended abruptly when a tip led to his arrest in Chicago en route to Saudi Arabia for yet another job; Swango would plead guilty to fraud and murder charges and is currently incarcerated.[9]

The Swango case, while shocking in many regards, regrettably was not unique. Several years later, Jayant Patel, a surgeon educated in India and trained in New York, embarked upon a dubious career in the U.S. and Australia. Disciplinary actions by the Oregon and New York medical boards that stemmed from his incompetence prompted his move to Queensland, Australia, where authorities apparently did not review his credentials from the United States well enough. After multiple complaints from patients, nurses and colleagues, and an investigation that began in 2005, Patel was accused of gross incompetence and convicted on three counts of manslaughter.[10] The Swango and Patel stories and other such cautionary tales infused the spirit of the policy discussions at IAMRA and other international conferences. Discussions led to more substantive cooperation, such as greater data sharing across national boundaries, a practice the Federation supports and facilitates.

At IAMRA's 2010 meeting, in Philadelphia, entitled "Best Practices in Medical Regulation" and cosponsored by ECFMG, Federation and the National Board, organizers and planners sought to actively engage attendees with three half-days devoted to small-group sessions that permitted unprecedented opportunities for information exchange, as well as plenary sessions and panel discussions on a range of medical regulatory subjects. Lefebvre noted at the close of the meeting that the half-day sessions had generated 223 stories from representatives across six continents, discussion of 123 principles of medical regulation and more than 1,875 person-hours of time that would be used to generate common norms and values for further discussion and adoption at the 2012 meeting.[11]

INTERNATIONAL MEDICAL SCHOOL (IMG) GRADUATES

During IAMRA's 2010 meeting, which had a record 226 registrants representing 90 organizations from 33 countries on 6 continents, the ECFMG president and CEO, Emmanuel Cassimatis, took the opportunity to announce publicly a substantive policy change that would impact future IMGs. Beginning in 2023, he reported, international medical graduates applying for ECFMG certification (the credential which enables them to participate in ACGME-accredited graduate medical education training in the United States and obtain medical licensure from state medical boards) would be required to graduate from a medical school that has been "appropriately" accredited, that is, with standards equivalent to those in the United States for its medical schools.[12] Concerns about the absence of accreditation systems for medical schools in many countries were not new, of course, just as concerns about the quality and capabilities of IMGs to practice in the United States led to the creation decades earlier of the ECFMG in the first place. It is useful to place the this historic policy decision in its larger context.

For more than a century, graduates of European medical schools sought opportunities to practice medicine in the United States. In the late nineteenth and early twentieth centuries, the uneven quality of U.S. medical education meant the credential presented by IMGs to state boards often carried more prestige than the diploma from many U.S. schools, even if not every state board was set up by statute to enable such physicians to practice without additional testing. However, as U.S. medical education improved rapidly beginning in the 1920s, state boards became increasingly less likely to infer greater knowledge or competence by European émigré physicians compared to U.S. graduates. Assessing IMG credentials and their fitness to practice remained a challenging issue that assumed greater visibility in the 1930s and 1940s as refugees fled Europe's turmoil, though their numbers remained relatively small compared with the post–World War II influx.[13] After the Immigration and Nationality Act of 1965, signed into law by President Lyndon Johnson and made effective in 1968, a national origin quota system for immigrant visas was replaced by a system that focused on immigrants' skills and expertise. The change would bring with it over time many IMGs from nations previously limited to small numbers of immigrants. While the preferential treatment of physicians in the granting of immigrant visas was formally ended in 1978, IMGs continued to migrate to the United States through a number of visa programs, including visa waiver programs that required physicians to work for a time in physician shortage areas following their training. Between 1958 and 2005, 658,813 physician candidates began the ECFMG certification process, and 292,287 (44.5 percent) were awarded the ECFMG certificate. Of the 850,085 actively licensed physicians in the United States in 2010, according to the Federation's census of physicians, 22 percent are graduates of international medical schools, primarily from India (23 percent), the Philippines (8 percent), Pakistan (5 percent), Mexico (5 percent) and Grenada (3 percent). Overall, actively licensed physicians in the United States have graduated from 1,926 medical schools in 161 countries around the world.[14]

While there is little debate that the United States has benefited from the medical expertise of such physicians and scientists who immigrated in large numbers since 1968, there have been concerns about human capital flight, also known as a "brain drain," by which the emigration of large numbers of educated and professional individuals with technical skills or knowledge depletes a developing country's efforts to thrive financially and modernize. Though better standards of living in countries like India may be prompting some international medical graduates to return following GME training in the United States, the brain drain concerns persist. The tragic events of September 11, 2001, meanwhile, led to some IMGs being denied or delayed in obtaining visas due to enhanced security measures and legislation such as the Border Security and Visa Entry Reform Act of 2002, signed into law by President George W. Bush.[15]

To satisfy the ECFMG's new requirement in the future, Cassimatis noted at the IAMRA meeting, an IMG physician's medical school will need to be accredited by 2023 through a formal process that uses criteria comparable to those established for U.S. allopathic medical schools by the Liaison Committee for Medical Education (LCME), or that uses globally accepted criteria such as those put forward by the World Federation for Medical Education (WFME). As a partial explanation for ECFMG's decision, he noted that unlike the United States and Canada, "there are no universally accepted standards for evaluating undergraduate medical education internationally."[16]

This development was welcomed by the Federation and state board community. Only six years earlier, Federation Chair Doris Brooker (Minnesota) appointed a Special Committee on the Evaluation of Undergraduate Medical Education, chaired by Kim LeBlanc (Louisiana), which concluded that "in many respects the requirements for initial medical licensure in the United States and the system for evaluating licensure candidates (both domestic and international) are stronger today than at any time in the past." The report, presented to the Federation's House of Delegates in 2005, noted that twenty years ago it was possible to be licensed in some jurisdictions in the United States without having completed any graduate medical education, but that "today, one to three years of GME is a standard requirement for initial licensure in all U.S. jurisdictions." Presaging ECFMG's announcement by several years, the report expressed concern about the quality of undergraduate medical education abroad.[17] The AMA's Council on Medical Education first published a list in 1950, the report noted, of recommended international medical schools whose graduates should be considered comparable to graduates of LCME-accredited schools, but abandoned that effort after a decade due to concerns about cost, fairness and legal defensibility.[18]

The committee's report noted that the Medical Board of California was the only state board that actively maintained a listing of approved international medical schools for licensing purposes based upon a formalized review process and, for a small number of schools, site visits of the school campus; at least six state or territorial medical boards, it further said, followed California's lead in approving or denying medical licensure to candidates based wholly or in part upon the school's status on California's list.[19] Though the report recommended that the ECFMG and the Federation jointly develop a national clearinghouse containing information and data about international medical schools, an effort that did not come to pass, it also called upon the Federation to monitor closely the efforts under way to establish approval or accreditation mechanisms for international medical schools and provide support for these initiatives as appropriate.[20] In October 2011, the Federation sponsored a webinar for its member boards to enable the ECFMG to present its new policy. Though this change in ECFMG's policies is more than a decade away from implementation, many state board members and several nations whose graduates train in the United States have already expressed their support.

DATA SHARING AND PHYSICIAN PROFILES

Several states between 1996 and 1999, as mentioned in the previous chapter, introduced physician profile initiatives and enacted profile laws. In April of 1999, Federation President Shumacher established an ad hoc Special Committee on Physician Profiling in response to increasing demand for public access to physician-specific information and growing efforts by member boards to address the need for consumer education and better protection by making physician profiles easily available to the public.[21] In so doing, the new committee reviewed models of physician profiles then being utilized by member boards and thoughtfully considered recommendations from several consumer advocacy groups regarding the types of information they believed to be useful to consumers in making health care decisions.

"A revolution is underway among American health-care consumers," said innovator Richard Reece in November 1999.[22] At the time, managed care—a term used to describe a variety of systems and programs of financing and delivering health care that catapulted to prominence since the adoption of the Health Maintenance Organization Act of 1973 and which was based upon a philosophy of business-style management—was progressing across the country and imposing significant limitations on consumer choice in health care provider selection. Where patients for many decades had relied on the advice of family, neighbors and friends when choosing a physician, they were now increasingly forced to choose from a prescribed list of "in-network" physicians they did not know and had little means to investigate. And with employers and consumers both frequently changing managed care plans, and thus often one's physician, there was suddenly a heightened need for publicly available information about health care providers of every background and specialty.

The Federation's profiling committee began by defining a physician profile as "a data record" that includes "personal, educational, demographic and professional information about an individual physician compiled for the purpose of assisting health care consumers when choosing a physician." In meetings during 1999 and 2000, the committee—chaired by Federation board member Ronald Agresta (Ohio)—reviewed historical information and noted that the first physician profile system mandated by statute in the United States had been established just three years earlier, in the Commonwealth of Massachusetts.[23] The adoption of that statute is a telling example of the types of discussion and politics that would play out to varying degrees in states across the country as consumer groups on one side, and organizations representing physicians on the other, sought compromise with state boards to satisfy the need-to-know concerns of the former with the confidentiality and accuracy concerns of the latter.

In 1993, the Massachusetts Teachers Association had supported legislation requiring a Massachusetts Rate Setting Commission to collect and publish information about individual physicians. Despite passage by both Houses of the Legislature, it was vetoed by Governor William Weld because of concerns raised by the Massachusetts Medical Society (MMS), which supported a competing bill that stressed verification of the information and additional privacy safeguards. To satisfy the concerns of all stakeholders, Governor Weld's secretary of consumer affairs appointed a special three-person committee to examine issues related to physician profiling and provide recommendations regarding what information should be disclosed to the public. In April 1995, the Kramer Commission, as the committee came to be known, issued its report, entitled "Making Informed Choices about Doctors," that contained elements favorable to all stakeholders. A revised physician profile bill was then introduced, with the support of the MMS and the Massachusetts Board of Registration of Medicine, and signed into law by the governor on August 9, 1996.[24] Of note, the statute did not appropriate any funds to prepare and implement the program, leaving the state board to its own resourcefulness in creating an effective profile system without compromising the board's regulatory obligations.

A year later, similar physician profile statutes were enacted in Florida, Rhode Island and California. In 1998, profiling laws were passed in Idaho, Tennessee and Virginia, with the Idaho and Tennessee statutes going a step further by requiring provider profiles on a wide range of health care professionals beyond physicians. By the time the FSMB's ad hoc committee met to finalize a policy for its House of Delegates to consider in 2000, profiling laws had also been enacted in Arizona, Connecticut, Maryland and Texas and legislation was pending in Hawaii, Illinois, New Jersey, New York, Ohio, Oklahoma and Pennsylvania.[25]

While the move by states to adopt physician profiling requirements was already well under way, the Federation's committee pointedly observed after reviewing the various state profiles that "there is no consistency in the types of information included." Some of the more basic profiles, it found, gave identifying information and details about a physician's medical education, licensure status and an indication of board disciplinary actions but only the more comprehensive profiles included criminal convictions, malpractice history and disciplinary actions taken by other entities. It further noted that several health-related organizations provided consumer access to a limited amount of information regarding physicians on their websites: American Board of Medical Specialties (ABMS), American Medical Association (AMA), Administrators in Medicine (AIM) and various proprietary sites that offered information to the general public, typically for a fee. None of these sources, however, contained information on criminal convictions or medical malpractice actions.[26]

In its final report, adopted as policy by the House of Delegates in 2000, the committee recommended that state boards include all of the following elements in a physician profile: demographic information (name, gender, business or practice address and birth date); medical education (medical school, medical school location, year of graduation, medical degree and approved graduate medical education training); license and certification information (license status, license number, license type, original license date, license renewal date, type of practice and if applicable, specialty board certification); criminal convictions; medical malpractice; and disciplinary information. It offered a Model Consumer Guide which could be adapted by a member board to apply to a particular profile system to help consumers understand the significance of individual profile components. To make sure profile components were accurate, it said all information should be verified and received directly from a primary source or attested to by the physician under penalty of discipline. The committee recommended and encouraged all state boards to provide public access to such information via the Internet and toll-free telephone numbers.[27]

In 2011, Illinois became the final state in the Union—and the sixty-fifth member board of the Federation—to adopt a physician profile statute, but not before a telling bureaucratic hiccup along the way. A 2008 provision of the Medical Practice Act of Illinois called for physician profiling, with the state's governor declaring, "It is not enough to make sure every Illinois family has access to health care. We need to make sure that people have enough information to make informed decisions about the doctors who treat them."[28] The provision was part of larger health care initiatives by the governor which were declared invalid by the Illinois Supreme Court when it declared that the larger initiatives, specifically the establishment of caps on noneconomic damages in medical malpractice cases, violated the separation of powers clause of the Illinois constitution.[29] On August 9, 2011, Illinois finally adopted a physician profiling statute as part of its new Patients Right to Know Act, which contains nearly all of the profile elements the Federation's policy had recommended a year earlier.[30]

Although such physician profiles are now freely available to the public online in each state, the Federation recognized that patients do not typically know all of the jurisdictions where their physician is licensed. Utilizing its comprehensive, nationally consolidated data bank of licensed physicians and physician assistants, an online service was created by the Federation (*DocInfo*) to provide the public for a nominal fee all professional license and disciplinary information that it maintains for physicians and physician assistants licensed in the United States.

ASSURING THE ONGOING CLINICAL COMPETENCE OF PHYSICIANS THROUGH MOL

As we have seen in the last few chapters, the granting of the initial privilege to practice medicine in the United States has for several decades been viewed as a robust process along a fairly rigorous continuum of medical education encompassing both undergraduate and graduate training with multiple assessments that must be cleared along a prescribed pathway. The process by which subsequent and continuing use of that privilege is granted, however, became the focus of increased commentary and recommendations in the last two decades as the nation, and a better informed public, developed greater awareness of patient safety concerns and medical errors.[31]

In 1995, the Pew Charitable Trust Health Professions Commission recommended that states "require each licensing board to develop, implement and evaluate continuing competency requirements to assure the continuing competence of regulated health professionals." In 1999, the Institute of Medicine (IOM) said that consumers generally believe they are protected within the health care arena because "licensure and accreditation confer, in the eyes of the public, a 'Good Housekeeping Seal of Approval,'" and suggested greater assessment of physicians' performance and skills after initial licensure." A year later, the IOM adroitly observed that in a profession with "a continually expanding knowledge base," a mechanism was needed to ensure that practitioners remain up to date with current best practices. More germane to state boards and practicing physicians, the report also noted that medical regulation, when properly conceived and executed, "can both protect the public's interest and support the ability of health care professionals and organizations to innovate and change to meet the needs of their patients."[32]

The 1990s were not the first time that the subject of a physician's ongoing clinical competence was raised, however. As early as 1947, the American Academy of General Practice (later the American Academy of Family Physicians) had implemented requirements that mandated continuing education as a condition for continued membership. Some critics of such directive measures disparagingly characterized these efforts as attempts to secure "brownie points" with the public rather than meaningful efforts to assure ongoing competence. Acceptance of the CME concept proved slow in coming as two decades passed before another major medical organization attempted to adopt similar measures. As New Mexico's Robert Derbyshire remembered it, broaching the subject of "more robust" licensure renewal amongst physician audiences at the time usually engendered awkward silences and outright opposition.[33]

Advocates for a strengthened license renewal process gained a measure of federal support as early as 1967, however. A presidential Commission on Medical Manpower recommended that "state governments . . . explore the possibility of periodic relicensing of physicians and other health professionals." More pointedly, the commission recommended license renewal contingent upon the acquisition of acceptable CME or upon assessment in the practitioner's area of specialty. In a report four years later, the U.S. Department of Health, Education and Welfare addressed the concerns of those challenging the status quo of medical regulation that provided a de facto lifelong medical license to most physicians. The commission described the current state requirements as safeguards adequate for entry into a profession but ineffective against "professional obsolescence."[34] Recognizing the importance of the issue, New York passed a regulation in 1971 for physicians not serving on a hospital staff or holding specialty board certified to demonstrate ongoing clinical competence by matching the CME requirements of the American Academy of Family Physicians.

In a prescient address to the attendees of the Federation's annual meeting in 1972, Robert Derbyshire expressed his personal support of continuing education as one means of assuring a physician's continuing clinical competence:

> I, trusting to my own personal observations, . . . firmly believe that participation in continuing education does improve patient care and changes habit patterns of physicians. Let any doctor who trained 20 years or more ago who has conscientiously fulfilled his educational needs since graduation reflect on the improvement in his methods during this period . . . he will be unable to escape the conclusion that most of the changes have been brought about by some form of continuing education, be it reading, attendance at meetings or listening to colleagues. Little faith is required to accept such a truth.[35]

In 1971, New Mexico became the first state to amend its Medical Practice Act to require participation in programs of continuing education for medical licensure renewal. In this effort, the medical board found an ally among progressive supporters within the state's medical society. The society proved instrumental in developing and delivering CME programming for the state's licensees. Derbyshire and others acknowledged that while the collaboration between the board and the medical society was critical in sustaining CME, ultimately the only way to assure the adoption of such practices was through legislative mandate linked with license renewal. Early discussions even considered reexamination as a component for licensure renewal but ultimately rejected it as "drastic and impractical."[36] Over the next four decades nearly all of the member boards would enact laws and regulations in support of continuing medical education as a requirement for licensure renewal. In 2011, forty years following New Mexico's action, the Vermont Board of Medical Practice became the sixty-fifth member board to require physicians to complete a certain number of CME credit hours in order to be eligible for medical license renewal.[37] Several state boards also require content-specific CME for license renewal, as mentioned in earlier chapters, in such areas as infection control, pain management or child abuse recognition. Most member boards, to be sure, now use a variety of information sources in the course of renewing a physician's license: hospital privilege reports, disciplinary data banks such as the Federation's Board Action Data Bank and/or the National Practitioner Data Bank, patient complaints and medical malpractice reports.

A quarter century after New Mexico's requirement for CME, the Federation's Special Committee on Evaluation of Quality of Care and Maintenance of Competence reviewed the function and role of state medical boards in assuring quality care and physician competence and recommended, in part, that states develop proactive methods of identifying physicians whose competence may be in question.[38] As the Pew Charitable Trust and IOM reports at the time suggested, however, there were nagging questions about whether the requirement of a physician's periodic completion of a specific number of hours of CME, coupled with a review of prior discipline, were sufficient to fulfill a state board's mission to protect the public and promote quality health care. Developments at other medical organizations would begin to set the foundation for a focused approach to the issue at the Federation.

The twenty-four specialty boards of the ABMS formally endorsed in 2000 the principles behind a comprehensive program for what it called "Maintenance of Certification" (MOC), for physicians to whom it had granted specialty board certification status. This program was initially proposed in 1998 to replace the relatively nominal recertification requirements that several ABMS boards had begun utilizing in the late 1970s.[39]

(However, it should be noted that most of the ABMS specialty boards that adopted MOC also agreed to a "grandfather clause" that exempted physicians from MOC if they had obtained specialty board certification prior to MOC implementation by that board.) In 2001, the Accreditation Council for Graduate Medical Education (ACGME) began implementation of its Outcome Project, which focused on the accomplishments and outcomes of accredited graduate medical education training programs rather than only on the potential of a program to educate its medical residents. Under the project, residency programs were required to provide educational experiences that enabled their resident physicians to achieve competency in six core areas: medical knowledge, patient care, practice-based learning and improvement, interpersonal and communication skills, professionalism and systems-based practice.[40] The six core competencies would quickly be endorsed by the ABMS and ultimately by the Association of American Medical Colleges (AAMC) and the American Osteopathic Association (which adopted the principles in 2006 but then added a seventh core competency focusing on osteopathic philosophy).

With such developments occurring around them and questions lingering about licensure renewal, Federation Chair Ronald Agresta and the board of directors agreed to formally consider the continued competence of licensed physicians as part of its strategic action plan. The following year, Federation Chair Thomas Kirksey (Texas) convened a Special Committee on Maintenance of Licensure (MOL)—the first time the term "Maintenance of Licensure" is used in Federation documents, having supplanted the term "Maintenance of Competence"—to make recommendations about the value of a possible system that state boards could consider for the periodic assessment of the clinical competence of actively licensed physicians. Following discussions and a review of existing practices at state boards, many of which were already considering creating committees of their own to examine the issue, the special committee recommended a seminal policy statement that was adopted in 2004 by the FSMB's House of Delegates: "State medical boards have a responsibility to the public to ensure the ongoing competence of physicians seeking relicensure."[41]

From 2004 to 2010, the Federation actively sought input and feedback on MOL from leaders and representatives of major health care organizations and a variety of governmental agencies. This outreach and information gathering extended to international audiences as well. Federation leadership sought greater insight about Continuous Professional Development (CPD) at a 2010 meeting in Sydney, Australia, and about Revalidation (a program of licensure renewal similar to MOL that the United Kingdom expects to implement in 2013) at a London meeting that same year that was sponsored by the General Medical Council, the

United Kingdom's Health Foundation and the Federation that same year. Outreach efforts such as these allowed the Federation to learn more about the efforts of international medical regulatory authorities seeking to assure the continued clinical competence of their physicians. The meetings enabled the Federation to better consider the options and programs by which state medical and osteopathic boards in the United States should or could implement a system of MOL.

The earliest Federation meetings about MOL included representatives from the IOM, the Pew Charitable Trust Health Professions Commission and the Joint Commission on Accreditation of Healthcare Organizations (later the Joint Commission). Indeed, from the very beginning the Federation wisely included representatives from medical organizations across the entire continuum of medical education and practice on its committees, task forces, working groups, advisory councils, and at several national summits (discussed later in this chapter) and ad hoc meetings: NBME, ABMS, NBOME, AMA, AOA and its Bureau of Osteopathic Specialists, Council of Medical Specialty Societies (CMSS), ECFMG, ACCME, ACGME, AAMC, Citizen Advocacy Center, American Association of Colleges of Osteopathic Medicine, Administrators in Medicine (AIM), American Association of Osteopathic Examiners, and seventeen state medical and osteopathic boards.[42]

A succession of Federation chairs continued guiding the MOL initiative through its early deliberative phases. Doris Brooker (Minnesota), Lee E. Smith (West Virginia), J. William McCord (Tennessee), and N. Stacy Lankford (Indiana) all played important roles in moving the dialogue forward in a constructive, collaborative and transparent fashion. In 2005 an Interim Report of the Federation's Special Committee on MOL stated that "the profession must implement some form of mandated assessment of competence beyond that required for entry to practice,"[43] but in subsequent deliberations the recommendation of a mandated examination for MOL was eliminated—echoing the comments of the New Mexico Medical Society thirty years earlier—though it would eventually be listed as an option by which a physician *could* meet the MOL requirements that a state board chose to adopt. The following year, the Accreditation Council on Continuing Medical Education released new standards for the accreditation of CME providers that focused on learning and change for both CME providers and learners. These standards aimed to improve physician practice by requiring CME providers to develop and implement CME programs that focused on improving physician competence, physician performance and patient outcomes.[44] In 2006 and again in 2008, the special committee (chaired by Stephen Schabel of South Carolina) issued interim reports to the Federation's Board and its House of Delegates, reviewing the history of ongoing clinical competence discussions and commenting on any relevant developments across the continuum of medical education and practice.[45] Behind the scenes but also in many of the formal meetings the Federation had with its many stakeholders on an issue that was of interest to many because it would impact all licensed physicians, FSMB chief executive James Thompson and his staff worked diligently to explain the Federation's nascent proposals for MOL, including its rationale and several potential ideas for its implementation.

Discussions around developing an MOL framework for state boards continued through 2008 under Federation Chair Regina Benjamin (Alabama), who appropriately established an MOL Impact Analysis Task Force to gauge the potential impact on board resources and practicing physicians should a state board adopt MOL. In 2009, Federation Chair Martin Crane (Massachusetts), who like a number of state board members initially had some concerns about how MOL would be implemented but over time felt more secure in supporting and later championing the proposal, began his term intent on moving ahead with MOL for consideration by the Federation's House of Delegates the following year, convening an Advisory Group on the Continued Competence of Licensed Physicians, chaired by J. Lee Dockery (Florida), a former chair of the AMA's Council on Medical Education and former executive vice president of the ABMS. The charge of Dockery's group was to issue an opinion to the Federation Board about whether the MOL framework that was being proposed in the report of the special committee was feasible, reasonable and consistent with a series of guiding principles adopted by the Federation's House of Delegates in May 2008. Dockery's group was also charged with determining whether the framework was suitable for use by state medical boards in assuring the continued competence of licensed physicians. In anticipation of the possible adoption of the MOL framework, Crane established an MOL Implementation Group in 2010 chaired by Steven Stack, who would go on in 2012 to become the youngest physician to be elected chair of the AMA's Board of Trustees.[46]

Crane also created a CEO Advisory Council on MOL, chaired by the Federation's new chief executive, Humayun Chaudhry, to keep the chief executives of more than a dozen medical organizations across the continuum of medical education and practice (AMA, AOA, CMSS, NBME, NBOME, ABMS, AOA-BOS, AAMC, AACOM, CAC, AIM, ECFMG, ACGME and ACCME) regularly apprised of developments related to MOL and to continuously obtain their feedback and input as MOL progressed. The group continues to meet periodically by conference call. In 2010, the Federation issued a peer-reviewed background paper that was approved by the Federation's Board and which summarized the history, rationale and framework for MOL.[47] In 2011, the Federation's Board approved an MOL Implementation paper that was published in 2012 in the *Journal of Medical Regulation*.

Thus in April 2010 in Chicago, more than seven years after it began to earnestly look at the issue and 250 years after the first medical regulatory board was created in colonial America, the Federation's House of Delegates voted to adopt a framework by which physicians in the United States would be required over time to demonstrate their continued clinical competence beyond initial licensure as a requirement for renewal of their medical license. The three components of MOL that all physicians would be expected to complete, as envisioned in the Federation's framework, incorporate the core competencies for physicians pioneered by the ACGME[48] (and endorsed by the ABMS, AAMC and the AOA) and focus on three primary areas: reflective self-assessment, an assessment of knowledge and skills, and performance in practice. The FSMB's House of Delegates also adopted a recommendation from the MOL Advisory Group that physicians actively engaged in the ABMS's MOC program, or the AOA-BOS's Osteopathic Continuous Certification (OCC) program, should be recognized as being in substantial compliance with any state's MOL requirements.[49] This step was important because a majority of physicians in the United States are specialty certified and MOL could be satisfied for this cohort of licensees by attestation of active involvement in MOC and/or OCC. Because not every physician is specialty certified, and because many are "grandfathered" for specialty certification and do not need to engage in recertification, and because some specialty certified physicians don't want to recertify for whatever reason, the Federation is working with a number of organizations with experience in specialty practice and assessment to identify activities outside of recertification that could meet a state's requirements for MOL.

The MOL Implementation Workgroup continued its work in 2010 and 2011 at the request of FSMB Chair Freda Bush (Mississippi) and provided additional recommendations beyond the framework: (1) MOL should be phased in over time (one component at a time, following a period of education for physicians, the public, and legislators in that jurisdiction); (2) the majority of CME required of physicians should be practice-relevant; and (3) the periodicity of MOL requirements should be annually for the first component (which is devoted to practice-relevant CME that supports performance improvement) and every five to six years for components two and three.[50]

By the summer of 2011, eleven state medical and osteopathic boards reported they were interested in participating in MOL implementation pilot projects with the Federation. To address the issue of how physicians actively licensed but not engaged in clinical practice (sometimes known as administrative physicians) could meet a state's MOL requirements, Federation Chair Janelle Rhyne in 2011 convened an MOL Workgroup on Non-Clinical Physicians, chaired by Claudette Dalton (Virginia), to examine the issue and report its recommendations to the Federation's House of Delegates by 2013. The movement by state boards to assure ongoing physician competence, it should be noted, is not unique to medicine but in actuality is a part of a growing trend around the world and across professions. The National Council of State Boards of Nursing, the National Association of Boards of Pharmacy and the National Commission on Certified Physician Assistants, for example, are also at various phases of adoption of a maintenance program for licensure and/or certification for nurses, pharmacists and physician assistants, as are a number of nations such as the United Kingdom, New Zealand and several provinces in Canada.[51]

SUPPORTING PHYSICIAN ACCOUNTABILITY THROUGH NATIONAL DIALOGUE

"Realizing that the task of ensuring the ongoing competence of all physicians is unattainable with the limited resources available to state medical boards," wrote Federation chief executive James Thompson in 2008, "the FSMB made an early effort to bring together a larger and more comprehensive constituency." He urged the Federation to organize a series of "Physician Accountability for Physician Competence" (PAPC) meetings beginning in 2005 as a national, multistakeholder forum to develop a valid, uniform system for measuring and evaluating a physician's competence during his or her professional career. Thompson felt the summits could also facilitate constructive dialogue that would advance the Federation's interest in MOL, a "main impetus" for the gatherings. Attendees from more than forty organizations, including representatives from medical regulators in the U.S. and Canada, organizations representing practicing physicians, insurers, academic health care centers, major education foundations and the public participated over time in a series of national invitational "summits"[52] coordinated by the Federation.[53]

The first summit, held over two days in March 2005 in Fort Worth, Texas, was supported by a Robert Wood Johnson grant and focused on developing various scenarios describing what the U.S. health care system could look like in 2020. A second summit in December of that same year in Chicago was jointly supported by the larger institutional participants and produced a draft definition of physician competence, a draft outline for a document describing "good medical practice"[54] and the conceptualization of a National Alliance for Physician Competence (NAPC). Subsequent summits were supported by a "fund drive" at the Chicago summit (proceeds were managed by the Federation's Foundation for Education and Research) that resulted in pledges adequate to support the direct costs of future summits. The Federation provided staff support for the organization of all of the summits, whose agenda were developed in collaboration with staff from several organizations and all made possible by generous contributions by several organizations. During the third summit, in Philadelphia in June 2006, participants continued to develop what would be called the "Good Medical Practice-USA" document, created a basic plan for the NAPC alliance, and proposed concepts for a portfolio tool that could be used by physicians to provide information about their competence to the public and to help physicians reflect on their performance. In preparation for the fourth summit, scheduled for January 2007, a draft proposal for NAPC was distributed for discussion by the participating organizations' governing boards. The proposal included a mission and purpose statement, possible governance structures, descriptions of pilot projects that could be pursued in support of measuring competence and even a proposed business plan and communications strategy.[55]

In 2009, as the Federation was preparing to move forward to actively propose a framework for MOL for consideration by its member boards, it signaled its desire to focus its energies on this effort rather than the summits. Though the NAPC Alliance did not formally continue beyond 2009 and interest in the "Good Medical Practice" document was not sustained in part because of concerns from organizations representing practicing physicians that its recommendations could be legally held against physicians as absolute standards, the summits did spawn collaborative efforts on various projects and achieved general support for the basic principles underpinning MOL. With the support of its Board and successive chief executives James Thompson and Barbara Schneidman, the Federation financially supported pilot projects in 2008 and 2009 with the NBME and AAMC to test the feasibility of an "eFolio" (or electronic portfolio) within a broader "Data Commons" platform that could link with FCVS and ultimately enable physicians to electronically access, within a protected and secure virtual space, documents of relevance along the milestones of their professional career from medical school through residency training through clinical practice.

Following the Federation's successful adoption of the MOL framework by its House of Delegates in 2010, and continuing interest by the leaders of organizations involved with the assessment, licensure, accreditation, credentialing and certification of physicians to get together for periodic discussions and consensus, Federation Chair Freda Bush and the board of directors agreed to participate in a series of national meetings that began later that year, though at a much smaller scale than the PAPC summits. The efforts of these organizations culminated, in 2011, in the creation of a Coalition for Physician Accountability that the Federation's Board agreed to support and whose principal members would include the National Board, NBOME, AAMC, the Federation, ACGME, ABMS,

ACCME, ECFMG, AOA and the AMA. The first Management Committee for the Coalition was elected at the charter meeting of the group at AAMC headquarters in Washington, D.C., on August 16, 2011, and consisted of the same individuals who agreed in 2010 to serve on an interim steering committee: Donald Melnick (NBME), Steve Minnick (ECFMG), Thomas Nasca (ACGME), Thomas Norris (ABMS), Humayun Chaudhry (FSMB) and Deborah Powell (AAMC). The Coalition's first consensus document, an important milestone because it demonstrated the ability of different organizations with different constituencies and governance but similar interests in protecting the public to come together, supported a call for sustained federal funding for graduate medical education. In agreeing to sign the letter, a majority of the Coalition's members felt that the current health care system was not adequately responsive to the physician workforce needs of society and that any funding reduction in graduate medical education could significantly hamper the medical profession's ability to meet the health care needs of the public.

COMPREHENSIVE REVIEW OF THE UNITED STATES MEDICAL LICENSING EXAMINATION (USMLE)

With progress being made in the plans for the assurance of the ongoing clinical competence of those providing health care it is perhaps appropriate that the examinations for entry into medical school and eligibility for medical licensure are also undergoing a comprehensive review and update. This activity has involved the AAMC for the Medical College Admissions Test (MCAT), which completed deliberations in 2011 as part of a comprehensive update for only the fifth time since the examination's creation in 1928; the NBOME for the COMLEX-USA examination and, in the narrative that follows, by the National Board and Federation for the USMLE program.[56]

The practice of medicine in the United States, as discussed in previous chapters and as referenced in the 2010 edition of the Federation's *Guide to the Essentials of a Modern Medical and Osteopathic Practice Act*, is a "privilege granted by the people acting through their elected representatives." One of the key credentials presented by physicians to state boards for the "privilege" of medical licensure is their successful completion of a licensing examination. The United States Medical Licensing Examination (USMLE) is the single, three-step examination pathway whose successful completion is required of all students receiving the M.D. degree from a Liaison Committee on Medical Education (LCME)-accredited U.S. or Canadian medical school and for all students trained outside the United States in order to be eligible for initial medical licensure by the FSMB's member boards. The exam is also taken by several thousand osteopathic medical students in the United States each year, though most take the COMLEX-USA, whose passage on Levels 1 and 2 is required by the Commission on Osteopathic College Accreditation for successful graduation from an American osteopathic medical school.

Currently, the USMLE program is in the midst of implementing its second strategic enhancement. The first concluded after the transition to computer-based testing (CBT) and the inclusion of a clinical skills component. The 1999 transition to CBT represented a significant improvement in test delivery and, more importantly, an opportunity to implement new testing modalities designed to assess critical physician skills such as diagnosis and patient management. This was exemplified by the introduction of Primum® Computer-based Case Simulations (CCS) into the USMLE Step 3 after several decades of research by the National Board of Medical Examiners.[57] The CCS presented a testing modality consistent with the assessment objectives of Step 3 to assess whether examinees can apply medical knowledge and understanding of biomedical and clinical science deemed essential for the unsupervised practice of medicine—a particularly relevant concern to state boards.

The introduction of a clinical skills component to USMLE represented something of a "return to the past." From 1916 through the early 1960s, the NBME certifying examination included a clinical bedside component. However, studies of the bedside oral exam that documented psychometric inadequacies, beginning in the 1950s, combined with high costs and logistical difficulties in administering this type of examination for the rapidly growing postwar cohort of medical students, ultimately contributed to its demise.[58] It was not until 1998 that a clinical skills component returned to the forefront in testing. In that year, the ECFMG added the Clinical Skills Assessment® to its requirements for certification. This meant that IMGs were now being asked to formally demonstrate acceptable proficiency in communication and clinical skills prior to entry into GME. The need for broadening such an assessment to include U.S. medical students had long been apparent. In 1995, the membership of the NBME and the Federation's House of Delegates adopted the original strategic plan for the USMLE calling for the inclusion of a clinical skills component to the USMLE when this could be done in a valid, reliable and feasible manner. Furthermore, arguments questioning the need for an independent assessment of clinical skills outside the confines of the U.S. medical schools were severely undercut by several studies outlining a wide variability in schools' assessment and insufficient evaluation methods.[59]

Despite significant opposition from the AMA, medical students and many medical educators, in 2004 a clinical skills examination using standardized patients was added to the USMLE Step 2.[60] Developed in collaboration with the ECFMG, the Step 2 Clinical Skills (CS) was designed to help ensure the public and the Federation's member boards that successful candidates for medical licensure are competent in the fundamental clinical skills required for safe and effective patient care. These clinical skills include taking a relevant medical history, performing an appropriate physical examination, communicating effectively with the patient, clearly and accurately documenting the findings and diagnostic hypotheses from the clinical encounter and listing appropriate initial diagnostic studies. The examination consists of a series of encounters with "live" standardized patients (SPs) portraying common and important clinical problems. Students graduating from M.D.-granting U.S. and Canadian medical schools in 2005 or later are required to take the Step 2 Clinical Skills examination as part of the requirements for licensure in all United States jurisdictions. The Step 2 CS also replaced the ECFMG's Clinical Skills Assessment as a requirement for ECFMG certification for graduates of medical schools located outside the U.S. and Canada seeking graduate medical education opportunities in the United States.[61]

Two important concepts and findings led the National Board, the Federation and ECFMG to move forward with the introduction of SP-based examinations to the USMLE program: a growing body of evidence and experience supporting the value of such testing and a reemerging acknowledgment that these patient-centered skills are critical to safe and effective patient care. The Step 2 CS examination is today recognized as an essential component of the USMLE, an enduring collaboration between the USMLE program and ECFMG, and has encouraged more formalized assessment of clinical skills at medical school campuses across the United States, Canada and abroad.[62]

With the introduction of the Step 2 CS in 2004 marking the completion of the program's first strategic plan, discussions soon arose as to future directions for the USMLE. As early work on a second strategic plan for USMLE unfolded in 2006–2007, the Federation board of directors determined that closure needed to be reached on an important proposal dating back several years earlier that called for a Common Medical Licensing Examination System (CMLES). In 2001, the Federation House of Delegates adopted a series of policy statements culminating from several years' work by the Special Committee on Licensing Examinations, chaired by William Fleming (Texas). The policy statements reaffirmed the organization's commitment to a "single pathway to licensure," acknowledged that both USMLE and the COMLEX were "valid for their stated purposes" and encouraged the Federation to work with the NBME and the NBOME on a plan for developing a "common examination system." Subsequent discussions progressed slowly among the three organizations for several reasons. Considerable staff resources were already being dedicated to the inclusion of a clinical skills component to both examinations. The targeted research necessary to determine the degree of comparability between the two examination programs was lacking and the projected resources (staff/financial) were substantial. Additionally, the Federation leadership understood that the timing for such work was inauspicious as the USMLE had just entered the early phase of its second strategic review with the prospect of potentially significant alterations to the program. Consequently, the Federation House of Delegates adopted a policy in 2008 acknowledging that the Federation may yet collaborate with other parties, along an unspecified timeline, on a "common licensing examination *system*" (italics added) advancing allopathic and osteopathic licensure and preserving the "distinctiveness" of both professions.[63]

With the CMLES initiative winding down, the Federation turned its attentions fully to the ongoing comprehensive review of the USMLE program. With the successful implementation of Step 2 CS nearing readiness, Federation President James Thompson encouraged the USMLE Composite Committee to undertake a formal, strategic review of the entire sequence of the program in light of the substantial attention received by the clinical skills issue. Subsequently, the USMLE formed a Committee to Evaluate the USMLE Program (CEUP) whose membership included medical students, residents, clinicians and members of the licensing, graduate and undergraduate medical education communities. The CEUP met between 2006 and 2008 at the behest of the USMLE Composite Committee, the governing body of the USMLE program, to determine if the mission and purpose of the USMLE exam were effectively and efficiently supported by the current design, structure and format of the three-step examination.[64] Except for the transition to computer-based testing and the introduction of the SP-based CS exam, the overall structure and approach to the examination had remained essentially unchanged since its inception in 1991. Several themes emerged during the CEUP deliberations. Among these were the concepts that the USMLE is primarily intended to support decisions for initial medical licensure, that USMLE should continue to assess readiness for supervised and unsupervised medical practice, and that USMLE should reflect the evolution of medical education, training and curricula.

The committee's primary recommendations, which were adopted in 2009 by the governance of the National Board and the Federation, are part of an evolutionary process of enhancement to the program known as the Comprehensive Review of the USMLE (CRU). Some of the more critical components of the proposed changes included the following:

- strengthening the focus of the examinations on two patient-centered decision points—one at the interface between undergraduate and graduate education and one at the beginning of independent practice;

- increasing the assessment of foundational medical sciences throughout the USMLE sequence;
- emphasizing the physician competencies that are deemed important to safe and effective patient care;
- enhancing the assessment of clinical skills within the USMLE; and
- introducing a testing format to assess examinees' ability to access and apply relevant information in solving clinical problems[65]

While the details of how the recommendations will be implemented over the next several years are being actively discussed by the staff and leadership of the Federation and the National Board, it is noteworthy that even during the development of the USMLE in the late 1980s there were no specific recommendations as to when the examination must be administered across the continuum of medical education. Both organizations have stressed that the emphasis on informing two decision points does not mean two examinations but rather a series of examinations to support the two general points in time—one during medical school and one following graduation from medical school—during which the various current examination components, newly formatted to better include the other recommendations, will be administered.

As with Maintenance of Licensure, it is likely that the Federation will be busy in the coming years talking with various groups of medical students, physicians-in-training and practicing physicians, as well as state boards and medical organizations across the continuum of medical education and practice about the changes envisioned in the Comprehensive Review of the USMLE. Both MOL and CRU, to be sure, represent substantive changes in the way in which physicians will be licensed and assessed in years to come but are positive trends that recognize a physician's commitment to lifelong learning and should assure the delivery of quality health care in the future.

EPILOGUE

While there may never be ironclad guarantees that the medical regulatory systems of today or tomorrow can prevent the tragedies of a Dr. Swango or a Dr. Patel, described in this chapter, many of the safeguards adopted by state medical and osteopathic boards in the United States, particularly during the last fifteen years, should offer considerable solace to the public.

The Federation's Board Action Data Bank remains this nation's primary central repository of physician and physician assistant disciplinary information, freely accessible to state boards and for individual public queries. The Federation's All-Licensed Physician Data Base continues to support the organization's Disciplinary Alert Service by promptly notifying any member board whenever any one of them takes a disciplinary action against one of their licensees. The Federation Credentials Verification Service (FCVS) continues to provide a valuable service to physicians and support state boards' licensing processes through the use of direct source verification of physician core credentials. The Federation continues to support multinational data-sharing agreements by which medical regulatory authorities in other countries can quickly determine a U.S.-based physician's verified credentials, including medical licensure and disciplinary history. The USMLE program's utilization of a clinical skills exam has stood the test of time and continues to provide medical boards and the public with an independent assessment of a prospective physician's skills in bedside manner, medical history taking and physical examination, and clinical reasoning. Similarly, the Maintenance of Licensure (MOL) framework, by which physicians would be required to periodically demonstrate ongoing clinical competency in their area of practice as a condition for medical licensure renewal, represents further evidence of progressive action by state boards to ensure public protection.

Finally, through such recent activities as the promotion of expedited telemedicine licenses (adopted thus far by eleven state boards), the Uniform Application for Physician Licensure (adopted by seventeen state boards and under consideration by two-dozen more) and a more robust and facile FCVS, the Federation continues to support its state and territorial boards of medicine and osteopathic medicine in strengthening state-based medical licensure and discipline as enshrined in the U.S. Constitution to better protect the public and promote quality health care.

A troubling 2009 incident serves as a potent reminder that the work of individual state board members, whom the Federation recognizes with the distinction of "Fellow," is not only little understood by members of the public they serve but can sometimes be fraught with danger: Trent Pierce, a family physician and chair of the Arkansas State Medical Board, was badly injured in a car bombing that year that required fifteen hours of surgery for burns on 18 percent of his body, two broken bones and damage to both eyes; a year later, a federal jury convicted a physician of conspiring to detonate the bomb outside Pierce's home in retaliation after the board twice sanctioned the doctor for overprescribing pain medication.[66] Pierce, who has since resumed his medical practice as well as his service on the board, received the Federation's Meritorious Service Award in 2010 and was recognized by FSMB Foundation President Nancy Achin Audesse with the establishment of the Dr. Trent Pierce Public Leaders' Safety and Violence Education (SAVE) Program that will utilize an education module to train state public servants on how to prevent and handle acts of violence.[67]

As the Federation begins a second century of services, it will undoubtedly continue on its quest to educate the public about its activities and those of its state boards. In doing so, it will address opportunities and challenges as they present themselves and create new opportunities where it is able for activities and services that ultimately serve the public good. Collaborative efforts with and among state medical boards, the Federation and the FSMB Foundation are already bearing fruit with tools and resources for professional, and to bolster educational outreach and bolstering public members' participation on state boards. Current Foundation President Stephen Heretick has taken on the work ably begun by his predecessors Nancy Audesse and Cheryl Vaught.[68]

If the business theorists are correct in positing a biological life cycle for organizations, then the Federation's evolution over the past several decades into a significant player on the national scene on behalf of the state board community represents a vibrant adulthood for the organization and augurs a promising future. A century of growth and accomplishment has given reality to the faith of the Federation's founders who hoped for the truth in a poet's words—"Mighty things from small beginnings grow."

NOTES

1. Alan Shumacher, "President's Message," *Journal of Medical Licensure and Discipline* 86, no. 1 (1999): 3; George Barrett, "Introduction," *Medical Licensure in the 21st Century* (Decatur, Georgia: St. Barthèlemy Press, 2002), 8–9.
2. Shumacher, "President's Message," 3.
3. Gary Johnson to Finlay Scott, April 25, 2001, FSMB Archives, Euless, Texas; IAMLA Interim Governing Committee Meeting Summary for January 25, 2001, FSMB Archives, Euless, Texas; *FSMB Public Policy Compendium* (Euless, Texas: Federation of State Medical Boards, 2011), 13.
4. "IAMLA Interim Governing Committee Meets," *BoardNet News* (Euless, Texas: Federation of State Medical Boards, March 8, 2002).
5. "IAMRA History," International Association of Medical Regulatory Authorities, accessed on January 31, 2012, http://www.iamra.com/history.asp.
6. Gerard Dillon, e-mail message to the authors, January 24, 2012.
7. "IAMRA ByLaw," International Association of Medical Regulatory Authorities, accessed on February 1, 2012, http://www.iamra.com/bylaws.asp.
8. "Committees" and "Conferences," International Association of Medical Regulatory Authorities, accessed on February 1, 2012, http://www.iamra.com.
9. James B. Stewart, *Blind Eye* (New York: Simon & Schuster, 1999).
10. Bill Wunner, "Dr. Death Shockwaves Ripple through Australia," accessed on January 31, 2012, http://edition.cnn.com/2010/WORLD/asiapcf/10/28/australia.doctor/index.html; *Queensland Public Hospitals Commission of Inquiry Report*, 2005, page 538, accessed on January 31, 2012, http://www.qphci.qld.gov.au/final_report/Chapter-08.pdf.
11. "Best Practices in Medical Regulation," 9th International Conference on Medical Regulation, accessed on January 31, 2012, http://iamra2010.nbme.org/.

12. "2010 Highlights," *Annual Report of the Educational Commission on Foreign Medical Graduates* (Philadelphia: Educational Commission for Foreign Medical Graduates, 2011), 4.

13. *International Medical Graduates in American Medicine: Contemporary Challenges and Opportunities* (Chicago: American Medical Association, 2010), 7–8.

14. *International Medical Graduates in American Medicine,* 10; Young, Chaudhry, et al., "Census of Actively Licensed Physicians in the United States," 10–20.

15. Fitzhugh Mullan, "The Metrics of the Physician Brain Drain," *New England Journal of Medicine* 353 (2005): 1810–1818; "IMGs in American Medicine," 30.

16. "ECFMG to Require Medical School Accreditation for International Medical School Graduates Seeking Certification Beginning in 2023," ECFMG Press Release issued September 21, 2010, accessed on January 31, 2012, http://www.iamra.com/pdf/nr-ecfmg-092110.pdf.

17. *Report of the Special Committee on the Evaluation of Undergraduate Medical Education* (Euless, Texas: Federation of State Medical Boards, 2004), 8.

18. Derbyshire, *Medical Licensure and Discipline,* 139.

19. The Education Department in New York State also maintains a review process for international schools but this is solely for the purpose of allowing these schools' students to participate in extended clerkship programs.

20. *Special Committee on Evaluation of Undergraduate Medical Education,* 11.

21. *Report of the Special Committee on Physician Profiling* (Euless, Texas: Federation of State Medical Boards, 2000), 1.

22. Richard L. Reece, "The Internet as an Equalizing, Energizing and Transforming Force in the Patient and Physician Relationship," *Connecticut Medicine* 63 (November 1999): 683.

23. *Special Committee on Physician Profiling,* 2.

24. M. Rothhouse and E. Kaiser, "Provider Profiles," Health Policy Tracking Service of National Conference of State Legislatures (September 22, 1999), 1.

25. *Special Committee on Physician Profiling,* 3.

26. Ibid.

27. Ibid., 4–8, 12–15.

28. "Illinois Announces Launch of Physician Profile Web Site," Government Technology, accessed on January 31, 2012, http://www.govtech.com/health/Illinois-Announces-Launch-of-Physician-Profile-Web_Site.html.

29. Larry Bodine, "In a Success for Plaintiffs, the Illinois Supreme Court Strikes Down Medical Malpractice Law," JDSUPRA, accessed on January 31, 2012, www.jdsupra.com/post/documentViewer.aspx?fid=68691928–98c1–43ce-a125–b247bc72e997.

30. "Public Act 097–0280, HB 0105," Illinois General Assembly, accessed on January 31, 2012, www.ilga.gov/legislation/publicacts/fulltext.asp?Name=097–0280.

31. Humayun Chaudhry, Janelle Rhyne, et al., "Maintenance of Licensure: Protecting the Public, Promoting Quality Health Care," *Journal of Medical Regulation* 96, no. 2 (2010): 13–20.

32. Pew Health Professions Commission, *Reforming Health Care Workforce Regulations: Policy Considerations for the 21st Century* (San Francisco: Pew Health Professions, 1995); Institute of Medicine, *To Err Is Human: Building a Safer Health System,* Linda Kohn, Janet Corrigan, and Molla Donaldson, eds. (Washington, DC: National Academy Press, 2000), 3, 116, 118; Institute of Medicine, *Crossing the Quality Chasm: A New Health System for the 21st Century,* R. Brier, Janet Corrigan, Molla Donaldson, and Linda Kohn, eds. (Washington, DC: National Academy Press, 2001), 25–26.

33. Robert Derbyshire, "Relicensure for Continued Practice," *Journal of Medical Licensure and Discipline* 89, no. 1 (2003): 16–22.

34. *Report of the National Advisory Commission on Health Manpower* (Washington, DC: Government Printing Office, 1967); U.S. Department of Health, Education and Welfare, *Report on Licensure and Related Health Personnel Credentialing* (Washington, DC: Government Printing Office, 1971).

35. Derbyshire, "Relicensure for Continued Practice," 18.

36. Ibid.

37. "Continuing Medical Education," Federation of State Medical Boards, accessed on January 31, 2012, http://www.fsmb.org/grpol_keyissues.html.

38. *Report of Special Committee on the Evaluation of Quality of Care and Maintenance of Competence* (Euless, Texas: Federation of State Medical Boards, 1999), 2–4.

39. "ABMS Maintenance of Certification," American Board of Medical Specialties, accessed on November 1, 2011, http://www.abms.org/Maintenance_of_Certification/ABMS_MOC.aspx.

40. "ACGME Outcome Project," Accreditation Council of Graduate Medical Education, accessed on November 1, 2011, http://www.acgme.org/outcome/project/glossary2.asp.

41. Humayun Chaudhry, "Charting Dynamism in Medical Education, Licensure and Regulation," *Journal of Medical Licensure and Regulation* 95, no. 3 (2009): 5–8.

42. "Summit Participants," Physician Accountability for Physician Competence, accessed on November 28, 2011, http://www.innovationlabs.com/summit/.

43. "Special Committee on Maintenance of Licensure Interim Report to the Board of Directors," February 2005, accessed January 31, 2012, http://www.fsmb.org/m_mol_reports.html.

44. "CME as a Bridge to Quality: The ACCME Announces Updated Accreditation Criteria," ACCME Press Release for September 5, 2006, accessed on January 31, 2012, http://www.accme.org/index.cfm/fa/news.home/News.cfm.

45. "MOL Timeline," Federation of State Medical Boards, accessed on January 31, 2012, http://www.fsmb.org/m_mol_timeline.html.

46. Ibid.

47. Chaudhry, Rhyne, et al., "Maintenance of Licensure: Protecting the Public, Promoting Quality Health Care," 13–20.

48. Medical Knowledge; patient care; interpersonal and communication skills; professionalism; practice-based learning and improvement; and systems-based practice.

49. "Board Report 10–3: Maintenance of Licensure," Federation of State Medical Boards, accessed on January 31, 2012, http://www.fsmb.org/m_mol_reports.html.

50. "Board Report 11–3: Report of the MOL Implementation Group," Federation of State Medical Boards, accessed on January 31, 2012, http://www.fsmb.org/m_mol_reports.html.

51. "MOL Timeline," accessed on February 1, 2012.

52. Attendees of the summit meetings included representatives of the AMA, AOA, AAMC, ACCME, ACGME, NBME, NBOME, ECFMG, ABMS, CMSS, FMRAC, Medical Council of Canada, Harvard School of Public Health, American Association of Osteopathic Examiners, American Board of Internal Medicine Foundation, American College of Cardiology, American Academy of Family Physicians, Association for Hospital Medical Education, Robert Wood Johnson Foundation, the Joint Commission, Commonwealth Fund, Consumers Union, Citizens Advocacy Center, Coalition for Physician Enhancement, American Association for Retired Persons, the state medical boards of Michigan, Iowa, Virginia, Kentucky, Minnesota, North Carolina, South Carolina, the District of Columbia and Oregon, and several regional health care systems and insurers, such as the BlueCross/BlueShield Association.

53. James N. Thompson, "Maintenance of Licensure and Continuing Medical Education," American Medical Association *CPPD Report* (Winter 2008): 1–2.

54. The document drew inspiration from a similarly titled work by the United Kingdom's General Medical Council, the CanMEDS project in Canada and the AAMC's Medical School Objectives Project (MSOP).

55. "Summit History," Physician Accountability for Physician Competence, accessed on January 31, 2012, http://innovationlabs.com/summit/overview.html.

56. "MR5: 5th Comprehensive Review of the MCAT," Association of American Medical Colleges, accessed on January 31, 2012; "Blue Ribbon Panel Making Progress on COMLEX-USA," *Osteopathic Examiner*, June 2011.

57. "NBME Historical Highlights," *National Board of Medical Examiners 2001 Annual Report*, 25.

58. Hubbard and Levit, *National Board of Medical Examiners*, 9; Gerard Dillon, John Boulet, et al., "Simulations in the United States Medical Licensing Examination," *Quality and Safety in Health Care* 13, Suppl. 1 (2004): i41–i45.

59. *Public Policy Compendium*, 5; Association of American Medical Colleges, *Report III, Contemporary Issues in Medicine: Communication in Medicine*; Donald Kassebaum, "Shortcomings in the Evaluation of Students' Clinical Skills and Behaviors in Medical School," *Academic Medicine* 74 (1999): 842–49.

60. Myrle Croasdale, "AMA Takes Aim at Skills Exam," *American Medical News*, July 5, 2004, accessed on January 31, 2012, http://www.ama-assn.org/amednews/2004/07/05/prsd0705.htm.

61. *USMLE Bulletin of Information* (Philadelphia: NBME and FSMB, 2011), 2, 4–5, 11.

62. W. R. Gilliland, J. LaRochelle, et al., "Changes in Clinical Skills Education Resulting from the Introduction of the USMLE Step 2 Clinical Skills," *Medical Teacher* 30, no. 3 (2008): 325.

63. FSMB Board of Directors, *Board Report 2008–1: Progress in the Development of a Common Medical Licensing Examination System*. FSMB Archives, Euless, Texas; *Public Policy Compendium*, 6.

64. Committee to Evaluate the USMLE Program, "Final Report and Recommendations," accessed on January 31, 2012, http://www.usmle.org/cru/updates/2009–06.html.

65. Ibid.

66. Robbie Brown, "A Town Takes a Car Bombing to Heart," *New York Times*, February 6, 2009; Robbie Brown, "Arkansas: Doctor Found Guilty in Bomb Attack," *New York Times*, August 9, 2010.

67. "Public Members Program," FSMB Foundation, accessed on February 1, 2012, http://www.fsmb.org/foundation2.html.

68. "FSMB Foundation," Federation of State Medical Boards, accessed on February 1, 2012, http://www.fsmb.org/foundation2.html.

List of Acronyms

The following list is intended to assist readers with a quick reference to the acronyms utilized within this text. In all instances within the text, the acronym is presented with the first reference to the organization, examination or community being alluded to. Afterward, the acronym or truncated version of the name is presented.

AAMC	Association of American Medical Colleges
ABMS	American Board of Medical Specialties
AIM	Administrators in Medicine
AMA	American Medical Association
AMA CME	American Medical Association's Council on Medical Education
AOA	American Osteopathic Association
AOA BOS	American Osteopathic Association Bureau of Osteopathic Specialtists
CAM	Complementary and Alternative Medicine
COMLEX-USA	Comprehensive Osteopathic Medical Licensing Examination
CMLES	Common Medical Licensing Examination System
DHHS	U.S. Department of Health and Human Services
ECFMG	Educational Commission for Foreign Medical Graduates
FLEX	Federation Licensing Examination
FMGEMS	Foreign Medical Graduates Examination in the Medical Sciences

FSMB	Federation of State Medical Boards; commonly cited in this text as the "Federation"
HRSA	U.S. Health Resources Services Administration
IMG	International Medical Graduate
JAMA	*Journal of the American Medical Association*
LCME	Liaison Committee on Medical Education
MPA	Medical Practice Act
NBME	National Board of Medical Examiners, also cited in this text as the "National Board"
NBOME	National Board of Osteopathic Medical Examiners
NPDB	National Practitioners Data Bank
OIG	Office of the Inspector General, Department of Health and Human Services
SPEX	Special Purpose Examination
USMLE	United States Medical Licensing Examination
VQE	Visa Qualifying Examination

Appendix 1: Original Constitution and Bylaws of the Federation of State Medical Boards

Constitution

Article I: The name of this organization shall be the Federation of State Medical Boards of the United States.

Article II: The object shall be to develop and maintain reasonably high and uniform standards of medical licensure in the United States. Contributing toward this end of the Federation shall endeavor (a) to obtain accurate knowledge of the standards of preliminary and of medical education; the rules adopted and methods employed by the medical boards of the various states of this country, and of other countries; (b) to publish a Bulletin by which this information may be disseminated among the members; and (c) to further interstate endorsement of medical licensure.

Article III: Section 1. The medical board of any state may become an active member of this Federation by making due application, if its standards, rules and methods are at least equal to the minimum requirements as set forth in the By-Laws, on the recommendations of the executive committee and a majority vote of the members of the Federation present at any regular meeting. (b) On the recommendation of the executive committee, any membership may be terminated at any annual meeting of the Federation by a majority vote of the membership present.

Section 2. The medical board of any state where, for good reasons, the standards, rules or methods are not as high as those required by this Federation, may be elected as an associate member on the recommendation of the executive committee, and by a majority vote of the active membership present at any regular meeting.

Section 3. Any individual not a member of a state medical board who is interested in medical education and state licensure may, on the recommendation of the executive committee and by a majority vote of the membership present at any regular meeting of the Federation, be elected as a fellow of the Federation

Section 4. Ex-members of state medical boards may, on recommendation of the executive committee and by a majority vote of the membership present at any regular meeting, be elected as honorary fellows, such honorary fellows being exempt from the payment of dues. Delegates from the U. S. Army, U. S. Navy, and U. S. Public Health and Marine-Hospital Service will be admitted to all sessions of the Federation, on the same basis as honorary fellows.

Article IV: There shall be an executive committee, consisting of five individual who are members or executive officers of state medical boards which are active members of the organization. The president and secretary of the Federation shall be ex-officio members of this executive committee. The remaining three members of the executive committee shall be elected by the Federation, one for three years, one for two years and one for one year, thereafter each year a member shall be elected for a term of three years. No two members of the executive committee shall be members of the same state board.

Article V: The Federation shall hold an annual meeting at such time and place as may be fixed at any previous session. The time and place may be changed, however, by the unanimous vote of the executive committee prior to two months of the time selected for the session.

Article VI: Section 1. The officers of the Federation shall be a president, a vice president and a secretary-treasurer.

Section 2. These officers shall be elected annually by the Federation to serve for one year or until their successors are elected and installed.

Section 3. Only individuals who are members or executive officers of state medical boards in active membership shall be eligible to office; except that provision may be made by the executive committee with the sanction of the Federation for a permanent secretary.

Article VII: Funds shall be raised by equal dues of not less than twenty-five dollars annually from each active member; ten dollars annually from each associate member, one dollar annually from each fellow and in any other manner approved by the Federation. Funds may be voted by the executive committee or by the Federation to defray the necessary expenses of the Federation. Funds for any special purpose may be paid by the executive committee when voted by the Federation.

Article VIII: This constitution may be amended at any annual meeting of the Federation, provided that the amendment has been submitted to the secretary in writing and sent to the members at least two months prior to the annual session; a three-fourths vote of the membership present at any regular annual meeting shall be required to secure the adoption of any amendment to this constitution.

By-Laws

Article I: Eligibility of State Boards for Membership

Section 1, Authority. A state medical board to be eligible for membership in this Federation must be operating under a medical practice act, which in the opinion of the executive committee gives it authority to uphold the minimum standards of the Federation.

Section 2, Standards. The minimum standards to be required for membership in this Federation are (a) Preliminary Education: Completion of at least 12 units, or its equivalent 60 counts, of work in and graduation from a recognized four-year high school or an equivalent credential. (b) Medical Education: At least four years of training in and graduation from a medical school having teachers, laboratory equipment, clinical facilities and property equipment equal to the minimum requirements of the Federation. (c) Examinations: These must be by such methods, must cover such subjects and be of sufficient duration to thoroughly test the candidates' fitness to practice medicine.

Section 3. Qualifications for Indorsement *(sic)* of State Licenses. (a) Prerequisite Credentials As a prerequisite to reciprocal registration the applicant therefore shall file, in the office of the board of the state of which he is a licentiate and of the state where reciprocal registration is sought, such evidence of good moral and professional character as may be demanded by said boards, and such evidence at the discretion of either board, and include proof of membership in a recognized medical society, and such membership may be considered in connection with the other evidences of character presented.

(b) Qualification 1: A certificate of registration showing that an examination has been made by the proper board of any state in which an average grade of not less than 75 per cent was awarded, the holder thereof having been at the time of said examination the legal possessor of a diploma from a medical college in good standing in the state where reciprocal registration is sought, may be accepted, in lieu of examination, as evidence of qualification. Provided, that in case the scope of the said examination was less than that prescribed by the state in which registration is sought, the applicant may be required to submit to a supplemental examination by the board thereof in such subjects as have not been covered.

(c) Qualification 2: A certificate of registration, or license issued by the proper board of any state. Provided, the holder of such certificate had been engaged in the reputable practice of medicine in such state at least one year, and also provided that the holder thereof was, at the time of such registration is sought, and tht the date of such diploma was prior to the legal requirement of the examination test in such state.

Section 4, Effectiveness. It is understood that the chief purpose of these standards, and requirements is to secure in each state a proper safeguard between the public and incompetent physicians. In deciding the eligibility of a state board for membership in the Federation, therefore, the executive committee shall convince itself that the board being granted membership is actually enforcing the minimum requirements of the Federation.

Article II: Delegates

Section 1. All members and executive officers of state medical boards are eligible as delegates, but only one vote may be cast by each state medical board in active membership and in good standing.

Section 2. *Credentials* Each delegate before having the right to vote shall deposit, with the secretary of Federation, a certificate signed by the secretary of his state medical board, showing that he has been duly authorized to represent that board.

Article III: Procedure at Business Sessions

Section 1, Order of Business. At the business sessions of the Federation the following order of business will be observed: (1) Call to order by the president; (2) Roll-call; (3) Reading and adopting of minutes; (4) Reports of officers; (5) Reports of committees: Special Committees and Executive; (6) Unfinished and New Business

Section 2, Rules of Order. The Federation shall be governed by Roberts' Rules of Order when not in conflict with these By-Laws or the fixed rules of the Federation.

Section 3, Quorum Seven voting members shall constitute a quorum for the transaction of business.

Section 4, Elections. All elections shall be by ballot.

Section 5, Special Meetings. Special meetings of the Federation may be called at such time and place as may be determined by the executive committee.

Article IV: Duties of the Executive Committee

Section 1. It shall be the duty of the executive committee to investigate and determine all matters in regard to qualifications for membership, subject to the approval of the Federation. Any charges or complaints regarding any member of the Federation coming to the knowledge or notice of the executive committee shall be investigated by the executive committee and reported with its recommendations to the Federation.

Section 2, Application of Membership. A state board desiring membership in the Federation shall make due application to the secretary on a blank provided for that purpose. The board by this application expresses its willingness to have its standards, methods of examination and its system of records investigated by the executive committee or its representative. At the next meeting of the Federation following such investigation the executive committee will report its decision if favorable for the final vote by the Federation.

Article V: Amendments

These By-Laws may be amended on a majority vote of the active members present at any regularly called meeting of the Federation, provided that such amendment has been referred to the members in writing at least two months prior to the meeting when final action is taken.

Source: *Quarterly of the Federation of State Medical Boards of the United States*, October 1913

Appendix 2: Original Charter Member Boards of the Federation of State Medical Boards of the United States

Board	*Date Enrolled*
Arkansas Eclectic Medical Board	January 23, 1913
Arkansas Regular Medical Board	February 13, 1913
Illinois State Board of Health	July 10, 1913
Iowa State Board of Health	March 5, 1913
Louisiana Board of Medical Examiners	February 7, 1913
Maryland Regular Board of Medical Examiners	January 29, 1913
Massachusetts Board of Registration in Medicine	February 20, 1913
Michigan State Board of Registration in Medicine	July 24, 1913
Minnesota State Board of Medical Examiners	July 17, 1913
Montana State Board of Medical Examiners	July 30, 1913
New Jersey State Board of Medical Examiners	May 1, 1913
New York State Board of Medical Examiners	February 17, 1913
North Dakota State Board of Medical Examiners	February 19, 1913
Ohio State Board of Medical Examiners	February 7, 1913
Oregon State Board of Medical Examiners	March 13, 1913
Pennsylvania Bureau of Medical Education and Licensure	March 25, 1913
Rhode Island State Board of Health	February 17, 1913
South Carolina State Board of Medical Examiners	July 30, 1913
Utah State Board of Medical Examiners	February 5, 1913

Board	*Date Enrolled*
Vermont State Board of Medical Registration	February 7, 1913
Virginia State Board of Medical Examiners	July 30, 1913
Wisconsin State Board of Medical Examiners	July 26, 1913

Source: *Quarterly of the Federation of State Medical Boards of the United States*, October 1913.

Appendix 3: Charter Fellows of the Federation of State Medical Boards of the United States

Under the original bylaws of the Federation, a "fellow" of the FSMB was defined as follows: "Any individual not a member of a state medical board who is interested in medical education and state licensure may, on the recommendation of the executive committee and by a majority vote at any regular meeting of the Federation, be elected as a fellow of the Federation."

Board	*City*	*Date Enrolled*
Dr. Emil Amberg	Detroit, MI	February 7, 1913
Dr. John P. Bennett	Chicago, IL	February 25, 1913
Dr. Arthur B. Brown	New Orleans, LA	February 25, 1913
Dr. George S. Brown	Conway, AR	May 6, 1913
Dr. Nathan Porter Colwell	Chicago, IL	February 10, 1913
Dr. Charles H. Cook	Natick, MA	February 25, 1913
Dr. R. D. Copeland	New York, NY	February 10, 1913
Dr. Homer Dupuy	New Orleans, LA	February 25, 1913
Dr. William P. Harlow	Boulder, CO	February 25, 1913
Dr. F. T. Isbell	Horatio, AR	May 6, 1913
Dr. F. F. Lawrence	Columbus, OH	February 25, 1913
Dr. J. G. Martin	Lake Charles, LA	February 25, 1913
Dr. Murray F. Motter	Washington, DC	February 11, 1913
Dr. F. T. Murphy	Brinkley, AR	February 25, 1913
Dr. George C. Tallerday	Belvidere, IL	February 25, 1913
Dr. Frederick C. Waite	Cleveland, OH	February 25, 1913

Board	*City*	*Date Enrolled*
Dr. S. L. White	Ruston, LA	February 25, 1913
Dr. Espey Williams	Patterson, LA	February 25, 1913
Dr. Fred C. Zapffe	Chicago, IL	February 10, 1913

Source: *Quarterly of the Federation of State Medical Boards of the United States*, October 1913.

Appendix 4: Past Presidents / Chairs of the Federation of State Medical Boards

Note: From 1912 to 2003, the FSMB's chief elected officer was called president. The title was changed to chair beginning in 2003.

1912–1913: Arthur B. Brown, M.D., Louisiana
1913–1916: Charles H. Cook, M.D., Massachusetts
1916–1925: David A. Strickler, M.D., Colorado
1925–1926: Thomas McDavitt, M.D., Minnesota
1926–1927: Samuel W. Welch, M.D., Alabama
1927–1928: Byron U. Richards, M.D., Rhode Island
1928–1929: Guy L. Connor, M.D., Michigan
1929–1930: Herbert M. Platter, M.D., Ohio
1930–1931: Charles B. Pinkham, M.D, California
1931–1932: Harold Rypins, M.D., New York
1932–1933: Thomas J. Crowe, M.D., Texas
1933–1934: G. M. Williamson, M.D., North Dakota
1934–1935: Henry M. Fitzhugh, M.D., Maryland
1935–1936: I. D. Metzger, M.D., Pennsylvania
1936–1937: James Norment Baker, M.D., Alabama
1937–1938: Jesse W. Bowers, M.D., Indiana
1938–1939: H. J. Lehnhoff, M.D., Nebraska
1939–1940: Roy B. Harrison, M.D., Louisiana
1940–1941: John Neal, M.D., Illinois
1941–1942: J. Earl McIntyre, M.D., Michigan
1942–1943: Julian F. DuBois, M.D., Minnesota
1943–1944: Frank M. Fuller, M.D., Iowa
1944–1945: J. F. Hassig, M.D., Kansas

1945–1946: Adam P. Leighton, M.D., Maine
1946–1947: N. D. Buie, M.D., Texas
1947–1948: R. N. Whitfield, M.D., Mississippi
1948–1949: Earle C. Johnson, M.D., Nebraska
1949–1950: Jacob L. Loehner, M.D., New York
1950–1951: Creighton Barker, M.D., Connecticut
1951–1952: Charles L. Shafer, M.D., Pennsylvania
1952–1953: Walter E. Vest, M.D., West Virginia
1953–1954: John M. McCann, M.D., Ohio
1954–1955: Elmer W. Schnoor, M.D., Michigan
1955–1956: McKinley H. Crabb, M.D., Texas
1956–1957: Joseph J. Combs, M.D., North Carolina
1957–1958: C. J. Glaspel, M.D., North Carolina
1958–1959: Wesley D. Richards, M.D., Pennsylvania
1959–1960: Edwin H. Lawson, M.D., Louisiana
1960–1961: Harold E. Jervey Jr., M.D., South Carolina
1961–1962: Louis E. Jones, M.D., California
1962–1963: Sam Poindexter, M.D., Idaho
1963–1964: E. C. Swanson, M.D., Michigan
1964–1965: Andrew M. Gehret, M.D., Delaware
1965–1966: Robert C. Derbyshire, M.D., New Mexico
1966–1967: George H. Lage, M.D., Oregon
1967–1968: Rhett McMahon, M.D., Louisiana
1968–1969: Leo T. Heywood, M.D., Nebraska
1969–1970: P. T. Lamey, M.D., Indiana
1970–1971: Frederick T. Merchant, M.D., Ohio
1971–1972: Frank Edmondson, M.D., North Carolina
1972–1973: Ray L. Casterline, M.D., Oregon
1973–1974: George L. Maltby, M.D., Maine
1974–1975: Howard L. Horns, M.D., Minnesota
1975–1976: Dan A. Nye, M.D., Nebraska
1976–1977: John H. Morton, M.D., New York
1977–1978: Harold E. Wilkins, M.D., California
1978–1979: Richard E. Flood, M.D., West Virginia
1979–1980: George S. Palmer, M.D., Florida
1980–1981: Henry G. Cramblett, M.D., Ohio
1981–1982: Bryant L. Galusha, M.D., North Carolina
1982–1983: John H. Clark, M.D., Utah
1983–1984: Charles B. Odom, M.D., Louisiana
1984–1985: Charles D. Godinez, M.D., Texas
1985–1986: John C. Sage, M.D., Nebraska
1986–1987: William E. Jacott, M.D., Minnesota
1987–1988: Howard G. McQuarrie, M.D., Utah

1988–1989: Anthony J. Cortese, D.O., Oregon
1989–1990: Susan F. Behrens, M.D., Wisconsin
1990–1991: Kenneth C. Yohn, M.D., Alabama
1991–1992: Barbara Schneidman, M.D., M.P.H., Washington
1992–1993: Melvin E. Sigel, M.D., Minnesota
1993–1994: Hormoz Rassekh, M.D., Iowa
1994–1995: Gerald J. Béchamps, M.D., Virginia
1995–1996: Robert E. Porter, M.D., New Hampshire
1996–1997: James E. West, M.D., Alabama
1997–1998: Susan M. Spaulding, Vermont
1998–1999: William H. Fleming III, M.D., Texas
1999–2000: Alan E. Shumacher, M.D., California
2000–2001: George C. Barrett, M.D., North Carolina
2001–2002: George J. Van Komen, M.D., Utah
2002–2003: Ronald C. Agresta, M.D., Ohio
2003–2004: Thomas D. Kirksey, M.D., Texas
2004–2005: Doris C. Brooker, M.D., Minnesota
2005–2006: Lee E. Smith, M.D., West Virginia
2006–2007: J. William McCord Jr., D.O., Tennessee
2007–2008: N. Stacy Lankford, M.D., Indiana
2008–2009: Regina M. Benjamin, M.D., M.B.A., Alabama
2009–2010: Martin Crane, M.D., Massachusetts
2010–2011: Freda McKissic Bush, M.D., Mississippi
2011–2012: Janelle Rhyne, M.D., North Carolina
2012–2013: Lance Talmage, M.D., Ohio

Appendix 5: Federation of State Medical Board Executive Committee and Board of Directors

The following is a complete list of all individuals with service on the Federation of State Medical Boards' executive committee or board of directors between 1912 and 2012. (Note: Individuals who served as FSMB president/chair are not duplicated on this list.)

Raymond Albert, MD (Ohio)
James Andriole, DO (Florida)
Nancy Achin Audese, JD (Massachusetts)
John Baldy, MD (Pennsylvania)
Dorothy Bernstein, MD (Minnesota)
Walter Bierring, MD (Iowa)
William Bird, MD (Delaware)
K. P. Bonner, MD (North Carolina)
Henry Briggs, MD (Delaware)
Andrew Bodnar, MD (Massachusetts)
Walter Bowers, MD (Massachusetts)
Leroy Buckler, MD (Delaware)
Ray Bumgarner, JD (Ohio)
Robin Hunter Buskey, MPAS (North Carolina)
Max Butler, MD (Texas)
George Carroll, MD (Virginia)
Douglas Cerf (Arizona)
Heddy Chang (California)
David Citron, MD (North Carolina)
Gary Clark (Oklahoma)
H. N. Connolly, MD (Texas)

Henry Cramblett, MD (Ohio)
William D. Cutter, MD (New York)
Albert de Bey, MD (Iowa)
Thomas Dilling, JD (Ohio)
Larry Dixon (Alabama)
E. J. Engberg, MD (Minnesota)
Wilmot C. Foster, MD (Oregon)
Linda Gage-White, MD (Louisiana)
Leslie Gallant (Alaska)
J. Daniel Gifford, MD (Alabama)
William Golden, MD (West Virginia)
K. D. Graves, MD (Virginia)
Kathleen Haley, JD (Oregon)
Edwin S. Hamilton, MD (Illinois)
Herbert Harlan, MD (Maryland)
Curtis Harris, MD, JD (Oklahoma)
Bruce Hasenkamp, JD (California)
Arthur Hengerer, MD (New York)
Stephen Heretick, JD (Virginia)
John Hinton, DO (Indiana)
Otto Huffman, MD (New York)
Philip Ingaglio, MD (Pennsylvania)
Galicano Inguito, MD (Delaware)
J. Craig Jackson, R.Ph. (Utah)
W. D. James (North Carolina)
S. L. Jepsen, MD (West Virginia)
Aldia A. Johnson, MD (Iowa)
Ronald Joseph (California)
Charles B. Kelley, MD (New Jersey)
Stephen Kelley, JD (Minnesota)
Edward Knowlton, MD (Massachusetts)
L. J. Kosminsky, MD (Arkansas)
Timothy Kowalski, DO (South Carolina)
Ram Krishna, MD (Arizona)
Donald Kuiper, MD (Michigan)
Lindy Kumagai, MD (California)
F. J. Lawliss, MD (Vermont)
Robert Leach, JD (Minnesota)
Kim Edward LeBlanc, MD, PhD (Louisiana)
Earle LeVoernois, MD (Oregon)
Rendel Levonian, MD (California)
Bruce Levy, MD (Texas)
Roger Lutz, MD (Florida)

Alexander MacAlister, MD (New Jersey)
John W. MacConnell, MD (North Carolina)
Randal Manning, MBA (Maine)
Blake Maresh, MPA (Washington)
Philip Margolis, MD (Michigan)
T. A. McCann, MD (Ohio)
J. D. McCarthy, MD (Nebraska)
A. T. McCormack, MD (Kentucky)
Tammy McGee, MBA (Minnesota)
Bruce McIntyre, JD (Rhode Island)
Larry McPherson, JD (Florida)
Josiah J. Moore, MD (Illinois)
Rev. Daniel J. Morrissey (Pennsylvania)
G. D. Murphy, MD (Arkansas)
W. Scott Nay, MD (Vermont)
Barbara Neuman, JD (Vermont)
Richard Nunnally, MD (Louisiana)
Harry Oberhelman, MD (California)
Bernard O'Hora, MD (Michigan)
John T. O'Mara, MD (Maryland)
James D. Osborn, MD (Oklahoma)
Dinesh Patel, MD (Massachusetts)
Tully Patrowicz, MD (Florida)
Carl G. Patterson, MD (Oregon)
Donald Polk, DO (Tennessee)
Maynard Pride, MD (West Virginia)
Salvatore Riggio, MD (Missouri)
Susan Rose, DO (Michigan)
Hubert Royster, MD (North Carolina)
John Rupel, MD (Wisconsin)
Harold J. Sauer, MD (Michigan)
Stephen Schabel, MD (South Carolina)
Kenneth Schnepp, MD (Illinois)
Stephen Seeling, JD (South Carolina)
Gregory Snyder, MD (Minnesota)
Bryan Spires, MD (Texas)
Scott Steingard, DO (Arizona)
George Sullivan, MD (Maine)
Conrad Suttner, MD (Washington)
Clyde Swett, MD (Maine)
Jon Thomas, MD (Minnesota)
Russell Thomas, DO (Texas)
Cheryl Vaught, JD (Oklahoma)

Michael Vitek, MD (Colorado)
F. C. Warnshuis, MD (Michigan)
Andrew Watry, MPA (North Carolina)
Richard Whitehouse, JD (Ohio)
Cheryl Winchell, MD (Maryland)
Edward Wolfson, MD (New York)

Appendix 6: Questions Taken from the Medical Licensing Examination of the Missouri State Board of Health, April and August 1906

ANATOMY

1. Give description with points of ossification of parietal, frontal, occipital bones and femur. 2. Describe superficial and deep palmar arch, brachial artery branches and relationship. 3. Describe brachial plexus and great sciatic nerve. 4. Describe the portal circulation. 5. Name flexor muscles of hand, extensor muscles of same. 6. Describe Scarpa's triangle, popliteal space. 7. Describe superior longitudinal sinus, lateral sinus, torcular herophili. 8. Give short description of pericardium. 9. Give short description of pleura. 10. Given anatomy of kidney.

CHEMISTRY

1. Give specific gravity of albuminated urine. Also two tests for albumin in the urine. 2. What are the antidotes for bichlorid of mercury? Treatment (chemically) of poisoning from the same? 3. Give properties of nitrous oxide or laughing gas. 4. What is the chemical composition of pancreatic juice? 5. Give chemical characteristics of hydrate of chloral?

PHYSIOLOGY

1. Give steps in the digestion of piece of buttered bread. 2. What effect does diet have on the secretion and constituents of milk? 3. Give function of thyroid body. What effect does its removal have? 4. Define metabolism.

5. What are some of the important characteristics of enzymes? 6. What are leucocytes? Give their functions in the normal body. 7. Locate and give function of cardio-inhibitory center and cardio-augmenter center. 8. Give brief description of secretion of urine. On what does the quantity depend? 9. What is diaphragmatic, what is costal respiration? Give examples. 10. Describe the pneumogastric nerve and give function of same.

PATHOLOGY

1. Discuss cell division and growth. 2. Discuss hereditary predisposition. 3. Give the pathology in contracted kidney. 4. What is a tumor? Give brief discussion of this formation. 5. Discuss caseation; discuss calcification.

BACTERIOLOGY

1. What is infection? What is immunity? Through what agencies may the body protect itself from the consequences of infection? 2. Name the common pyogenic micro-organisms and describe the microscopic appearance and the behavior of the staphylococcus pyogences aureus in osteomyelitis. 3. What is meant by an antitoxin? What is serum therapy? Illustrate by two disease conditions in which it is successfully employed. 4. Describe in detail Widal's test in typhoid fever and explain the principle on which it is based. 5. Give the characters of the tetanus bacillus. How does it induce its effects? On what theory is tetanus antitoxin administered?

PRACTICE

1. Give etiology, symptoms and treatment in the following: Pyelitis; Acute ascending (Landry's) paralysis; Pneumothorax; Dilatation of the heart. 2. How would you diagnose cerebral hemorrhage? Give treatment and general management in such case. 3. What are the most reliable signs of death? 4. What is meant by sympathetic disturbance? Give an example. 5. Discuss autoinfection. 6. Give symptoms and treatment of Grave's or Basedow's disease.

SURGERY

1. Give in detail the treatment of a recent open fracture of the tibia. 2. What are the symptoms of a subglenoid dislocation of the humerus? Describe the steps in its reduction by manipulation and mention the dangers which may be connected with the reduction. 3. Given a wound of the scalp, what investigation of the wound is necessary? Describe in detail the

surgical treatment. 4. What are the symptoms and what is the treatment of a gunshot wound of the kidney? 5. Give and explain the symptoms of a strangulated inguinal hernia? 6. How would you differentiate between a fracture at the neck of the femur without impaction and a dislocation? Give Bryant's and Nélaton's lines for making the measurements. 7. Detail the clinical symptoms and the surgical treatment of an empyema. 8. What are the clinical symptoms and what is the surgical treatment of a purulent effusion into the knee joint? 9. Describe the different avenues through which the urinary bladder in the male may be emptied surgically. 10. Give the differential diagnosis between an aneurism of the popliteal artery and an abscess in the popliteal space.

OBSTETRICS

1. Give diagnosis, prognosis and treatment of placenta prævia. Give same for puerperal eclampsia. 2. Describe normal labor in L.O.A. presentation. Give care of mother before, during and after labor. 3. Describe asphyxia neonatorum. Give forms and treatment. 4. Give different presentations that may be met in obstetrical practice. Differentiate a foot from a hand presentation; knee from elbow. Give treatment of each. 5. What is the bag of waters? What is its function during pregnancy? During labor? 6. How would you diagnose pregnancy at the third month, fifth month, full term? 7. How to diagnose hour-glass contractions with retained placenta? Give treatment. 8. Define involution and define subinvolution. Give cause and treatment of same. 9. After the fifth month how may death of fetus in utero be recognized? What should be done?

GYNECOLOGY

1. What is salpingitis? Give causes, pathology and treatment. 2. When should the uterine cavity be curetted? What are the dangers to be avoided? 3. Diagnose simple from gonorrheal vaginitis. Give treatment of each. 4. Define amenorrhea, dysmenorrhea, menorrhagia and leucorrhea. Give probable cause of each. 5. What is the difference between anteversion, retroversion and prolapsus of the uterus? To what extent does each influence the pregnant uterus?

MEDICAL JURISPRUDENCE

1. What is tyrotoxicon and in what is it found? 2. What are ptomains and in what are they found? 3. What is insanity? 4. Give different forms of insanity. 5. Give appearance of gunshot wound, at entrance and at exit.

THERAPEUTICS

Give therapeutic action of the following: aconite, belladonna, digitalis, nux vomica, opium, veratrum, and mercury. Give medical treatment of the following: measles, diarrhea and scarlet fever.

HYGIENE

1. What precautions are necessary and what is length of quarantine of (a) variola, (b) scarlatina, (c) diphtheria, (d) yellow fever? 2. Give composition of milk. How is it sterilized? How peptonized? How modified? Why is it necessary to modify milk for infant feeding? 3. Give percent of oxygen and nitrogen (in air). What effect has burning lamp (or gas) on atmosphere? Mention deleterious substances existing in sewer gas. 4. How much water per day in ounces should be consumed by an average adult? Mention most frequent pollution of water. Give test for organic matter in same. 5. Give general outline for disinfection and fumigation and comparative value of the following: formaldehyde, sulphur and chlorine.

Source: "Medical Education and State Boards of Registration," *Journal of the American Medical Association* 47 (October 27, 1906): 1410–1411.

Appendix 7: Current Fellows of the FSMB

The following alphabetical listing contains all individuals serving on a state medical board in 2011. Under the organization's bylaws these individuals are "fellows" of the Federation of State Medical Boards, a status they retain for a period of three years after the completion of their service on the state medical board.

Current Fellow	*Board*
Kathy Abeles	New Mexico Medical Board
Steven A. Acker, DO	Michigan Board of Osteopathic Medicine and Surgery
Gregory D. Adams, MD	Delaware Board of Medical Licensure and Discipline
Radheshyam M. Agrawal, MD	Pennsylvania State Board of Medicine
Rohit K. Agrawal, DO, MBA, FACEP	Pennsylvania State Board of Osteopathic Medicine
Busharat Ahmad, MD, FACS	Michigan Board of Medicine
Gerard Akaka, MD	Hawaii Medical Board
Ahmad Al-Alou, MD	Commonwealth of the Northern Mariana Islands
Raymond J. Albert	State Medical Board of Ohio
Kenneth W. Aldridge, MD	Alabama State Board of Medical Examiners
Richard H. Alfred, MD	New York State Board for Medicine
Abd A. Alghanem, MD	Michigan Board of Medicine

Current Fellow	*Board*
Subhi D. Ali, MD, FACS, FICS	Tennessee Board of Medical Examiners
Robert L. Allen, MD	Medical Licensing Board of Indiana
Jandel T. Allen-Davis, MD	Colorado Medical Board
Ricardo Almaguer, DO	Nevada State Board of Osteopathic Medicine
Jack C. Amato, MD	State Medical Board of Ohio
Kweli J. Amusa, MD	Louisiana State Board of Medical Examiners
Robert Andelman, MD	New Hampshire Board of Medicine
Alfred V. Anderson, DC, MD	Minnesota Board of Medical Practice
James A. Anderson, MD	Wyoming Board of Medicine
Mickey D. Anderson, MD	Kentucky Board of Medical Licensure
Bruce J. Andison, MD	Washington State Medical Quality Assurance Commission
David R. Andrews, MD	Maine Board of Licensure in Medicine
John S. Antalis, MD	Georgia Composite Medical Board
James Anthony, DO, JD, MBA	Nevada State Board of Osteopathic Medicine
Javaid Anwar, MD	Nevada State Board of Medical Examiners
Jeffrey L. Apfelbaum, MD	Illinois Department of Financial and Professional Regulation
Michael R. Arambula, MD, PharmD	Texas Medical Board
R. Curtis Arnold, DPM	West Virginia Board of Medicine
Regina Arrigoni	New Mexico Board of Osteopathic Medical Examiners
Omar T. Atiq, MD	Arkansas State Medical Board
Julie K. Attebury	Texas Medical Board
Evelyn Ayala	Delaware Board of Medical Licensure and Discipline
Larry B. Aycock, MD	Mississippi State Board of Medical Licensure
Marc E. Babitz, MD	Utah Physicians Licensing Board
Brenda G. Baker	Maryland Board of Physicians
Zeyad Baker, MD	New Jersey State Board of Medical Examiners
Jerry Ray Balentine, DO	New York State Board for Medicine

Current Fellow	*Board*
Robert T. Ball Jr., MD	South Carolina Board of Medical Examiners
John W. Banks	Delaware Board of Medical Licensure and Discipline
Bharat H. Barai, MD	Medical Licensing Board of Indiana
Gail Barba	New Hampshire Board of Medicine
William R. Barnette, CSW	New York State Board for Medicine
Louisa Barnhart, MD	Maine Board of Licensure in Medicine
Michael J. Baron, MD, MPH	Tennessee Board of Medical Examiners
Patrick C. Barry, Esq.	Rhode Island Board of Medical Licensure and Discipline
John P. Bart, DO	Pennsylvania State Board of Osteopathic Medicine
Deeni Bassam, MD	Virginia Board of Medicine
Charles David Baucom	Texas Medical Board
Robert E. Baute, MD	Rhode Island Board of Medical Licensure and Discipline
Fred Bearison, MD	Florida Board of Medicine
Evelyn T. Beasley	Maryland Board of Physicians
Joseph M. Beck II, MD	Arkansas State Medical Board
Neal S. Beckford, MD	Tennessee Board of Medical Examiners
Michael J. Beezley, MD	Kansas State Board of Healing Arts
Sandra Anderson Bell, MD	Virginia Board of Medicine
Barry F. Bennett, MD	Idaho State Board of Medicine
John W. Bennion, PhD	Utah Physicians Licensing Board
Susan M. Berberich, MD	Kentucky Board of Medical Licensure
Keith Berge, MD	Minnesota Board of Medical Practice
Stewart Berkowitz, MD	New Jersey State Board of Medical Examiners
Theodore B. Berndt, MD	Nevada State Board of Medical Examiners
Steven V. Berson, JD	Colorado Medical Board
Harold B. Betton, MD	Arkansas State Medical Board
Habib A. Bhutta, MD	Maryland Board of Physicians
Kay Bills Kazimi, PA	Montana Board of Medical Examiners
Sharon Bintliff, MD	Hawaii Medical Board

Current Fellow	*Board*
Michael J. Bittles, MD	Nebraska Board of Medicine and Surgery
Richard C. Bittner, Esq.	Maryland Board of Physicians
Jackie D. Black	South Carolina Board of Medical Examiners
Patricia S. Blackwell	Texas Medical Board
Elizabeth Blatt, PhD	West Virginia Board of Osteopathy
Pamela L. Blizzard, MBA	North Carolina Medical Board
Debbie J. Boe	Minnesota Board of Medical Practice
Pat Bollinger, MS, RD	Montana Board of Medical Examiners
Leticia Borja, MD	Commonwealth of the Northern Mariana Islands
Albert Bourbon, MPAS, PA-C	New Mexico Medical Board
Melvin G. Bourgeois, MD	Louisiana State Board of Medical Examiners
Rev. O. Richard Bowyer	West Virginia Board of Medicine
Jenny Boyer, PhD, MD, JD	Oklahoma State Board of Medical Licensure and Supervision
Richard D. Brantner, MD	Washington State Medical Quality Assurance Commission
Thomas G. Breslin, MD	Rhode Island Board of Medical Licensure and Discipline
John Brewer	Kentucky Board of Medical Licensure
Richard M. Bridburg, MD	Connecticut Medical Examining Board
C. William Briscoe, MD	Kentucky Board of Medical Licensure
Carolyn H. Bronston	Wisconsin Medical Examining Board
Gary L. Brooks, JD	Oklahoma State Board of Medical Licensure and Supervision
George E. Brown	Delaware Board of Medical Licensure and Discipline
Jane W. Brown	Utah Osteopathic Physicians and Surgeons Licensing Board
Claude D. Brunson, MD	Mississippi State Board of Medical Licensure
Lori G. Buhler	Utah Physicians Licensing Board
Patrick J. Burchill	South Dakota Board of Medical and Osteopathic Examiners
John Michael Burdine, MD	Louisiana State Board of Medical Examiners

Current Fellow	*Board*
Leslie M. Burger, MD, FACP	Washington State Medical Quality Assurance Commission
Ryan Burke, EMT-P	Montana Board of Medical Examiners
Richard E. Burney, MD	Michigan Board of Medicine
Ronald R. Burns, DO	Florida Board of Osteopathic Medicine
Boyd R. Buser, DO	Kentucky Board of Medical Licensure
Lisa R. Butler, DO	Colorado Medical Board
William J. Butler, MD	Georgia Composite Medical Board
Tariq H. Butt, MD	Illinois Department of Financial and Professional Regulation
Norman T. Byers, MD	North Dakota State Board of Medical Examiners
David D. Byrd, MD	Utah Physicians Licensing Board
Rusty L. Cain, DPM	West Virginia Board of Medicine
Vonda Calhoun	Delaware Board of Medical Licensure and Discipline
Ned Calonge, MD	Colorado Medical Board
Oliver G. Cameron, MD, PhD	Michigan Board of Medicine
Paul S. Camnitz, MD	North Carolina Medical Board
Pam Carhill, PT	Commonwealth of the Northern Mariana Islands
Walter O. Carlson, MD	South Dakota Board of Medical and Osteopathic Examiners
Kathleen M. Carney	Michigan Board of Osteopathic Medicine and Surgery
Mary S. Carpenter, MD	South Dakota Board of Medical and Osteopathic Examiners
Jorge Carreon, MD	Medical Board of California
Jeffrey D. Carter, MD	Missouri Board of Registration for the Healing Arts
G. David Casper, MD	Oklahoma State Board of Medical Licensure and Supervision
Tamella B. Cassis, MD	Kentucky Board of Medical Licensure
Judy L. Cates, JD	Illinois Department of Financial and Professional Regulation
Steven L. Cathey, MD	Arkansas State Medical Board
Robert F. Centeno, MD	Virgin Islands Board of Medical Examiners
Dean Center, MD	Montana Board of Medical Examiners

Current Fellow	*Board*
Robert Cervenka, MD	New Hampshire Board of Medicine
Rickey L. Chance, DO	Mississippi State Board of Medical Licensure
Hedy L. Chang, MS	Medical Board of California
Richard W. Chapa, MD	Utah Physicians Licensing Board
Norm Chapman	Rhode Island Board of Medical Licensure and Discipline
Eddie R. Cheeks, MD	Georgia Composite Medical Board
H. Mahmood Cheema, MD	New Jersey State Board of Medical Examiners
Peter C. Chin, MD	Hawaii Medical Board
Jim C. Chow, MD	South Carolina Board of Medical Examiners
Bernie Christenson	South Dakota Board of Medical and Osteopathic Examiners
George J. Ciechanowski, MD	New Jersey State Board of Medical Examiners
Jim C. Citty, MD	Arkansas State Medical Board
Diane Clark	Iowa Board of Medicine
Valerie J. Clark, BSN, RHU, LUTCF	Nevada State Board of Medical Examiners
J. Randolph Clements, DPM	Virginia Board of Medicine
Athalia Clower, PA-C	Washington State Medical Quality Assurance Commission
Cheryl D. Clukey	Maine Board of Licensure in Medicine
Rebecca Cochran, CPMSM, CPCS	New Mexico Medical Board
Brian E. Cody	Hawaii Medical Board
Bob E. Cogburn, MD	Arkansas State Medical Board
Manuel Colón, MD	North Dakota State Board of Medical Examiners
Michael T. Concannon, JD	Washington State Medical Quality Assurance Commission
William A. Cone, MD	Idaho State Board of Medicine
Ray N. Conley, DC	Kansas State Board of Healing Arts
Carmen M. Contee	Maryland Board of Physicians
James P. Conterato, MD	Wisconsin Medical Examining Board
Joanne M. Coolen	Pennsylvania State Board of Osteopathic Medicine

Current Fellow	*Board*
Stephen Cooper, MD	Delaware Board of Medical Licensure and Discipline
Mary Reich Cooper, MD, JD	Rhode Island Board of Medical Licensure and Discipline
Samuel E. Coor, DO	Washington Board of Osteopathic Medicine and Surgery
Lisa A. Cornelius, DPM	Oregon Medical Board
Louis E. Costa III, MD	South Carolina Board of Medical Examiners
Margaret C. Coughlin	Rhode Island Board of Medical Licensure and Discipline
Gary Counselman, DC	Kansas State Board of Healing Arts
William Cove, DO	Vermont Board of Osteopathic Physicians and Surgeons
Rose Crane	Arkansas State Medical Board
Virginia M. Crawford, MD	Mississippi State Board of Medical Licensure
Joan A. Crawley	Rhode Island Board of Medical Licensure and Discipline
Karen Criss, RN, CNM	New Jersey State Board of Medical Examiners
Patrick J. Crocker, DO	Texas Medical Board
Charles Cronin III, DO	Rhode Island Board of Medical Licensure and Discipline
Coquilla Deborah Cross, MD	New York State Office of Professional Medical Conduct
John S. Cullen, MD	Alaska State Medical Board
Bruce F. Cullen, MD	Washington State Medical Quality Assurance Commission
Douglas L. Cunningham, DO	Arizona Board of Osteopathic Examiners in Medicine and Surgery
William Cunningham, DO	Michigan Board of Osteopathic Medicine and Surgery
Jay D. Cunningham, DO	Oklahoma State Board of Osteopathic Examiners
Jack Cvitanovic	Washington State Medical Quality Assurance Commission
Claudette E. Dalton, MD	Virginia Board of Medicine
James G. Davis, MD	Alabama State Board of Medical Examiners

Current Fellow	*Board*
James S. Davis, MD	Kentucky Board of Medical Licensure
Mark Henry Dawson, MD	Louisiana State Board of Medical Examiners
Robert Earl Dawson, MD, MPH	Louisiana State Board of Medical Examiners
Steven H. Dayan, MD	Illinois Department of Financial and Professional Regulation
Richard M. De Andino-Lorenzon, MD	Puerto Rico Board of Medical Licensure and Discipline
Frederick C. De Beer, MD	Kentucky Board of Medical Licensure
Jacqueline DeGregorio, Esq.	New Jersey State Board of Medical Examiners
John David DeHoll, MD	South Carolina Board of Medical Examiners
Joseph S. DeJames, MD	Virgin Islands Board of Medical Examiners
Joseph R. D. DeKay, DO	Maine Board of Osteopathic Licensure
Dominique Delma, MD	New York State Board for Medicine
Niraj Desai, MD	Hawaii Medical Board
Thomas Desperito, MD	Delaware Board of Medical Licensure and Discipline
Constance G. Diamond, DA	New York State Board for Medicine
	New York State Office of Professional Medical Conduct
Silvia Diego, MD	Medical Board of California
William P. Dillon, MD	New York State Office of Professional Medical Conduct
Priscilla Dillon	Wyoming Board of Medicine
Robert G. Dinwoodie, DO	Rhode Island Board of Medical Licensure and Discipline
James A. DiRenna Jr., DO	Missouri Board of Registration for the Healing Arts
Michelle Dizon, MD	Virgin Islands Board of Medical Examiners
Dennis Dobritt, DO	Michigan Board of Osteopathic Medicine and Surgery
Frederick H. Dore Jr., MD	Washington State Medical Quality Assurance Commission

Current Fellow	*Board*
Anne C. Doremus	Connecticut Medical Examining Board
Michael Drew, MD	Vermont Board of Medical Practice
Tom Drew	Iowa Board of Medicine
William F. Dudding, MD	Arkansas State Medical Board
David L. Dull, MD	Michigan Board of Medicine
David H. Dumont, MD	Maine Board of Licensure in Medicine
Shelton Duruisseau, PhD	Medical Board of California
Monica Michele Dweck, MD	New York State Board for Medicine
Dana D. Dyer	Maine Board of Licensure in Medicine
Anna Earl, MD	Montana Board of Medical Examiners
S. Randall Easterling, MD	Mississippi State Board of Medical Licensure
Gale E. Easton, PA	Michigan Board of Osteopathic Medicine and Surgery
Jeremy Edmonds, DO	New Mexico Board of Osteopathic Medical Examiners
Steven Paul Edwards, Esq.	Nevada State Board of Osteopathic Medicine
Mark A. Eggen, MD	Minnesota Board of Medical Practice
Nabil El Sanadi, MD	Florida Board of Medicine
Paul T. Elder, MD	Maryland Board of Physicians
Theresa J. Elders, LCSW	Washington State Medical Quality Assurance Commission
Vincent John Ella, JD	Minnesota Board of Medical Practice
John D. Ellis Jr.	Texas Medical Board
Laurie O. Elsass	State Medical Board of Ohio
William H. Epstein, MD	Virginia Board of Medicine
Carole Erickson	Montana Board of Medical Examiners
David Erickson, MD	South Dakota Board of Medical and Osteopathic Examiners
Allan R. Escher, DO	Florida Board of Osteopathic Medicine
Trina Espinola, MD	Florida Board of Medicine
Aurelio Espinola, MD	Guam Board of Medical Examiners
Sarah L. Evenson, JD, MBA	Minnesota Board of Medical Practice
Ahmed Faheem, MD	West Virginia Board of Medicine

Current Fellow	*Board*
H. Joseph Falgout, MD	Alabama State Board of Medical Examiners
Irina Farquhar, PhD	Virginia Board of Medicine
Richard R. Fay, DC	Illinois Department of Financial and Professional Regulation
Amy Feitelson, MD	New Hampshire Board of Medicine
Douglas W. Fellows, MD	Connecticut Medical Examining Board
Keith C. Ferdinand, MD	Louisiana State Board of Medical Examiners
Michael L. Ferrebee, MD	West Virginia Board of Medicine
Robert L. Ferrell, MD	South Dakota Board of Medical and Osteopathic Examiners
Jon B. Fiegen, JD	Arizona Board of Osteopathic Examiners in Medicine and Surgery
John G. Finch Jr., DO	Washington Board of Osteopathic Medicine and Surgery
Michael Fine, MD	Rhode Island Board of Medical Licensure and Discipline
Michael J. Fischer, MD	Nevada State Board of Medical Examiners
James R. Fowler, MD	Utah Physicians Licensing Board
Jamie Frain	Michigan Board of Medicine
Theresa L. Fraley	Michigan Board of Medicine
Monica Franklin	Tennessee Board of Medical Examiners
LaMarr Franklin	Wisconsin Medical Examining Board
Wayne A. I. Frederick, MD, FACS	District of Columbia Board of Medicine
Richard M. Freeman, MD	Alabama State Board of Medical Examiners
Bradley D. Freeman, MD	Missouri Board of Registration for the Healing Arts
James W. Freeman, MD	Pennsylvania State Board of Medicine
Alfred T. Frontera, MD	New York State Board for Medicine
Cathy M. Funk, MD	West Virginia Board of Medicine
Steven P. Furr, MD	Alabama State Board of Medical Examiners
John F. Gaddis, DO	Maine Board of Osteopathic Licensure

Current Fellow	*Board*
Ramiro Gaitan	Oregon Medical Board
Frank K. Galbraith, DPM	Kansas State Board of Healing Arts
Joseph C. Gallagher Jr., DO	Pennsylvania State Board of Osteopathic Medicine
Janice M. Gallant, MD	Vermont Board of Medical Practice
William L. Gant, MEd	Washington Board of Osteopathic Medicine and Surgery
William F. Ganz, MD	Idaho State Board of Medicine
Stephen R. Gardner, MD	South Carolina Board of Medical Examiners
Samuel J. Garloff, DO	Pennsylvania State Board of Osteopathic Medicine
Jude Genereaux	Wisconsin Medical Examining Board
Karen R. Gerancher, MD	North Carolina Medical Board
Randel C. Gibson, DO	Kentucky Board of Medical Licensure
J. Daniel Gifford, MD	Alabama State Board of Medical Examiners
Joan Gill, MD	Guam Board of Medical Examiners
James Gillard, MD	Arizona Medical Board
Donald E. Girard, MD	Oregon Medical Board
Maroulla S. Gleaton, MD	Maine Board of Licensure in Medicine
Brigitte Rivera Goersch	Florida Board of Medicine
William E. Goetter, MD	Alabama State Board of Medical Examiners
David M. Goldenberg, MD	Connecticut Medical Examining Board
Michael R. Golding, MD, FACS	New York State Office of Professional Medical Conduct
Carmen Gonzales-Keelan, MD	Puerto Rico Board of Medical Licensure and Discipline
William E. Gotthold, MD	Washington State Medical Quality Assurance Commission
Peter T. Graham, MD	Michigan Board of Medicine
Cheryl Graham Solomon, MA	Michigan Board of Medicine
J. William Graves, JD	Kentucky Board of Medical Licensure
Robert A. Green, MD	Connecticut Medical Examining Board
Thomas M. Green, MD	Washington State Medical Quality Assurance Commission

Current Fellow	*Board*
Eleanor E. Greene, MD, MPH	North Carolina Medical Board
Rabbi Dov Greer	Connecticut Medical Examining Board
A. Neal Gregory, MD	New York State Board for Medicine
Eric R. Groce, DO	Colorado Medical Board
Alexander S. Gross, MD	Georgia Composite Medical Board
Manuel G. Guajardo, MD	Texas Medical Board
Rao V. C. Gudipati, MD	Michigan Board of Medicine
Mary Anne Guggenheim, MD	Montana Board of Medical Examiners
Suresh K. Gupta, MD	Maryland Board of Physicians
Analisa Haberman, DO	Iowa Board of Medicine
W. Frank Hairston Jr.	State Medical Board of Ohio
Edward A. Hall, PA-C	Alaska State Medical Board
Edward C. Halperin, MD	Kentucky Board of Medical Licensure
Azeta G. Hamedani, MD, MPH	Wisconsin Medical Examining Board
Melissa P. Hankins, MD	Massachusetts Board of Registration in Medicine
Ellen J. Harder, PA-C	Washington State Medical Quality Assurance Commission
Leo S. Harf, MD	Idaho State Board of Medicine
Kristin E. Harkin, MD	New York State Board for Medicine
Roger Harmon, PD	Arkansas State Medical Board
T. Michael Harrington, MD	Alabama State Board of Medical Examiners
Mary Jo Harris, JD	Massachusetts Board of Registration in Medicine
David Harris, MD, MPH	New York State Office of Professional Medical Conduct
Scott J. Harris, Esq.	Osteopathic Medical Board of California
B. Jerome Harrison, MD	Alabama State Board of Medical Examiners
Susan M. Harvey, MD	Washington State Medical Quality Assurance Commission
M. Khalid Hasan, MD	West Virginia Board of Medicine
Gary R. Hatfield, MD	Maine Board of Licensure in Medicine
Anna Z. Hayden, DO	Florida Board of Osteopathic Medicine

Current Fellow	*Board*
Beth P. Hays, MA	West Virginia Board of Medicine
Bruce Hayward, DO	Montana Board of Medical Examiners
Robert G. Hayward, MD	Vermont Board of Medical Practice
John E. Hearnsberger II, MD	Arkansas State Medical Board
Ronald Hedger, DO	Nevada State Board of Osteopathic Medicine
Jeffrey A. Heebner, DO	Pennsylvania State Board of Osteopathic Medicine
Laura E. Henderson, MD	Maryland Board of Physicians
Cheryl Henderson, JD	West Virginia Board of Medicine
Arthur S. Hengerer, MD, FACS	New York State Office of Professional Medical Conduct
Merle James Henkenius	Nebraska Board of Medicine and Surgery
Robert G. Hennessy, MD, MBA	Maryland Board of Physicians
Frank M. Hensley, MBA	Washington State Medical Quality Assurance Commission
Stephen E. Heretick, JD	Virginia Board of Medicine
Layne A. Hermansen, DO	Utah Osteopathic Physicians and Surgeons Licensing Board
David P. Herrick, MD	Alabama State Board of Medical Examiners
Candis A. Hewitt	Colorado Medical Board
Dennis A. Higdon, MD	Tennessee Board of Medical Examiners
Karen M. Higgins, MD	Nebraska Board of Medicine and Surgery
Thomas R. Hill, MD	North Carolina Medical Board
Samuel K. Himmelrich Sr.	Maryland Board of Physicians
Merle J. Hodges, MD	Kansas State Board of Healing Arts
Honorable Herbert H. Hodos, JD	Massachusetts Board of Registration in Medicine
Kent R. Hoerauf, MD	North Dakota State Board of Medical Examiners
Valerie Lowe Hoffman, DC	Virginia Board of Medicine
James Scott Holliday, DO	Texas Medical Board
Worthe S. Holt Jr., MD	Medical Licensing Board of Indiana
Jody M. Holzinger	Wyoming Board of Medicine

Current Fellow	Board
Bruce G. Hopkins, MD	Washington State Medical Quality Assurance Commission
Ruth Horowitz, PhD	New York State Office of Professional Medical Conduct
William K. Hoser, PA-C	Vermont Board of Medical Practice
Alice R. House, MD	Georgia Composite Medical Board
Greg Hoversten, DO	Iowa Board of Medicine
Heather Howard	New Jersey State Board of Medical Examiners
Alan R. Howard	Osteopathic Medical Board of California
Elizabeth F. Howell, MD	Utah Physicians Licensing Board
Jeffrey L. Howorth	Nebraska Board of Medicine and Surgery
James L. Hubbard, DO	South Carolina Board of Medical Examiners
Stephen Huddleston, JD	Medical Licensing Board of Indiana
Deborah Huff, MD	Oklahoma State Board of Medical Licensure and Supervision
Janice E. Huff, MD	North Carolina Medical Board
Catherine A. Hunter, DO	Washington Board of Osteopathic Medicine and Surgery
Richard P. Iacobucci, MD	Rhode Island Board of Medical Licensure and Discipline
Peter J. Iannuzzi, DPM	New Jersey State Board of Medical Examiners
Andrea E. Ibanez	Arizona Medical Board
Eileen M. Illuzzi	Vermont Board of Medical Practice
Subbarao Inampudi, MD, FACR	Minnesota Board of Medical Practice
Rabbi Solomon Isaacson	Pennsylvania State Board of Medicine
Donald E. Jablonski, DO, FACOFP	North Carolina Medical Board
Jane L. Jackman, MD	Illinois Department of Financial and Professional Regulation
Gary L. Jackson, DO	New Mexico Board of Osteopathic Medical Examiners
Trudy Jackson	Idaho State Board of Medicine
Henry Jacobs, MD, JD	Connecticut Medical Examining Board
Gopinath R. Jadhav, MD	Virginia Board of Medicine

Current Fellow	*Board*
Sanjay K. Jain, MD	New York State Board for Medicine
Thea L. James, MD	Massachusetts Board of Registration in Medicine
David A. Jenkins, JD	Vermont Board of Medical Practice
Jody L. Jenkins, MD	Arizona Medical Board
Steve Jenkusky, MD	New Mexico Medical Board
Carlton Jennings	Colorado Medical Board
Carlos C. Jimenez, MD	West Virginia Board of Medicine
Bradley S. Johnson, MD	Minnesota Board of Medical Practice
Juan Johnson, MD	Alabama State Board of Medical Examiners
Kelli Johnson, MBA	Minnesota Board of Medical Practice
Larry E. Johnson, MD	North Dakota State Board of Medical Examiners
Linda B. Johnson, MD	Oregon Medical Board
Mark L. Johnson, MD	Washington State Medical Quality Assurance Commission
Nathalie M. Johnson, MD	Oregon Medical Board
Ray B. Johnson, PA-C	Wyoming Board of Medicine
Ronald L. Johnson, MD	Illinois Department of Financial and Professional Regulation
Howard S. Jonas, DO	Vermont Board of Osteopathic Physicians and Surgeons
David D. Jones, MD	Maine Board of Licensure in Medicine
William B. Jones, MD	Mississippi State Board of Medical Licensure
Paul M. Jordan, MD	New Jersey State Board of Medical Examiners
Sujatha Kailas, MD, MBA	Wisconsin Medical Examining Board
Paul Kalekas, DO	Nevada State Board of Osteopathic Medicine
Barry C. Kane	Michigan Board of Osteopathic Medicine and Surgery
Sambaiah Kankanala, MD	New Mexico Medical Board
Gerald T. Kaplan, MA, LP	Minnesota Board of Medical Practice
Gaylord Kavlie, MD	North Dakota State Board of Medical Examiners
Lynn M. Keil, RPA	New York State Board for Medicine

Current Fellow	*Board*
Charles E. Kelly, DO	Michigan Board of Osteopathic Medicine and Surgery
Kathy Kemle, PA-C	Georgia Composite Medical Board
Noubar Kessimian, MD	Rhode Island Board of Medical Licensure and Discipline
Mimi S. Kevan, MS	Vermont Board of Osteopathic Physicians and Surgeons
Fareesa Khan, MD	Missouri Board of Registration for the Healing Arts
Gordi S. Khera, MD, FACC	Arizona Medical Board
Peter V. Kilburn, DO	Washington Board of Osteopathic Medicine and Surgery
Patricia A. King, MD, PhD	Vermont Board of Medical Practice
Kathleen Kinlaw, MDiv	Georgia Composite Medical Board
John William Kinsinger, MD	Oklahoma State Board of Medical Licensure and Supervision
Kyle Kirkpatrick, PA-C	Colorado Medical Board
Harry C. Knipp, MD	Maryland Board of Physicians
Steven Komadina, MD	New Mexico Medical Board
John P. Kopetski	Oregon Medical Board
George Koval, MD	Oregon Medical Board
Paul J. Kovnat, MD	New Mexico Medical Board
Timothy J. Kowalski, DO, FACN	South Carolina Board of Medical Examiners
Ram R. Krishna, MD	Arizona Medical Board
Rhonda W. Kunes	Georgia Composite Medical Board
Onelia Garcia Lage, MD	Florida Board of Medicine
Gordon P. Laird, DO	Oklahoma State Board of Osteopathic Examiners
Kathryn Lambert, DO	New Jersey State Board of Medical Examiners
Ernest W. Lampe II, MD	Minnesota Board of Medical Practice
Benjamin A. Lampert, MD	Missouri Board of Registration for the Healing Arts
R. Fletcher Lance	Tennessee Board of Osteopathic Examiners
Jerry G. Landau, JD	Arizona Board of Osteopathic Examiners in Medicine and Surgery
James Langland, MD	Minnesota Board of Medical Practice

Current Fellow	*Board*
Maria Laporta, MD	Illinois Department of Financial and Professional Regulation
Lynn M. Larson	Michigan Board of Medicine
Lonnie C. Lauer, DO	Maine Board of Osteopathic Licensure
Kim Edward LeBlanc, MD, PhD	Louisiana State Board of Medical Examiners
Douglas D. Lee, MD	Arizona Medical Board
Jennifer S. Lee, MD	Virginia Board of Medicine
Marion O. Lee Jr., MD, MBA	Georgia Composite Medical Board
M. Myron Leinwetter, DO	Kansas State Board of Healing Arts
Thelma C. Lennon	North Carolina Medical Board
Jonathan Lerner, PA-C	Maryland Board of Physicians
Vivian W. Leung	Michigan Board of Medicine
Bradley Levine	Florida Board of Medicine
Sharon Levine, MD	Medical Board of California
John B. Lewis Jr., LLB	North Carolina Medical Board
Mary Jo Lewis, MD	North Dakota State Board of Medical Examiners
Maureen Liegeot	Connecticut Medical Examining Board
John R. Lilly, MD	Maryland Board of Physicians
Reynald T. Lim, MD	Guam Board of Medical Examiners
Michael C. Lindberg, MD	Connecticut Medical Examining Board
Brent Lindbloom, DO	South Dakota Board of Medical and Osteopathic Examiners
James R. Little Sr., MD	Wyoming Board of Medicine
Florencio T. Lizama, MD	Guam Board of Medical Examiners
Vincent G. Lobo, DO	Delaware Board of Medical Licensure and Discipline
Steven Lomazow, MD	New Jersey State Board of Medical Examiners
Ralph C. Loomis, MD	North Carolina Medical Board
Gary Keith Lovelady, MD, MPH	Tennessee Board of Medical Examiners
Patricia S. Loving, PA-C	Connecticut Medical Examining Board
Reginald Low, MD	Medical Board of California

Current Fellow	*Board*
Sue Lowden	Nevada State Board of Medical Examiners
Georgia D. Lubben, MD	Illinois Department of Financial and Professional Regulation
John Joseph Lynch, MD	District of Columbia Board of Medicine
Richard A. Macias, JD	Kansas State Board of Healing Arts
Stuart F. Mackler, MD	Virginia Board of Medicine
Jane Sheffield Maddux	Virginia Board of Medicine
Dalsukh A. Madia, MD	State Medical Board of Ohio
Harold Magalnick, MD	Arizona Medical Board
Raymond P. Mager, DO	Wisconsin Medical Examining Board
Christopher Magiera, MD	Wisconsin Medical Examining Board
Darshan Mahajan, MD	State Medical Board of Ohio
Rina A. Malan	Florida Board of Osteopathic Medicine
Ravinder Mamtani, MD	New York State Office of Professional Medical Conduct
Lawrence A. Manning, MD	District of Columbia Board of Medicine
Luis R. Marcos, MD	New York State Board for Medicine
Burton T. Mark, DO	Pennsylvania State Board of Osteopathic Medicine
Miriam A. Markowitz, MSc	District of Columbia Board of Medicine
Peter Marsh, MD	Washington State Medical Quality Assurance Commission
Kent Martin, MD	North Dakota State Board of Medical Examiners
Margaret Funk Martin	Vermont Board of Medical Practice
David P. Martinez, DO	Washington Board of Osteopathic Medicine and Surgery
Sarita M. Massey, MD	Illinois Department of Financial and Professional Regulation
Kirk Masten, DO	Medical Licensing Board of Indiana
Michael J. Mastrangelo Jr., MD	Oregon Medical Board
Curtis D. Mather, DO	Missouri Board of Registration for the Healing Arts
Kathleen Matthews, MD	Colorado Medical Board

Current Fellow	*Board*
William S. Mayo, DO	Mississippi State Board of Medical Licensure
Peter McAndrews III, DO	Michigan Board of Osteopathic Medicine and Surgery
Janet McCullough, PhD	Commonwealth of the Northern Mariana Islands
Annette S. McDaniel-Turner, MD	Pennsylvania State Board of Medicine
Karl W. McIntosh, MD	Delaware Board of Medical Licensure and Discipline
Marty W. McIntyre	Maine Board of Osteopathic Licensure
Roger McKimmy, MD	Oregon Medical Board
Andrew McLean, MD	North Dakota State Board of Medical Examiners
Melinda McMichael, MD	Texas Medical Board
Margaret C. McNeese, MD	Texas Medical Board
B. Joyce McRoberts	Idaho State Board of Medicine
John S. Meigs Jr., MD	Alabama State Board of Medical Examiners
Edwin Mejias	Puerto Rico Board of Medical Licensure and Discipline
Jose A. Melendez, MD	Colorado Medical Board
Susan Y. Melvin, DO	Osteopathic Medical Board of California
Paul C. Mendelowitz, MD	New Jersey State Board of Medical Examiners
Philip T. Merideth, MD, JD	Mississippi State Board of Medical Licensure
Linda Platt Meyer, EdD, ATC	Pennsylvania State Board of Osteopathic Medicine
Scott W. Meyers, MD	Oklahoma State Board of Medical Licensure and Supervision
Ambreen Mian	Iowa Board of Medicine
Charles D. Miles, MD	Mississippi State Board of Medical Licensure
Kathleen M. Millar	Alaska State Medical Board
Cory R. Miller, MD	North Dakota State Board of Medical Examiners
David A. Miller, MD, FACS	Alaska State Medical Board
Ernest E. Miller Jr., DO	West Virginia Board of Osteopathy

Current Fellow	*Board*
Roger Miller, MD	New Mexico Medical Board
C. Dean Milne, DO, FACP	Nevada State Board of Osteopathic Medicine
Richard D. Milone, MD	New York State Office of Professional Medical Conduct
Garold O. Minns, MD	Kansas State Board of Healing Arts
Suresh K. Misra, MD	Wisconsin Medical Examining Board
Juan M. Montero II, MD	Virginia Board of Medicine
Cynthia Gail Montgomery, MD	Louisiana State Board of Medical Examiners
Raymond L. Moore Sr., MS	Delaware Board of Medical Licensure and Discipline
Mary Lynn Moran, MD, FACS	Medical Board of California
G. Mark Moreland, MD	West Virginia Board of Medicine
Rev. Daniel W. Morrissey, OP	New Hampshire Board of Medicine
Dawn Morton-Rias, RPA	New York State Board for Medicine
Donald E. Mullins	Florida Board of Medicine
Wayne Eugene Musser Jr., MD	Wisconsin Medical Examining Board
Sylvia G. Mustonen, DO	Michigan Board of Osteopathic Medicine and Surgery
Mitchell L. Mutter, MD	Tennessee Board of Medical Examiners
Paul M. Nagrodzki, MD	Alabama State Board of Medical Examiners
Tom Najjar	Florida Board of Osteopathic Medicine
Kenneth C. Nanners, MD	West Virginia Board of Medicine
Lewis D. Neace, DO	Oregon Medical Board
LaQuandra S. Nesbitt, MD, MPH	District of Columbia Board of Medicine
Grace A. Newton, JD	Illinois Department of Financial and Professional Regulation
Beverly A. Neyland, MD	Nevada State Board of Medical Examiners
David Mark Nierman, MD	New York State Board for Medicine
Diane L. Noton, MD	Wyoming Board of Medicine
Preston P. Nunnelley, MD	Kentucky Board of Medical Licensure
Robert C. Nuss, MD	Florida Board of Medicine

Current Fellow	*Board*
David Nyberg, PhD	Maine Board of Licensure in Medicine
Noel C. Nye, DO	Utah Osteopathic Physicians and Surgeons Licensing Board
Frank A. Odlum, MD, FACS	Virgin Islands Board of Medical Examiners
Bekoe Ohene-Agyei	New York State Board for Medicine
Hilary T. O'Herlihy, MD, FACC	Maryland Board of Physicians
Kevin F. O'Malley	Missouri Board of Registration for the Healing Arts
Janis M. Orlowski, MD, MACP	District of Columbia Board of Medicine
James W. Orr, MD	Florida Board of Medicine
Sandra L. Osborn, MD	Wisconsin Medical Examining Board
Geraldine T. O'Shea, DO	Osteopathic Medical Board of California
Roger M. Oskvig, MD	New York State Board for Medicine
Stephen M. Ostroff, MD	Pennsylvania State Board of Medicine
Leticia M. Overholt, MD	Colorado Medical Board
Peter Paige, MD, MMM	Massachusetts Board of Registration in Medicine
Gary E. Palman, DO	Maine Board of Osteopathic Licensure
Dennis D. Palmer, DO	Illinois Department of Financial and Professional Regulation
Joseph M. Parise, DO	Delaware Board of Medical Licensure and Discipline
Daniel J. Parker, MD	Utah Physicians Licensing Board
F. Don Parsa, MD	Hawaii Medical Board
Cynthia Pasky	Michigan Board of Medicine
Marilyn E. Pattison, MD	Washington State Medical Quality Assurance Commission
Sindy M. Paul, MD, MPH, FACPM	New Jersey State Board of Medical Examiners
Nick Perencevich, MD	New Hampshire Board of Medicine
John T. Perry, MD	Georgia Composite Medical Board
John M. Peterson, DO	Vermont Board of Osteopathic Physicians and Surgeons
Warren A. Peterson, DO	Utah Osteopathic Physicians and Surgeons Licensing Board

Current Fellow	*Board*
Sara L. Petrosky, Esq.	Pennsylvania State Board of Medicine
Carl B. Pettigrew, DO	Oklahoma State Board of Osteopathic Examiners
Jack G. Pettigrew, DO	Tennessee Board of Osteopathic Examiners
Patty K. Pettway, DO	Arkansas State Medical Board
Dennis Phelps, MD	Colorado Medical Board
Mary Ann Picardo, DO	Arizona Board of Osteopathic Examiners in Medicine and Surgery
Thomas R. Pickard, DO	Oklahoma State Board of Osteopathic Examiners
Trent P. Pierce, MD	Arkansas State Medical Board
Ken Pierson, DDS	Commonwealth of the Northern Mariana Islands
Jane E. Piness, MD	Virginia Board of Medicine
James H. Pingree, MD	Utah Physicians Licensing Board
Asim R. Piracha, MD	Kentucky Board of Medical Licensure
Joshua A. Plavin, MD	Vermont Board of Medical Practice
David A. Poggemeier, MD	Missouri Board of Registration for the Healing Arts
Alfred J. Poggi, DO	Pennsylvania State Board of Osteopathic Medicine
Anthony M. Policastro, MD	Delaware Board of Medical Licensure and Discipline
Donald H. Polk, DO	Tennessee Board of Osteopathic Examiners
David J. Powers, MD	Alaska State Medical Board
Linda Prescott Wilson	New York State Office of Professional Medical Conduct
Germaine Proulx	Arizona Medical Board
Joseph J. Provenzano, DO	Osteopathic Medical Board of California
Palasi Puletasi	Hawaii Medical Board
William J. Rademacher, DC	Illinois Department of Financial and Professional Regulation
Kia Rahmani, MD	Guam Board of Medical Examiners
Frank Raines, III	Michigan Board of Medicine
Illays Rajput, MD	New Jersey State Board of Medical Examiners
Nallan C. Ramakrishna, MD	Maryland Board of Physicians

Current Fellow	*Board*
Krishnamurthi Ramprasad, MD	State Medical Board of Ohio
Keith P. Ramsey, DO	Utah Osteopathic Physicians and Surgeons Licensing Board
Thangam Rangaswamy, PhD	Kentucky Board of Medical Licensure
Marc Espy Rankin, MD	District of Columbia Board of Medicine
Karen A. Ransone, MD	Virginia Board of Medicine
Karyl Rattay, MD	Delaware Board of Medical Licensure and Discipline
Harvey S. Reich, MD	Vermont Board of Medical Practice
William W. Resinger, MD	Alaska State Medical Board
David W. Retterbush, MD	Georgia Composite Medical Board
James R. Reynolds, MD	South Dakota Board of Medical and Osteopathic Examiners
Wayne J. Reynolds, DO, FAAFP	Virginia Board of Medicine
Kristen M. Ries, MD	Utah Physicians Licensing Board
Meghan Riley, PA-C	Michigan Board of Medicine
Robert R. Rinaldi, DPM	Vermont Board of Medical Practice
Thomas L. Rine	Oklahoma State Board of Medical Licensure and Supervision
Burt L. Riskedahl	North Dakota State Board of Medical Examiners
Daniel Rissi, MD	Connecticut Medical Examining Board
George Roberts, MEd, ATC	Pennsylvania State Board of Medicine
Vonn E. Roberts, MD	Nebraska Board of Medicine and Surgery
Deborah Jane Robinett, DO	Wyoming Board of Medicine
Jill Robinson, DO	Tennessee Board of Osteopathic Examiners
Peggy R. Robinson, PA-C	North Carolina Medical Board
Benjamin J. Rodriguez, MD	Nevada State Board of Medical Examiners
Alejandro Roman, MD	Puerto Rico Board of Medical Licensure and Discipline
Rota Rosaschi, MPA	Nevada State Board of Osteopathic Medicine
Carol E. Rose, MD	Pennsylvania State Board of Medicine
Edward P. Rose, MD	Illinois Department of Financial and Professional Regulation

Current Fellow	*Board*
Harold A. Rose	Maryland Board of Physicians
Joel B. Rose, DO	Florida Board of Osteopathic Medicine
Barrett F. Rosen, MD	Tennessee Board of Medical Examiners
Jason J. Rosenberg, MD, FACS	Florida Board of Medicine
Beryl J. Rosenstein, MD	Maryland Board of Physicians
Barry M. Rosenthal, MD	New York State Board for Medicine
Louis E. Rosenthall, MD	New Hampshire Board of Medicine
Arthur Rubin, DO	West Virginia Board of Osteopathy
Linda A. Ruiz, JD	Washington State Medical Quality Assurance Commission
G. Jerry Russell	Idaho State Board of Medicine
Donna A. Ruthe	Nevada State Board of Medical Examiners
Sister Janice E. Ryan, RSM	Vermont Board of Medical Practice
Mary K. Ryan	Delaware Board of Medical Licensure and Discipline
David J. Rydell, DO	Maine Board of Osteopathic Licensure
Vas N. Sabeeh, DO	Arizona Board of Osteopathic Examiners in Medicine and Surgery
Howard Sadinsky, DO	Connecticut Medical Examining Board
Toby R. Sadkin, MD	Vermont Board of Medical Practice
Richard W. Saiser	New Mexico Board of Osteopathic Medical Examiners
Janet K. Salomonson, MD, FACS	Medical Board of California
Shirley U. Salvatore, MD	Colorado Medical Board
Leticia J. San Diego, PhD	Michigan Board of Medicine
Kenneth L. Schaecher, MD	Utah Physicians Licensing Board
Evelyn Schipske, RNP, JD	Medical Board of California
Amy J. Schneider, MD, FACOG	Arizona Medical Board
Stephen D. Schoenmakers, MS	Colorado Medical Board
Joseph Schreiber, DO	West Virginia Board of Osteopathy
Stephen L. Schwartz, MD	Pennsylvania State Board of Medicine
George J. Scott, DPM, DO	New Jersey State Board of Medical Examiners

Current Fellow	*Board*
Judith A. Scott, DO	Nebraska Board of Medicine and Surgery
Kendrick A. Sears, MD	New York State Office of Professional Medical Conduct
Anjan K. Sen, MD	Washington State Medical Quality Assurance Commission
Oluseyi N. Senu-oke, MD	Delaware Board of Medical Licensure and Discipline
John F. Settich, PhD	Kansas State Board of Healing Arts
Susan Sevensma, DO	Michigan Board of Osteopathic Medicine and Surgery
George Shade Jr., MD	Michigan Board of Medicine
Dhiren K. Shah, MD	New York State Board for Medicine
Daryl Sharman, MD	Delaware Board of Medical Licensure and Discipline
Brenda R. Sharpe	Kansas State Board of Healing Arts
B. Frank Shaw Jr., DO	Oklahoma State Board of Osteopathic Examiners
Myra B. Shayevitz, MD	New York State Board for Medicine
Eileen Sheehy	Montana Board of Medical Examiners
Thomas N. Shelton, DO	Washington Board of Osteopathic Medicine and Surgery
Karen R. Shepherd, DO	Tennessee Board of Osteopathic Examiners
Siroos S. Shirazi, MD	Iowa Board of Medicine
James Shiveley, DO	New Mexico Board of Osteopathic Medical Examiners
Allan Shulkin, MD	Texas Medical Board
William Sightler, DO	Georgia Composite Medical Board
Michael Signer, PhD, JD	Virginia Board of Medicine
E. Scott Sills, MD, FACOG, FACS	New York State Board for Medicine
Antonio R. Silva-Iglecia, MD	Puerto Rico Board of Medical Licensure and Discipline
Ronald Simmons, PhD	District of Columbia Board of Medicine
Sylvia D. Simon, MD	Arkansas State Medical Board
Calvin J. Simons, MD	New York State Office of Professional Medical Conduct
Kenneth B. Simons, MD	Wisconsin Medical Examining Board

Current Fellow	Board
Riaz A. Sirajuddin, MD	Oklahoma State Board of Medical Licensure and Supervision
Michael Sitorious, MD	Nebraska Board of Medicine and Surgery
Catherine Slemp, MD, MPH	West Virginia Board of Medicine
Robert H. Small, MD	Washington State Medical Quality Assurance Commission
Lynda Smirz, MD	Medical Licensing Board of Indiana
Carl V. Smith, MD	Nebraska Board of Medicine and Surgery
George C. Smith Jr., MD	Alabama State Board of Medical Examiners
Paul G. Smith Jr., DO	Tennessee Board of Osteopathic Examiners
Wynne M. Snoots, MD	Texas Medical Board
Gregory B. Snyder, MD, DABR	Minnesota Board of Medical Practice
Jeffrey T. Snyder, MD	Iowa Board of Medicine
Carolina M. Soria, DO	Kansas State Board of Healing Arts
Paulette B. Southard	Texas Medical Board
Kristin Spanjian, MD	Montana Board of Medical Examiners
James S. St. Louis, DO	Florida Board of Osteopathic Medicine
William Stanley, MD	New Jersey State Board of Medical Examiners
Anita M. Steinbergh, DO	State Medical Board of Ohio
Scott A. Steingard, DO	Arizona Board of Osteopathic Examiners in Medicine and Surgery
Susan E. Stephens, MD	State Medical Board of Ohio
Timothy A. Stewart, MD	Alabama State Board of Medical Examiners
Colleen Stockdale, MD	Iowa Board of Medicine
Jeffrey D. Storey, MD	Wyoming Board of Medicine
William H. Stouch, MD	Vermont Board of Medical Practice
J. Craig Strafford, MD, MPH	State Medical Board of Ohio
Susan T. Strahan, MD	Maryland Board of Physicians
Merle P. Stringer, MD	Florida Board of Medicine
J. Andy Sullivan, MD	Oklahoma State Board of Medical Licensure and Supervision
Mark Sullivan, PA	New Hampshire Board of Medicine

Current Fellow	*Board*
Roland S. Summers, MD	Georgia Composite Medical Board
Jean Rawlings Sumner, BSN, MSN, MD	Georgia Composite Medical Board
Marchelle L. Suppan, DPM, MBA	State Medical Board of Ohio
Ralph Marc Sutherlin, DO	Idaho State Board of Medicine
Danny M. Takanishi Jr., MD, FACS	Hawaii Medical Board
Lance A. Talmage, MD	State Medical Board of Ohio
Robert Tanous, DO	North Dakota State Board of Medical Examiners
Michael J. Tauriainen	Alaska State Medical Board
Catherine C. Taylor, JD	Oklahoma State Board of Osteopathic Examiners
John B. Tedeschi, MD	New Jersey State Board of Medical Examiners
Kimberly J. Templeton, MD	Kansas State Board of Healing Arts
W. Jeff Terry, MD	Alabama State Board of Medical Examiners
Hamed Tewfik, MD	Iowa Board of Medicine
George Thomas, MD	Florida Board of Medicine
Jon V. Thomas, MD, MBA	Minnesota Board of Medical Practice
Nathan Thomas, DPM	Montana Board of Medical Examiners
Scott A. Thomas, DO	Maine Board of Osteopathic Licensure
Peter Thomashow, MD	Vermont Board of Medical Practice
Suzanne H. Thomashow, MD, PhD	Michigan Board of Medicine
Dwight Thompson, PA-C	Montana Board of Medical Examiners
Tricia J. Thompson Handel, DO	Maryland Board of Physicians
William Thrift, MD	Arizona Medical Board
Tracy Tomac McCauley, MD	Minnesota Board of Medical Practice
Joseph E. Toner, III	Pennsylvania State Board of Osteopathic Medicine
Carmela Torrelli, BBA	New York State Office of Professional Medical Conduct
Russell L. Travis, MD	Kentucky Board of Medical Licensure
Jean M. Tsigonis, MD	Alaska State Medical Board
Elisabeth Tucker, MD	Florida Board of Medicine

Current Fellow	*Board*
Robert E. Turner III, MD	South Carolina Board of Medical Examiners
Timothy J. Turner, BBA	Texas Medical Board
Laurie S. Y. Tyau, MD	Maryland Board of Physicians
James Upchurch, MD	Montana Board of Medical Examiners
Dale J. Utt, DO	Colorado Medical Board
Ronald V. Uva, MD	New York State Board for Medicine
Douglas P. Vanator, DO	Michigan Board of Osteopathic Medicine and Surgery
John C. Vander Woude, MD	South Dakota Board of Medical and Osteopathic Examiners
Robert M. Vanecko, MD	Illinois Department of Financial and Professional Regulation
Cheryl A. Vaught, JD	Oklahoma State Board of Osteopathic Examiners
Donald Vennekotter, MD	Medical Licensing Board of Indiana
Rosaire Verna, MD	Maryland Board of Physicians
Robert Vidaver, MD	New Hampshire Board of Medicine
Veronica Vuksich, DO	Osteopathic Medical Board of California
Datta G. Wagle, MD	New York State Office of Professional Medical Conduct
Paul E. Wakim, DO	Osteopathic Medical Board of California
John B. Waldman, MD	New York State Office of Professional Medical Conduct
Kathy Walker, LMSW	Maine Board of Osteopathic Licensure
William A. Walker, MD, FACS	North Carolina Medical Board
Kevin Walsh, PA	New Jersey State Board of Medical Examiners
Stanley S. Wang, MD	Texas Medical Board
Michael P. Ward, DO	Arizona Board of Osteopathic Examiners in Medicine and Surgery
Robert M. Ward Jr., MD	Idaho State Board of Medicine
Kayleen Wardner	North Dakota State Board of Medical Examiners
Sheldon A. Wasserman, MD	Wisconsin Medical Examining Board
Edmund J. Waters Jr., Esq.	New Hampshire Board of Medicine

Current Fellow	*Board*
Thelma R. Watson, MD	Virgin Islands Board of Medical Examiners
Mark C. Watts, MD	Colorado Medical Board
Joyce Vista Wayne, MD	Iowa Board of Medicine
Badshah J. Wazir, MD	West Virginia Board of Medicine
Terry L. Webb, DC	Kansas State Board of Healing Arts
Timothy M. Webb, JD	Texas Medical Board
John B. Webber	Vermont Board of Medical Practice
Regine A. Webster	Tennessee Board of Medical Examiners
Richard L. Weil, MD	Georgia Composite Medical Board
Steven Weiner, MD	New Mexico Medical Board
David S. Weingarden, MD	Michigan Board of Medicine
Daniel Weiss	New Jersey State Board of Medical Examiners
John B. Weiss, MD	Arkansas State Medical Board
John J. Welch, JD	Vermont Board of Osteopathic Physicians and Surgeons
Irene E. Wells	Tennessee Board of Medical Examiners
Jeffrey A. Welsh, MD	South Carolina Board of Medical Examiners
Nancy J. Welsh, MD	Kansas State Board of Healing Arts
John H. Wheeler, DO	New Hampshire Board of Medicine
Charles L. White, DO	Georgia Composite Medical Board
Charles W. White Sr., MD	Tennessee Board of Medical Examiners
Keith A. White, MD	Oregon Medical Board
Robert D. Whitler	West Virginia Board of Osteopathy
Ronald N. Whitmer, DO	Kansas State Board of Healing Arts
George Willeford III, MD	Texas Medical Board
Joseph Willett, DO	Minnesota Board of Medical Practice
Joseph H. Williams, MD	Idaho State Board of Medicine
W. Kent Williamson, MD	Oregon Medical Board
Gary E. Winchester, MD	Florida Board of Medicine
Mimi Winslow, JD	Washington State Medical Quality Assurance Commission
C. Steven Wolf, MD	Connecticut Medical Examining Board

Current Fellow	*Board*
Kenneth Dean Wright, PA-C	West Virginia Board of Medicine
Barbara Yaroslavsky	Medical Board of California
Ralph A. Yates, DO	Oregon Medical Board
Carl K. Yorita, MD	Hawaii Medical Board
Florence Young	Vermont Board of Medical Practice
LeRoy Young, DO	Oklahoma State Board of Osteopathic Examiners
Zachariah P. Zachariah, MD	Florida Board of Medicine
Michael D. Zanolli, MD	Tennessee Board of Medical Examiners
Irvin E. Zeitler Jr., DO	Texas Medical Board

Bibliographical Essay

MEDICAL LICENSURE AND REGULATION

The publications of the Federation of State Medical Boards constitute an invaluable resource for the researcher interested in America's medical regulatory system, both in its current form and in its historical development. The organization's official publication has been issued continuously in either monthly or quarterly fashion since 1913. Despite a series of name changes—*Quarterly of the Federation of State Medical Boards* (1913–1914); *Monthly Bulletin* (1915–1920); *Federation Bulletin* (1921–1998); *Journal of Medical Licensure and Discipline* (1999–2010); and now the *Journal of Medical Regulation* (2010–present)—this periodical remains one of the best sources of insight into the evolution of medical regulation in the United States. The *Bulletin* is a rich trove of information on the Federation's early years when other records are scanty or nonexistent and a hidden gem for researchers exploring the multiple issues, trends, and forces at work in medical regulation.

There are several book-length treatments of medical regulation focusing on the role of state medical boards. Though now dated, Robert Derbyshire's *Medical Licensure and Discipline in the United States* (Johns Hopkins University Press, 1969) and Richard Harrison Shryock's *Medical Licensing in America, 1650–1965* (Johns Hopkins University Press, 1967) are the starting point for most researchers seeking a quick overview of the field. Derbyshire's text is somewhat unique in its blend of historical research and firsthand observations based upon his years of experience on New Mexico's medical board and the Federation's board of directors. The most important recent contribution to the field is Carl Ameringer's

State Medical Boards and the Politics of Public Protection (Johns Hopkins University Press, 1999), though his focus centers primarily on the disciplinary role of state medical boards. This book offers a valuable addition to the Derbyshire and Shryock works as Ameringer scrutinizes the critical period of the 1970s through 1990s when state boards fully embraced their disciplinary role.

Shorter historical treatments of nineteenth-century medical regulation and the second wave of licensing laws can be found in Samuel L. Baker's "Physician Licensure Laws in the United States, 1865–1915," *Journal of the History of Medicine* (April 1984), and Ronald Hamowy's "The Early Development of Medical Licensing Laws in the United States, 1875–1900," *Journal of Libertarian Studies* (1979). Both are excellent works that draw heavily from the nineteenth-century medical practice laws and feature helpful appendix materials guiding researchers to the individual state statutes. A number of state-specific studies of licensure laws have been produced. Toby Appel supplied an interesting case study on the Thomsonian movement's impact on licensing laws in Connecticut—see "The Thomsonian Movement, the Regular Profession and the State in Antebellum Connecticut: A Case Study of the Repeal of Early Medical Licensing Laws," *Journal of the History of Medicine and Allied Sciences* (April 2010). Clinton Sandvick and Kenneth H. Schnepp provide insight into Illinois's unique experience with their respective works, "Enforcing Medical Licensing in Illinois: 1877–1890," *Yale Journal of Biology and Medicine* (June 2009), and "Medical Licensure in Illinois: An Historical Review," *Federation Bulletin* (March 1977). An interesting contemporary assessment on the impact of homeopathic and eclectic practitioners on the rebirth of licensing laws can be found in Reginald Fitz's "Legislative Control of Medical Practice" (*Boston Medical and Surgical Journal,* June 21, 1894).

Medical regulation and the role of state medical boards have been covered by Paul Starr and Rosemary Stevens within the pages of their larger narratives covering the sociopolitical and economic development of medicine in America. Chapter 3 of Starr's *The Social Transformation of American Medicine: The Rise of a Sovereign Profession and the Making of a Vast Industry* (Basic Books, 1982) addresses the consolidation of professional authority spanning the late nineteenth and early twentieth centuries. This Pulitzer Prize–winning work remains one of the most commonly cited sources on the evolution of medical regulation. Rosemary Stevens's *American Medicine and the Public Interest: A History of Specialization* (University of California Press, 1998 edition) presents a similarly ambitious narrative. The subtitle of this impressive history underscores Stevens's narrative focus on increasing specialization in all aspects of medicine in the twentieth century. However, medical licensure and regulation figure less prominently in Stevens's text than that of Starr.

There is no single source for the history of the Federation's two predecessor organizations—the National Confederation of State Medical Examining and Licensing Boards and the American Confederation of Reciprocating Examining and Licensing Boards. However, a wide variety of original source material from the medical journals of the day (1890–1912) is extant through the Internet and Google books search. Much of this appeared as news items in periodicals such as the *Journal of the American Medical Association (JAMA)* and the *Bulletin of the American Academy of Medicine*. These items were often reproduced in the publications of various state medical associations. Prior published work on the history of the Federation includes Derbyshire's chapter on the organization in *Medical Licensure and Discipline in the United States*. The *Federation Bulletin* has published numerous shorter pieces on the organization's history, including Walter Bierring's "Medical Licensure after Forty Years" (April 1956); James Norment Baker's "The Federation: Its Origin, History and Obligations" (March 1937); and a series of articles that appeared in the 1987 issues of the *Bulletin*.

Economic theorists have weighed in frequently on the utility of licensing and professional regulation. For the field of medical regulation, a number of interesting works are available though they may be strongly ideological in nature, such as Harris Cohen's "On Professional Power and Conflict of Interest: State Licensing Boards on Trial," *Journal of Health Politics, Policy and Law* (1980). Shirley Svorny has also written extensively in this area. Articles representative of her work include "Physician Licensure: A New Approach to Examining the Role of Professional Interests," *Economic Inquiry* (July 1987), and "Licensing Doctors: Do Economists Agree?" *Economic Journal Watch* (August 2002). A more recent contribution comes from Randall Holcombe, "Does Licensing of Health Care Professionals Improve Health Care?" *Journal of Medical Licensure and Discipline* (2007). One of the earlier works attracting considerable attention was *Of Foxes and Hen Houses: Licensing and the Health Professions* (Greenwood Press, 1984) by Stanley J. Gross.

While much of the literature on medical licensure and discipline is data-driven and focused on contemporary issues, thoughtful, forward-looking pieces on medical regulation attempting to look into the future appear on occasion. Notable among these are Leroy Buckler's "Medical Licensure in the 21st Century: Are We Ready?" *Federation Bulletin* (1995); James N. Thompson's "The Future of Medical Licensure in the United States," *Academic Medicine* (December 2006); and Humayun Chaudhry's "Charting Dynamism in Medical Education, Licensure and Regulation," *Journal of Medical Licensure and Discipline* (2009). The published proceedings of a Federation symposium held in 2000 spotlight many of the emergent issues garnering the attention of state medical board at the opening of this century—see *Medical Licensure in the 21st Century* (St. Barthélemy Press, 2002).

STATE BOARD HISTORIES

Published histories are available for a number of state boards. Usually written by board staff, these histories provide insightful looks at the multiple issues and local, regional and national forces at work impacting the work of these state agencies. Among the more notable are Linda McCready and Billie Harris's excellent history of the California board in *From Quackery to Quality Assurance: The First Twelve Decades of the Medical Board of California* (State of California, 1995). This concise but richly detailed history is excellent though surprisingly silent on the state's osteopathic controversy in the 1960s. Warren Koontz Jr. and staff associated with the Virginia medical board produced an illustrated in-house history entitled *The Virginia Board of Medicine: 1884 to 2000 and Beyond*. The Federation's holdings include an unpublished work on the Virginia board drafted by one of its former board members, Carroll H. Lippard, entitled "The First Century: A History of the Virginia State Board of Medicine, 1984–1994" (1984, unpublished ms.) The Nevada State Board of Medical Examiners collaborated with the University of Nevada's Oral History Program for their history in Anita Ernst Watson's *Reflection, Recollection and Change: The Nevada State Board of Medical Examiners* (University of Nevada Oral History Program, 1996). An appendix to this work included the questions comprising the first examination administered by the board in 1899.

The long history of the North Carolina board has been captured twice in print. A centennial history of the board by Ivan M. Proctor and Dorothy Long covered not only the history and evolution of the board but board policies extant in the 1950s and decisions of the North Carolina Supreme Court pertaining to that state's medical practice act. See *One Hundred Year History of the North Carolina State Board of Medical Examiners, 1859–1959* (Edwards & Broughton, 1959). The board's more recent history was captured in Christina Apperson's *Protecting the Public, Strengthening the Profession: A One Hundred Fifty Year History of the North Carolina Medical Board* (HF Group, 2009). This contains a particularly useful bibliography identifying news stories related to the board, its decisions and policies.

While not a history of medical licensing in Illinois, the annual reports of the Illinois Board of Health beginning in 1878 represent a valuable resource for insight into the major challenges facing licensing boards (spurious degrees; diploma mills; unlicensed practitioners) at the time of their resurrection in the late nineteenth century. Detailed information on medical schools and the official register of physicians and midwives licensed in the state provides substantial raw material for researchers interested in the history of medicine and medical regulation. Many other state medical boards produced similar reports (e.g., Indiana, Massachusetts) that provide a detailed state-specific snapshot into the genesis of early licensing systems.

State board histories are often imbedded in broader narratives of medicine drafted by state medical associations. For example, Nancy Rockafellar and James W. Haviland discuss the Washington state board within the historical context of the practice of medicine within that state in *Saddlebags to Scanners: The First 100 Years of Medicine in Washington State* (Washington State Medical Association, 1989). Pat Ireland Nixon's *History of Texas Medical Association, 1853–1953* (University of Texas Press, 1953) contains helpful references to that state's medical board. Oklahoma's state medical association produced a two-part history of that state's medical board spanning its territorial origins through the modern era. See *Journal of the Oklahoma State Medical Association* 96, nos. 11–12, 2003.

The story of homeopathic, eclectic and physio-medical practitioners in gaining representation on medical boards, and in some instances acquiring independent licensing boards, has not been fully told. Some insight into these groups' successes can be found within select chapters of John Haller Jr.'s work in *Kindly Medicine: Physio-Medicalism in America, 1836–*1911 (Kent State University Press, 1997) and *Medical Protestants: The Eclectics in American Medicine, 1825–1939* (Illinois University Press, 1994).

The role of the public members on state medical boards has been a frequent topic in Federation publications. Noteworthy articles on this topic include the following: Stephen Heretick, "The Role of Public Members on State Medical Boards," *Journal of Medical Regulation* (2010); Linda Wasmer Andrews, "Public Members: The Voice of the Public," *Journal of Medical Licensure and Discipline* (2002); Gwen Andrew and Harold Sauer, "Do Boards of Medicine Really Matter? The Future of Professional Regulation," *Federation Bulletin* (1996); and David McPhee, "The Public on the Boards . . . What Is the Role of the Consumer Members?" *Federation Bulletin* (January 1978). Elizabeth Graddy and Michael Nichol have provided data driven analyses of board performance focusing on the impact of public members in "Structural Reforms and Licensing Board Performance," *American Politics Quarterly* (July 1990), and "Public Members on Occupational Licensing Boards: Effects on Legislative Regulatory Reforms," *Southern Economic Journal* (January 1989). See also Andreas Broscheid and Paul Teske, "Public Members on Medical Licensing Boards and the Choice of Entry Barriers" in *Public Choice* (March 2003).

HISTORY OF MEDICINE

Two of the better works covering the colonial and pre–Civil War era of medicine are William G. Rothstein's *American Physicians in the 19th Century: From Sects to Science* (Johns Hopkins University Press, 1972) and Joseph Kett's *The Formation of the American Medical Profession: The Role of Institutions, 1780–1860* (Yale University Press, 1968). Both works are strong in addressing the rise of sectarian medicine (e.g., Thomsonians, homeopaths, eclectics), with Kett particularly insightful in relating the sociopolitical and cultural aspects of sectarian medicine. Though not a particular emphasis of either work, both authors discuss nineteenth-century medical licensure. Rothstein addresses medical societies and their relationship to licensure at length. Licensure in the post–Civil War era is presented in the context of the "institutionalization" of medical sects. Kett offers numerous examples of state and territorial efforts seeking to regulate medicine through legislation and medical societies. Also worth noting are Maurice Gordon's *Aesculapius Comes to the Colonies* (Ventnor Publishers,1949) and John Tate Lanning's, *The Royal Protomedicato: The Regulation of the Medical Profession in the Spanish Empire* (Duke University Press, 1985). An older work of surprisingly comprehensive scope on colonial medicine comes from Joseph M. Toner in *Contributions to the Annals of Medical Progress and Medical Education . . . before and during the War of Independence* (Washington, DC: Government Printing Office, 1874).

John S. Haller Jr.'s *American Medicine in Transition, 1840–1910* (University of Illinois Press, 1981) takes the history of medicine into the second half of the nineteenth century. However, his treatment of licensure is surprisingly cursory considering the time period covered by this text coincides with the second wave of licensing laws in the United States beginning in the 1870s. Another very readable account of the development of American medical practice can be found in John Duffy's *From Humors to Medical Science: A History of American Medicine* (University of Illinois Press, 1993). However, like Haller's *American Medicine,* this text is limited in its discussion of medical licensure.

Mainstream medical practitioners of the nineteenth century tightly guarded their professional identity and often looked askance at what they deemed "irregular" practitioners. A strong sense for this can be obtained from Morris Fishbein's *A History of the American Medical Association, 1847–1947* (W. B. Saunders, 1947). John S. Haller related the story of several medical "sects," including eclectic and homeopathic practitioners and their ultimate absorption into the medical mainstream through a series of insightful works. See *The History of American Homeopathy: The Academic Years, 1820–1935* (Haworth Press, 2005) and the aforementioned *Kindly Medicine* and *Medical Protestants.* Osteopathic medicine proved to be the most successful of the nineteenth-century challengers to conventional medical practice in its ability to gain broader acceptance without relinquishing its identity. Norman Gevitz drafted an excellent overview with *The DOs: Osteopathic Medicine in America* (Johns Hopkins University Press, 1982). Interwoven through this text is the success of osteopathic practitioners in gaining recognition from the regulatory community and the broader profession.

MEDICAL LICENSING EXAMINATIONS

A vast body of research into educational and professional assessment has developed over the past sixty years. Highly technical analyses of the examinations required today for medical licensure appear frequently in *Academic Medicine*, the *Journal of the American Medical Association (JAMA)* and the *Journal of the American Osteopathic Association*. Some of the best technical literature tying performance on medical licensing examinations to patient care and treatment comes from Canada and the research of Robyn Tamblyn. See "Association Between Licensing Examination Scores and Resource Use and Quality of Care in Primary Care Practice," *JAMA* (September 16, 1998); "Association Between Licensing Examination Scores and Practice in Primary Care," *JAMA* (December 18, 2002); and "Physician Scores on a National Clinical Skills Examination as Predictors of Complaints to Medical Regulatory Authorities," *JAMA* (September 5, 2007).

The best book-length treatments of medical licensing examinations are John Hubbard and Edithe Levit's *The National Board of Medical Examiners: The First Seventy Years* (Philadelphia: National Board of Medical Examiners, 1985) and Betty Burnett's *In the Public Trust: The National Board of Osteopathic Examiners, 1934–2009* (Chicago: NBOME, 2010). These provide an overview of the two professional agencies responsible for multiple examinations recognized for licensure in the twentieth century: the NBME Parts certifying examination, Federation Licensing Examination (FLEX) and the Comprehensive Osteopathic Medical Licensing Examination or COMLEX-USA (previously the NBOME Parts). Detailed articles on the FLEX, including annual statistical and informational reports, appeared throughout the history of this examination (1968–1994) in the pages of the *Federation Bulletin*.

Articles providing information on the United States Medical Licensing Examination (USMLE) within the broader history of medical licensing examinations include Donald E. Melnick, "Licensing Examinations in North America: Is External Audit Valuable?" *Medical Teacher* (2009) and Melnick, Gerard F. Dillon, and David B. Swanson, "Medical Licensing Examinations in the United States," *Journal of Dental Education* (May 2002). Possible future directions and enhancements for the USMLE are presented in the *Final Report and Recommendations of the Committee to Evaluate the USMLE Program*, which can be accessed on the program's website at www.usmle.org. Similar strategic enhancements are under way with the "Blue Ribbon Panel for Enhancing the COMLEX-USA," whose progress reports are available at www.nbome.org.

Two of the best overviews of the basic science examinations that spread among the states beginning in the mid-1920s are provided by Leo P.

Clements, "The Basic Science Laws," *Academic Medicine* (March 1943), and Norman Gevitz, "A Coarse Sieve: Basic Science Boards and Medical Licensure in the United States," *Journal of the History of Medicine and Allied Sciences* (1988). The state board issues of *JAMA* routinely provided performance data on these examinations.

The literature covering licensing examinations during the late nineteenth and early twentieth centuries is less robust. One can gather a strong sense for content on these examinations from Rudolph Max Goepp's *State Board Questions and Answers* (Philadelphia: W. B. Saunders, 1908). This popular compilation of questions that had appeared on medical licensing examinations went through multiple revised editions. The best resource on licensing remains the state board statistics issues of the *Journal of the American Medical Association (JAMA)* which appeared from 1903 to 1966. These offer the data and context for a national perspective on issues in the medical regulatory arena pertaining to examinations.

MEDICAL EDUCATION

Perhaps the best work on the development of medical education over the past century and a half comes from Kenneth M. Ludmerer. Through two works—*Learning to Heal: The Development of American Medical Education* and *Time to Heal: American Medical Education from the Turn of the Century to the Era of Managed Care*—Ludmerer crafts a seamless narrative tracing the evolution of U.S. medical education from its haphazard conditions in an unregulated environment in the mid-nineteenth century to the current era of managed care (Johns Hopkins University Press, 1985, and Oxford University Press, 1999). In *Learning to Heal,* he contends that state medical boards' primary contribution to medical education stemmed from their efforts (in concert with the AAMC and the AMA) in shutting down substandard proprietary schools during the two decades after the Flexner report. Dean F. Smiley's "History of the Association of American Medical Colleges, 1876–1956," found in the *Journal of Medical Education* (July 1957) provides a helpful supplement explaining the genesis and contribution of this important organization to U.S. medical education. This important organization's story is told more fully in Mark Bowles and Virginia Dawson's *With One Voice: The Association of the American Medical Colleges, 1876–2002* (AAMC, 2003). The role of the AAMC and the AMA Council on Medical Education in accreditation for medical education is outlined by Donald G. Kassebaum in "Origin of the LCME, the AAMC-AMA Partnership for Accreditation," *Academic Medicine* (February 1992). Susan Skochelak's "A Century of Progress in Medical Education: What About the Next 10 Years?" *Academic Medicine*

(February 2010) provides a more current contribution to the field in looking to the future of medical education.

For a concise history of osteopathic medical education, see Norman Gevitz's piece in *Academic Medicine*, "The Transformation of Osteopathic Medical Education" (June 2009). Stephen Shannon and Howard Teitelbaum offer a forward-looking assessment of osteopathic education in "The Status and Future of Osteopathic Medical Education in the United States," *Academic Medicine* (June 2009).

The era of medical educational reform represented by the Carnegie Foundation report of Abraham Flexner has been discussed extensively. A good starting point remains *Beyond Flexner: Medical Education in the 20th Century* (New York: Greenwood Press, 1992) from editors Barbara Barzansky and Norman Gevitz. Another excellent multiperspective assessment of this key report and the era within which it appeared can be found in the February 2010 issue of *Academic Medicine*. Two excellent additions to this resource are Andrew Beck's "The Flexner Report and the Standardization of American Medical Education," *JAMA* (May 5, 2004), and Barbara Barzansky's "Abraham Flexner and the Era of Medical Education Reform," *Academic Medicine* (September 2010). Too often overlooked, however, is chapter 11 of Flexner's report which acknowledged the critical role played by state medical boards as the "instrument" effectively supporting much of the reform movement.

The various aspects of the diploma mill scandals of the 1920s, including the fallout on a few state boards, were captured by Frederick Waite in a series of articles in the *Federation Bulletin* (May, June, and September 1926). Google book searches under "Buchanan diploma mill" bring up a number of articles by the contemporary press on this scandal from 1880 to 1881.

INTERNATIONAL MEDICAL GRADUATES

Eric Kohler offers one of the more critical pieces on the role of state boards and their handling of émigré physicians in the 1930s and 1940s. See "Relicensing Central European Refugee Physicians in the United States, 1933–1945," *Simon Wiesenthal Center Annual* 6 (Los Angeles, 1989). Reflective of the era and prevailing sentiment is the Michigan board's J. Earl McIntyre in "Citizenship and Medical Licensure," *Federation Bulletin* (March 1939).

The history and critical role of the Educational Commission for Foreign Medical Graduates as well as the contributions of international physicians to U.S. medicine are captured succinctly in the proceedings from the ECFMG's fiftieth anniversary symposium in a special issue of *Academic Medicine* (December 2006). Data and trend information on IMGs covering more recent years can be found in the annual reports of the ECFMG and the extensive publications of their Foundation for the Advancement of International Medical Education and Research (http://www.faimer.org/).

STATE BOARDS AND POLICY DEVELOPMENT

State medical boards have become more proactive in guiding their licensees through the development and dissemination of board policies covering a range of topics. Often these policies are backed by research and policy work undertaken by the Federation of State Medical Boards. The advocacy and policy section of the Federation website (www.fsmb.org) provides complete copies of all Federation policy documents. All policy documents referenced in this narrative are available on the website. These publicly accessible documents represent the official policy of the organization, meaning they have been adopted by the assembled representatives of state medical boards convened as the Federation's House of Delegates at the organization's annual meeting.

PHYSICIAN CONTINUING COMPETENCE AND MAINTENANCE OF LICENSURE

The concept that physician license renewal should be tied to more than updated personal/practice information and a renewal fee is not new. Robert Derbyshire captured the historic introduction of the first continuing medical education requirement by a state medical board (New Mexico) in "Relicensure for Continued Practice," *Federation Bulletin* (July 1972). The literature on physician competence and related issues/challenges has developed considerably in recent decades. The Pew Health Professions Commission's *Reforming Health Care Workforce Regulation* and a series of Institutes of Medicine reports (*To Err Is Human; Crossing the Quality Chasm;* and *Health Professions Education: A Bridge to Quality*) address broad competence issues as a key component in patient safety and professional expectations for physicians. A sense for public perceptions and expectations for physician competence can be gleaned from several reports on the Citizen Advocacy Center website: *Maintaining and Improving Health Professional Competence; Implementing Continuing Competency Requirements for Health Care Practitioners;* and *Measuring Continuing Competence of Health Care Practitioners.*

A number of studies have explored the efficacy of physician self-assessment as a means of practice improvement. An excellent starting point is the *Journal of Continuing Education in the Health Professions,* whose Winter

2008 issue covered this subject as part of the foundation for continuing education. Particularly noteworthy was the article by Kevin Ewa and Glenn Regehr, "I'll Never Play Professional Football and Other Fallacies of Self-Assessment." An excellent companion piece comes from David Davis et al. in "Accuracy of Physician Self-Assessment Compared with Observed Measures of Competence," *JAMA* (2006). Collectively, these works demonstrate the flaws of "unguided" physician self-assessment. However, both these and other studies attest to the usefulness of self-assessment when guided by objective assessment data compared with external standards. See also Robert Galbraith et al. in "Making Self-Assessment More Effective," *Journal of Continuing Education in the Health Professions* (Winter 2008), and F. Daniel Duffy et al. in "Self-Assessment in Lifelong Learning and Improving Performance in Practice: Physician Know Thyself," *JAMA* (2006). Important related works by Ewa and Niteesh K. Choudhry challenge the conventional wisdom assumption of experience equating to greater expertise by showing an inverse relationship between age or years in practice and performance. See "The Aging Physician: Changes in Cognitive Processes and Their Impact on Medical Practice," *Academic Medicine* (2002), and "Systematic Review: The Relationship Between Clinical Experience and Quality of Health Care," *Annals of Internal Medicine* (2005).

The best summary of the Maintenance of Licensure (MOL) initiative comes from Humayun Chaudhry, Janelle Rhyne and colleagues in "Maintenance of Licensure: Protecting the Public, Promoting Quality Health Care," in the *Journal of Medical Regulation* (2010). The Federation of State Medical Boards' website houses all the major reports and documents from this multiyear initiative. Perhaps most helpful to the reader are *Board Report 11–3: Report of the MOL Implementation Group* (April 2011); *Board Report 10–3: Maintenance of Licensure* (April 2010); and the *Special Committee on Maintenance of Licensure Draft Report on Maintenance of Licensure* (February 2008). A broader look exploring the traditional role of licensing authorities, including their role in ensuring continued competence, can be found in the 2008 Milbank Memorial Fund report, *Medical Regulatory Authorities and the Quality of Medical Services in Canada and the United States.*

DISCIPLINARY ROLE OF STATE BOARDS

A seminal work on the transition of state medical boards toward a more robust disciplinary role can be found in the American Medical Association's "Report of the Medical Disciplinary Committee to the Board of Trustees" as part of the proceedings for the 1961 AMA House of Delegates. This report and Lall Montgomery's article "Panel on Problems of Discipline: Unprofessional Conduct," in the *Federation Bulletin* (September 1960), offer contextual insight into the transition beginning in the medical regulatory arena toward a stronger disciplinary focus in the early 1960s. Several publications by Robert Derbyshire cited in chapters 6 and 7 of this text provide quantitative measures of the actions taken by state medical boards in the 1960s and 1970s.

Scholarly work in this realm accelerated beginning in the 1980s. Important contributions to the field came from Richard Kusserow, "An Overview of State Medical Discipline," *Journal of the American Medical Association* (February 13, 1987); Andrew Dolan and Nicole Urban, "Determinants of the Effectiveness of Medical Disciplinary Boards: 1960–1970," *Law and Human Behavior* (1983); Elizabeth Graddy and Michael B. Nichol, "Structural Reforms and Licensing Board Performance," *American Politics Quarterly* (July 1990); Darren Grant and Kelly Alfred, "Sanctions and Recidivism: An Evaluation of Physician Discipline by State Medical Boards," *Journal of Health Politics, Policy and Law* (October 2007); Marc Law and Zeynep Hansen, "Medical Licensing Board Characteristics and Physician Discipline," *Journal of Health Politics, Policy and Law* (2010); and Nadia Sawicki, "Character, Competence, and the Principles of Medical Discipline," *Journal of Health Care Law and Policy* (2010).

The best book-length treatment of state medical boards and their disciplinary function comes from Carl Ameringer's *State Medical Boards and the Politics of Public Protection*. Ameringer deftly interweaves the forces of consumerism and corporate medicine into his analysis of state medical boards and their sometimes uneven transition into the disciplinary role envisioned for them by the public. His narrative picks up the story of state medical boards' disciplinary efforts begun by Derbyshire and updates their efforts through the 1980s and 1990s.

Invariably discussion and assessment of state boards' performance of their disciplinary role centers upon data—in particular, the number of actions/sanctions taken by a state medical board. The most complete national data on state board disciplinary actions have been published by the Federation since 1981. Data covering 1981–1989 were published annually in the *Federation Bulletin*. A summary of board actions spanning 1990–2010 is available on the Physician Data Center section of the Federation website at www.fsmb.org. For information on the National Practitioner Data Bank (NPDB) and its role in medical discipline, see http://www.npdb-hipdb.hrsa.gov/. See also P. Jesilow and J. Ohlander for evidence of the positive impact of the NPDB on state medical board activity in "Impact of the National Practitioner Data Bank on Licensing Actions by State Medical Licensing Boards," *Journal of Health and Human Services Administration* (Summer 2010).

Some of the best work exploring possible indicators for subsequent likely discipline by a state medical board comes from Maxine Papadakis in a pair of articles from 2004–2005. See Papadakis's "Disciplinary Action by Medical Boards and Prior Behavior in Medical School," *New England Journal of Medicine* (December 22, 2005), and "Unprofessional Behavior in Medical School Is Associated with Subsequent Disciplinary Action by a State Medical Board," *Academic Medicine* (March 2004).

Index

About the Authors

David A. Johnson holds a graduate degree in history from the University of Texas-Arlington (2001) and serves as the vice president for assessment services at the Federation of State Medical Boards. His published works have appeared in *Academic Medicine, Journal of Medical Regulation, Journal of Medical Licensure and Discipline, Journal of Continuing Education in the Health Professions* and *The Guide to Medical Education in the Teaching Hospital* (fourth edition).

Dr. Humayun J. Chaudhry is a general internist and president and CEO of the Federation of State Medical Boards. He holds a master's degree in health care management from the Harvard School of Public Health (2001). He is the recipient of a Laureate Award from the American College of Physicians and has been inducted into the American Osteopathic Association's Mentor Hall of Fame. Prior to his tenure at the Federation, he served as Commissioner for the Suffolk County (New York) Department of Health Services. He is the principal author of *Fundamentals of Clinical Medicine* (Lippincott, Williams & Wilkins, 2004).